Strategic Management in Small and Medium Enterprises

Strategic Management in Small and Medium Enterprises

Farhad Analoui and Azhdar Karami

THOMSON

Australia · Canada · Mexico · Singapore · Spain · United Kingdom · United States

Strategic Management in Small and Medium Enterprises
Copyright © Farhad Analoui and Azhdar Karami 2003

For more information, contact Thomson Learning, High Holborn House, 50–51 Bedford Row, London WC1R 4LR or visit us on the World Wide Web at: http://www.thomsonlearning.co.uk

British Library Cataloguing-in-Publication Data
A catalogue record for this book is available from the British Library

ISBN 1-86152-962-7

First edition published by Thomson Learning, 2003

Typeset by LaserScript, Mitcham, Surrey

Printed in Great Britain by TJ International

Contents

List of figures

List of tables

List of boxes

1 Introduction to the strategic management concept and small business

> ## Learning objectives
>
> By the end of this chapter you should be able to:
>
> - Explain the importance of small and medium-sized enterprises.
>
> - Explore and define the terms strategic and strategic management.
>
> - Explain the process of strategic management in the context of the organisation.
>
> - Describe the study of strategic management in small and medium-sized enterprises.
>
> - Explain the benefits and limitations of strategic management.
>
> - Describe the concepts of strategy and entrepreneurship.
>
> - Explain who the strategic managers are.
>
> - Describe the role of entrepreneurs as strategists of the firm and the characteristics of successful entrepreneurs.

The first objective of this chapter is to determine why we study strategic management in small and medium-sized enterprises (SMEs); the second is to introduce the concept and process of strategic management. Our third objective is a brief review of literature on strategic management in small and medium-sized enterprises (pros and cons). Accordingly, the benefits and limitations of strategic management in small businesses will be discussed. Finally, the last objective will be to find out who the strategists in the firm are and what the salient characteristics of these successful entrepreneurs in small businesses are.

Strategy and small and medium-sized enterprises

Strategic management researchers have recently been concerned with small and medium-sized enterprises (SMEs) (Chan and Foster, 2001; Analoui and Karami, 2002). Recognition of the importance of this sector as a major contributor to job creation and economic growth, especially during the 1990s, has led to a dramatic increase in the academic research being carried out on small businesses and related management practices in this period. This progress in the theoretical development of the concept of strategic management in small businesses is largely due to the importance of this sector in the well-being and economy of most countries in the world.

In the 1990s, small business became one of the mainstays of the economy (for example, for the USA see Schwenk and Shrader 1993; for the UK see Storey, 1994; McKiernan and Morris, 1995; Webb and Pettigrew, 1999). Arguably, one of the reasons for this is the increasing number of employees who were laid off by the larger corporations in the 1980s and early 1990s and who subsequently joined the small business workforce (Robinson, *et al.* 1986). Second, there has been an increasing trend in large firms to outsource some of their activities to smaller organisations, a process which has been facilitated to some extent by the growth of the Internet. Third, the relative stability of the economies of the UK and USA since the early 1990s has encouraged more entrepreneurial activities. Fourth, the emergence of new economies around the world has accelerated global development which has encouraged more entrepreneurial activity in the UK. Small businesses will, therefore, continue to play a major role in both job creation and economic growth throughout the next decade and topics such as strategic growth of small businesses have received considerable attention from researchers (Krishnan, 2001).

The sheer numbers of SMEs make them an important constituent of local, regional and national economics and as such a potential target for policy intervention. According to the Official UK Labour Market Statistics (1998) small businesses account for 84 per cent of all business units in the UK. Business

---

Box 1.1

Practical and theoretical progress in the field of strategic management in small businesses is largely due to the importance of the contribution of this sector to the well-being of the economy of a country as the whole. Some of the main reasons for this are:

- Small businesses' contribution to employment and job creation
- Small businesses' contribution to innovation and high technology development
- An increasing trend on the part of large firms to outsource some of their activities to smaller ones, because of the widespread use of Internet facilities
- An increase in entrepreneurial activities since the early 1990s
- The globalisation and internationalisation of small businesses.

support policy interventions have shifted their focus from job creation through business start-ups in the 1980s towards increasing the competitiveness of existing businesses with a view to their sustained growth and development in the 1990s. The recent DTI White Paper, *Competitiveness* (1998) with its focus on the provision of advice to at least 10,000 business start-ups a year by the year 2001, suggests once again the presence of an increased emphasis on the formulation and implementation of small business strategies.

It would be wise, however, to remember that the importance of SMEs to an economy largely depends on their ability to fulfil these roles effectively. Economic strategies that aim to support SMEs will have to focus on the factors that either encourage or inhibit their growth. Company strategies specifically formulated for the SMEs to grow and become successful will be based upon either a technological or commercial innovation, or on a focused niche strategy with a differentiated product or services. For any growing company these strategies can lead to severe problems as they proceed through different phases of their life cycle (Hitt and Ireland, 2000; Venkataraman and Sarasvathy, 2001; Karami, 2002).

Generally speaking, it could be concluded that small businesses have acted as the backbone of the economy (Schwenk and Shrader, 1993), thus accounting for more than half of its total employment – and over 80 per cent of its growth – during the 1990s (Wheelen and Hunger, 1998). Small firms are also often innovative and challenging to manage strategically (Bracker and Pearson, 1986). Consequently, it is important to assess the value of adopting approaches like strategic management to improve the performance of these firms.

The strategic management concept

What is strategic management? What are its main components and does it differ from other types of management? In order to answer these questions we will review various definitions of strategic management.

The dominant paradigm in strategic management is characterised by two principal functions: strategy formulation and implementation. The major contributors to these approaches are Ansoff (1965), Andrews (1971, 1986) and Porter (1979, 1980, 1985, 1998). Generally speaking, strategic management is about how the strategy is developed and implemented (Stacey 1993; Karami, 2002). Strategy formulation, on the other hand, is about how the firm chooses to define its strategy and how it approaches its implementation through strategic management (Bowman, 1998). The approach to strategy formulation will ultimately dictate the eventual management style. In contrast, the managerial style and the degree of effectiveness of the senior managers involved can influence the nature of strategy formulation in organisations (Analoui, 1997). It results in the adoption of a specific approach to strategic management. Only after a firm has determined how it will formulate strategy can the path of strategic management be effectively undertaken. The development of a strategy can be either formal or rational (Mintzberg, 1994), emergent or progressed (Whittington, 2001) under a logical incremental path. Strategic management handles how a strategy is developed and where the organisation's environment is analysed before the appropriate strategy is selected and implemented (Hambrick, 1981; Thompson, 1995; Wheelen and Hunger, 1998).

Before discussing the process of strategic management, it would be beneficial to provide a definition of the term. What, then, *is* strategic management? Thompson has argued that the area addressed by strategic management has been defined as 'the management processes and decisions, which determine the long term structure and activities of the organisation' (1996: 6). This definition incorporates five key themes: management process, management decisions, timescales, structure of the organisation and activities of the organisation.

Let's review other definitions of strategic management. Ansoff and McDonnell (1990) separated goal setting (concerned with ends) from strategy (concerned with means). On the subject of strategic management, they defined the process as a systematic approach for managing strategic change which consists of positioning the firm through strategy and capability planning, real time strategic response through issue management and systematic management of resistance during strategic implementation. This definition favours an adaptive approach to strategic management.

Johnson and Scholes (1993) suggest that it is not enough to say that strategic management is the management of the process of strategic decision-making, because strategic management is different in nature from other aspects of management. An individual manager is most often required to deal with problems of operational control, such as production, sales management and financial management. These tasks are vital to the effective implementation of strategy but they are not the same as strategic management. Johnson and Scholes propose that strategic management is not only concerned with taking decisions about major issues facing the organisation, but also with ensuring that the strategy is put into effect. Johnson and Scholes propose three main elements for strategic management – 'strategic analysis, strategic choice and strategy implementation' (1993: 16).

In contrast, Stacey (1993) defines strategic management as a process. He suggests that strategic management is a process directed by top management to determine the fundamental aims or goals of the organisation. Within the process of strategic management, top management ensure a range of decisions which will allow for the achievement of those aims or goals in the long term, whilst providing for adaptive responses in the shorter term.

Goldsmith argued that, rather than being preoccupied with analysis of the firm, its environment and the formulation of strategies, the emerging subfield

---

Box 1.2

Strategic management is a systematic approach for managing strategic change which consists of:

- Positioning the firm through strategy and capability planning
- A real time strategic response through issue management
- Systematic management of resistance during strategic implementation (Ansoff and McDonnell, 1990).

began to feature implementation and evaluation as critical components of the organisation's success. These are the action and assessment phases of the strategic management process. He further asserts that 'strategic management, to sum up, is a broad activity that encompasses mapping out strategy, putting strategy into action and modifying strategy or its implementation to ensure that the desired outcomes are reached' (1995: 4).

It has been argued that strategic management is fundamentally about setting the underpinning aims of an organisation, choosing the most appropriate goals towards those aims and fulfilling both over time. David (1995) holds that strategic management can be defined as the art and science of formulating, implementing and evaluating cross-functional decisions that enable an organisation to achieve its objectives. As this definition implies, strategic management focuses on integrating managerial abilities and techniques such as marketing, financial/accounting, human resource management, production management and research and development to achieve organisational success (Analoui, 2002).

Therefore, strategic management is that set of managerial decisions and actions that determines the long term performance of a corporation (Wheelen and Hunger, 1998). Wheelen and Hunger contend that strategic management includes environmental scanning (both internal and external), strategy formulation (strategic or long range planning), strategy implementation and evaluation and control. The study of strategic management emphasises the monitoring and evaluation of external opportunities and threats in light of a corporation's strengths and weaknesses.

The strategic management process

There are different models of the strategic management process and scholars have proposed different models of the strategy process within the organisation. These models are generally similar in the phases of strategic management process. They start with environmental analysis, continue with strategy development and implementation and end with evaluation of the implemented strategies. For instance, Pitts and Lei (1996) assert that a management process designed to satisfy strategic imperatives that push forward the firm's vision and mission is called a strategic management process. It usually consists of four major steps: analysis, formulation, implementation and adjustment/evaluation (Figure 1.1).

Figure 1.1

The strategic management process

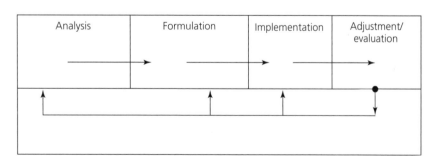

Source: Adapted from Pitts and Lei (1996: 10).

The strategic management process thereby begins with a careful analysis of a firm's internal strengths and weaknesses and external opportunities and threats, commonly referred to as SWOT analysis. Information derived from SWOT analysis is used to construct strategies that will enable the firm to pursue its mission. Similarly, a strategic management model has started the process by defining the company mission in light of the company profile, external environment and operating industry analysis. Strategies must now be formulated in such a way that they match the external opportunities found in the environment with the firm's internal strengths.

For each firm this match is likely to be different. Pitts and Lei (1996) contend that in order to gain maximum competitive advantage, individual firms need to identify the activities they perform best and seek ways to maximise their effect. Effective strategy formulation is based on identifying, understanding and using the firm's distinctive competencies and strengths in a way that other firms cannot (Ansoff and McDonnell, 1990; Pitts and Lei, 1996; Bowman, 1998; Mintzberg and Quinn, 1998). In some models, the strategy formulation is illustrated as the first step toward formulating the strategic management process. The second element of the strategic management process is implementation. Implementation measures include organising the firm's tasks, hiring individuals to perform designated activities properly and rewarding them for carrying out these responsibilities effectively. Third and finally, the environment within which a firm operates inevitably changes over time (Bowman and Faulkner, 1997). In addition to these changes to the environment a firm's performance may occasionally fall below desired levels. Either event compels a firm to re-examine its existing approach and make any necessary adjustments to regain high performance. Mechanisms must be put into place to monitor potential environment changes and alert managers to developments that require modification or adjustment of mission, goals, strategies and implementation practices (Pitts and Lei, 1996).

In order to identify and compare the characteristics of typical strategic management, some of the strategic management models have been reviewed. These have proved seminal to the development of a three-stage strategic management model. Despite differences in details and variations in wording, the three models show three common features: strategy formulation, strategy implementation and strategy evaluation (Figure 1.2).

First, in the strategy formulation section, there is an emphasis on company mission, business goals and their relationship to the international nature of the external environment in which opportunities and threats are present.

Figure 1.2

The process of strategic management

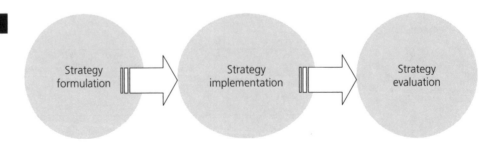

Strategy formulation → Strategy implementation → Strategy evaluation

Second, in the strategy implementation section, there is an emphasis on leadership, organisation structure, organisational culture and their relationship to functional policies and resource allocation decisions.

Finally, the last section is that of strategy evaluation. Here, there is an emphasis on control of activities, using performance appraisal to provide positive feedback, motivating, improvement of policies and operational procedures in line with the grand strategy.

The study of strategic management in small businesses: the pros and cons

It would be helpful briefly to review the work that has been carried out in this area. Research into strategy formulation and implementation, particularly in small and medium-sized enterprises (SMEs), has become one of the main focuses of academia and industry (Watts and Ormsby, 1990; Boyd, 1991; Berry, 1998; Hitt and Ireland, 2000; Beal, 2000; Krishnan, 2001). This is because with the accelerating dynamics of competition SMEs play a key role in generating employment, promoting innovation, creating competition and generating economic wealth (Bantel and Jackson, 1989; Smith, 1998; Bridge and Peel, 1999).

While the volume of literature on strategic management in large organisations is extensive (Hambrick, 1983; Stacey, 1993; Pearce and Robinson, 1994; Hitt *et al.* 1998; Wheelen and Hunger, 1998; Lowry *et al.* 1999; Hoskisson, 2000; Phillips and Moutinho, 2000), the literature on SMEs, in particular strategic management, is more limited (McKiernan and Morris, 1995; Berry, 1998; Smith, 1998; O'Gorman and Doran, 1999; Beal, 2000; Chan and Foster, 2000). Strategic management as a field of enquiry typically deals with large, established business corporations and neglects SMEs. Generally, SMEs are defined as firms that employ up to 250 people and have up to £50 million turnover (d'Amboise and Muldowney, 1988; Berry, 1998; Beal, 2000).

Some writers have argued forcefully that formal strategic management procedures are particularly inappropriate for small and medium-sized firms which have neither the management nor financial resources to indulge in elaborate strategic management techniques (Cragg and King, 1988; Shrader *et al.* 1989; Watts and Ormsby, 1990). For companies operating within the turbulent environment of high technology industries, where conditions are subject to constant change, the process of environmental forecasting becomes almost meaningless and long-range planning of questionable value (Smith and Fleck, 1987; Shrader *et al.* 1989).

A number of studies have concluded that there is little or no significant relationship between strategic planning and the performance of small firms (Unni, 1981; Robinson *et al.* 1984; Orpen, 1985; Robinson *et al.* 1986; Gable and Topol, 1987; Cragg and King, 1988; Shrader *et al.* 1989; Watts and Ormsby, 1990). These studies report mixed planning/performance relations and most suggest that the value of planning is mitigated by factors such as environmental uncertainty, managerial expertise and the firm's stage of development.

While some have concluded that small firms do not commonly practice strategic management (Gable and Topol, 1987) several studies have found a positive relationship between strategic planning and performance in these companies. For example Robinson (1982), found that small businesses that employed consultants to help with strategic planning tended to perform better than firms that did not. Bracker *et al.* (1988) found that small electronics firms that engaged in sophisticated strategic planning performed better than unstructured planners. Several other studies have reported positive relationships between formal strategic planning and financial performance in small firms (Jones, 1982; Ackelsberg and Arlow, 1985; Sexton and Van Auken, 1985; Bracker and Pearson, 1986; Wood *et al.* 1988; Watts and Ormsby, 1990). Still others have reported positive relationships among various measures of strategy content and small firm performance (Miller and Toulouse, 1986; Segev, 1987; Bracker *et al.* 1988). Proponents of strategic management in SMEs have suggested that the type of planning employed will be contingent upon its stage of development and that this activity will evolve and become more formal and sophisticated over the life cycle of the business (Robinson and Pearce, 1984; Scott and Bruce, 1987).

The literature suggests that as the activities and supporting functional areas of the organisations become more complex, strategic management will develop through various stages from its beginnings as simple financial plans and budgets, through to forecast-based planning, externally oriented planning. It is at the last stage that managers begin to think strategically, using formal strategic management techniques to plan the firm's future (Goodwin and Hodgett, 1991; Foster, 1993; Berry, 1998; Beal, 2000; Apfelthaler, 2000). It is often argued that managers must make this necessary progression toward a strategic orientation and more sophisticated strategic management techniques as the business grows in order to ensure the future survival and long term success of the company (Ward, 1988; Stone, 1999; Hitt and Ireland, 2000; Wolff, 2000).

Benefits and limitations of strategic management in SMEs

It has further been argued (Goldsmith, 1995; Bowman and Kakabadse, 1997) that strategic management's main teachings are: First: look to the future. Know what markets you are in and want to be in. Second, pay ongoing attention to external factors – technological, economic, political and social factors. Third, establish and keep a match among those external factors and internal organisational variables. Fourth, remember that strategic management is an interactive process. It is not something that can be done at the front end of an operation and then dropped; it entails feedback and learning (Goldsmith, 1995).

These teachings may seem like common sense, but that does not make them easy to follow. Because managing strategy is a process and not an event, it demands action and follow-up. Therefore, strategic management is concerned with those decisions to do with choosing the appropriate market or product. Strategic management helps the strategists to understand the current situation and set the goals and objectives of the firm. First pose the question 'where is the organisation now?' Second enquire, 'where do we hope it would be?' For instance, in which market and with what environmental characteristics are we operating? Third, determine where the organisation will be in a specific period of time, for example in one year, three years or five years. Fourth, prepare the means to achieve the ends – the goals and objectives of the organisation.

To be effective, especially in SMEs, the process of strategic management need not always take a formal course. Research shows that firms that frequently engage in strategic management generally outperform those that do not

---

Box 1.3

The benefits of strategic management

There are many benefits in adopting a strategic management system. It:

- Helps the strategists to understand the current situation of the firm
- Gives a clear sense of vision and mission for the firm
- Assesses the strengths and weaknesses of the firm and enables it to focus on what is strategically important
- Helps strategists to set the proper goals and objectives of the firm
- Prepares the means to achieve the goals and objectives of the organisation
- Allows an organisation to be more proactive
- Prepares the firm to get ready to confront any controlled and/or uncontrolled issues
- Creates a process of communication within an organisation, thus facilitating commitment to the achievement of specified goals
- Evaluates the implementation of the strategy of the firm, providing information on the issue of 'fit' with the environment, and aids understanding of the nature of the environmental change
- Allows ethics and corporate social responsibility to infuse the strategy process.

The limitations of strategic management in SMEs

Despite the many advantages for managers of small businesses in using strategic management, there are still some who avoid the process because they:

- Lack knowledge of strategic management techniques
- Lack time and planning
- May be unaware of the importance of strategic management
- Lack the necessary knowledge and information about strategic planning and its advantages
- Pay less attention to financial indicators such as cash flow
- Lack the necessary managerial skills
- Are heavily involved in the daily and routine operations
- Feel uncertainty about the future
- Have few employees
- Lack effective MIS, especially ineffective and poor data recording systems.

(Wheelen and Hunger, 1998). Strategic management allows an organisation to be more proactive than reactive, preparing it to confront any controlled or uncontrolled issues. Strategic management gives a clear sense of vision and mission for the firm. Having clear vision will create synergy and combine the firm's energies together. It helps effectively to communicate the plans and therefore facilitates the attainment of commitment to the achievement of the organisational goals. Strategic management assesses the strengths and weaknesses of the firm and thus focuses on what is strategically important. By evaluating the implementation of the strategy the firm receives relevant information about the issue of 'fit' with the environment and begins to understand the environment as it changes. Moreover, it allows ethics and corporate social responsibility to infuse the strategy process.

As discussed earlier, although there are many advantages for small businesses in using strategic management, still there are some managers who, for one reason or another, avoid using strategic management. These are:

- SME managers who may be unaware of the importance of strategic management for their business. They may lack the necessary knowledge and information about the process and its advantages for them and their firms. Some managers of small businesses are not familiar with strategic management techniques. It may be that they think the process is only useful for large organisations or that they do not believe in long term planning.

- SME managers who may lack the relevant managerial skills necessary to initiate and use the process in running their business. They might be aware that long term planning can help, but they do not know how to achieve it.

- Finally and more importantly, many small business managers are heavily involved in the daily operations. Those day-to-day routine operations may take up the time necessary for strategic and long term planning. They do not wish to spend time and money on strategic planning because they feel that they do not know what will happen in the future.

Entrepreneurship and strategy

As discussed in the beginning of this chapter, small and medium-sized enterprises are key drivers of economic growth and job creation in the United Kingdom (Bryson, *et al.* 1992; McKiernan and Morris, 1995; Webb and Pettigrew, 1999). The shift to a knowledge-based, global economy is opening up new opportunities and challenges for these small businesses. While the fields of strategic management and small businesses have developed largely independently of each other, they are both focused on how firms adapt to environmental change and exploit opportunities created by uncertainties and discontinuities in the creation of wealth (Hitt and Ireland, 2000; Venkataraman and Sarasvathy, 2001). Entrepreneurship is about creation; strategic management is about how advantage is established and maintained from what is created (Venkataraman and Sarasvathy, 2001). As such, several scholars have recently called for the integration of strategic and entrepreneurial thinking (McGrath and MacMillan, 2000). Accordingly, Meyer and Heppard (2000) argue that the two are really inseparable. McGrath and MacMillan (2000) assert that strategists must exploit an entrepreneurial mindset and thus have no choice but to embrace it to seize opportunities, mobilise resources and act to exploit these opportunities, especially under highly uncertain conditions.

Venkataraman and Sarasvathy (2001) use a metaphor based on Shakespeare's *Romeo and Juliet*. They suggest that strategic management research that does not integrate an entrepreneurial perspective is like the balcony without Romeo. Alternatively, they argue that entrepreneurship research without integration of a strategic perspective is like Romeo without a balcony.

It is important to recognise that in studying strategic management practice in small and medium-sized firms the role of the entrepreneur is critical (Brown, 1995; McGrath and McMillan, 2000; Meyer and Heppard, 2000). In business, preparation comes through strategic planning (Schwenk and Shrader, 1993). Many owners and managers of small businesses routinely plan their day-to-day operations, but do not believe that strategic planning applies to them. However, it has been argued that no business is too small to require a sound strategy and few strategies are so simple that they need not be developed into a strategic plan (Sandberg *et al.* 2001). The entrepreneur's personal goals, characteristics and strategic awareness will all significantly impact on the development of the business (Schlegelmich and Ross 1987; Daft *et al.* 1988; McKenna, 1996). Previous studies have already shown that whether or not an effective process of strategy development is implemented will be heavily influenced by the firms' owner-manager, and that the ability to comprehend and make appropriate use of sophisticated strategic management practice is a function of the entrepreneur's previous experience (Robinson *et al.* 1986; McKenna, 1996; Berry, 1998; Chan and Foster, 2001).

Who are the strategic managers?

It is now appropriate to consider who has the responsibility for making strategic decisions in the organisations. Strategic management is meant to be useful for managers and tends to see the organisation from the top downward – from the manager's point of view. Determined strategic managers are always trying to build on the organisation's strength and capitalise on favourable circumstances, while minimising weaknesses and attempting to overcome potential threats to the organisation (Goldsmith, 1995; Kakabadse *et al.* 1996).

Therefore the task of managing strategy is the duty of strategic managers in the organisation. But who are they? The term strategic manager is being used here to describe the chairman, chief executive or managing directors who are visibly responsible for strategic decisions and changes in the firm. The strategic leader (manager) can be a single person or a team of executives responsible for the board of directors and through the board, to the stakeholders of the business (Barney, 1986; Analoui, 2000).

An effective strategic leader ensures the organisation has a strategic vision and an appropriate structure which allows the implementation of a successful strategy. Consequently, it is vital that the strategic leader ensures that there is a strong, competent and balanced executive team at the head of the organisation.

> **Box 1.4 Who are the strategists in SMEs?**
>
> Entrepreneurs, CEOs and business owner-managers are the main strategists and decision-makers in small businesses. They are involved in all three levels of the strategic decision-making processes within the firm – corporate, business and functional.

Additionally, it is important that the strategic leader ensures the necessary coordination between other strategic leadership factors, such as structure, culture and resources in the organisation.

The board of directors and senior management are the main strategic managers of large corporations. Chief executive officers (CEOs) or owner-managers are the main strategic managers in SMEs. The CEO of the corporation usually conducts the top management function with the chief operating officer (COO) or president, executive vice president and vice presidents of divisions and functional areas. Usually there are two kinds of senior managers who are most directly responsible for strategy – business managers and corporate strategists. Business managers are in charge of strategic business units (SBUs). In a diversified multibusiness firm, the executives in charge of strategic business units are business managers and go by a variety of titles including business manager, division manager and strategic business unit manager. The president and a chairperson of a single business enterprise also act as business managers.

Corporate managers are responsible for the portfolio of the business. Consequently, corporate managers exist only in multibusiness firms. The president and chairperson of such an enterprise are corporate managers. They go by a variety of titles including group vice president and executive vice president. Both business and corporate managers play pivotal roles in the strategic management process. They are the key people who bring all other assets into play when competing with other firms. They also present the highest levels of power within the firm or subunit. Thus these senior managers perform multiple tasks at the highest level of an organisation and bear the highest responsibility for their firm's strategies (Pitts and Lei, 1996).

The entrepreneur as strategist

As discussed earlier, in large organisations, the board of directors, senior management team and chief executive offices play the role of strategic managers. In multibusiness firms, strategic business unit (SBU) managers act as strategists – in small businesses, the business owner-manager or entrepreneur who organises and manages the business is the ultimate strategist. Entrepreneurs and business owner-managers make all strategic as well as operational decisions in the firm. They are simultaneously involved in all three levels of strategic decision-making processes – corporate, business and functional. Entrepreneurs develop the vision and mission of the business and thus formulate and implement the business strategies of the firm.

Characteristics of successful entrepreneurs

What are the key characteristics of successful entrepreneurs as ultimate strategists in SMEs? What does it take to be a successful entrepreneur and is there a perfect combination of attributes that can be used to predict success? Are there different characteristics for successful entrepreneurs?

A great deal of research has been carried out in this area and we do know that there are some key characteristics of successful entrepreneurs. Generally speaking, successful entrepreneurs are the strategists who are well motivated, flexible, creative and risk takers. They are proactive leaders and use strategic planning and organisation in their decision-making process. Successful entrepreneurs are skilled managers with previous experiences in the business.

They are self-motivated individuals who begin the business on their own and successful entrepreneurs are often self-financed. Some of the characteristics of successful entrepreneurs are discussed in more detail below.

Motivation

Successful entrepreneurs are extremely self-motivated and enthusiastic. Starting and running a business from the beginning requires enormous energy and successful entrepreneurs are very excited and enthused about their businesses. Determination to succeed is vital for the success of any business. Highly motivated individuals believe in themselves and their ability to develop the business – and they transmit that enthusiasm to others. They encourage the other employees to be active and enthusiastic in achieving organisational goals and objectives. The entrepreneurs' motivated behaviour is a good pattern for the employees in adapting to the organisational environment.

Box 1.5

Successful entrepreneurs are characterised as:

- Highly motivated
- Innovative and flexible
- Risk takers
- Proactive leaders
- Good planners and organisers
- Benefiting from previous experiences
- Having technical knowledge
- Hard workers
- Self-starters
- Having personal financial resources.

Flexibility and innovation

Successful entrepreneurs are creative and have dreams and goals. They are flexible, listen to their customers and adapt to meet those needs. They do not operate exclusively on their own preconceived notions about the marketplace. Successful entrepreneurs use innovative approaches to deal with organisational issues.

Risk takers

Successful entrepreneurs are able to determine the level of risk and have the courage to take risks, but they are not gamblers. The research reveals that there seems to be positive association between risk and output – a high level of risk normally comes with outstanding outputs. Successful entrepreneurs are aware and accept that their decisions may have positive or negative outcomes.

Proactive leader

Successful entrepreneurs are proactive leaders. They like challenge, enjoy competing with others, do not wait for the future with ideal conditions to react and they seek out, evaluate and act on professional advice. They are constantly looking for ways to improve their operations. Successful entrepreneurs inspire other people to help them achieve their goals. They are comfortable with people and good at communicating their vision and needs. Successful entrepreneurs also know how to monitor and supervise people to make sure that their instructions are carried out properly.

Planning and organising

Successful entrepreneurs are good planners and organisers. The business world is too complex for the sloppy or disorganised to succeed for any length of time. They stick to their time management. The myth of the entrepreneur flying by the seat of his pants is just that, a myth. Whether you're running a one-person business or a large company success is in the details. Successful entrepreneurs develop a system for managing their time and following up on important items. Because entrepreneurs often juggle many tasks – including sales, marketing, production and paying bills – they must be flexible and able to tolerate some degree of chaos.

Previous experience

Prior experience in starting a business is one of the top characteristics shared by successful entrepreneurs. Because starting a business is so complex, with uncontrollable external and internal factors and so many potential pitfalls, especially taxes and government regulations and economical and technological changes, having gone through the experience in the past is an important prerequisite for the entrepreneur. Accordingly, successful and experienced entrepreneurs have a better understanding of the marketplace. The more experience individuals have, the better able they are to understand what it is that customers want and value and then devise a successful competitive strategy to serve those customers. Successful entrepreneurs are good business people. Every business must eventually make a profit and successful entrepreneurs keep their eye on the bottom line. They understand how to read financial statements, how to plan cash flows and how to obtain financing. They also understand marketing issues, production techniques and the business climate. Successful entrepreneurs have good business sense and make decisions based on a realistic appraisal of their business and the marketplace.

Technical knowledge

Successful entrepreneurs have managerial and technical knowledge of their business. They know how to manage the business and have the balance of skills required for running the business. A sound working knowledge of both general business practices and the processes used to deliver goods and services is a must: the more skill sets that entrepreneurs have, particularly in the early stages of the new business, the better off they are likely to be. Entrepreneurs are trained and have developed their managerial skills in the areas of marketing, accounting, administration and managing people. Today's entrepreneurs are better educated than ever. Research shows that the successful entrepreneur has, alongside technical skills, a managerial and a good educational background. In addition, there are a variety of highly skilled consultants who can help entrepreneurial ventures be successful.

Hard workers

Successful entrepreneurs have a high level of energy and are hardworking people who are willing to stick with their business. Entrepreneurs generally work long hours and take responsibility for the hundreds of details involved in managing their business. They continue to work hard even when they are bored, tired or discouraged. Successful entrepreneurs are thoroughly committed to their idea, which keeps them focused even when things do go wrong. Despite difficult times, successful entrepreneurs continue to take the steps needed to make their business dreams come true.

Self-starters

Entrepreneurs are self-motivated people who begin projects on their own. They don't wait for anybody's approval or for somebody else to motivate them, but begin developing their business because of their own vision and instincts.

Personal financial resources

The vast majority of new ventures are still launched on the strength of the entrepreneur's personal financial resources. Family and friends support successful entrepreneurs financially. Successful entrepreneurs consider the impact of the business on their personal life. They explain the changes that the new business will bring – such as long hours or extensive travel – and develop a plan that family and friends can live with.

The organisation of this book

The discussions in this volume revolve around the concept of strategy for small and medium-sized businesses. They are organised sequentially in ten separate but interrelated chapters.

After briefly introducing the field and its importance for small enterprises, the remaining part of Chapter 1 deals with the concept and process of strategic management. It sets the scene for the remaining chapters by exploring the benefits and limitations of strategic management for SMEs and delineating the salient characteristics of successful entrepreneurs. The intention is to show the crucial role of the managers as strategists. The structure and organisation of the discussions in this book clearly reinforce this point.

Chapter 2 is concerned with the condition and role of small businesses in the UK. It opens the discussion by defining SMEs using theoretical and practical examples. Consequently, the advantages and disadvantages of small businesses and their importance to the UK economy are explored providing the grounds for reaching the conclusion that, given future uncertainties and intense competition, there is a need for SME managers begin to think strategically.

In Chapter 3, the process of strategic management for SMEs, the evolution of the concept, its definitions and four main approaches to strategic management are dealt with in detail. These provide a basis for the introduction of a dynamic model of strategic management in SMEs followed by detailed explanations of each stage; namely awareness, strategy formulation and implementation.

The competitive nature of the environment and its analysis is dealt with in Chapter 4. Here attention is paid to the process of environmental analysis in SMEs using a comprehensive overview of the research background in the sector. This discussion is followed by analysis of the external political, economic, sociocultural and technological aspects of (PEST) the environment, focusing on issues such as resource, value chain and finally SWOT analysis.

Now that a clear distinction has been made between small and large corporate organisations, Chapter 5 focuses on the concept of strategy formulation, especially in SMEs. The discussion begins by exploring vision and mission statements and goes on to review the theoretical background and practical aspects of dealing with the task of strategy formulation. Since the issue of strategy has always been associated with planning, particular attention is paid to this ongoing debate prior to the introduction of generic and business strategies at corporate levels. Then the relationship between vision as the property of senior management and the nature and types of strategy formulated by the senior management of small firms are clearly set out.

No matter how perfect the formulation of the strategy may be, much can still go wrong during implementation. Therefore, Chapter 6 is dedicated to task of strategic planning and the sequence of the activities necessary for the development of a business plan. Following the review of the concept and the exploration of its importance for small enterprises, the types of planning are discussed in some depth. Attention is therefore drawn to the preparation of an effective strategic plan and its practical applications in SMEs.

The issue of implementing strategy in SMEs is discussed in Chapter 7. Here we focus first on the constituent elements of a successful strategy; then the vital role and contributions of the related organisational issues in SMEs such as structure, leadership, human resources, culture and budgeting in implementing a strategy are emphasised. This holistic view and analysis is then extended to an in-depth discussion of the role that human resources play in the successful implementation of business strategy. The need for the presence of effective management of the different phases of implementation is emphasised.

The management of a successful business not only go about implementing their plan strategically, they also ensure strategic control by evaluating the activities undertaken, hence the focus for Chapter 8. To exercise effective control there is a need for systematic and continual evaluation of the business performance. This and other related concepts, such as different approaches to the measurement of firms' performance, are discussed to ensure that the reader is made aware of the relationship between evaluation and control and the need for alteration, modification and even change of a particular strategy. Without effective evaluation managers as strategists will not be able to determine how well or badly the firm is doing at any given time in the market.

A methodical and strategic approach to the functional strategies such as marketing, pricing, advertising, financing and human resources is the main concern of the discussions in Chapter 9. After introducing the essential functions of the firm each concept is dealt with comprehensively, thus providing the reader with the opportunity to gain an expert understanding of the subject and simultaneously benefit from coherent practical viewpoints. These detailed discussions remind scholars and practitioners that without paying attention to methodical collection of data, analysis and their interpretation, it would be impossible to contemplate gaining a competitive advantage in the market.

Of course, the adoption of the correct pricing strategy, be it pricing the product or service on a discounting basis or psychologically, is as important as their promotion and advertising. In this chapter we further consider how SMEs, like other businesses, have to make a financing decision and more importantly have to adopt a realistic strategy to recruit, select, train, develop and reward the human resources of the organisation in order to make the goals of their business realisable. The strategic nature of these issues for the success of the business can not be understated.

Finally, in Chapter 10, it is contended that in the global competitive market small firms play a decisive role in the economy and can provide successful enterprises for their owners, managers or shareholders. However, given the strategic nature of business nowadays, faced with an intense constant flux and global competitive organisations, managers as leaders and strategists are in an unenviable position to either make or break a business.

In order to make it, however, and survive through this and the next decade, it is vital that owner-managers and/or the top management team begin to think strategically. It is only in this way that a competitive advantage for SMEs can be successfully secured.

Summary

- Small and medium-sized enterprises are the backbone of the economy, accounting for more than half of total employment and over 80 per cent of employment growth in the past decade. Moreover, small firms are often innovative and challenging to manage strategically. Therefore it is important to assess the value of approaches like strategic management for improving the performance of these firms.

- Strategy as an aspect of management is concerned with the general direction and long term policy of the firm and is a means to achieve organisational goals and objectives. Strategic management is that set of managerial decisions and actions that determines the long term performance of a firm. It is the process by which the strategists determine the firm's mission and objectives, formulate and craft the strategies to achieve those goals and objectives, implement the chosen strategies and evaluate the results. Strategic management includes environmental analysis, strategy formulation, strategy implementation and control.

- There are many benefits in adapting a strategic management system for these organisations. Some of those benefits are listed here. Strategic management helps the strategists to understand the current situation of the firm and have a clear sense of vision and mission for the firm. It enables the managers to assess the strengths and weaknesses of the firm and focus on what is strategically important. Strategic management helps strategists to establish proper goals and objectives for the firm and prepare the means to achieve those goals and objectives successfully. It allows an organisation to be more proactive than reactive and to be ready to face any controlled or uncontrolled issues and situations. By evaluating the strategy for the implementation of a plan the strategists benefit from information about the issue of 'fit' with the environment and begin to understand the environmental changes which may impact on their business.

- There are still some managers of small businesses who avoid using strategic management. This is largely due to a lack of knowledge of the strategic management techniques, a lack of time and/or the inability to plan. SME managers may be unaware of the importance of strategic management for their business. Their lack of knowledge and information about strategic planning and its advantages will lead to an inability to establish a strategic management system within their firms. Other reasons include lack of attention paid to the financial indicators such as cash flow; lack of necessary managerial skills; excessive involvement in daily and routine operations; anxiety about the uncertain future; low number of employees and poor management information system (MIS), especially ineffective data recording systems.

- The responsibility for effective management of strategy in the organisation ought to be the remit of the strategic managers. The term strategic manager is being used to describe the chairman, chief executive or managing director who is clearly responsible for taking strategic decisions and initiating and managing change in the firm. The strategic leader (manager) can be a single person or a team of executives and in that sense they are accountable to the board of directors and through the board to the stakeholders of the business. The board of directors and top management are the main strategic managers of large corporations. However, chief executive officers (CEOs) or owner-managers are the main strategic managers in SMEs. In multibusiness firms, managers of strategic business units (SBU) act as strategists while in small businesses, the business owner-manager and the entrepreneur who organise and manage the business are the ultimate strategist. They are involved in three levels of corporate, business and functional levels of strategic decision-making processes within the firm.

- There are different characteristics for successful entrepreneurs as strategists in small businesses. Successful entrepreneurs are the strategists who are motivated, flexible, creative and are risk takers. They are proactive leaders and use strategic planning and organisation in the decision-making process. Successful entrepreneurs are skilled managers with previous experiences in business who begin the business on their own. Finally, successful entrepreneurs are often self-financed.

Discussion questions

1. Due to which dimensions of the small and medium-sized enterprises does studying strategy in SMEs gain importance?
2. How would you define strategic management?
3. What is the process of strategic management? List and explain the three steps involved in a typical strategic management process.
4. Compare the pros and cons of studying strategic management in small businesses.
5. What do you consider the relationship between strategy and entrepreneurship to be?
6. Who are the strategic managers in the organisation? Compare large firms with small and medium-sized enterprises.
7. Who is an entrepreneur? List and explain at least five of the characteristics of the successful entrepreneur.

Case study *Developing a successful small business*

Late in December Kevin, a computer engineer, received a phone call from his college friend Tony. After wishing each other merry Christmas and a happy new year, the conversation turned to business. Tony, a graduate from business school, was inviting Kevin to become a coinvestor in his business.

Until the previous year his father had run the company, Computer Technology (CT) Ltd. However, he had recently died and the company had become Tony's responsibility. As a business graduate Tony had little knowledge of computer engineering and had come to the

conclusion that somebody with these skills and knowledge was needed in order for the company to continue to thrive.

Background

Kevin, a computer engineering graduate from a reputable university, had always shown an aptitude for engineering and for assuming leadership roles; although he does not come from an entrepreneurial family he has always harboured an ambition to own and run his own company within the computer industry.

▶

His father, also an engineer, had worked for the same company for 30 years but was now retired due to the closure of the firm. His mother is a housewife and his sister is studying accounting at college. Kevin's business experience comes from his three years working with an international computer company.

After giving consideration to his experience and personal interests and Tony's business experience, Kevin decided to join forces with Tony.

Tony transferred all his assets, cash, inventory, equipment, equity and liabilities to the new company, Kevin borrowed money from the bank and invested it in computer assembly equipment and together they set up a new company – Sunrise Computer Technology (SCT) Ltd. (Table 1.1 illustrates the balance sheet.)

Now Kevin and Tony are trying to introduce their firm and product into the market. Their main priority is to compete with other firms and give the same quality products for cheaper prices. They see many opportunities for future expansion. Profit is not a priority for SCT at the moment. Kevin says he gains satisfaction and happiness from running a successful business.

Table 1.1

Balance sheet: Sunrise Computer Technology Ltd

January 30, beginning of the first year

Assets		Liabilities and equity	
Cash	6284	Accounts payable	6230
Inventory	4672	Notes payable	5000
Total current assets	10956	Total current liabilities	11230
Office equipments	2395	Stock	30000
Assembly line machinery	18 456		
Unassembled parts	3567		
Furniture and fixtures	5856		
Total fixed assets	30274		
Total assets	41230	**Total liabilities and equity**	41230

Case study questions

1. What consideration did Kevin give to the business proposition by Tony?
2. Why did Kevin decide to join forces with Tony and start a joint venture?
3. Did Tony take a risk by transferring all his assets to SCT Ltd?
4. Why, in your opinion, did Tony contact Kevin?
5. What does the balance sheet tell you about the state of the company?
6. In your opinion, is Kevin likely to come up with his own small business in the near future?
7. What, in your opinion, is Kevin's main motivation for remaining in the business with Tony?

References

Ackelsberg, R. and Arlow, P. (1985) Small businesses do plan and it pays off, *Long Range Planning*, 18 (5), 61–67.

d'Amboise, G. and Muldowney, M. (1988) Management theory for small business: Attempts and requirements, *Academy of Management Review*, 13 (2), 226–240.

Analoui, F. (1997) *Senior Managers and Their Increased Effectiveness*, Avebury, Aldershot, UK.

Analoui, F. (2000) What motivates senior managers? The case of Romania, *Journal of Managerial Psychology*, 15 (4), 324–326.

Analoui, F. (ed.) (2002) *The Changing Patterns of Human Resource Management*, Ashgate, Aldershot, UK.

Analoui, F. and Karami, A. (2002) CEOs and development of the meaningful mission statement, *Corporate Governance The International Journal of Effective Board Performance*, 2 (3), 13–21.

Andrews, K. (1971) *The Concept of Corporate Strategy*, Irwin, Homewood, IL.

Andrews, K. (1986) *The Concept of Corporate Strategy*, Irwin, Homewood, IL.

Ansoff, H. I. (1965) *Corporate Strategy*, McGraw Hill, New York.

Ansoff, H. I. and McDonnell, I. (1990) *Implementing Strategic Management*, Prentice Hall, Englewood Cliffs, NJ.

Apfelthaler, G. (2000) Why small enterprises invest abroad: The case of four Austrian firms with U.S. operations, *Journal of Small Business Management*, 38 (3), 92–99.

Bantel, K. A. and Jackson, S. E. (1989) Top management and innovations in banking: Does the composition of the top management team make a difference?, *Strategic Management Journal*, 10, 107–124.

Barney, J. B. (1986) Organisational culture: Can it be a source of sustained competitive advantage?, *Academy of Management Review*, 11, 656–665.

Beal, R. M. (2000) Competing effectively: Environmental scanning, competitive strategy and organisational performance in small manufacturing firms, *Journal of Small Business Management*, 38 (1), 27–47.

Berry, M. (1998) Strategic planning in small high-tech companies, *Long Range Planning*, 31 (3), 455–466.

Bowman. C. (1998) *Strategy in Practice*, Prentice Hall Inc., London.

Bowman, C. and Faulkner, D. (1997) *Competitive Corporate Strategy*, Irwin, London.

Bowman, C. and Kakabadse, A. (1997) Top management ownership of the strategy problem, *Long Range Planning*, 30 (2), 197–208.

Boyd, B. K. (1991) Strategic planning and financial performance: A meta-analytic review, *Journal of Management Studies*, 28, 353–374.

Bracker, J. S. and Pearson, J. N. (1986) Planning and financial performance of small, mature firms, *Strategic Management Journal*, 7, 503–522.

Bracker, J. S., Keats, B. W. and Pearson, J. N. (1988) Planning and financial performance among small firms in a growth industry, *Strategic Management Journal*, 9, 591–603.

Bridge, J. and Peel, M. J. (1999) A study of computer usage and strategic planning in the SME sector, *International Small Business Journal*, 17 (4), 82–87.

Brown, R. (1995) Family business: Rethinking strategic planning, paper presented at the 40th Annual International Council on Small Business, Sydney, Australia, June.

Bryson, J., Keeble, D. and Wood, P. (1992) *Business networks flexibility and regional development in UK business services*, Working Paper No. 19, Small Business Research Centre, University of Cambridge.

Chan, S. Y. and Foster, J. M. (2001) Strategy formulation in small business: The Hong Kong experiences, *International Small Business Journal*, April–June, 56–71.

Cragg, P. B. and King, M. (1988) Organisational characteristics and small firms' performance revisited, *Entrepreneurship Theory and Practice*, 13 (2), 49–64.

Daft, R. L., Sormunen, L. and Parks, D. (1988) Chief Executive scanning, environmental characteristics and company performance: An empirical study, *Strategic Management Journal*, 9, 123–139.

David, F. R. (1995) *Cases in Management*, Prentice Hall, Englewood Cliffs, NJ.

DTI (1998) White Paper *Competitiveness*, http://www.dti.gov.uk/er/inform.htm.

Foster, M. J. (1993) Scenario planning for small businesses, *Long Range Planning*, 26 (1), 123–129.

Gable, M. and Topol, M. T. (1987) Planning practices of small-scale retailers, *American Journal of Small Business*, 12 (2), 19–32.

Goldsmith, A. (1995) Making managers more effective: Applications of strategic management, Working Paper No. 9, USAID March.

Goodwin, D. R. and Hodgett, R. A. (19991) Strategic planning in medium size companies, *Australian Accountant*, 61 (2), 71–83.

Hambrick, D. C. (1981) Environment, strategy and power within top management teams, *Administrative Science Quarterly*, 26, 253–276.

Hambrick, D. C. (1983) Some tests of the effectiveness and functional attributes of Miles and Snow's strategic types, *Academy of Management Journal*, 2 (6), 5–25.

Hitt, M. A. and Ireland R. D. (2000) The intersection of entrepreneurship and strategic management research. In D. L. Sexton and H. A. Landstrom (eds) *Handbook of Entrepreneurship*, Blackwell, Oxford, 45–63.

Hitt, M. A., Gimeno, J. and Hoskisson, R. E. (1998) Current and future research methods in strategic management, *Organisational Research Methods*, 1, 6–44.

Hoskisson, R. E. (2000) Strategy in emerging economics, *Academy of Management Journal*, 43 (3), 249–268.

Johnson, G. and Scholes, K. (1993) *Exploring Corporate Strategy: Text and Cases*, 3rd edn, Prentice Hall Publications, London.

Jones, W. D. (1982). The characteristics of planning in small firms, *Journal of Small Business Management*, 20 (3), 15–19.

Kakabadse, A., Kakabadse, N. and Myers, A. (1996) Leadership and the public sector: An internationally comparative bench marking analysis, *Public Administration and Development*, 16 (4), 377–396.

Karami, A. (2002) Corporate strategy: Evidence from British Airways plc., in F. Analoui (ed.) *The Changing Patterns of Human Resource Management*, Ashgate, Aldershot, 46–65.

Krishnan, H. A. (2001) Supplier selection practices among small firms in the United States: Testing three models, *Journal of Small Business Management*, 39 (3), 259–271.

Lowry, J. R., Avila, S. M. and Baird, T. R. (1999) Developing a niche strategy for insurance agents, *CPCU Journal*, 52 (2), 74–83.

McGrath R. G. and MacMillan, I. (2000) *The Entrepreneurial Mindset*, Harvard Business School Press, Boston, MA.

McKenna, S. D. (1996) The darker side of the entrepreneur, *Leadership and Organisational Development Journal*, 17 (5), 41.

McKiernan, P. and Morris, C. (1995) Strategic planning and financial performance in UK SMEs: Does formality matter?, *British Journal of Management*, 5, 31–41.

Meyer, G. D and Heppard, K. A. (2000) *Entrepreneurship as Strategy: Competing on the Entrepreneurial Edge*, Sage, Thousand Oaks, CA.

Miller, D. and Toulouse, J. M. (1986) Strategy, structure, CEO personality and performance in small firms, *American Journal of Small Businesses*, Winter, 47–62.

Mintzberg, H. (1994) *The Rise and Fall of Strategic Planning*, Free Press, New York.

Mintzberg, H. and Quinn, J. B. (1998) *Reading in the Strategy Process*, 3rd edn, Prentice Hall Inc., New Jersey.

O'Gorman, C. and Doran, R. (1999) Mission statements in small and medium sized businesses, *Journal of Small Business Management*, 37 (4), 59–66.

Official UK Labour Market Statistics (1998) *Annual Employment Survey*, http://www.nomisweb.co.uk/news/april01.html#ABI

Orpen, C. (1985) The effects of long-range planning on small business performance: A further examination, *Journal of Small Business Management*, 23 (1), 16–23.

Pearce, J. and R. Robinson (1994) *Strategic Management: Strategy Formulation and Implementation*, 5th edn, Irwin, Boston, MS.

Phillips, P. A. and Moutinho, L. (2000) The strategic planning index: A tool for measuring strategic planning effectiveness, *Journal of Travel Research*, 38 (4), 369–370.

Pitts, R. A. and Lei, D. (1996) *Strategic Management Building and Sustaining Competitive Advantage*, West Publishing Company, Minneapolis, MN.

Porter, M. (1979) How competitive forces shape strategy, *Harvard Business Review*, March–April.

Porter, M. (1980) *Competitive Strategy*, Free Press, New York.

Porter, M. (1985) *Competitive Advantage: Creating and Sustaining Superior Performance*, Free Press, New York.

Porter, M. (1998) *On Competition*, Harvard Business School Press, Boston, MA.

Robinson, R. B. (1982) The importance of outsiders in small firm strategic planning, *Academy of Management Journal*, 25 (1), 80–93.

Robinson, R. B. and Pearce, J. A. (1984) Research trusts in small firm strategic planning, *Academy of Management Review*, 9 (1), 128–137.

Robinson, R. B., Pearce, J. A., Vozikis, G. and Mescon, T. (1984) The relationship between stage of development and small firm planning and performance, *Journal of Small Business Management*, 22 (2), 45–52.

Robinson, R. B., Salem, M. Y., Logan, J. E. and Pearce, J. A. (1986) Planning activities related to independent retail firm performance, *American Journal of Small Business*, 11 (1), 19–26.

Sandberg, W. R., Robinson, R. B. and Pearce, J. A. (2001) Why small businesses need a strategic plan, *Business and Economic Review*, 48 (1), 12–15.

Schlegelmilch, B. and Ross, A. G. (1987) The influence of managerial characteristics on different measures of export success, *Journal of Marketing Management*, 3 (2), 145–158.

Schwenk, C. R. and Shrader, C. R. (1993) Effects of formal strategic planning on financial performance in small firms: A meta-analysis, *Entrepreneurship Theory and Practice*, 17 (3), 53–72.

Scott, M. and Bruce, R. (1987) Five stages of growth in small business, *Long Range Planning*, 20 (3), 45–52.

Segev, E. (1987) Strategy, strategy making and performance: An empirical investigation, *Strategic Management Journal*, 8, 565–577.

Sexton, D. L. and Van Auken, P. (1985) A longitudinal study of small business strategic planning, *Journal of Small Business Management*, 23 (1), 7–15.

Shrader, C. B., Mulford, C. L. and Blackburn, V. L. (1989) Strategic and operational planning, uncertainty and performance in small firms, *Journal of Small Business Management*, 27 (4), 45–60.

Smith, J. A. (1998) Strategies for start-ups, *Long Range Planning*, 31 (6), 857–872.

Smith, J. G. and Fleck, V. (1987) Business strategies in small high technology companies, *Long Range Planning*, 20 (2), 61–68.

Stacey, R. D. (1993) *Strategic Management and Organisational Dynamic*, Pitman Publishing, London.

Stone, B. (1999) Ergonomics and the small to medium sized organisation, *The Safety & Health Practitioner*, 17 (7), 15–16.

Storey, D. J. (1994) *Understanding the Small Business Sector*, Routledge, London.

Thompson, J. L. (1995) *Strategy in Action*, Chapman & Hall Publications, London.

Thompson, J. L. (1996) *Strategic Management: Awareness and Change*, 2nd edn, Chapman & Hall Publications, London.

Unni, V. K. (1981) The role of strategic planning in small business, *Long Range Planning*, 14 (2), 54–58.

Venkataraman, S. and Sarasvathy, S. D. (2001) Strategy and entrepreneurship: Outlines of an untold story, in M. A. Hitt, E. Freeman and J. S. Harrison (eds) *The Blackwell Handbook of Strategic Management*, Blackwell, Oxford.

Ward, J. L. (1988) The special role of strategic planning for family business, *Family Business Review*, 1 (2), 105–117.

Watts, L. R. and Ormsby, J. C. (1990) Small business performance as a function of planning formality: A laboratory study, *Journal of Business and Entrepreneurship*, 2 (1), 1–8.

Webb, D. and Pettigrew, A. (1999) The temporal development of strategy: Patterns in the UK insurance industry, *Organisation Science*, 10 (5), 601–621.

Wheelen, T. L. and Hunger, J. D. (1998) *Strategic Management and Business Policy*, Addison-Wesley, Reading, MA.

Whittington, R. (2001) *What Is Strategy and Does It Matter?*, Thomson Learning, London.

Wolff, J. A. (2000) Internationalisation of small firms: An examination of export competitive patterns, firm size and export performance, *Journal of Small Business Management*, 38 (2), 34–48.

Wood, D. R., Johnston, R. A. and DeGenaro, G. J. (1988) The impact of formal planning on the financial performance of real estate firms, *Journal of Business Strategies*, 5 (1), 44–51.

2 Small businesses in the UK

Learning objectives

By the end of this chapter you should be able to:

- Define the term small and medium-sized enterprises.

- Describe the advantages of small businesses.

- Describe the disadvantages of small businesses.

- Explore the importance of small businesses to the UK economy.

- Define what is meant by small business failure.

- Discuss the future of small businesses and the need for strategy.

The first objective of this chapter is to define the term 'small and medium-sized enterprises' (SMEs) by using theoretical backgrounds and practical examples. Our second objective is to study the advantages and disadvantages of small businesses. A review and explanation of the importance of the SMEs to the UK economy is the third objective and finally, the fourth objective is to discuss the future of SMEs and the need on the part of their managers to think strategically.

The definition of SMEs

The vast majority of enterprises in the UK are SMEs – 3.7 million businesses across the UK. It is important to define what we mean by SMEs in this book and what the characteristics of these SMEs are. Of course, identifying the 'size' of the firms is complicated by the lack of a generally agreed definition of an 'SME', either internationally or within the United Kingdom. Rigorously defining SMEs has always been difficult.

The term SME covers a variety of firms (Hertz, 1982) and most writers use the term rather loosely (d'Amboise and Muldowney, 1988). Researchers and other interested parties have used specific criteria to operationalise SME as a construct: value added, value of assets, annual sales and number of employees. The last two are most often used to delimit the category (d'Amboise and Muldowney, 1988). For a growing number of researchers and reporting organisations, the SME is generally considered to employ no more than 250 persons and to have annual sales of less than £50 million.

According to Preston *et al.* (1986) the SME is one which is independently owned and operated and which is not dominant in its field of operation. Although the term small and medium-sized enterprises (SMEs) is perceived by many authors as an ambiguous parameter which does not lend itself to simple definition, defining an SME is necessary to avoid misunderstanding of the term (Box 2.1).

Quantitatively, measure of sales revenue or numbers of employees are used, although a number of authors employ a variety of scales and sectional differences among industries are sometimes recognised (Gupta, 1988). In a more recent thorough review of financial assistance available to SMEs, it is noted that wide variations are apparent where quantitative parameters are applied to determine eligibility of the small to medium-sized firms: for example, turnover limits ranging from £50,000 to £50 million; and number of employees varying between 50 and 250 (Berry, 1998). In contrast some scholars (Scott and Bruce, 1987; Gupta, 1988) suggest that employing additional qualitative criteria can enhance quantitative definition of SME.

For instance, Scott and Bruce (1987) provided the qualitative definition of an SME. They indicated that an SME is one which has three characteristics:

1. Management is independent; usually managers are also the owners.
2. Capital is supplied and ownership is held by an individual or small group.
3. Area of operations is mainly local. Workers and owners are in one home community, but markets need not be located in the same community.

As discussed earlier, there is no single definition of a small firm, mainly because of the wide diversity of businesses. The best description of the key characteristics of a small firm remains that used by the Bolton Committee in its 1971 Report on Small Firms (Bolton, 1971). This stated that a small firm is an

---

Box 2.1 General definition of an SME

A small firm is one that has only a small share of its market, is managed in a personalised way by its owner or part-owner and not through the medium of an elaborate management structure. It is, therefore, not sufficiently large to have access to the capital market for the public issue or placement of securities.

A branch of a large company cannot be regarded as a small firm because, although it is small and may even be independent with regard to decision-making, it will still have access to capital and technical assistance from the parent company (Bannock, 1981).

independent business, managed by its owner or part-owners and having a small market share. The Bolton Report also adopted a number of different statistical definitions. It recognized that size is relevant to the sector – i.e. a firm of a given size could be small in relation to one sector where the market is large and there are many competitors; whereas a firm of similar proportions could be considered large in another sector with fewer players and/or generally smaller firms within it. A qualitative approach, based on the Bolton Committee view, would suggest that a small firm is one:

- that has a relatively small share of a competitive market;
- that is unable to influence prices or, if it is a non-profit organisation makes little significant impact in its area;
- in which the management has close personal involvement in all aspects of decision-making. In a commercial organisation they are likely to be the owners or part-owners;
- is independent, with the owners/managers having effective control of the business or activities of the organisation, although they might be limited in their freedom of action by obligations to financial institutions or founders.

Similarly, it is recognised that it may be more appropriate to define size by the number of employees in some sectors but more appropriate to use turnover in others (Small Business Services, 2000). Across government it is most usual to measure size according to numbers of full-time employees or their equivalent.

Section 247 (Qualifications of company as small or medium-sized) of the Companies Act of 1989 states that a company is 'small' if it satisfies two or more of the following requirements (Companies Act 1989):

- Turnover not more than £2 million.
- Balance sheet total not more than £975,000.
- Number of employees not more than 50.

A medium-sized company must satisfy at least two of the following requirements:

- Turnover not more than £8 million.
- Balance sheet total not more than £3.9 million.
- Number of employees not more than 250.

For statistical purposes, the Department of Trade and Industry (DTI) usually employs the following definitions:

- Micro firm: 0–9 employees
- Small firm: 0–49 employees (includes micro)
- Medium firm: 50–249 employees
- Large firm: over 250 employees.

However, in practice, schemes which are nominally targeted at small firms adopt a variety of working definition depending on their particular objectives.

The European Commission (2001) recently adopted a communication setting out a single definition of SMEs (Table 2.1). The communication also includes a (non-binding) recommendation to Member States, the European Investment Bank and the European Investment Fund encouraging them to adopt the same definitions for their programmes.

The communication permits them to use lower threshold figures, if desired. By examining the general consensus within the literature and through the combination of quantitative and qualitative approaches, the following definition for SME has been developed and employed throughout this book. SMEs exhibit the following characteristics:

- Employing up to 250 employees;
- Having an annual turnover of up to £50 million;
- Management is independent and free from outside control in taking principal decisions.

SMEs' advantages

As discussed earlier, SMEs play a key role in generating employment, promoting innovation, creating competition and generating economic wealth (Bannock, 1981). The importance of SMEs to the economy depends on their ability to fulfil these roles. Company strategies for SMEs to grow and be successful could be based either upon a technological or commercial innovation, or on a focused niche strategy with a differentiated product or services. The role of small business in the economy will be discussed in detail in the next section.

The next questions to be considered are why people go into small businesses and what are the advantages of the small business for business owners? The research reveals that there are many advantages associated with SMEs, some of which have been summarised in Box 2.2.

One of the advantages of going into the small business is the challenge that accompanies the undertaking. People who are interested in challenging jobs and are likely to be dynamic opt for small businesses. In a small business, the CEO or owner-manager is normally involved in decision-making, planning,

Table 2.1	Criteria	Micro	Small	Medium
European Commission's definition of an SME	Maximum number of employees	9	49	249
	Maximum annual turnover	n/a	7 million Euros	40 million Euros
	Maximum annual balance sheet total	n/a	5 million Euros	27 million Euros
	Independence	n/a	Not more than the 25% of the capital or voting rights held by one or more enterprises which are not themselves SMEs	

Source: European Commission (2001: 16).

Box 2.2 Small businesses' advantages

There are many advantages in going into small businesses. Some of these are:

- Involvement in a challenging situation
- Psychological satisfaction
- To be one's own boss
- Job security
- Increasing family employment opportunities
- Increasing financial benefits.

---

organising and the other duties of senior management. So involvement in a challenging job satisfies the business owners psychologically. Research reveals that most successful small business managers like to feel that they have a chance to succeed as well as a chance to fail. They want to win or fail on their own abilities and competences. They know that the final outcome depends heavily on their skills, abilities, competencies and using the opportunities in the marketplace. Most small business owners enjoy being their own boss. There is a sting in the tail, of course, in that often a great deal of responsibility is associated with the freedom to manage the business independently. Entrepreneurs, nevertheless, are willing to accept the responsibility. Also, when one owns a business job security is ensured for as long as they want with no set retirement age. Eventually the business will create more jobs if it grows successfully. Another advantage of small business is the opportunity to provide family members with a place of employment. The main advantage of having a small business, of course, is increasing financial opportunities for the business owner. Many small business owners make more money running their own company than working for someone else. There are many opportunities for success and financial benefits for business owners (Box 2.3).

Box 2.3 A move toward independence

Bill Robinson worked as a salesman for 20 years. During this time he noticed that the best sale people were not always listened to by management. The senior management of the firm made decisions without consulting with Bill. Last year, relying on his sales experience, Bill went into business for himself. Today, he has a firm with a turnover of £6 million and four sales employees. Bill admits that it feels good being the owner of a business. By running the business he has created employment opportunities for his wife and sons, he is his own boss and his job is secure. 'I don't know why I waited so long to set up my own company,' he said recently. 'I love the independence and freedom of running things my own way.'

SMEs' disadvantages

Although small businesses offer many advantages, numerous disadvantages are also associated with them (Box 2.4) including sale fluctuations, competition, increased responsibilities, financial losses, employee relations, laws and regulations and the risk of failure (Hodgetts and Kuratko, 2001). Small businesses face a sale fluctuation problem which influences their cash flow balance. In some seasons sales are high, while in others they drop significantly. Business owner-managers need to balance the cash inflow and outflow so that there are always enough funds to meet day-to-day expenses. More importantly, small businesses' failure to respond quickly to the changes in customers' values and expectations is a disadvantage. For example, in many cases small businesses are not able to adapt themselves to the rapid changes in technology and market.

Small businesses are faced with the ever present risk of competition. For many reasons, such as weak capital structure, low marketing channels, low market share and the like, they tend to face more competition that the larger concerns. For instance, rapid changes in technology can impact the small businesses dramatically. Another disadvantage for the owner of a small business is the acceptance of full responsibility for the whole business. Business owners should be highly motivated in order to accept such responsibility and develop their managerial skills in different areas of the business such as marketing, operation, financial management, human resource management and so on. Failure to develop their managerial skills and competences in all aspects of the business will inevitably lead to business failure. Fluctuation in market, technology level, customers' favourites and expectations could impact on small business dramatically. Small businesses are more susceptible to the problem of financial losses than are large corporations. Mistakes in making strategic decisions will potentially impose much higher costs to the small business – operating in the wrong market or investing money in the production of a product which is in the declining stage of its life cycle could lead to a great deal of financial loss. Another disadvantage for small businesses is that they are subject to a multitude of laws and regulations; for example, small businesses are required to secure a licence before embarking on operations. Finally, when small

---

Box 2.4 Small businesses' disadvantages

- Sale fluctuations
- Competition
- Increased responsibilities
- Financial losses
- Employee relations
- Laws and regulations
- Risk of failure (Hodgetts and Kuratko, 2001).

fail the owners often face financial ruin because most of their money is invested in the business. Generally speaking these disadvantages could either be minimised or converted to opportunities if the business owner-manager thinks strategically and considers their strengths, weaknesses, opportunities and threats when developing the business plan.

The role of SMEs in the UK economy

During the 1980s, turnover, employment and stocks of firms in a range of business services and activities in the United Kingdom all grew spectacularly (Bryson *et al.* 1992). Both large and small businesses are included. However, much of this growth, especially in the stock of business firms, has been dominated by SMEs. Small businesses play a significant role in the UK economy (Box 2.5). The majority of the United Kingdom's 3.7 million business enterprises employ fewer than 500 people, though these large firms account for almost one-third of non-government employment, but the number of SMEs increased rapidly during the 1980s and 1990s from 57 to 67 per cent.

The increase in the role of SMEs in the United Kingdom seems to have been greater than elsewhere, but most of the new firms are very small and the share of SMEs in employment and GDP appears to be less than in most other OECD countries (OECD, 1996, 1997). Nevertheless, SMEs have made a significant contribution to innovation, the maintenance of competition, the spread of entrepreneurial culture and the flexibility of the economy. Their importance in the UK economy is illustrated in Table 2.2. Whilst the UK economy, as a whole, is highly globalised, there is little reliable statistical information on the role of SMEs in its overseas activities. There is some evidence that in manufacturing, for instance, relatively fewer SMEs are globalised in the United Kingdom than in some other major OECD countries. This may not be true of the service sector, where SMEs account for a large and possibly growing proportion of exports, especially in travel, consultation, entertainment, education, computer and software and other services (OECD, 1997). There is a wide variety of approaches to globalisation and developing strategic management in SMEs. In assessing the economic impacts of globalisation, returns on foreign investment by UK companies benefit the UK economy. The benefits of a strategic management approach and globalisation are, in short, similar in nature to those of the growth of international trade in general (OECD, 1997). The UK is

---

Box 2.5 Importance of SMEs to the UK economy at a glance

The UK's 3.7 million SMEs account for approximately 40 per cent of the GDP and have an annual turnover of one trillion pounds. Employing over 12 million people, they account for 85 per cent of the 2.3 million extra jobs created by new businesses in the private sector between 1995–1999 and more than 50 per cent of the 3.5 million jobs gained from expansion over the same period (Small Business Services, 2000).

Table 2.2 Importance of SMEs by sector in the UK (percentages)

Sector	SIC	Sectoral share of total GDP	Sectoral share of total employment	Share of firms in sector which are SMEs	Share of sectoral employment (SMEs)	Share of sectoral GDP (SMEs)
Agriculture, forestry and fishing	0	1.8	2.7	100.0	99.7	
Energy and water supply	1	8.6	2.1	97.4	9.4	6.1
Manufacturing	2–4					
Metals	21, 22	0.9	0.6	98.5	29.4	
Other mineral and mineral products	23, 24	1.1	1.1	99.2	44.1	
Chemical	25	2.6	1.4	98.2	31.0	
Man-made fibres	26	0.1	0.0	88.2	15.0	
Metal goods	31	1.1	2.1	99.7	60.5	
Mechanical engineering	32	2.6	3.7	99.7	55.5	
Electrical and instrument engineering	33, 34, 37	3.7	3.2	99.3	41.8	
Motor vehicles and parts	35	1.8	0.9	98.3	31.6	
Other transport equipment including aerospace	36	1.4	0.9	98.8	27.2	
Food, drink and tobacco	41, 42	2.9	2.2	99.4	36.0	
Textile	43	0.5	1.0	99.4	45.9	
Clothing, footwear and leather	44, 45	0.7	1.6	99.8	58.8	
Paper, printing and publishing	47	2.7	2.7	99.8	56.8	
Other manufacturing (inc. timber, furniture, rubber)	46, 48, 49	2.1	3.2	99.8	67.0	
Construction	5	6.4	6.9	100.0	86.9	64.9
Distribution, hotels and catering repairs	6	14.0	25.9	99.9	86.5	29.8
Transport and communication	7	7.6	7.4	99.9	43.4	28.4
Banking, finance, insurance, business services and leasing, ownership of dwelling	8	24.2	14.8	99.9	56.5	12.2
Other services	9	20.5	15.5	99.9	77.9	48.4
Adjustment for financial services		-6.7				
Total	100.0	100.0	99.9	67.2	30.3	

Source: *Globalisation and small and medium-sized enterprises. Vol. I Synthesis Report, Vol. II Country Studies*, p. 290. Table: SMEs by sector in the UK (Vol. II) Copyright OECD 1997.

prioritising SMEs in terms of its policies and activities and a national network of business links has just been established in England.

Business links are a partnership of local business support agencies. They are the main vehicle through which government support for SMEs will be delivered locally. The UK SMEs sector is made up of a significant number of SMEs which often account for up to 90 per cent of an area's economic activity (Quayle *et al.* 1999). Many trade and industry observers noted a trend during the 1990s for technological innovation to shift away from the previously active leviathans of industry and move towards the SME. The big names in defence and engineering are, it seems, no longer able to plan proactively for, or even respond quickly to, the demands of the technology-hungry markets they once exploited on an exclusive basis. Today, as a consequence, they are turning to the innovative SME in an attempt to preserve their own longevity. The number of fact finding seminars being hosted by blue chip companies, with free invitations sent to local SMEs, is increasing. As the number of SMEs active in information technology and other commercial pursuits expands, so too will a reliance by larger companies on outsourcing for innovation and progress (Stone, 1999).

Share of SMEs in the UK industry sector

Different resources, such as Kompass UK vols 1 and 2 (1998–9) and Small Business Services, supply the statistics of the small and medium-sized enterprises in the United Kingdom. Small Business Services, the agency within government championing small businesses, have published headline statistics for the year 2000 with regard to SMEs in the UK. It is estimated that there were 3.7 million active businesses in the UK at the start of the year 2000. These statistics contain a size breakdown of the number of businesses in the UK, from small traders with no employees to those with 500 or more employees (Table 2.3). They also show the contribution made to employment and turnover by businesses of different sizes, industry by industry.

Of the entire business population of 3.7 million enterprises only 25,000 were medium sized (50 to 249 employees) and fewer than 7000 were large (250 or more employees). Small businesses, including those without employees, accounted for over 99 per cent of businesses, 44 per cent of non-government employment and 37 per cent of turnover. In contrast, the 7000 largest businesses accounted for 45 per cent of non-government employment and 49 per cent of turnover (Figure 2.1). Of the 3.7 million businesses trading at the start of 2000, nearly 2.6 million were sole proprietorships and partnerships comprising only the self-employed owner-manager(s) and companies comprising only an employee director.

Only 1.1 million enterprises were employers. The stock of enterprises has now been at a similar level for the sixth successive year following falls in 1992 and 1993. The business stock is 1.3 million higher than in 1980, the first year for which comparable figures are available. Most of the moderate growth in the business population between 1995 and 2000 has been in the number of micro businesses employing fewer than ten people and in the number of one-person companies. Table 2.3 shows the number of enterprises, employment and turnover in the private sector by size of the enterprises and industry groups in

Table 2.3   Number of enterprises – summary by size of enterprise and industry section, 2000

		Size (number of employees)			
	= 100%	None	Small (1–49)	Medium (50–249)	Large (250+)
All industries	3 722 610	69.6	29.5	0.7	0.2
A, B Agriculture, forestry and fishing	190 390	69.2	30.7	0.1	0.0
C, E Mining, quarrying, energy, water	3720	57.0	36.3	3.9	2.8
D Manufacturing	332 085	62.2	34.5	2.5	0.7
F Construction	678 515	81.8	18.0	0.2	0.0
G Wholesale, retail and repairs	536 040	51.3	47.8	0.8	0.2
H Hotels and restaurants	157 310	34.3	64.6	1.0	0.2
I Transport, storage, communication	228 075	80.6	18.6	0.6	0.2
J Financial intermediation	59 040	70.7	27.7	1.0	0.6
K Real estate, business activities	826 125	69.6	29.8	0.5	0.1
M Education	111 035	89.9	9.7	0.4	0.1
N Health and social work	207 375	75.3	23.5	1.0	0.3
O Other social/personal services	392 900	79.3	20.4	0.3	0.1

Source: Small Business Services (2000).

Figure 2.1

Share of private sector businesses, employment and turnover by size of businesses, UK, 2001

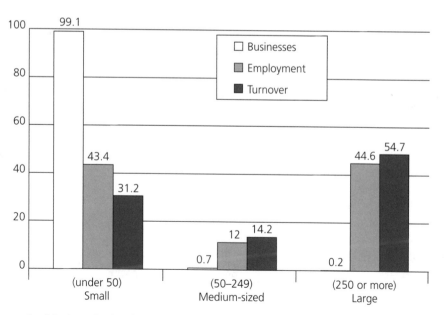

Source: Small Business Services (2000).

the UK. At the start of 2000, at least 95 per cent of businesses in all but the electricity, gas and water supply sector were small or medium sized. The share of employment provided by small businesses (with under 50 employees) varies greatly from one industry to the next. In construction it is 76 per cent while in finance it is only 14 per cent.

Table 2.4 shows the importance of the share of SMEs in the UK economy in terms of creating job opportunities, turnover and innovation and development of the technology.

Small business failure

Why do SMEs fail, and how many SMEs fail throughout the UK annually? Answers to these questions reveal the importance of strategic thinking to small businesses success. One of the methods in determining the level of business failure is to use the registration and deregistration statistics of the firms. First, let's look at the trend of the rate of small business failure in the UK from 1994 to 2000. Small Business Services (SBS) provides the official statistics for the small and medium-sized enterprises in the UK. SBS uses the VAT registrations and deregistrations as the best official guide to the pattern of business start-ups and closures. They are indicators of the levels of entrepreneurship and of the health of the business population. As such they are used widely in regional and local economic planning. Table 2.5 shows VAT registrations and deregistrations for the period 1994–2000 in the UK.

As SBS reported, there were 183 300 registrations and 177 100 deregistrations in the UK in 2000. Figure 2.2 shows the trend for SMEs' stock at the year end from 1994 to 2000. There was a net gain of 6200 registered enterprises during the year, increasing the stock of VAT-registered businesses to 1.67 million at the start of 2001. In 2000 there were 39 registrations for every 10 000 people aged 16 or over in the UK. There were 37 deregistrations for every 10 000 people aged 16 or over. The number of registrations rose by 4900 (or 3 per cent) between 1999 and 2000. The number of deregistrations rose by 5100 (or 3 per cent). The net

Table 2.4 Number of enterprises, employment and turnover in the private sector by size of enterprise and industry group, 2000 (all industries*)

	Enterprises	Employment ('000)	Turnover (£ million)	Enterprises %	Employment	Turnover
All employers	1 130 835	19 136	1 882 317	100.0	100.0	100.0
Micro (1–9)	944 775	3697	313 365	83.5	19.3	16.6
Small (10–49)	154 230	2956	291 830	13.6	15.4	15.5
Medium (50–249)	25 085	2536	282 953	2.2	13.3	15.0
Large (250+)	6745	9946	994 169	0.6	52.0	52.8

Source: Small Business Services (2000).
(*See Table 2.3 for definition of 'all industries'.)

gain of 6200 enterprises during 2000 represents a rise in the total business stock for the fifth consecutive year (Small Business Services, 2001).

Every year many small businesses fail. There are numerous reasons why businesses have problems that might ultimately prove to be fatal – lack of investment, cash flow problems, disappointing sales etc. – or because of less obvious factors such as poor planning or a lack of business experience. The major reasons are related to managerial causes. Hodgetts and Kuratko (2001) provide ten of the more specific managerial causes of small business failure, based on an SBA study of businesses that had failed. (The SBA is the Small Business Administration Service, a US governmental agency that aids small businesses by providing financial, consulting, and managerial assistance.) These are:

- Inadequate records
- Expansion beyond resources

Table 2.5

VAT registrations and deregistrations, 1994–2000

UK, thousands and rate per 10,000 resident adults					
	Registrations		Deregistrations		Stock at year end
Year	*000*	*Rate*	*000*	*Rate*	
1994	168.2	36	188.1	40	1609.30
1995	164.0	35	173.2	37	1600.10
1996	168.2	36	165.1	35	1603.20
1997	182.6	39	164.5	35	1621.30
1998	186.3	40	155.9	33	1651.60
1999	178.5	38	172.0	37	1658.10
2000	183.3	39	177.1	37	1664.40

Source: Small Business Services (2000).

Figure 2.2

Net change in the stock of VAT registered enterprises, 1998–2000

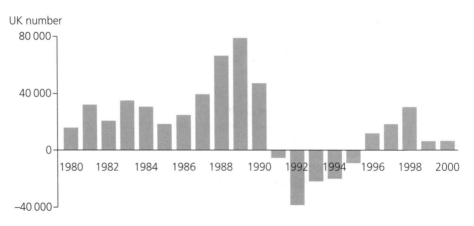

Source: Small Business Services (2000).

- Lack of information about customers
- Failure to diversify markets
- Lack of marketing research
- Legal problems
- Nepotism
- One-person management
- Lack of technical competencies
- Absentee management.

Generally speaking, the first common reason for the SMEs' failure is that of the managers, simply because they do not know how to run the business. In other words, they do not have a long term plan for the business and do not think strategically. They make major mistakes in strategic decision-making, where an experienced SME manager would quickly see and easily solve the problem. A manager's competencies and core capabilities are a considerable factor in the success of an SME and lack of managerial experience in the strategic activities of the business, such as long range planning, leads to inevitable business failure. Analoui (1993, 2000) contends that the other main reason is the unbalanced managerial skills of the SME managers. SME managers need to balance their self-related skills with the other two categories of managerial skills – people and task-related skills. More importantly, most SME managers do not possess sufficient experience in the main areas of the business: marketing, finance, operation and production. This lack of managerial skills in the main activities of the business and a limited range of managerial skills can cause the business to decline gradually.

The future of SMEs

Globalisation and change in the economical and commercial environment is accelerating because of changing technology and social patterns. Global markets have already arrived for many products. For example, Microsoft operating systems are used by 90 per cent of PCs worldwide. At the same time, markets have become more dispersed as barriers to enter national or local markets decrease (Burns, 1996). There is also a growing trend towards fragmentation of the market segments, with niches becoming ever smaller (Box 2.6).

Globalisation and the trend towards narrower market niches create opportunities for SMEs in the marketplace. The number of SMEs in the UK is growing and it is predicted that this number will continue to rise over the next decade, bringing the total to around 4.5 million. This means that SMEs will expand as large corporations shrink, thus transferring over two million jobs (SBS, 2000).

Small businesses' need for strategy

As discussed earlier, SMEs play a key role in the UK economy. Studying the impact of numerous managerial factors in SMEs' performance is important in

---

Box 2.6 A vision of 2010 by the Small Business Services

- There will be over 4.5 million SMEs in the UK
- They will have created over 2 million new jobs
- The sectoral mix of smaller businesses will have changed significantly, with fewer in manufacturing, construction and transport and more in services particularly knowledge, care, creative and leisure industries
- More businesses will trade internationally – using the Euro as currency even if the UK is not a member
- Many small businesses will be 'New Economy' companies, which are not readily amenable to traditional valuation techniques
- Almost all businesses will have Internet access and will bank electronically by 2010 (Small Business Services, 2000).

---

order to help these enterprises to fulfil their roles in the economy as a whole. One of these crucial factors is the implication for the use of strategic management in SMEs. Do SMEs need to develop a strategic plan? There is considerable debate about the application of strategy in small businesses, but the positive impacts of strategy on a firm's performance cannot be ignored. Company strategies required for SMEs to grow and be successful could be based either upon a technological or commercial innovation, or on a focused niche strategy with a differentiated product or services. Even if implementing these strategies, any growing company will face several problems as it proceeds through different phases of its life cycle; they can, however, still be considered powerful tools in managing the firm successfully in a competitive landscape.

Summary

- The term small business has been defined in a number of ways. By examining the general consensus within the literature and through the combination of quantitative and qualitative approaches, the following definition for a SME is employed throughout this book. Small and medium-sized enterprises (SMEs) exhibit the following characteristics: employing up to 250 employees; having an annual turnover of up to £50 million; and independent management who are free from outside control in taking principal decisions.
- There are numerous advantages and disadvantages in entering this sector. The advantages for individuals of going into small businesses include involvement in a challenging situation, psychological satisfaction, being one's own boss, job security, increasing family employment opportunities and finally increasing financial benefits. On the other hand, there are also risks and disadvantages associated with SMEs. These include sale fluctuations, competition, increased responsibilities, financial losses, employee relations, laws and regulations and risk of failure.

- Small businesses play a significant role in generating employment, promoting innovation, creating competition and generating economic wealth in the UK economy. The majority of the UK's 3.7 million business enterprises employ fewer than 500 people, though these large firms account for almost one-third of non-government employment. SMEs also make an important contribution to innovation, the maintenance of competition, the spread of entrepreneurial culture and the flexibility of the economy. The UK's 3.7 million SMEs account for approximately 40 per cent of the GDP and have an annual turnover of one trillion pounds.

- There are a considerable number of business failures in the SME sector every year often due to managerial causes. Some of these include lack of long term planning; lack of technical competencies, imbalance between managerial skills and competencies; failure to diversify markets; one-person decision-making; and inadequate information about customers, market, resources and technology.

Discussion questions

1. How do you define the term 'small and medium-sized enterprises'? What criteria do you use to determine your definition?

2. What are the advantages in going into small businesses? List and explain at least five factors.

3. Are there any disadvantages in small businesses? Support your answer.

4. Explain the role of SMEs in the UK economy. Support your answer.

5. What is the future of SMEs in the UK?

6. What are the major reasons for small business failure?

References

d'Amboise, G. and Muldowney, M. (1988) Management theory for small business: Attempts and requirements, *Academy of Management Review,* 13 (2), 226–240.

Analoui, F. (1993) *Skills of Management*, Longman Scientific and Technical, England.

Analoui, F. (2000) What motivates senior managers? The case of Romania, *Journal of Managerial Psychology,* 15 (4), 324–326.

Bannock, G. (1981) *The Economics of Small Firms: Return from the Wilderness*, Blackwell, Oxford.

Berry, M. (1998) Strategic planning in small high tech companies, *Long Range Planning,* 31 (3), 455–466.

Bolton, J. E. (1971) *Small firms*, Report of the commission of inquiry on small firms, HMSO, London, Cmnd. 4811.

Bryson, J., Keeble, D. and Wood, P. (1992) *Business networks flexibility and regional development in UK business services*, Working Paper No. 19, Small Business Research Centre, University of Cambridge.

Burns, P. (1996) The significance of small firms, in P. Burns and J. Dewhurst, *Small Business and Entrepreneurship*, Macmillan Education, Basingstoke.

Companies Act (1989) http://www.hmso.gov.uk/acts/acts1989/Ukpga_19890040_en_2.htm#mdiv13

European Commission (2001) *Creating an entrepreneurial Europe: the activities of the European Union for small and medium-sized enterprises (SMEs)*, Final report from the Commission to the Council, The European Parliament, The Economic and Social Committee and The Committee of the Regions, Brussels.

Gupta, A. (1988) A stakeholder analysis approach for inter organisational systems, *Industrial Management and Data Systems*, 95 (6), 3–7.

Hertz, L. (1982) *In Search of a Small Business Definition*, University Press of America, Washington, DC.

Hodgetts, R. M. and Kuratko, D. F. (2001) *Effective Small Business Management*, 7th edn, Harcourt, Inc., Orlando.

Kompass UK (1998–99) *Kompass: United Kingdom, Vol. 1, Product and Services*, Kompass, East Grinstead.

Kompass UK (1998–99) *Kompass: United Kingdom, Vol. 2*, Kompass, East Grinstead.

OECD (1996) *Best Practice Policies for Small and Medium-sized Enterprises*, OECD, Paris.

OECD (1997) *Globalisation and Small and Medium Enterprises*, Country Studies, Vol. 2, OECD, Paris.

Preston R. A., Albaum, G. and Kozmetsky, G. (1986) The public's definition of small business, *Journal of Small Business Management*, 24 (3), 63–69.

Quayle, M., Whithead, M. and Arkin, A. (1999) A small concern, *Supply Management*, 4 (22), 26–30.

Scott, M. and Bruce, R. (1987) Five stages of growth in small business, *Long Range Planning*, 20 (3), 45–52.

Small Business Services (2000) UK Small Business Services at www.sbs.gov.uk

Small Business Services (2001) UK Small Business Services at www.sbs.gov.uk

Stone, B. (1999) Ergonomics and the small to medium sized organisation, *The Safety and Health Practitioner*, 17 (7), 15–16.

3

The strategic management process in small businesses

Learning objectives

By the end of this chapter you should be able to:

- Briefly review the evolution of strategic management.

- Compare the definitions of strategy and provide a general definition of strategy.

- Discuss the four approaches to strategy: classical, evolutionary, processual and systemic approaches.

- Explore the process of strategic management in small and medium-sized enterprises.

- Explore and explain the dynamic model of strategic management in small businesses.

- Explain the steps of strategic management in small businesses.

The general objective of this chapter is to introduce the process of strategic management in SMEs. First, the evolution of the strategic management concept will be overviewed. Second, the term strategy and its definitions in management will be explored. Third, based on the recent literature, the four main approaches to strategy in management will be discussed. Reviewing the process of strategic management in small businesses is the fourth objective of this chapter. Consequently, introducing a dynamic model of the strategic management in SMEs is the next objective and finally the stages of strategic management in small businesses, including awareness, strategy formulation and implementation will be explained in the last section.

Evolution in strategic management theories

To understand what strategic management is all about, it is helpful to look at its history and review its core ideas. Strategic management grew out of both teaching and research in the field of business administration. On the teaching side, the roots were the business policy or general management classes that by the 1960s most business schools required as the 'capstone' course at the end of the business curriculum (Goldsmith, 1995). Business policy professors were forced to try to think systematically about company strategies, which eventually led them into the self-styled study of strategic management (Schendel and Cool, 1988).

On the research side, the strategic management theories evolved during four main distinct periods (Figure 3.1). Theoretically, the recent theories of strategic management such as the resource-based view of the firm (Boxall, 1996), have turned their attention towards the internal aspects of the firm whose characteristics represented the crucial research domain in the early development of strategic management (Hoskisson *et al.* 1999). Early strategy researchers such as Andrews (1971) and Ansoff (1965) were more concerned with identifying firms' 'best practices' that contribute to the firms' success. The researchers in this stream share an interest in pondering the inner growth engines or 'the black box' of the firm, and argue that a firm's continued success is chiefly a function of its internal and unique competitive resources (Hoskisson *et al.* 1999).

Figure 3.1

Evolution in strategic management theories

Source: Based on Hosskisson *et al.* (1999) Theory and research in strategic management: Swings of a pendulum, *Journal of Management*, 25 (3), 421.

During the next development period, strategic management departed, theoretically and methodologically, from the early period to the industrial organisation (IO) economics period. Developments in the field, beginning in the 1970s, fostered a move toward IO economics (Porter, 1980, 1985), with its theoretical roots based on Mason (1939) and Bain (1968). Hoskisson *et al.* (1999) argued that this swing shifted attention externally toward industry structure and securing a competitive position in the industry. Industrial organisation economics considers the structural aspect of an industry, whereas works on strategic groups are largely focused on firm grouping within an industry (Hoskisson *et al.* 1999). Strategic groups and competitive dynamics are popular research areas in the current field of strategic management.

Within the third period of developing strategic management theories, the trend to swing back toward the firm can be clearly observed. Re-emergence of internal firm characteristics is evident in the emphasis which has been placed on competitive dynamics and boundary relationships between the firm and its environment (Hill and Jones, 1995; Heene, 1997; Hoskisson *et al.* 1999). Compared to industrial organisation economics, strategic management moves much closer to the firm and direct competitive rivalry between specific firms in the competitive environment (Chen, 1996). Finally, and more recently, the popularity of the resource-based view of the firm has once again returned the focus to the inside of the firm. Theoretically, the central premise of the resource-based view of the firm addresses the fundamental questions of why firms are different and how firms achieve and sustain competitive advantage (Boxall, 1992, 1996; Grant, 1998; Hoskisson *et al.* 1999).

Strategic management and small businesses

Over the last 30 years there have been many developments in the field of strategic management in large firms as well as small and medium-sized enterprises. Many of the concepts that form the current approaches were developed over recent decades. Among the main concepts developed during the 1960s and 1970s were the product life cycle, the experiences curve, the strategic business unit (SBU), and the growth share (portfolio) matrix. The Boston Consulting Group was the dominant influence (Leavy, 1996) in forming these views. In the 1960s and 1970s the emphasis was primarily on strategies for growth, diversification and vertical integration. However, the 1980s were dominated by the contribution of Michael Porter in the field of strategic management including the five-force model (1979), generic strategies (1985) and the value chain (1985).

During the low growth of the 1980s, the emphasis in the field shifted towards competitive and renewal strategy, particularly in the core, and often in the nature of the business. There is a growing belief that the business world in the twenty-first century is facing a new set of priorities such as increasing globalisation of competition, new information and technology (Leavy, 1996). These developments are changing the nature of business and competition in several ways. The scholars in the field of strategy (Ansoff, 1965; Mintzberg, 1978; Henderson, 1979; Williamson, 1991; Stacey, 1993; Whittington, 1993) have produced a variety of definitions of business strategy, reflecting in some cases significantly differing approaches to the subject. Perhaps strategy is the main essence of management, pulling together all the strands required in running any organisation in response to competition in the operative environment.

Although much work has been undertaken to analyse and investigate strategy in large corporations, until recently there has been little concern with strategic management in SMEs (Aram and Cowan, 1990; Foster, 1993; Lang *et al.* 1997; Smith, 1998). Strategic management in small businesses has emerged as an important new conceptualisation in the field of strategic management. Traditional thinkers on strategic management were inclined to define the concept in terms of formulation of plans, hence the quest was to arrive at the optimum strategy for a given context in large organisations.

SMEs are a novel subject in strategic management research (Chell, 2001). According to Hanlon and Scott (1995), the dominant perspective in relation to strategy in smaller organisations has been the rational planning model. Planning is often seen as the key to company success (Leidecker and Bruno, 1986; Monck *et al.* 1988) since it reduces uncertainty, it ensures that alternatives are considered and assists managers in dealing with investors (O'Gorman and Cunningham, 1997). Researchers suggest that planning is contingent upon the nature of the business (Monck *et al.* 1988) the skills of the owner-manager and his or her predisposition to planning, company size and stage of development/ life cycle stage (Scott and Bruce, 1987). A survey by Berry (1998) of 257 companies found that small high tech firms do use strategic planning to direct their long term growth. However, it was found that the planning processes become more sophisticated as firms grow. Other authors have questioned the value and applicability of strategic management for the small firm (Bhide 1994). It has been argued that strategic planning loses its meaning in a dynamic environment, where innovation, flexibility and responsiveness to perishable opportunities are the key conditions for survival (Mintzberg and Quinn, 1998).

Thompson (1999) however, argued that entrepreneurs require the ability to think and act strategically. The majority of researchers view strategic management as a necessity while acknowledging that development and implementation of business strategies in small firms tends to be different from that of large firms (Carson *et al.* 1995).

In summary, the treatment of strategy in the small business literature has lagged behind that of the mainstream strategic management literature. The majority of studies have been normative in their orientation (Covin, 1991; Smallbone *et al.* 1995). However, recent studies suggest that an optimal strategy for all firms in a given context does not exist, due to variations in learning, culture, personalities, experiences and the goals of actors within the firms. In this chapter an attempt has been made to study the application of strategic management in SMEs.

What is strategy?

Let's begin with the question, what is the meaning of strategy in management? It would be useful first to review different definitions of the term strategy by management theorists. The word strategy has long been used implicitly in different ways (Chandler, 1962; Bowman and Kakabadse, 1997; Mintzberg and

Quinn, 1998) and has been conceptualised in diverse forms according to the parent social science discipline of numerous authors (Mintzberg, 1994; Marsh, 1999; Webb and Pettigrew, 1999). The concept of strategy in business and management is analogous to that of war (Luttwak, 1987). Explicit recognition of multiple definitions can help us to manoeuvre this battlefield.

Accordingly, some definitions of strategy in management are presented here and their relevant interrelationships are then carefully considered. The American business historian, Alfred D. Chandler (1962), who provided one early definition of strategy said 'strategy is the determination of the basic long term goals and objectives of an enterprise, and the adoption of courses of action and the allocation of resources for carrying out those goals' (1962: 13). Chandler subscribes to the widely held view that strategy is as much about planning and defining goals and objectives as it is about providing the means for achieving them. Hofer and Schendel (1978) provided a more continuous and interactive definition of strategy. They defined the strategy as 'a fundamental pattern of present and planned resource deployments and environmental interactions that, indicate how the organisation will achieve its objectives' (1978: 25) (Box 3.1).

We have witnessed the emergence of different, and at times novel, definitions of strategy in the 1980s. For instance, Ohmae defined strategy as 'the way in which a corporation endeavours to differentiate itself positively from its competitors, using its relative corporate strengths to better satisfy corporate needs'(1983: 93). Chaffee (1985) presented three models – linear strategy, adaptive strategy and interpretive strategy (Box 3.2). For Chaffee a tripartite classification of strategy ought to pay attention to and focus more on means, with goals seen as an alignment of the organisation and its environment. Lower level changes in style and marketing of quality are also seen as strategically important.

Although top managers are still seen as responsible for guiding strategy, other managers are clearly involved in the process (Chaffee, 1985). Of the associated terms regarded as important variables by Chaffee, strategic management appears in each of his three classifications. When strategy is linear, strategic management takes the form of long-range planning; when strategy is adaptive, strategic management balances strategic fit to company predisposition. Finally, when strategy is interpretive, strategic management can be regarded as a vital capability for the continuous improvement of quality performance.

Kenneth Andrews (1986) combines goal setting with the policies and plans needed to achieve goals. In his definition of strategy the distinction between

---

Box 3.1 What is strategy?

Strategies are means to ends, and these ends concern the purpose and objectives of the organization. They are the things that businesses do, the paths they follow and the decisions they take, in order to reach certain points and levels of success.

(Thompson, 2001: 9)

Box 3.2 Three models of strategy

Variable	Linear strategy	Adaptive strategy	Interpretive strategy
Sample definition	'determination of the basic long term goals of an enterprise, and the adaption of courses of action and the allocation of resources necessary for carrying out these goals' (Chandler, 1962: 13).	'strategy is fundamental pattern of present and planned resources deployments and environmental interactions that, indicates how the organization will achieve its objectives' (Hofer and Schendel, 1978: 25).	'Orienting metaphors constructed for the purpose of conceptualizing and guiding individual attitudes of organizational participants' (Chaffee, 1985: 94).
Nature of strategy	Decisions, actions, plans integrated	Achieving a 'match' Multifaceted	Metaphor interpretive
Focus for strategy	Means, ends	Means	Participants and potential participants in the organisation
Aim of strategy	Goal achievement	Co-alignment with the environment	Legitimacy
Strategic behaviour	Change markets, products	Change style, marketing quality	Develop symbols, improve interactions and relationships
Associated terms	Strategic planning, strategy formulation and implementation	Strategic management, strategic choice, strategic predisposition, strategic trust, strategic design, strategic fit, niche	Strategic norms, emergent strategic management, strategy and flexibility
Associated measures	Formal planning, new products, configuration of products or business, market segmentation and focus, market share, merger/acquisition, product diversity	Price, distribution policy, marketing expenditure and intensity, product differentiation, authority changes, proactiveness, risk taking, multiplexity, integration, futurity, adaptivity, and uniqueness	Measures must be derived from context and may require qualitative evaluation, demand responsiveness

Source: Adapted from Chaffee (1985) 'Three models of strategy', *Academy of Management Review*, 10 (1), 89–98.

corporate strategy – the lead strategy – and business strategy is explored. He believes that strategy is:

a pattern of decisions … [which represent] … the unity, coherence and internal consistency of a company's strategic decisions that position a company in its environment and give the firm its identity, its power to mobilise its strengths, and its likelihood of success in the marketplace.

(Andrews, 1986: 112)

Accordingly, Glueck and Jauch have defined strategy in management as a unified, comprehensive and integrated plan. They maintain that:

Strategy is a unified, comprehensive, and integrated plan that relates the strategic advantages of the firm to the challenges of the environment. It is designed to ensure that the basic objectives of the enterprise are achieved through proper execution by the organisation.

(1988: 11)

Johnson and Scholes (1993) describe strategy from a different point of view. They discuss how strategy is concerned with the full scope of an organisation's activity; the process of matching the organisation's activities to its environment and resource capabilities; having major resource implications; and being affected by the values and beliefs of those who have power in an organisation. In their empirically grounded text on exploring corporate strategy they categorise a number of different approaches:

- Natural selection: where organisations are under great environmental pressure and have to constantly adapt to changes in their environment.
- Planning: where strategy comes about through highly systematised forms of planning; this is the rational approach to strategy.
- Logical incremental: an evolutionary step-by-step approach to strategy; it is an adaptive approach but one which is more controlled by them than the natural selection example mentioned above.
- Cultural: an approach to strategy based on the experiences, assumptions and beliefs of management over time and which may eventually permeate the whole organisation.
- Political: where strategy emerges after a variety of internal battles, in which managers, individuals and groups bargain and trade their interests and information.
- Visionary: where the strategy is dominated by one individual, or sometimes a small group, who have a particular vision of where the organisation can and should be; this is a particularly intuitive approach.

More recently, Mintzberg and Quinn (1998) identified four interrelated definitions of strategy as plan, perspective, pattern, and position. They posed that strategy is first a plan – some sort of consciously intended course of actions, a guideline to deal with a situation. For example, a corporation has a plan to capture a market. As a plan, strategies may be general or they can be specific.

They discuss how a strategy is the pattern or plan that integrates an organisation's major goals, policies and action sequences into a cohesive whole (Mintzberg and Quinn, 1998: 3) (Box 3.3).

Second, strategy is defined as a pattern. It is argued that defining strategy as a plan is not sufficient; there is also a need for a definition that encompasses the resulting behaviour. Thus, strategy is proposed as a pattern, 'specifically a pattern in a stream of actions' (Mintzberg and Quinn, 1998: 11). The definition of strategy whether as plan or pattern can be quite independent of each other: plans may go unrealised, while patterns may appear without preconception. They argue that:

> If we label the first definition 'intended' strategy and the second 'realized' strategy, then we can distinguish deliberate strategies, where intentions that existed previously were realized, from 'emergent' strategies, where patterns developed in the absence of intentions, or despite them which went 'unrealised'.
>
> (1998: 15)

The third definition is that strategy is a position. By this definition, strategy becomes the mediating force or match between the organisation and its external and internal environment. Strategy as a position looks outside the organisation, seeking to locate the organisation in the external environment and place it in a concrete position (Mintzberg and Quinn, 1998).

The fourth definition is strategy as a perspective, which looks inside of the organisation. Strategy in this respect is to the organisation what personality is to the individual (Mintzberg, *et al.* 1995). The definition of strategy as perspective, suggests that strategy is a concept. In this case, strategy is a perspective shared by the members of an organisation through their intentions and/or by their actions (Mintzberg and Quinn, 1998). Strategy as both position and perspective can be compatible with strategy as plan and/or pattern. But in reality, the relationships between these different definitions can be more involved than that.

Segal-Horn (1998) discusses strategy as an area of management that is concerned with the general direction and long term policy of the business as distinct from short term tactics and day-to-day operations. Hence, the strategy

---

Box 3.3 Strategy as a plan that guides small business

In 1999 Express Inc., a distributor of the parts for home appliances, needed to retrench, having lost a large sum of money on one venture and having neglected its core business. Victor Adams, Express Inc.'s Managing Director, with the help of a management consultant and his own management team, put together a comprehensive plan designed to turn strategies into action. The plan was distinctive in that it was constructed for use as a management tool to be followed during the year rather than being placed on a shelf and forgotten. Each department had a summary of the plan that laid out its activities by calendar periods. Victor and the management team hold monthly meetings to monitor progress, and they update the plan annually. The plan as a sales strategy was credited with helping the business to double its 2000 sales in the plan's first year.

of business may be defined as its long term objectives and the general means by which it intends to achieve them (Segal-Horn, 1998).

Hax (2001) believes that the *concept* of strategy should be considered separately from the *process* of strategy. He introduced the following six critical dimensions of strategy which must included in any unified definition of strategy concept:

- Strategy as a unifying and integrative pattern of decisions.
- Strategy as a means of establishing an organisation's purpose in terms of its long term objectives.
- Strategy as a definition of a firm's competitive domain.
- Response to external opportunities and threats and to internal strengths and weaknesses as a means of achieving competitive advantage.
- Strategy as a logical system for differentiating managerial tasks at corporate, business and functional level.
- Strategy as a definition of the economic and non-economic contribution that the firm intends to make to its stakeholders (Hax, 2001).

Strategies are means to ends – the ends would be the goals and objectives of the organisations. Therefore the concept of strategy covers all purposes and aspects of the organisations. In order to achieve the organisational goals, the organisations go through the process of strategic management.

The strategy approaches

Within the field of management, strategy has been defined and conceptualised in a wide variety of ways. Most concepts in the field of strategy were developed in the first half of the twentieth century. Perhaps the pioneer in demonstrating the importance of strategy in business organisations was Newman (1951). The best review of the different approaches to strategy is Whittington's recent work (2001). Generally, Whittington has addressed four approaches to strategy including classical, evolutionary, processual and systemic (Figure 3.2). As shown in Figure 3.2 the four approaches differ fundamentally along two dimensions: the 'outcome' of strategies and the 'process' by which they are made.

The vertical axis measures the degree to which strategy either produces profit-maximising outcomes or deviates to allow other possibilities to intrude. The horizontal axis considers processes, reflecting how far strategies are the product of deliberate calculation or whether they emerge by accident, muddle or inertia. The classical and evolutionary approaches see profit maximisation as the natural outcome of strategy making, while the systemic and processual approaches are more pluralistic, envisioning other possible outcomes as well as just profit. We will endeavour an overview of these approaches (Box 3.4).

Classical approach

The classical approach stresses rationality and analysis. For the classical approach, the strategy should be formal and explicit and its objective ought to be unambiguous acts of profit maximisation. The classical approach to business strategy was established in the 1960s, with the writings of the American business historian Chandler (1962) and theorist Ansoff (1965). For the classical approach, profitability is the main goal of organisations and the firms use rational planning to achieve their goals and objectives. As Whittington discussed, the classical approach places great confidence in the readiness and capacity of managers to adopt profit-maximising strategies through rational long term planning (2001). Implicit in Chandler's (1962) definition of strategy is also the idea that strategy involves rational planning. Ansoff (1965, 1984) and Mintzberg (1994) made the main contribution in developing the classical view of strategic management. From this base the essence of strategic planning, known as the design or strategic planning school, was developed by Mintzberg (1994). This view centres upon finding a path between organisation capabilities and opportunities within the competitive environment. As Aaker discussed, the basic assumption is that 'past extrapolations are inadequate and that discontinuities from past projections and new trends will require strategic adjustments' (Aaker, 1998: 9). This strategic planning approach marks the start of what has been termed the classical paradigm in the development of strategy theory and development. The organisation is depicted as choosing its goals, identifying the course of actions or strategies that best enable it to fulfil its goals and allocating resources accordingly (Hill and Jones, 1995).

After the evolution of strategic management, there then followed a period of research aimed at generalising the application of design school techniques. This concentrated on quantitative studies using scientific methods. Analytical tools such as life cycle analysis, the Boston Consulting Groups (BCG) growth/share matrix and McKinsey/GE's market attractiveness strategic position matrix, amongst others, typify the approach at this time. Ohmae (1983) has also made a major contribution to the classical approach and the school of competitive

Figure 3.2

Whittington's four generic approaches to strategy

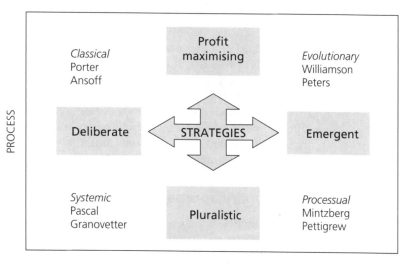

Source: Adapted from Whittington, R. (2001) *What is Strategy and Does it Matter?*, Thomson Learning, London, p. 10. Reprinted by permission.

Box 3.4 The four perspectives on strategy

	Classical	Processual	Evolutionary	Systemic
Strategy	Formal	Crafted	Efficient	Embedded
Rationale	Profit maximisation	Vague	Survival	Local
Focus	Internal (plans)	Internal (political/ cognitions)	External (markets)	External (societies)
Key influence	Economic/ military	Psychology	Economics/ biology	Sociology
Key authors	Chandler Ansoff Porter	Cyert and March Mintzberg Pettigrew	Hannan and Freeman Williamson	Granovetter Whitley
Key period	1960s	1970s	1980s	1990s

Source: Whittington (2001) *What is Strategy and Does it Matter?*, Thomson Learning, London, p. 39. Reprinted by permission.

advantage. He contended that strategy is the way in which a corporation endeavours to differentiate itself positively from its competitors, using its relative corporate strengths better to satisfy corporate needs (Ohmae, 1983: 93).

Finally Porter (1985) has expanded the strategy theory to competitive advantage as a subparadigm of the classical approach. The notion of the subparadigm was that it was possible to prescribe universal rules and concepts in order to enable organisations to pursue generic strategies based on considered analysis of forces driving competition within their industry sector. This work extended into the 1980s as researchers and industrialists realised that superior performance could not be explained through generic strategies or organisation characteristics alone and the focus shifted towards competitive advantage (Smallman, 1997).

Evolutionary approach

The proponents of the evolutionary approach believe that high profitability and efficiency are essential for the survival of the firm. They stress the unpredictability of the environment which makes irrelevant much of what is traditionally regarded as strategic analysis (Teece *et al.* 1997). In the evolutionary approach to strategy, the focus is transferred from managers to market behaviour. As Whittington (2001) aptly contends, the evolutionary approach to strategy is less confident about top management's ability to plan and act rationally and it is expected that the markets will secure profit maximisation. As Whittington has argued stressing competitive processes of natural selection, evolutionary theorists do not necessarily prescribe rational planning methods; rather, they argue that 'whatever methods managers adapt, it will only be the best performers that survive' (1993: 17). Based on this approach to strategy, there is an explicit parallel between economic competition and the natural law of the jungle. Therefore it has some intriguing implications for managerial strategy.

Henderson (1979) has drawn evolutionary aspects of strategy from the biological principle of competitive exclusion, which was established by Gause in 1934. As Montgomery and Porter have discussed

> In 1934 Professor G. F. Gause of Moscow University published the result of a set of experiments in which he put two very small animals (protozoas) of the same genus in a bottle with an adequate supply of food. If the animals were of different species, they could survive and persist together. If they were of the same species, they could not. This observation led to Gause's principles of competitive exclusion: No two species can co-exist that make their living in an identical way.
>
> (Montgomery and Porter, 1991: 4)

The evolutionary approach to strategy 'stresses the unpredictability of the environment which makes irrelevant much of what is traditionally regarded as strategic analysis. It is analogous to the biological survival of the fittest model' (Segal-Horn, 1998: 413). The evolutionary strategy then can be a dangerous delusion, except for the minority of firms with significant market power. In this approach, economy is the best strategy (Williamson, 1991). Managers must concentrate on their costs, especially the transaction costs of organising and coordinating. The evolutionary approach to strategy advises that, in searching for the best strategy, it is best to let the environment do the selecting, not the managers (Whittington, 1993) (Box 3.5).

Processual approach

The processual approach to strategy was developed during the 1970s by Cyert and March (1963), Pettigrew (1973) and Mintzberg (1978). It generally shares the evolutionary scepticism about rational strategy making, but is less confident about markets ensuring profit-maximising outcomes. The processual approach is a pragmatic view of strategy: the world and our knowledge are imperfect, so organisations have to take this into account in their strategic processes (Segal-Horn, 1998: 413). Processualists agree that long range planning is largely futile, but they are less pessimistic about the fate of businesses that do not somehow optimise environmental fit. Whittington has argued that:

> For processualists, both organisations and markets are often sticky messy phenomena, from which strategies emerge with much confusion and in smaller forms. The best processual advice is not to strive after the unattainable idea of rational fluid action, but to accept and work with the world as it is.
>
> (Whittington, 1993: 22–23)

> **Box 3.5 Key points of Whittington's four approaches to strategy**
>
> - Classical approach: the classical approach stresses rationality and analysis. Strategy should be formal and explicit, and its objective ought to be unambiguous acts of profit maximisation.
> - Evolutionary approach: evolutionists believe that high profitability and efficiency are essential for survival but stress the unpredictability of the environment, which makes irrelevant much of what is traditionally regarded as strategic analysis.
> - The processual approach: the processual approach is a pragmatic view of strategy. It shares the evolutionary scepticism about rational strategy making, but is less confident about markets ensuring profit-maximising outcomes.
> - Systemic approach: considers the social system and the rationales underlying strategy as peculiar to particular sociological contexts.

Processual theorists too dismiss classical formality, viewing strategy as 'crafted'; its goals are vague and any logic often emerges in retrospect (Whittington, 1993).

Systemic approach

The systemic approach is based on the classical philosophy which places stress on the rational approach and the value of the analysis. For the proponents of the classical approach, strategy should be formal and explicit, its objective should be unambiguous profit maximisation. Here, the link between the contingency school of organisation behaviour and the strategic management theory is established and developed by Mintzberg.

This is further reinforced by systemic thinkers (Granovetter, 1985; Shrivastava, 1986; Checkland and Scholes, 1990; Stacey, 1993). Strategy in this school of thought is 'directly contingent upon political, economic, social, technological and cultural contexts' (Smallman, 1997). The strategy therefore stresses the importance and to an extent the uniqueness of social systems within which diverse attitudes to and conceptualisations about strategic issues occur. Strategy will thus, in part, reflect the social system in which it occurs (Segal-Horn, 1998). Against propositions of evolutionary and processual theorists, strategist theorists do retain faith in the capacity of organisations to forward plan and to act effectively within their environment. They insist that the rational underlying strategies are peculiar to a particular sociological context. A central tendency of strategic theory is that 'decision makers are not simply detached calculating individuals interacting in purely economic transactions, but people rooted deeply in a densely interwoven social system' (Whittington, 1993: 28).

The system approach challenges the universality of any single model of strategy. The objectives of strategy and the modes of strategy making depend on the strategist's social characteristics and the social context within which they operate.

Levels of strategy

Strategists in the organisations deal with three levels of strategy development. It has been debated that the various hierarchical levels in the organisations have different managerial responsibilities in terms of their contribution to defining the strategy of the firm (Hax, 2001). A corporations' strategy forms a unified, comprehensive and integrated plan stating how the corporation will achieve its mission and objectives. The firm's strategy maximises competitive advantages and, at the same time, minimises the competitive disadvantages of the firm. The typical business firm usually considers three linked and interdependent levels of strategy consisting of corporate strategy, business strategy and functional strategy (Figure 3.3 and Box 3.6).

The first level of strategy is concerned with determining the corporate strategy. It is essentially and simply concerned with deciding what businesses the organisation should be in and how the overall group of activities should be structured and managed (Analoui, 1990, 1991; Thompson, 1995). One of the pioneers of strategic management, Kenneth Andrews, has noted that 'corporate strategy is the pattern of major objectives, purposes or goals and essential policies and plans for achieving these goals, stated in such a way as to define what business the company is in or is to be in' (1971: 28). It is also argued that corporate strategy describes a company's overall direction in terms of its general attitude toward growth and the management of its various business and product lines (Wheelen and Hunger, 1998). The corporate level strategy is responsible for defining the firm's overall mission and objectives, validating

Figure 3.3

Three levels of strategy

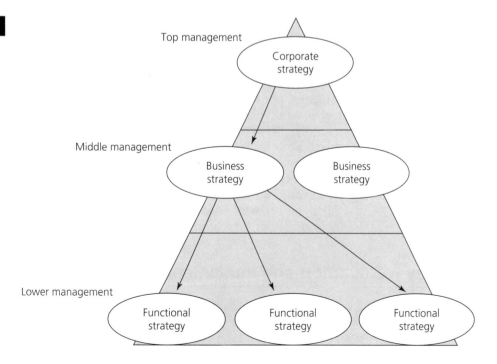

Box 3.6 Three levels of strategy

- Corporate level strategy. The strategy for a multi-business company which determines the overall scope of the business in terms of markets and products. It covers all the business and functional strategies of the firm.
- Business level strategy. Concerned with creating a competitive advantage in each of the strategic business units of the firm.
- Functional level strategy. Concerned with functional areas of the firm such as operations, marketing, financial, human resources, and research and development.

---

proposals emerging from business and functional levels, and allocating resources with a sense of strategic priorities (Hax, 2001).

The second level of strategy is business strategy. Business level strategy is concerned with creating and maintaining a competitive advantage in each strategic business unit. It can be achieved through any one function, or a combination of several (Thompson, 1995). Business strategy usually occurs at the business unit or product level and it emphasises the importance of the competitive position of a corporation's products or services in the specific industry or market segment served by that business unit (Wheelen and Hunger, 1998). The business level strategy enhances the competitive position of the business units.

Accordingly, the third level of strategy is the functional one. Functional strategy is concerned with the functional areas of the firm such as operation, marketing, financial, human resources, and research and development. It is the approach taken by a functional area to achieve the corporate and business objectives of the unit strategically by maximising resource productivity (Wheelen and Hunger, 1998). It is critical that these functional strategies are designed and managed in a coordinated way, so that they interrelate with each other and at the same time collectively allow the competitive strategies to be implemented properly (Thompson, 1995). Successful functional and competitive strategies add value which is perceived as important by the company's shareholders, especially its customers, and which helps distinguish the organisation from its competitors. Internal linkages and cooperation between functions can add value. External networks which create synergy by linking a company closely with its suppliers, distributors and customers are also a source of added value, but these are an aspect of the corporate strategy. Business firms use all three types of strategy simultaneously. Functional strategies support business strategies, which, in turn, support the corporate strategy.

Strategy formulation and implementation

SMEs increase their chances of success by making a serious attempt to work through the strategic issues embedded in the strategic management model. For SMEs the key point is to focus on what is important – the set of managerial decisions that determines the long-run performance of the firm. These decisions include strategy formulation and strategy implementation. By formulation of the business strategies, we meant that SMEs' managers decide what to do and consequently by implementation of the chosen strategies, the results of the strategy are achieved (Figure 3.4).

Strategy formulation and implementation have been considered as inter-related elements of corporate strategy. Corporate strategy is inherently an organisational process, in many ways inseparable from the structure, behaviour and culture of the company in which it takes place. The process of setting out corporate strategy includes two phases; formulation of strategy and implementation of strategy. Mintzberg *et al.* (1995) argue that the principal subactivities of strategy formulation, as a logical activity, include identifying opportunities and threats in the company's environment; determining the company's resources; personal values of senior managers and acknowledgement of non-economic responsibility to society. Naturally, the main subelements of strategy implementation include organisational structure; organisational processes and top leadership (Mintzberg *et al.* 1995).

The process of strategic management in SMEs

Does the process of strategic management in small and medium-sized enterprises differ from that of the large firms? Basically, what is the process

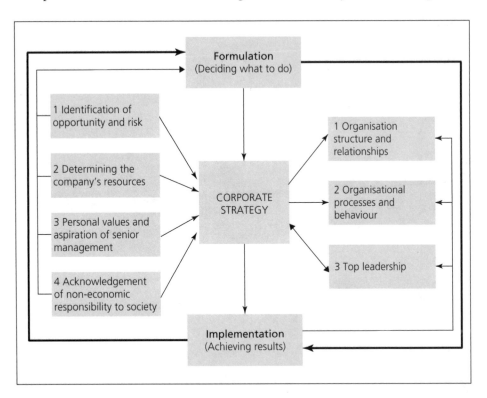

Figure 3.4

Formulation and implementation of strategy as a pattern of interrelated decisions

Source: Adapted from Mintzberg *et al.* (1995: 58).

of strategy formulation and implementation in small businesses? In the last section, the concept of strategic management was introduced. It included environmental scanning, formulation, implementation and evaluation of strategy. Wheelen and Hunger (1998) contended that the discussed process does not fit the small businesses and new entrepreneurial ventures. These companies must have new missions, objectives, strategies and policies out of a comparison of their external opportunities and threats to their potential strengths and weaknesses. Consequently, they proposed a modified version of the strategic management model, which is more closely suited to the new entrepreneurial businesses. Figure 3.5. shows the appropriate strategic management model for small businesses which is composed of the following eight interrelated steps (Wheelen and Hunger, 1998):

- Develop the basic business idea – a product and/or service having target customers and/or markets. The idea can be developed from a person's experiences or generated in a moment of creative insight.
- Scan and assess the external environment, to locate factors in the societal and task environments that pose opportunities and threats. The scanning should focus particularly on market potential and resource accessibility.
- Scan and assess the internal factors relevant to the new businesses. The entrepreneur should objectively consider personal assets, areas of expertise,

Figure 3.5   Strategic decision-making for SMEs (new ventures)

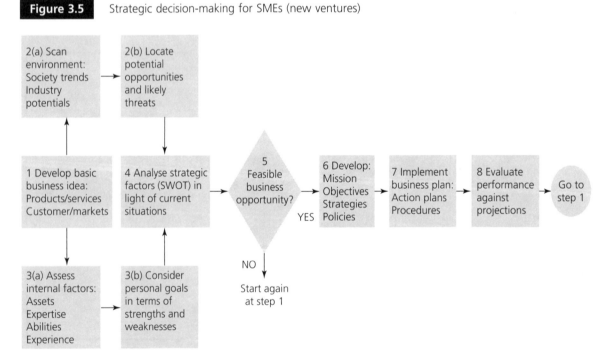

Source: T. L. Wheelen and D. Hunger *Strategic Management and Business Policy*, 6th edn, pp. 306–307; source T. L. Wheelen and C. E. Michaels, *Model for the Strategic Decision-making Process for New Ventures*. Copyright © 1987 by T. L. Wheelen. Reprinted by permission.

abilities and experience, all in terms of organisational needs for the new venture.

- Analyse the strategic factors in light of the current situation using SWOT. The venture's potential strengths and weaknesses must be evaluated in light of opportunities and threats.
- Decide on go or no go. If the basic business idea appears to be a feasible business opportunity, the process should be continued. Otherwise, further development of the idea should be cancelled unless the strategic factors have changed.
- Generate a business plan, specifying how the idea will be transformed into reality.
- Implement the business plan through the use of action plans and procedures.
- Evaluate the implemented business plan through comparison of actual performance against projected performance results. To the extent that actual results are less than or much greater than the anticipated results, the entrepreneur needs to reconsider the company's current mission, objectives, strategies, policies and programmes and possibly make changes to the original business plan.

The details of each step of strategic management in small businesses will be discussed in the different chapters of this book.

The dynamic SME strategic management model

The literature suggests that a number of models have been proposed for strategic management in SMEs (Linneman, 1980; Green and Jones, 1982; Shuman and Seeger, 1986; Aram and Cowan, 1990; Foster, 1993; Berry, 1998; Beal, 2000). Basically, there is no substantial difference between the above proposed strategic management models for small businesses – the basis for all is similar in their employed concepts. Many of the concepts and techniques dealing with strategic management have been developed and used successfully by business firms. As managers attempt to better deal with their changing world, a firm generally evolves through four phases of strategic management, financial planning, forecast-based planning, externally oriented planning (strategic planning) and strategic management (Dyson and O'Brien, 1998). Strategic management itself consists of four basic elements: environmental scanning, strategy formulation, strategy implementation and evaluation and control (Wheelen and Hunger, 1998). Environmental scanning is the monitoring, evaluating and disseminating of information from the external and internal environment to key people within the corporation. Its purpose is to identify strategic factors, those external and internal elements that will determine the future of the corporation.

The simplest way to conduct environmental scanning is through strengths, weakness, opportunities and threat (SWOT) analysis (Wheelen and Hunger, 1998). Strategy formulation is the development of long range plans for the effective management of environmental opportunities and threats, in light of corporate strengths and weaknesses. It includes defining the corporate mission, specifying achievable objectives, developing strategies and setting policy guidelines. Strategy implementation is the process by which strategies are put into action through the development of programmes, budget and procedures (Phillips and Moutinho, 2000). The process might involve changes within the overall culture, structure and management of the organisation (Peel and Bridge, 1998).

Finally, evaluation and control is the process by which corporate activities and performance results are monitored so that actual performance can be compared with the desired one. Although evaluation and control is the final major element of strategic management, it can also pinpoint weaknesses in previously implemented strategic plans and stimulate the entire process to begin again. In this book, the conceptual framework for the construction of a strategic management model for SMEs has been developed based on the insight gained from the work of scholars in this field, first hand observation by the authors and the result of a first time empirical research which has been carried out in the electronics industry in the UK. This we believe provides a sound realistic and structured format for directing the examination of SME strategies under the headings of awareness, strategy formulation, strategy implementation and strategy control and development.

Traditionally, the strategic management process models have attempted to answer six basic questions: What is our business? Where are we now? Where do we want to be? How are we going to get there? Which way is the best? And shall we do it? Most models of the strategic management process take a broad view of stakeholders and are competitor driven rather than customer oriented. The dynamic SME's strategic management as an extension of the basic strategic management model introduces a customer value-based model of strategic management (Figure 3.6).

The dynamic SME strategic management model consists of four stages:

1. Awareness: understanding the strategic situation
2. Strategy formulation: prepare suitable strategies
3. Strategy implementation: making the determined strategies happen
4. Strategy control and development: review and learn for future development.

The dynamic SME strategic management model describes a process by which small and medium-sized enterprises determine their purposes, objectives and desired levels of attainment; decide upon actions for achieving those objectives in an appropriate timescale and frequently in a changing environment; implement the actions and assess progress made by evaluating the result. This will form a basis for learning from the actions taken for future development. It is suggested here that the strategic management process in SMEs is profiled by a dynamic sequence of the following activities:

- An analysis of the present situation of the SME in terms of its products, markets, its distinctive competitive advantages, the personal objectives of the owner-manager and consequently, defining the business in terms of mission, objectives, and values for meeting specified customer needs.

- External environment analysis: Assessing opportunities and threats in terms of its competitors, suppliers, the economy socio-political influences and technology in order to improve customer value.
- Internal environment analysis: Assessing internal capabilities, strengths and weaknesses.
- Identifying key improvement factors and strategic issues of the company, which will influence the future direction of the SME.
- Defining strategic alternatives in terms of objectives and grand strategies.
- Implementing change to enhance process (product and service) by improving people capability.
- Monitoring improved customer value and business performance.
- Review and learn from the strategies adopted with a view to further developing the strategic management capability of the firm (decision-making).

Figure 3.6

Dynamic SME's strategic management model

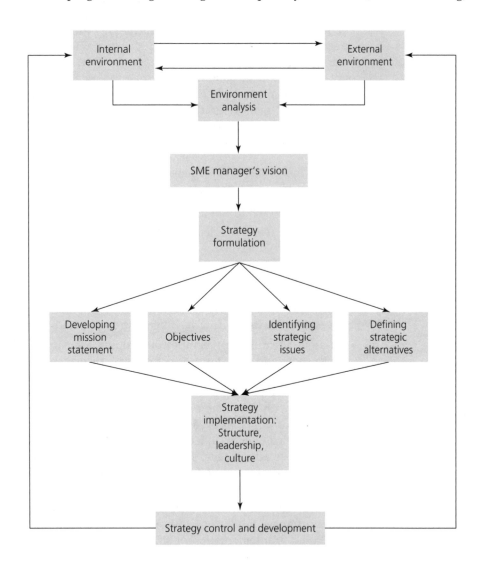

The eight basic issues referred to above are essentially dynamic; that is, they address the problem of deciding action priorities for companies that wish to prosper by developing and maintaining competitive strategy through the formulation, implementation and evaluation of strategies that not only bring satisfaction to customers but also provide a basis for action learning and the future development of the strategic capability for the firm.

Stages of strategic management in SMEs

Strategies constitute means to ends and these ends are concerned with the purpose and objectives of the organisation. They are the things that businesses do, the paths they follow and the decisions they take, in order to reach certain points and levels of success. Strategic management is a process that needs to be understood as more than just a discipline. It is the process by which organisations determine their purpose, objectives and desired levels of attainment, decide upon actions for achieving these objectives in an appropriate timescale and frequently in a changing environment, implement the actions and assess progress and results. Whenever and wherever necessary the changes may be introduced and actions may be altered, modified or completely changed. The magnitude of these changes can range from being dramatic and revolutionary or more gradual and evolutionary (Thompson, 1995).

It is possible to interpret the sequence of elements that comprise the four selected strategic management models as:

1. Understand the strategic situation.
2. Formulate suitable strategies.
3. Make the determined strategies happen.
4. Exercise (evaluate, learn and develop further as a result).

The strategic management process can thus be claimed to consist of four stages: awareness, strategy formulation, strategy implementation and control:

- Awareness: identifying an organisation's external opportunities and threats in relation to its internal resources, strengths and weakness.
- Strategy formulation: includes developing a business mission, deciding on both short and long term objectives and prioritising which strategies to pursue. Strategy formulation is also concerned with resource allocation, taking decisions about diversifications, entry into international markets, merging with suppliers or sale agencies and participation in joint ventures. Strategy commits an organisation to specific products, markets and technologies over an extended period of time. They determine long term competitive advantages. Top managers bear responsibility for the ramification of strategic formulation decisions, this reflects their authority to commit company resources for implementation of strategy.
- Strategy implementation: Strategy implementation seeks to create the right circumstances within organisations so that formulated strategies can be executed. Implementation of strategy is achieved by developing a strategy-

supportive culture, creating an effective organisational structure and motivating individuals to learn new ways of contributing to improved performance. Often considered to be the most difficult stage in strategic management, strategy implementation requires personal discipline, commitment and sacrifice. Successful strategy implementation relies on the managerial ability to lead employees, assist in the redesign of products, improve organisational process and adjust to environmental constraints.

- Strategy control and development: culminates the activity inherent in the design, application and eventual assessment of strategy. Strategy evaluation is needed because current success does not guarantee that such success will continue in the future: an organisation that becomes complacent loses the drive required for survival in an increasingly competitive environment. Essential to realistic control of the company performance is the development of performance indicators linked to key improvement factors and attributes that influence the improvement of people, product and process elements that have been adopted for realising organisational performance. Strategic control begins by noting external and internal circumstances, continues by measuring performance and ends by critical assessment of achievement against strategic objectives.

Environmental analysis, strategy formulation, strategy implementation and evaluation activities occur at three managerial levels in a large organisation: corporate, strategic business unit (SBU) and functional levels. By fostering effective communications and interaction among managers and employees across hierarchical levels, strategic management helps a firm to function by virtue of team structure that links the corporate, SBU and functional levels of the strategically driven organisation. Most small business do not have divisions or business units. It is therefore essential to reiterate that in most small firms, the manager or owner-manager constitutes the strategic management capability of the firm. Since the performance of the firm is largely determined as a result of their awareness of the circumstances and analysis of the factors involved, it is imperative that the analysis is focused on them as formulators of the plans, the action takers, controllers and, most importantly, as agents actively involved in a process of reflective learning and development of their capabilities as strategists.

Summary

- Strategy is a unified, comprehensive and integrated plan that relates the strategic advantages of the firm to the challenges of the environment. It is designed to ensure that the basic objectives of the enterprise are achieved through proper execution by the organisation.
- Strategic management is a systematic approach for managing strategic change which consists of positioning the firm through strategy and capability planning, real time strategic response through issue management and systematic management of resistance during strategic implementation. Having a strategic approach helps small businesses to increase their competencies in a turbulent environment. The typical business firm usually

considers three linked and interdependent levels of strategy consisting of corporate, business and functional strategies.

- The dynamic SME's strategic management as an extension of the basic strategic management model, introduces a customer value-based model of strategic management which consists of four stages – awareness: understanding the strategic situation; strategy formulation: preparing suitable strategies; strategy implementation: making the determined chosen strategies happen and finally, control and development, which involves evaluation of the results and action learning reflectively for the purpose of the future development of strategic management capability.

- Awareness is identifying an organisation's external opportunities and threats in relation to its internal strengths and weaknesses. Strategy formulation includes developing a business mission, deciding both short and long term objectives and prioritising strategies to pursue. Strategy implementation seeks to create the right circumstances within organisations so that formulated strategies can be executed. Implementation of strategy is achieved by developing a strategy supportive culture, creating an effective organisational structure and motivating individuals to learn new ways of contributing to improved performance. Finally, strategy control and development not only devises the systems and measures for control, it also extends the responsibilities of the management to become learning strategists in order to improve the capability of firm's strategic decision-making.

Discussion questions

1. What is the meaning of strategy? Compare at least two definitions of strategy.
2. What are different approaches to strategy in management? Explain Whittington's approaches to strategy.
3. What are the differences between the classical, evolutionary, processual and systemic approaches to strategy? Which approach focuses on profit maximisation?
4. How does strategic management typically evolve in a small business?
5. What are the basic strategic management process components in a small business?
6. Explain briefly awareness, strategy formulation, implementation, and control and development in SMEs.

Case study *Strategic planning in SMEs*

Strategic planning! Does it work in small businesses? Recently David retired from a high tech manufacturing company. He is a skilled computer engineer. Having nearly 20 years of experience in computer hardware, he is thinking of developing a small business of his own in computer hardware. Although he has a strong intrinsic motivation for running such a business he does not know how, where and when he can start. Since he has never attended

▶

any business courses, he decided to consult a small business development expert. It was then that he realised that for developing a small business he needs to have answers to some basic questions. He was advised first to develop a business plan. Yes, he was told, 'starting and managing a small business takes motivation, talent AND strategic planning'. The process of developing a business plan will help David think through some notable problems which he may not have considered already. So, he should think strategically and answer the following questions before developing his business plan:

What are the main reasons for wanting to go into the computer hardware business? The first and very important reason is that David is 'a computer man'. He wants to use his skills and 20 years of earned work experience. Moreover, he now thinks it's time to be his own boss. Therefore, he wants to experience new and challenging responsibilities as a technical entrepreneur.

The next step for David is to determine precisely what business is right for him. So he has to identify his own level of technical skills and competencies, time, financial support and so on. For instance, it is imperative for David to realise that although he may be very good at computer hardware, he is not so competent in computer software. He has a budget limit up to £1 million and his children have grown up so he has enough time to run such a business.

The third step for David is to identify his business niche in the market. He needs to determine the service or products which he intends to sell. Given that he is thinking of assembling the computers and selling to home users, who are David's competitors and how can he create a demand for his business? What are the advantages and disadvantages of such a business? Can he deliver a better quality product than the current competitors? These are the questions that David should consider and have answers for before embarking on the next stage.

Apart from the above questions, David needs to take into account general considerations before developing his strategic business plan. Some of these considerations include: clearing his vision about the future of the business, financial resources, technology and equipment, the firm's structure, political and legal considerations, skills and knowledge required, location of the business and support of his family.

David's thinking and answers to the questions will help him to create and develop a well-structured strategic business plan, which should detail how his business will be operated, financed and managed.

References

Aaker, D. A. (1998) *Developing Business Strategies*, 5th edn, John Wiley & Sons Inc., New York.

Analoui, F. (1990) Managerial skills for senior managers, *International Journal of Public Sector Management*, 3 (2), 26–38.

Analoui, F. (1991) Toward achieving the optimum fit between managers and project organisation, *Project Appraisal*, 6 (4), 217–222.

Andrews, K. (1971) *The Concept of Corporate Strategy*, Irwin, Homewood, IL.

Andrews, K. (1986) *The Concept of Corporate Strategy*, 2nd edn, Irwin, Homewood, IL.

Ansoff, H. I. (1965) *Corporate Strategy*, McGraw-Hill, New York.

Ansoff, H. I. (1984) *Implementing Strategic Management*, Prentice Hall, Englewood Cliffs, NJ.

Aram, D. J. and Cowan, S. S. (1990) Strategic planning for increased profit in the small businesses, *Long Range Planning*, 23 (6), 63–70.

Bain, J. S. (1968) *Industrial Organisations*, 2nd edn, John Wiley & Sons Inc., New York.

Beal, R. M. (2000) Competing effectively: Environmental scanning, competitive strategy and organisational performance in small manufacturing firms, *Journal of Small Business Management*, 38 (1), 27–47.

Berry, M. (1998) Strategic planning in small high tech companies, *Long Range Planning*, 31 (3), 455–466.

Bhide, A. (1994) How entrepreneurs craft strategy that works, *Harvard Business Review*, March/April, 150–161.

Bowman, C. and Kakabadse, A. (1997) Top management ownership of the strategy problem, *Long Range Planning*, 30 (2), 197–208.

Boxall, P. (1992) Strategic human resource management: Beginnings of a new theoretical sophistication?, *Human Resource Management Journal*, 2 (3), 60–79.

Boxall, P. (1996) The strategic HRM debate and the resource-based view of the firm, *Human Resource Management Journal*, 6 (3), 59–75.

Carson, D., Cromie, S., McGowan, P. and Hill, J. (1995) *Marketing and Entrepreneurship in SMEs: An Innovative Approach*, Prentice Hall, London.

Chaffee, E. E. (1985) Three models of strategy, *Academy of Management Review*, 10 (1), 89–98.

Chandler, A. (1962) *Strategy and Structure*, MIT Press, Cambridge, MA.

Checkland, P. B. and Scholes, J. (1990) *Soft Systems Methodology in Action*, John Wiley & Sons, Chichester.

Chell, E. (2001) *Entrepreneurship: Globalisation, Innovation and Development*, Thomson Learning, London.

Chen, M. J. (1996) Competitor analysis and inter-firm rivalry: Toward a theoretical integration, *Academy of Management Review*, 21, 100–134.

Covin, J. (1991) Entrepreneurial versus conservative firms: A comparison of strategies and performance, *Journal of Management Studies*, 28 (5), 439–462.

Cyert, R. M. and March, J. G. (1963) *A Behavioural Theory of The Firm*, Prentice Hall, Englewood Cliffs, NJ.

Dyson, R. G. and O'Brien. F. A. (1998) *Strategic Development*, John Wiley & Sons, New York.

Foster, M. J. (1993) Scenario planning for small businesses, *Long Range Planning*, 26 (1), 123–129.

Glueck, W. L. and Jauch, L. R. (1988) *Business Policy and Strategic Management*, 5th edn, McGraw Hill, New York.

Goldsmith, A. (1995) Making managers more effective: Applications of strategic management, Working Paper No. 9, USAID, March.

Granovetter, M. (1985) Economic action and social structure: The problem of embeddedness, *American Journal of Sociology*, 91 (3), 481–510.

Grant, R. M. (1998) The resource-based theory of competitive advantage: Implications for strategy formulation, in H. Costin (ed.) *Reading in Strategy and Strategic Planning*, The Dryden Press, London.

Green, G. J. L. and Jones, E. G. (1982) Strategic management step by step, *Long Range Planning*, 15 (3), 61–70.

Hanlon, D. and Scott, M. (1995) Strategy formulation in entrepreneurial small firms, in S. Birley and I. Macmillan (eds) *International Entrepreneurship*, Routledge, London, 17–38.

Hax, A. (2001) Defining the concept of strategy, in R. Wit and R. Meyer (eds) *Strategy, Content, Context*, Thomson Learning, London, 28–32.

Heene, A. (1997) The nature of strategic management, *Long Range Planning*, 30 (6), 933–938.

Henderson, B. D. (1979) *Henderson on Corporate Strategy*, Abt books, Cambridge.

Hill, C. H. and Jones, G. R (1995) *Strategic Management Theory: An Integrated Approach*, 3rd edn, Houghton Mifflin Company, Boston.

Hofer, C. W. and Schendel, D. (1978) *Strategy Formulation: Analytical Concept*, West Publishing Company, New York.

Hoskisson, R. E., Hitt, M. A., Wan, W. P. and Yiu, D. (1999) Theory and research in strategic management: Swings of a pendulum, *Journal of Management*, 25 (3), 417–456.

Johnson, G. and Scholes, K. (1993) *Exploring Corporate Strategy: Text and Cases*, 3rd edn, Prentice Hall Publications, London.

Lang, J. R., Calatone, R. J. and Gudmundson, D. (1997) Small firm information seeking as a response to environmental threats and opportunities, *Journal of Small Business Management* 35, 11–23.

Leavy, B. (1996) *Key Process in Strategy*, International Thomson Business Press, UK.

Leidecker, L. and Bruno, A. (1986) Identifying and using critical success factors, *Long Range Planning*, 17 (1), 23–32.

Linneman, R. E. (1980) *Shirt-sleeve Approach to Long Range Planning for the Smaller Growing Corporations*, Prentice Hall, Englewood Cliffs, NJ.

Luttwak, E. (1987) *Strategy the Logic of War and Peace*, Belknap Harvard University Press, Cambridge, MA.

Marsh, I. (1999) Program strategy and coalition building as facets of new public management, *Australian Journal of Public Administration,* 58 (4), 54–68.

Mason, E. S. (1939) Price and production policies of large scale enterprises, *American Economic Review,* 29, 61–74.

Mintzberg, H. (1978) Patterns in strategy formations, *Management Science,* 24 (9), 934–948.

Mintzberg, H. (1994) The fall and rise of strategic planning, *Harvard Business Review,* 72 (1), 107–114.

Mintzberg, H. and Quinn, J. B. (1998) *Reading in the Strategy Process,* 3rd edn, Prentice Hall Inc., Englewood Cliffs, NJ.

Mintzberg, H., Quinn, J. B. and Ghoshal, S. (1995) *The Strategy Process* (European edition), Prentice Hall International, UK.

Monck, C., Porter, B., Quintas, P., Story, D. and Wynarczyk, P. (1988) *Science Parks and the Growth of High Technology Firms,* Croom Helm, Beckenham, Kent.

Montgomery, C. A. and Porter, M. E. (1991) *Strategy: Seeking and Securing Competitive Advantage,* Harvard Business Review.

Newman, W. H. (1951) *Administrative Action: The Technique of Organisation and Management,* Prentice Hall, Englewood Cliffs, NJ.

O'Gorman, C. and Cunningham, J. (1997) *Enterprise in Action: An Introduction to Entrepreneurship in an Irish Context,* Oak Tree Press, Dublin.

Ohmae, K. (1983) *The Mind of the Strategist,* Penguin Books, Harmondsworth.

Peel, M. J. and Bridge, J. (1998) How planning and capital budgeting improve SME performance, *Long Range Planning,* 31 (6), 848–856.

Pettigrew, A. M. (1973) *The Politics of Organisational Decision Making,* Tavistock, London.

Phillips, P. A. and Moutinho, L. (2000) The strategic planning index: A tool for measuring strategic planning effectiveness, *Journal of Travel Research,* 38 (4), 369–370.

Porter, M. (1979) How competitive forces shape strategy, *Harvard Business Review,* March–April, 137–145.

Porter, M. (1980) *Competitive Strategy,* Free Press, New York.

Porter, M. (1985) *Competitive Advantage: Creating and Sustaining Superior Performance,* Free Press, New York.

Schendel, D. E. and Cool, K. O. (1988) Development of the strategic management field, in J. H. Grant (ed.) *Strategic Management Frontiers,* JAI Press, Greenwich, CT, 17–31.

Scott, M. and Bruce, R. (1987) Five stages of growth in small businesses, *Long Range Planning,* 20 (3), 45–52.

Segal-Horn, S. (1998) *The Strategy Reader,* Blackwell Publishers Ltd, Oxford.

Shrivastava, P. (1986) Is strategic management ideological?, *Journal of Management,* 12 (3), 363–377.

Shuman, J. C. and Seeger, J. A. (1986) The theory and practice of strategic management in smaller rapid growth firms, *American Journal of Small Business,* 11 (1), 7–18.

Smallbone, D., Leig, R. and North, D. (1995) The characteristics of strategies of high growth SMEs, *International Journal of Entrepreneurial Behaviour and Research,* 1 (3), 44–62.

Smallman, C. (1997) Risk and strategic management, PhD thesis, University of Bradford.

Smith, J. A. (1998) Strategies for start-ups, *Long Range Planning,* 31 (6), 857–872.

Stacey, R. D. (1993) *Strategic Management and Organisational Dynamic,* Pitman Publishing, London.

Teece, D. J., Pisano, G. and Shuen, A. (1997) Dynamic capabilities and strategic management, *Strategic Management Journal,* 18, 509–533.

Thompson, J. L. (1995) *Strategy in Action,* Chapman & Hall Publications, London.

Thompson, J. L. (2001) *Strategic Management,* 4th edn, Thomson Learning, London.

Thompson, J. (1999) A strategic perspective of entrepreneurship, *International Journal of Entrepreneurial Behaviour and Research,* 5 (6), 279–296.

Webb, D. and Pettigrew, A. (1999) The temporal development of strategy: Patterns in the UK insurance industry, *Organisation Science,* 10 (5), 601–621.

Wheelen, T. L. and Hunger, J. D. (1998) *Strategic Management and Business Policy,* 6th edn, Addison-Wesley Publications, New York.

Whittington, R. (1993) *What is Strategy and Does it Matter?,* Routledge, London.

Whittington, R. (2001) *What is Strategy and Does it Matter?,* Thomson Learning, London.

Williamson, O. E. (1991) Competitive economic organisation: The analysis of discrete structural alternatives, *Administrative Science Quarterly,* 36, 269–29.

4 Environmental competitive analysis

Learning objectives

By the end of this chapter you should be able to:

- Define the term 'environmental analysis' and explore its process in SMEs.

- Discuss the importance of environmental analysis in small businesses.

- Identify environmental factors in an SME.

- Explore the process of PEST analysis in small and medium-sized enterprises.

- Explore and explain the industry analysis in small businesses.

- Explain the competitive environmental analysis and application of five-force model in SMEs.

- Define the nature of recourses and explore the resource-based approach to strategy analysis.

- Describe the value chain analysis in SMEs.

- Finally, explain the SWOT analysis and key success factors in small businesses.

The general objective of this chapter is to introduce the process of environmental analysis in SMEs. In detail, first the term environmental analysis will be defined, then the research background in environmental analysis of SMEs will be examined. Second, the external analysis (including PEST political, economical, sociocultural and technological analysis) and industry analysis will be explained. Third, the internal analysis and its components such as resource analysis and value chain analysis will be discussed in some detail. Finally, SWOT analysis and its implication in SMEs will be dealt with.

Analysis and diagnosis of the environment

The organisation is surrounded by the environment and the term environment has been used in different ways (Fahr, Hoffman and Hegarty, 1984; Beal, 2000). By environment we mean factors which should be considered in the development of a strategy for small businesses. Since organisations are assumed to be an open system, interaction between the organisations and their environment is inevitable. The organisation impacts on environmental factors, and in turn, environmental factors impact on the performance of the organisation. In this two-way interaction the role of the strategist is to determine and diagnose the presence of strategic environmental factors. In order to develop the relevant business strategies of the firm, managers should also analyse the impacts of the environmental factors on the firm's strategy (Pitts and Lei, 1996). In this regard, environmental factors are divided into two main groups: external and internal. The relationship between the external and internal environments of the business and the formulation of the strategy for the firm is illustrated in Figure 4.1.

External environmental factors are those that are generally out of the control of the firm such as competitors, government, the industry, technological changes, economical, and sociocultural factors. Internal environmental factors are those related to the internal aspects of the organisation like organisational culture, organisational structure, leadership and resources of the organisation. Therefore, the strategists should diagnose the external and internal strategic factors and analyse the impact of those factors on the firm. Consequently, in light of the environmental analysis it will be possible to formulate and implement a successful business strategy. Arguably, the CEOs or the owner-managers in SMEs have tended in the past to neglect this aspect of strategic management. The general purpose of this chapter is to provide a theoretical discussion of the environmental analysis as well as assessing managers' perception of the importance of environmental analysis when developing business strategy in small firms.

Figure 4.1

External and internal analysis in SMEs

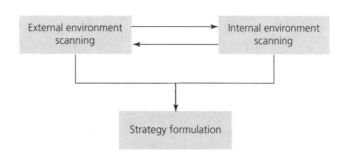

What is environmental analysis?

What do we mean by environmental analysis in strategic management? Let's suppose that a small firm in the textile industry operates nationally. The owner-manager of the firm is thinking about exporting some of the products to specific countries in South America. The first question faced would be concern with the economical, cultural and political situations in the targeted countries. Accordingly, the SME manager ought to investigate all those environmental factors as well as possible competition before entering the market. What are the opportunities and threats for the firm in the new market? What are the strengths and weaknesses of the firm, for instance, in terms of marketing, resources and competitive advantages? Environmental analysis is an organised way of answering these question (Box 4.1).

Therefore, before an organisation begins the process of formulating a strategy, it must analyse its external environment to identify possible opportunities and threats on the one hand, and analyse its internal environment to establish its strengths and weaknesses, on the other (Hambrick, 1981). From this point of view, environmental analysis can be regarded as a process which consists of monitoring, evaluating and disseminating information obtained from the external and internal environments to strategists within the organisation. Environmental analysis is a process through which the strategists study the environment of the firm and determine the strengths, weaknesses, opportunities, and threats (SWOT) facing the firm. Choo (1999) argues that environmental scanning is the acquisition and use of information about events, trends and relationships in an organisation's external environment, the knowledge of which would assist management in planning the organisation's future course of action.

Analysing the environment, according to Gable and Topol (1987) and Goldsmith (1995) consists of external analysis – often referred to as environmental scanning (this includes general and industrial environment) – and internal analysis (sometimes known as doing a strategic audit). Logically, the external analysis involves developing a better understanding of the industry while internal analysis is chiefly concerned with the study of the firm itself. In

---

Box 4.1 What is environmental analysis?

Environmental analysis is a process of studying external and internal environments in which SMEs operate. An effective environmental analysis leads to the identification of factors that have impact on the firm and its operations. These are:

- Strengths
- Weaknesses
- Opportunities
- Threats.

other words, the organisations scan the environment in order to understand external forces of change so that they may develop effective responses that can secure or improve their position in the future market (Gable and Topol, 1987). Since the organisation's ability to adapt to its outside environment is primarily determined by its knowledge of and capability to interpret the ongoing external changes, it could be argued that environmental scanning constitutes a primary mode of organisational learning.

Environmental analysis in SMEs: research background

Before starting a theoretical discussion of the environmental analysis in the organisations in general and in SMEs in particular, it would be helpful to review some of the findings of the recent research projects in the field. Most empirical studies on environmental scanning have focused on the relationships between scanning behaviours (for example, frequency, scope, sources used and interests) and environmental conditions such as environmental uncertainty, perceived threats and perceived opportunities (Daft *et al.* 1988; Tyler *et al.* 1989; Sawyer, 1993; Lang *et al.* 1997). Other studies have investigated the relationships between competitive strategies and environmental scanning (for example, Tyler *et al.* 1989; Jennings and Lumpkin, 1992; Yasai-Ardekani and Nystrom, 1993; Bantel and Osborn, 1995). For instance, Tyler *et al.* (1989) in their investigation of the relationship between different environmental conditions and the usage of different types of information sources by executives in formulating competitive strategy found that (1) high and low rich information sources were used less under highly changing, unpredictable environmental conditions than under stable, predictable conditions; and (2) low rich information sources (such as income statements, memos or letters) were used more than high rich sources (face-to-face discussions with workers, customers or suppliers) under stable, predictable conditions. They also found that the executives in the 28 firms in their sample tended to use more high rich information sources in formulating differentiation strategies than in formulating low cost strategies. These results suggest that environmental conditions affect the type of sources (low rich versus high rich) used by executives in selecting a competitive strategy (that is, low cost leadership or differentiation). Jennings and Lumpkin (1992) argued that the types of information that CEOs seek differ according to their firm's competitive strategies. This implies that strategy can determine scanning behaviour as well as being affected by it. This perspective deviated from the traditional view of proponents of the design school who claim that environmental scanning and analysis are determinants of strategy rather than the products of it (Mintzberg, 1994). Jennings and Lumpkin (1982) found support for their hypotheses that (1) firms following a differentiation strategy, scanned their environments in search of opportunities; and (2) firms following a low cost strategy looked for threats to their survival. However, because the study included firms in only one industry, the generalisability of the results is limited. In a comprehensive study of the scanning systems of 179 small (50 employees) to large (more than 200,000 employees) manufacturing and service firms, the relationships that Yasai-Ardekani and Nystrom, (1993) examined included the one between firms pursuing low cost leadership and the scope and frequency with which they scanned their environments. Results indicated that firms with effective scanning systems pursuing low cost leadership subsequently scanned their environments more frequently and more broadly than those firms with ineffective scanning systems which pursued the same competitive strategy. Simultaneously, Sven (1998) developed a theory of the nature of spontaneous environmental scanning based on theories in cognitive psychology, psychiatry, organisation theory, and other empirical findings from case studies of four Swedish organisations. The theory covers the cognitive base for this behaviour and how it is influenced by organisational factors.

Other findings indicated that organisational size was not a determinant of the effectiveness of scanning systems. That is, small as well as medium-sized and large organisations were able to develop effective scanning systems (Yasai-Ardekani and Nystrom, 1993; Beal, 2000). However, some other researches show a positive relationship between firm size and environmental analysis (see Box 4.2).

Beal (2000) indicated that there are some explanations for his recent research on SME and environmental scanning results. First, the set of questions used to measure scanning frequency may lack content validity. Beal (2000) believes that the set of questions designed to capture CEOs' frequency of scanning constitute adequate coverage of the various environmental sectors including scanned competitors, customers, suppliers, manufacturing and product development technology, economies (local, state and national) and the frequency (daily, weekly, monthly, quarterly and annually) with which the sectors are scanned. Second, CEOs of SMEs in the manufacturing sector are constrained by their involvement in their firms' daily operations, and as a result, may not have time for carrying out frequent scanning of their external environments. Naturally, the environmental scanning may be relatively infrequent. It is further concluded that scanning of the environmental sectors that arguably have the most impact on firm performance and the formulation/implementation of competitive strategy occurs relatively infrequently. Third, the frequency at which CEOs of SMEs scan their environments may not be critical to aligning their firms' competitive strategies with the stage of the industry life cycle in which the firms compete. Other factors such as scope of scanning, accurate assessment of opportunities and threats and effective use of competitive information may be the key. As a final point, the CEOs' awareness, which is gained from environmental analysis, is a crucial factor in organisational performance. No strategic planning will be formulated and implemented in SMEs where the senior managers or entrepreneurs (McKenna, 1996) exhibit a lack of strategic awareness.

Why is environmental analysis in SMEs so important?

From the theorists and practitioners' point of view understanding of the environment in which a firm operates is an essential phase of the strategic management process (Hitt and Ireland, 2000). There are, of course, many reasons for analysing the environment. In general, it could be posited that the firms which are systematically involved in environmental scanning seem to be more successful than those which are not seriously involved in such activity. For

---

Box 4.2 Research note: environmental analysis and firm size

The results of a recent survey show that the majority of the CEOs of SMEs (94 per cent) indicated that they were generally involved in environmental scanning for the purpose of formulating their firm's business strategies. Only 89 per cent claimed to use formal environmental analysis. Accordingly, the CEOs were asked to rate the importance of formal or informal environmental scanning within their organisations. The responses were varied in terms of the size of organisations. The following table shows the variation in the perception of the CEOs of the importance of environmental analysis within the studied firms.

Environmental analysis by organisation size (%)

Extent of importance of environmental analysis	Size of organisation by number of employees			
	Micro enterprises	*Small enterprises*	*Medium enterprises*	*Total*
Not important	2.27	0.70	0.00	2.97
Limited importance	1.53	12.12	0.00	13.65
Important	1.53	28.78	2.27	32.58
Very important	0.70	16.11	9.09	25.81
Essential	0.00	3.78	21.21	24.99
Total				**132 (100%)**

Some 2.97 per cent of the firms considered environmental analysis as not an important factor in the firm's strategy formulation. In contrast, some 50.08 per cent of the respondents described environmental analysis as a very important and essential factor in formulating their firm's strategic management process. The findings seem to indicate that the perception concerning the importance of environmental analysis seems to increase as firms get bigger. Almost all managers in medium-sized enterprises (N = 40 out of 43) felt that environmental analysis is important and therefore forms an essential factor in developing their business strategy. In contrast, only one micro enterprise CEO (N = 1 out of 8) rated environmental analysis as a very important factor. Simultaneously, a slightly lower proportion of the smaller enterprises than the medium-sized ones (N = 26 out of 81) felt that environmental analysis must be considered as very important in developing business strategies.

example, Thomas *et al.* (1993) have found that there is a positive relation between environmental scanning and profit. Some of the reasons for analysing the environment are listed below.

SMEs' managers' awareness

The general awareness of strategists plays an important role in developing a proper strategy. Are managers aware of the changes in the environment? Are they aware of the expectations and values of the customers? It has been argued (Berry, 1998; McGrath and MacMillan, 2000) that the entrepreneurs' strategic awareness and their perception of the benefits arising from environmental scanning within the SME will be a significant determinant of the success and survival of the SME in the long term. Berry (1998) in her recent research concluded that:

> The technical entrepreneur's strategic awareness will determine the nature of planning used within the SME. The strategic awareness of the entrepreneur will be heightened by exposure to strategic management techniques within another organisation prior to business start-up or alternatively through contact with individuals who are aware of the benefits that strategic planning may bring to the business.
>
> (1998: 464)

Uncertainty and changing environmental conditions

As we have seen, environmental factors are those which influence the performance of the strategy. Since these factors are changing, logically, it is important to analyse the environment frequently. In order to adapt to the changes in the environment, it is imperative to be aware of these changes. Accordingly, the environmental analysis enables SMEs to cope with the uncertainty and changes of their environment (Meyer and Heppard, 2000). For example, when a SME intends to introduce a new product to the market, it needs to investigate the expectations of the customers. Niv *et al.* (1998) in their recent research interviewed CEOs in 46 firms with regard to the pattern of the environmental scanning they performed. The study points to significant differences in the level of environmental scanning and in the use of information systems between firms that were more successful in introducing new products into the market and those that were not. The differences are in the pattern and the frequency of conducting environmental scanning, in the number of computerised applications, and in the number of advanced marketing information systems (Niv *et al.* 1998).

Determine the challenging environmental factors

The SMEs' strategist should determine the kind of opportunities that might be explored (McGrath and MacMillan, 2000). These opportunities may come from competitors, changes in technology, government, sociocultural and many other factors. Accordingly, SMEs need to find out what threats are they facing. For instance, new tools such as e-commerce in marketing and sales could be considered an opportunity for SMEs. Another example is business links between small firms. As discussed earlier (see Lynch, 2000), there are opportunities for sale networks and other linkages which lead to sustainable cooperative linkage between the firms. Such business links may strengthen the position of small firms in their environment by providing mutual support for others.

Identifying environmental factors

In order to gain a better understanding of the environment in which the firm operates, managers should identify related factors. These can be classified into two main groups; external and internal. The external environmental factors can be further classified into two groups; those which include general environmental factors and those which are related to the industry. Figure 4.2. illustrates the related environmental factors of an organisation.

The general environmental factors include the four main societal environmental factors – political and legal, economical, sociocultural, and technological (Wheelen and Hunger, 1998; Beal, 2000). These general environmental factors are outside the control of the firm. They influence and are consequently affected by the firm. However, they are not under control of the management in the short term. The second group of external environmental factors are the industry environmental factors. These include the factors within the particular industry in which the firm operates, for example suppliers, competitors, customers and government and shareholders. Using various analytical techniques, the managers indicate the opportunities and threats of the organisation in the environment. In contrast, the internal environmental factors of a firm consist of the factors that are within the organisation itself. These factors determine the strengths and weaknesses of the firm. They include the firm's structure, culture and resources.

Figure 4.2

External and internal environment of firms

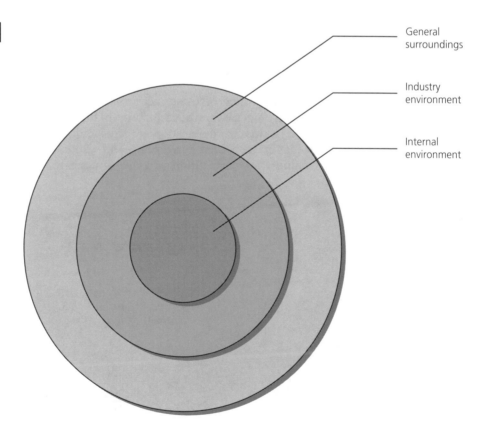

General surroundings

Industry environment

Internal environment

External environment analysis

As discussed earlier, the external environment of the organisation includes both general environmental factors and industry factors. Therefore, the process of external environmental analysis entails, first, the analysis of the political, economical, sociocultural and technological factors and, second, industry-competitive environment analysis which leads to determining the firm's opportunities and threats (Lynch, 2000). The process of external environmental analysis is shown in Figure 4.3.

In this section the external environmental analysis will be discussed in some detail.

Political, economical, sociocultural and technological (PEST) analysis

All organisations are surrounded by environmental factors which influence their activities. The first step in analysing the environment is to determine the degree of the impact of the general environmental factors on the firm's performance. The number of possible environmental factors is very high and they have been classified in different ways. In this book, we classify these general environmental factors as including:

- Political and legal factors
- Economical factors
- Sociocultural factors
- Technological factors.

It is clear that some of these factors may differ from country to country. However, in some cases we can observe the similarities present between countries in terms of their strategic environmental factors. For instance, countries like South Korea, Singapore, and China have many similarities in cultural values but very different views on the role of business in society.

Figure 4.3

External environmental analysis

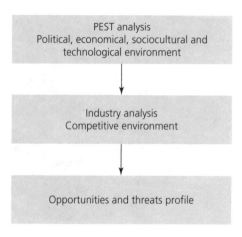

PEST analysis
Political, economical, sociocultural and technological environment

Industry analysis
Competitive environment

Opportunities and threats profile

Hence the question, what is the nature of these environmental factors? Is it important to be aware of these environmental variables when developing a strategy? The answer is simply 'yes'. Before developing a strategy CEOs must be aware of the nature and the impact of general environmental factors on their strategy. This awareness could be gained by systematic (PEST) analysis of the firm's environment. Figure 4.4 illustrates the process involved in the analysis of external environmental factors.

The political environmental factors include taxation law, political changes at different levels, changes in employment law, green issues, political stability, critical situations and war. However, there are many other political factors which are not listed here. For instance, in Europe, the formation of the European Union has led to an increase in merger activities across national boundaries. It has encouraged SMEs to be involved in exporting their products and services to the other markets in Europe. Trends and changes in the political aspects of society have been shown to have significant impact on business firms. For example, the attack on the World Trade Center on 11 September 2001 in the USA had a huge impact on the airline industry, regardless of location. Many job opportunities were lost. Since then, the demand for travel has been drastically decreased so the airline industry has faced a critical economical situation. Table 4.1 illustrates some of the external environmental factors.

Any development in the economic part of the environment can have a significant impact on SMEs and their activities. These include factors such as total GNP trends, GDP per head, inflation rate, exchange rate, energy and raw materials availability and cost, employment level, interest rate, monetary and fiscal policies, banking policies and investment. Strategists should therefore be aware of the trends and changes in the economical side of the environment in which they operate. For instance, an increase in the exchange rate can result in a

Figure 4.4

PEST analysis

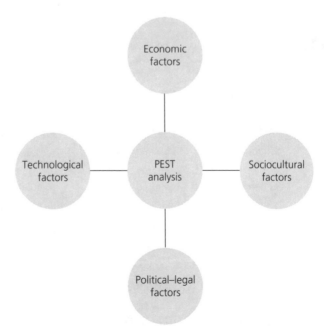

decrease in export activities. SMEs operating in a foreign market should be aware of any changes in the exchange rate and calculate its likely effects on their business. Another example would be the consequences of an increase in energy and/or employment cost for SMEs' profit margin. Naturally, the rising cost of the human resources and energy tend to be reflected in higher production costs. As a consequence, the demand for the product tends to suffer. Finally, a reduction in sales and production translates into a reduced profit for every SME in the industry.

The third element of the environmental factors is the sociocultural variable. This variable includes any factors related to the cultural aspects of the environment such as cultural change, customers' values, demographic changes, age and geographical distribution of the population, birth and death rate, income distribution patterns, life expectations, music, education level and health level. For instance, strategists ought to be aware of the cultural values of the community and the country, as a whole, in which they plan to make investment. Customers' values in one country will certainly be different in another and considering customers' expectations and needs is crucial in developing a successful business strategy.

Demographic trends are another aspect of the sociocultural environment. What is the age distribution of the population? What is the geographical distribution of the population of the target market? More importantly, in order to formulate an effective marketing strategy strategists should know the distribution of the population of the target market. In short, sociocultural factors have significant impact on the performance of the SMEs.

Last but certainly not least is technology – another important environmental factor. Nowadays, technological changes, especially in the field of e-commerce and information technology, strongly impact the performance of the SMEs. For example, improvements in computer microprocessors have not only led to the extensive use of home PCs, it has also provided the opportunity to work and

Table 4.1	Political factors	Economical factors	Sociocultural factors	Technological factors
General environmental factors	Taxation law	The total GNP trends	Cultural changes	Investment in R & D
	Political changes at different levels	GDP per head	Customers' values	Total SME spending for R & D
	Changes in employment law	Rate of inflation	Demographic changes	Spread of technological changes within the industry
	Green issues	Exchange rate	Age and geographical distribution of the population	
	Political stability	Energy availability and cost	Birth and death rate	Product substitutions
	Critical situations	Inflation	Income distribution patterns	Information technology
	War	Employment level	Life expectations	Electronic commerce
		Interest rate	Education level	Internet and intranet
		Banking policies	Health level	
		Investment		

shop from home – possibly another step towards a better quality of life. Strategists in small businesses should be aware of many aspects of technological changes in the industry. Factors such as the speed of technological changes within the industry, products substitutions, information technology (IT), electronic commerce (e-commerce) development, Internet development and many more should be considered carefully prior to formulation of the strategy. Equally, it is important to allocate a portion of the financial resource of the firm to research and development (R & D), in order to be able to keep up with increasing technological changes within the industry.

Industry analysis

The second step in analysing the environment of the firm is commonly referred to as industry analysis. As mentioned earlier, the attractiveness of a firm within the industry is undoubtedly an important determination for its profitability. Therefore, it is important for strategists to include the industry in which the firm operates in their analysis. There are various different methods of analysing the industry. In this book we propose a framework for industry analysis which includes industry profile analysis, competitive industry environment analysis, defining the strategic groups and determining the key success factors in the industry. The process of industry analysis is illustrated in Figure 4.5.

Industry profile analysis

It is essential to analyse the industry profile in which a firm operates. This, however, necessitates defining what is meant by the term industry: an industry is generally defined as a group of firms or organisations producing and/or

Figure 4.5

Process of industry analysis in SMEs

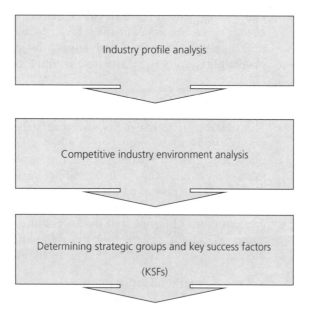

providing essentially the same products and services. The task of profiling the relevant industry for a SME involves listing its limits and boundaries with respect to customers, rivals, suppliers, production and services and any other factors relevant to its operation. Some industries may have to be defined by more than just their function. For instance, the Digit Software Company's operation involves developing a computer program for an ordering system in local warehouses. While such a firm is a part of the software industry, the relevant segment, as far as our analysis is concerned, is the one that deals only with warehouse ordering services for smaller businesses. Therefore, the potential customers of the Digit Software Company would only be the warehouses which are located in the area. The potential rivals, however, could be software firms of any size, based anywhere. Some of the main criteria when attempting to analyse the industry profile are (Lasher, 1999):

- The industry's profitability
- Market size and structure
- Industry life cycle
- Technological change.

The industry's profitability

Probably the first criterion to be seriously considered prior to entering a market or industry is profitability. The current average level of profitability among firms in the industry is an important indicator and ought to be considered carefully. As a rule, in the short term, maximising the profit is the main objective of the small businesses. For the strategist, therefore, it is imperative to have a clear vision of the future of the industry. Lasher (1999) asserts that a chronically depressed profit level in an industry is a strategically important issue and it is worth understanding the reasons for it presence. It can be an indicator of things like a long run of decline in demand, too many competitors or technical obsolescence. For small businesses profitability is one of the main considerations in assessing 'industry attractiveness'; the sting in the tail is that normally high profitability tends to attract new competitors.

Market analysis

The market, in terms of its size and structure, is the second major criterion which needs to be considered when analysing an industry profile. Should managers of small businesses wish to be successful, they must understand the market in which they are operating very well. This understanding is vital because the success of a business is largely determined by the manager's ability to serve that market better than his or her competitors (Wickham, 2001). There are a number of issues that managers of small businesses ought to be warned about. Wickham asserts that the following aspects of the market should be included in any serious market analysis:

- General market conditions
- The attractiveness of the innovation

- Initiation and position of the new venture in the marketplace
- The way in which competitors might react to the new venture.

Since many SMEs compete in geographically limited markets, it is essential to carry out market analysis as part of our industry profiling. Once the relevant market has been defined, its size can be estimated. The size of the market is the sales volume that is potentially available to the firm.

The second aspect of the market is its structure. Market structure relates to the number of rivals participating in an industry. It is important to consider the number of rivals as well as their size. In other words, it is important to gain a thorough understanding of the type of market that we intend or are currently operating in. For example, in an oligopoly condition the industry is typically dominated by a few large firms while a fragmented industry consists of a large number of firms with no one dominating the others. Obviously, SMEs do not operate in an oligopoly market. As Lasher (1999) aptly asserts, the selling side of the market structure is a key determinant of the way participating firms behave. It is essential to learn about the industry's structure, whether or not it is changing and why. Apart from the selling side of the market, the number and size of the buyers is also significant and ought to be included in the analysis of a market structure. For example, it makes a big difference whether a firm sells its product and/or services to a large number of individuals or offers them to a few big-spending customers.

Industry life cycle

Industries, by and large, go through a predictable growth pattern known as the industry life cycle. The basic concept which is developed to predict the probable course of industry evolution is commonly referred to as product life cycle theory (Porter, 1980). This is based on the notion that an industry passes through a number of stages including introduction, growth, maturity and decline throughout its life cycle (see Figure 4.6).

At the introduction stage, the organisation begins to develop new products or services and offers them to the market – industry growth at this stage is rather flat. This reflects the difficulty of overcoming reluctant buyers to stimulate trials of the new product. Unlike the first stage, the second stage of the product life

Figure 4.6

Industry life cycle

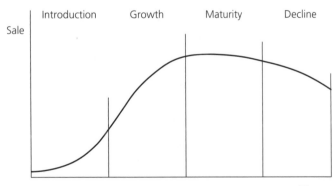

cycle is normally characterized by growth. If the product is successful an expansion period of rapid growth follows. Rapid growth signifies the rush of many buyers into the market once the product and/or service have proved themselves successful. The growth, whether rapid or otherwise, is inevitably followed by the third stage – maturity. This stage of the industry life cycle is normally characterized by the stabilization of demand and supply. Often the sale growth deceases or even stops. In this stage, potential buyers have been reached and the rapid growth will stop and reach a plateau stage (Porter, 1980). Finally, new substitute products will penetrate the market and begin their growth as the old one begins to decline.

Lasher (1999) goes on to suggest that a rapid intensification of rivalry as an industry transitions from the expansion into the maturity phase is expected. As a result the prices generally fall and because of intense competition only the strong firms survive. Thus, we believe it is imperative for SMEs to analyse the industry life cycle of the produce in order to understand their position in the industry. However, this is mainly determined by the manager's ability to define the industry in which he operates, otherwise the life cycle analysis will not be beneficial for decision-making. For the sake of argument, suppose that the recent trends show that the tourism industry is shrinking nationwide.

Technological changes

Consideration of the technology and its changes is an important factor in analysis of the industry profile, especially in SMEs where recently we have witnessed the rapid development of high tech industries. This development is a direct result of the rapid technological changes whose impact on the industry ought to be considered carefully. For example, the arrival of e-commerce as a new technological tool in marketing and sales could potentially increase the market share of the small businesses and expand their sales level. Apart from studying the impact of technological changes on small business operations, it is important to know the extent of the competition as a result of the technological changes itself. In some cases, the technology could be considered as a competitive advantage. If the firm cannot adapt itself to the emerging technological changes it will inevitably shrink out of existence.

The factors discussed above are the main variables in analysing an industry profile, but there are some other variables such as barriers to entry, product differentiation and vertical integration which are equally important when analysing the industry profile.

Generally speaking, the analysis of the industry profile is the first step. It provides a clear view of the industry in which the firm is either going to be or is currently operating. The second step in analysing the industry environment, as pointed out earlier, is analysis of the competitive environment. This important step will be discussed in the next section.

Competitive industry environment analysis

Identification of the potential and actual competitors constitutes the second step in the analysis of the industry competitive environment (Miller, 1988; Shay and Rothaermel, 1999). One of the best known techniques is that of Porter's five-force model (Porter, 1979, 1985). Porter argues that, in any industry, whether it is domestic or international, whether it is involved in the production of products or provision of services, the role of competition can be seen in terms of five forces: the entry of new competitors, the threats of substitutes, the bargaining power of buyers, the bargaining power of suppliers, and the rivalry among the existing operators (Porter, 1985). The collective strength of these five competitive forces by and large determines the ability of firms in any industry to earn, on average, the rates of return on their investment in excess of the cost of capital. Of course, the collective strength of the above forces tend to vary from industry to industry, and can change as an industry evolves. The analysis of the five force elements has been regarded as an important factor for SMEs as well as large organisations (see Box 4.3).

The five forces, in collective form, determine the industry profitability, because they influence the price, costs and the required investment of the firm in an industry. The strength of each of the five competitive forces is a function of industry structure (Porter, 1985). The five-force framework allows the firm to see through the complexity and pinpoint those factors that are critical to competition in its industry as well as identify those strategic innovations that would improve the industry's profitability (Box 4.4).

This will direct the managers' creative energies toward those aspects of industry structure that are most important to the long-run profitability of their firms. Finally, the process results in raising the odds of discovering a desirable strategic innovation (Wit and Meyer, 1998).

Box 4.3 Research note: the five competitive forces of strategy

In our recent research, we investigated the effects of the five competitive factors within the industry. The results of the analysis showed that the collective strength of the five external forces including bargaining power of customers (mean = 3.71, standard deviation (SD) = 0.88), bargaining power of suppliers (mean = 3.09, SD = 0.91), rivalry among existing firms (mean = 3.73, SD = 0.99), threat of new entrants (mean = 3.12, SD = 0.95) and finally threat of substitute products (mean = 3.32, SD = 1.12) tend to influence strategy formulation in the electrical and electronic industry. Accordingly, the respondents were asked to rank the above factors based on their perceived importance on the firm's strategy formulation process. We found that the bargaining power of customers (62.8 per cent) seemed to be regarded as the most important factor. The rivalry among existing firms (62.1 per cent) formed the second and the threat of substitute new products (40.7 per cent) formed the third priority. In contrast, the threat of new entrants (28.1 per cent) and the bargaining power of suppliers (25 per cent) did not seem strongly to influence the formulation of strategy in the targeted firms.

Box 4.4 Porter's five-force model

The five-force model of Porter is one of the best known techniques used to analyse the industry. This framework enables SMEs to see through the complex market and develop their very own competitive advantages. The five-force strategic factors are:

- The entry of new competitors
- The threats of substitutes
- The bargaining power of buyers
- The bargaining power of suppliers
- The rivalry among the existing competitors.

Whilst each force should be treated as important, it is the collective strength of all five which determines the profitability of a firm in a specific industry.

The threat of new entrants

In the main, it could be safely argued that new entrants to an industry bring to it new capacity for production, a desire to gain a market share (competition) and substantial resources. Naturally, new firms will be confronted by numerous barriers and threats which are largely determined by the reaction of the existing firms in the industry. If the existing firms ensure access to substitute resources, they can control the prices and reduce the production costs. This will enable them to see off the new firms entering the industry. Otherwise the new firms, possibly with new competitive advantages, will enter into the industry and pose a threat to established firms. In other words, the extent of the threat of new entrants into the industry largely depends on the presence of effective barriers to their entry. For instance, if an existing small firm develops a new product on which the firm has a patent, the other firms may not produce this product, thus the patent in this case will act as a barrier to newcomers to the industry and protects the firm from potential rivals. To sum up, an entry barrier is an obstruction that makes it difficult for a firm to enter an industry. Some of the factors which act as possible entry barriers to an industry are:

- Low production costs
- Economies of scale
- Governmental policies and restrictions
- Access to resources such as financial or skilled human resources
- Product differentiation
- Access to marketing and distribution channels.

This implies that industry analysis should include identification of the potential barriers to entry. If the profit rate is higher than the average rate in industry, there will be potential interest in entering into the industry from new firms. Consideration of the profitability alone is not sufficient analysis of the industry – we also need to take into account the presence and/or absence of the entry barriers as well. By considering these criteria we can predict the success possibilities of the new entrants into the industry.

Rivalry among existing firms

Competitors are considered as an external factor in environmental analysis; however in most industries the firms are dependent on each other. A competitive move by one firm can be expected to have an effect on the other competitors. For instance, the development of new technology by an existing firm can increase its market share. Accordingly the application of Internet and intranets in SMEs is expected to lead to an increase in sale volume. According to Porter (1985) intense rivalry is related to the presence of several factors. Some of those are:

- Industry growth rate and capacity
- Fixed costs and value added
- Product or services characteristics
- Brand identification
- Switching costs
- Informational complexity
- Diversity of competitors
- Exit barriers.

Lasher maintains that rivalry among existing firms ranges from mild to a level of intensity described as 'cut-throat' (1999). He goes on to suggest that the mild form of competition means that the firms strive to prevent new entrants into the industry, but make only mild efforts to attract customers away from existing competitors. In contrast, intense competition means that the players actively target customers who currently buy from other companies using attractions strategies such as publicity and advertising.

Threat of substitute products or services

The third element of Porter's five-force model is the threat of substitute products and services. Substitute products are those products that appear to be different but are not. They can satisfy the same need as another product and hence pose a threat to the existing producers and providers of the services. For example, one bottled mineral water can be a substitute for another; or tea is a substitute of coffee. So, if the price of coffee increases, the customers will tend to buy tea instead of the coffee. According to Porter (1985) the following factors are the determinants of effective substitution threat:

- Relative price performance of substitutes
- Switching costs
- Buyer propensity to substitute.

The existence of substitutes enables buyers to make a comparison of products in terms of prices and quality, and to generally benefit from the presence of the substitutes in the market. Therefore, existing substitutes limit the firms' market power. In other words, if the customers are not happy with a particular product or service, they can switch to alternatives and consequently the sellers lose their captured customers.

Bargaining power of buyers

It has been suggested that satisfying buyers' needs is at the core of the success of any businesses and it is indeed a crucial factor for an industry and the firms that operate within it. As discussed earlier, buyers affect an industry through their ability to compare and bargain for higher quality and lower priced commodities. In a monopoly condition the buyers are at a distinct disadvantage since the lack of such bargaining power prevents them from playing one firm against the other(s). In monopoly situations only a few supply the products or services; or in some cases only one firm. There exists virtually no competition in the market. In contrast, in a fragmented market in which many firms supply the same products or services, competitive prices will emerge and as a result a buyer or a group of buyers will be able to play one firm against another, force down the prices and so benefit from the intense competition According to Porter (1985) the following factors are the determinants of buyer power:

- Bargaining leverage
- Price sensitivity.

Porter argues that bargaining leverage includes factors such as buyer concentration, buyer volume, buyer switching costs, buyer information, ability to step back and substitute products. Accordingly the price sensitivity impacts on quality performance, buyer profit and decision-makers' incentives. A bargaining power analysis includes an assessment of the current buyer power in an industry. In some cases it is difficult to identify the exact group of buyers, in others the firm will be able actively to target the specific group of customers. For example, suppose that a small business operates in manufacturing and selling children's shoes. It produces the shoes in terms of the age size of the children up to 10 years old. So the buyers will be the families who have children up to 10 years old. McDonald's 'happy meal' product is another interesting example where only children are targeted. In general, the bargaining power of the buyer will be weaker if the firm knows the customers and their needs and can satisfy their expectations comprehensively.

Bargaining power of the suppliers

The bargaining power of suppliers can also affect the industry profile. A supplier's power is critical when they provide a special input that the firm cannot get elsewhere. For instance, suppose that a small firm is producing PVCs. One of the chemical materials is provided by only one leading firm, which has a patent on it. Since the small business cannot buy the same material from another source, it has to pay the price asked for the chemical. In this way, the source of any input for production could be considered as a supplier. Even the labour unions or market that provide the human resources could be considered to be a supplier.

Firms can reduce the bargaining power of suppliers by vertical integration, or long term supply arrangements. According to Porter (1985) the following factors are some of the determinants of the supply power:

- Differentiation of inputs
- Switching costs of suppliers
- Supplier's concentrations
- Importance of volume to supplier
- Cost relative to total purchases in the industry
- Impacts of inputs on cost or differentiation.

Recently, Kleindl (2000) has applied the five-force model to analysis of the industry structure and the new competitive forces that impact on SMEs (see Figure 4.7).

Figure 4.7   Information technology base threats to traditional SMEs

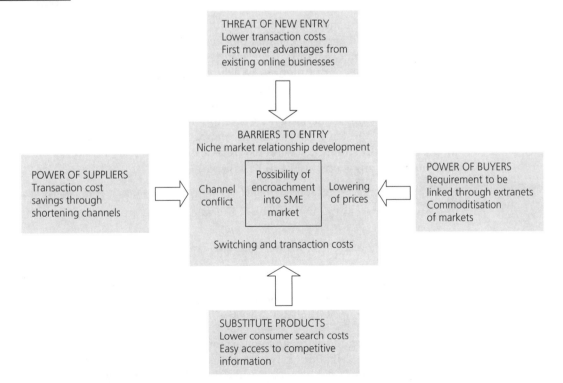

The traditional barriers to competition enjoyed by SMEs have been created largely by their ability to serve niche markets and develop strong relationships with customers. These, however, have increasingly been threatened by Internet-enabled businesses. Nowadays, there is a real threat of entry from larger regional, national and international firms (Wolff, 2000). Generally, the lower transaction costs involved enable competitors to enter markets primarily dominated by SMEs. These new entrants sometimes represent industries quite far removed from those with which the SMEs are familiar. In the case of new entrants with an established Web presence, consumers may have either formed relationships with that business or may see the business as the brand name. There is also an incentive for the suppliers to eliminate intermediaries to save costs. This pattern has been made possible because of the increased Web-based efficiencies in both information flows and distribution flows. The easy access to competitive information is challenging existing prices and hence encouraging customers to search for substitutes. Not all industries will face this challenge. The ultimate needs of the customer will determine how quickly businesses go online. Those businesses that rely on person-to-person interface may become the latecomers to the world of e-commerce. However, online communication through email and Web pages, developing extranet links to suppliers and changing internal communication systems are impacting on almost all businesses.

Determining strategic groups

After analysing the industry we need to determine the main competitors of the firm. As discussed already, in small businesses the industry could be defined in terms of geographical region; therefore it is imperative to locate the strategic groups within the environment in which the firm operates. A strategic group is a set of businesses that pursue similar strategies with similar resources. Categorising firms, in any industry, into a set of strategic groups is useful as a way of better understanding the competitive environment (Wheelen and Hunger, 1998). Strategic groups can be mapped by plotting the market positions of the competitors in industry on two relevant attributes on the axes. To achieve this the following steps ought to be taken:

1. Choosing the two characteristics of the industry, which differ from firm to firm. For example we can select the sale volume and product or service quality.
2. Plotting the selected firms using two characteristics as the dimensions of the plot.
3. Drawing a circle around those firms that are closest to each other as one strategic group. The size of the circles determines the share of each strategic group within the industry.

When analysing industry, it is important to carry out market segmentation to identify who the SMEs are competing with. For instance, suppose that a small business operates in the catering industry in a moderate-sized city. In order to determine if there is any competition between restaurants in the city the active restaurants ought to be categorised into different segments or strategic groups.

It could be argued that each strategic group acts as an independent strategy in small businesses. Figure 4.8 shows the strategic group map of the local restaurant industry.

A strategic group map is a helpful technique for analysing the structure of an industry. Once we categorise and recognise our main competitors, it will be possible to develop and implement appropriate business strategies and to successfully compete with rivals.

Key success factors

The last step in industry analysis is the identification of the key success factors (KSFs) in the industry. Providing KSFs can help small business managers to focus on what they can do better than their competitors. KSFs consist of the distinctive skills, abilities and attributes which are normally related to the product, service or technology, which can be used to create a competitive advantage for the firm in the industry (Box 4.5).

Figure 4.8

Strategic group map in local restaurants

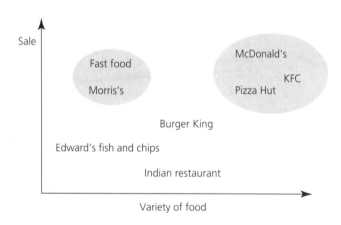

Box 4.5 Key success factors (KSFs)

Key success factors consist of the distinctive skills, abilities and attributes normally related to the product or service or technology, which can be used to create a competitive advantage for the firm in the industry. Providing KSFs can help small business managers to focus on what they can do better than their competitors.

Strategic group

A strategic group is a set of businesses that follow similar strategies with similar resources. Categorising SMEs in any industry into a set of strategic groups is useful as a way of better identifying with whom the small and medium-sized enterprises are competing.

There are a few things in any business that *have* to be done to compete with the competitors successfully. For example, a bakery has to be able to cook good quality bread. A garment manufacturer has to be able to produce goods of good quality and at a reasonable price. A university has to demonstrate a high quality in research. These examples show that quality for the baker, reasonable price for the manufacturer and high quality research for the university are the key success factors. In other words, if a university cannot produce outstanding research, or a bakery cannot provide quality bread, they will not be able to survive. Therefore, KSFs are those aspects or characteristics that an organisation must be able to do or possess should it wish to succeed. Table 4.2 illustrates some of the key success factors in different industries.

It is strategically important for SMEs to identify the key success factors for the industry or the strategic group in which they operate. Once the KSFs for the industry are identified and listed, the SMEs can compare their individual abilities, skills or competencies with those of the industry or strategic group. Bearing in mind that in small businesses we need to consider the entrepreneurs' skills as a crucial factor in the success of the firm.

Internal environment analysis

In the last section, we discussed how analysing the external environment of the organisation could lead to the identification of the opportunities and threats for the firm in the market. However, analysing the external environment is not enough to provide a firm with a distinct competitive advantage – the SMEs need to assess their internal environment strengths and weaknesses too. Analysing the internal environment of the firm is concerned with identifying and developing the firm's resources.

The resource-based approach concept

The resource-based approach in organisational analysis has emerged as an important new conceptualisation in the field of strategic management (Black

Table 4.2	Industry	KSFs
Key success factors (KSFs) in some industries	Consumer goods manufacturer	Brand management
	Higher education institution (university)	High quality research
	Charities	Fund raising and public relation
	Dairy industry	Access to distribution channels
	Insurance industry	Access to financing
	Heavy manufacturing	Capital
	Software development	Design knowledge
	Small high tech industry	Technology
	Tourism industry	Customer satisfaction skills

and Boal, 1994; Zajac, 1995; Teece *et al.* 1997; Hoskisson *et al.* 1999). Hoskisson *et al.* argue that 'theoretically, the central premise of resource-based view (RBV) addresses the fundamental question of why firms are different and how firms achieve and sustain competitive advantage' (1999: 437). It also focuses on specific types of resources inside a firm, such as strategic leadership.

The origin of the resource-based view can be traced to early management researches (Selznick, 1957; Chandler, 1962; Andrews, 1971). Since the early 1980s, researchers have been developing and defining resource-based concepts, and seeking to relate how resources can give rise to firm competitive advantage (Hoskisson *et al.* 1999). Another group of researchers (Barney, 1986; Spender, 1989; Hitt and Ireland, 2000) focused on examining specific resources which give rise to sustainable competitive advantages. During the 1990s the resource-based theory was developed significantly. In the early 1990s, Barney presented a more comprehensive framework to identify the resource characteristics required by a firm in order to generate sustainable competitive advantages (Barney, 1991). Four criteria were proposed to assess the economic implications of the resources: value, rareness, inimitability and sustainability. Supporting this thesis some researchers discussed the dynamic aspects of the theory. Grant (1991) suggested that there is a need to examine the dynamic interrelationships among the resources. Accordingly, Amit and Schoemaker (1993) presented the framework in which values such as those included the subdimensions of an external link were complementarily overlapping with strategic factors in industry and the internal.

Recently, the researches on the resource-based view have become further specialised (Leonard-Barton, 1992; Hoskisson *et al.* 1999). In this regard, Hoskisson *et al.* (1999) argued, 'first, rigidities in acquiring resources may be different from the rigidities in shedding resources, and some resources may have negative value by creating core rigidities. Second, a controversy has evolved concerning the potential of the RBV to be a theory' (Hoskisson *et al.* 1999: 439). The resource-based view of the firm may form the kernel of a unifying paradigm for strategic management research (Boxall, 1996). It provides a framework for increasing dialogue between scholars from different disciplines within the conversation of strategic management.

Firms' resources and competitive advantage

A resource is an asset, competency, process, skill or knowledge controlled by the firm and is a strength if it provides a company with a competitive advantage. It is something that the firm does or has the potential to do particularly well relative to the abilities of existing or potential competitors. A resource could be a weakness if it is something that the firm or business, regardless of size, does not have the capacity to achieve or does poorly in comparison with its competitors (Box 4.6).

It has been claimed (Wheelen and Hunger, 1998; Beal, 2000) that scanning and analysing the external environment for opportunities and threats is not enough to provide an organisation with advantage(s). Analysts must also look within the business itself to identify internal strategic factors – those critical strengths and weaknesses – that are likely to enable the firm to take advantage of opportunities while avoiding threats in its environment (Wheelen and

> **Box 4.6 What is a resource?**
>
> A resource is an asset, competency, process, skill or knowledge controlled by the corporation. A resource is considered as a strength if it provides an SME with a competitive advantage. Normally, resources of the firms are categorised into three types:
>
> - Tangible resources
> - Intangible resources
> - Organisational capabilities.

Hunger, 1998). The resource-based approach to strategic management accentuates the link between the internal characteristics of the firm and that firm's performance (Barney, 1991; Grant, 1991). The resource-based perspective has been used to analyse many aspects of the firm, including strategic planning, information system, positive reputation (Barney, 1991) and strategic groups (Mehra, 1994).

The development of resource-based theory within the field of strategic management has certainly contributed to the increased understanding of organisations differentiated by many types of characteristics, one being competitive advantage (Green, 1997). Other scholars have considered the resource-based approach from other points of view. For instance, Lynch (2000) argues that the resourced-based approach consists of seven main elements. These are:

- Priority to acquire resources
- Innovative capability
- Being truly competitive
- Substitutability
- Appropriability
- Durability
- Imitability.

Grant (1998) proposed a five-step, resource-based approach to strategy analysis. He proposes that a firm's sustained competitive advantage is primarily determined by its resource endowments. These are:

1. Identifying resources – identifying and classifying the firm's resources in terms of strengths and weaknesses.
2. Identifying and appraising capabilities – the combining of the firm's strengths into specific capabilities. Corporate capabilities are the things that a corporation can do exceedingly well. Resource-based theory recognises the intangibles in a business as an important source of capabilities. Hall (1992) describes intangible assets as including intellectual property rights, contracts, trade secrets, reputation and networks and describes intangible skills as consisting of knowledge and culture.

3. Evaluating sustainability of resources – to appraise the profit potential of resources and capabilities in terms of their potential for sustainable competitive advantage and the ability to harvest the profits resulting from the use of these resources and capabilities. Four conditions are considered necessary to the development of sustainable competitive advantage (Flynn, 1993; Green, 1997):

- First, the resource must be valuable, contributing significantly to the increased effectiveness and efficiency of the business.
- Second, the resource must be rare among both current and potential competitors.
- Third, the resource must be imperfectly imitable, that is due to unique historical conditions, the link between the sustained competitive advantage and the complex social dynamic of the resource cannot be determined clearly enough to enable its duplication elsewhere.
- Fourth, the resource must not have any strategic equivalent substitutes.

4. Formulating strategy – selecting the strategy that best exploits the firm's resources and capabilities relative to external opportunities. The essence of strategy formulation is to design a strategy that makes the most effective use of these core resources and capabilities.

5. Identifying resource gaps and investing in upgrading weaknesses – a resource-based approach to strategy is concerned not only with the development of existing resources, but also with the development of the firm's resources base. This includes investment and sometimes replacement to ensure the continuity of the firm's stock of resources and supplementing the existing resources to further competitive advantage and broaden the firm's strategic opportunities.

Resource-based view and SMEs

Like many strategic management theories, the resource-based view of the firm applies to SMEs as well as to large organisations. The general notion is that whilst SMEs have access to resources which are not vast in comparison to the large firms, their resource base tends to be more flexible and entrepreneurial. SMEs typically concentrate on developing strategies which might be different from large organisations. For instance, Lynch (2000) contends that SMEs develop strategies that might include a higher level of personal services, specialist expertise, design skills, regional knowledge and bespoke solutions. As he aptly argues, all these can be contained within the seven elements of the resource-based approach.

Analysing the firm's resources

Perhaps the main reasons for analysing the resources of an organisation are to explore and identify those resources that enable an organisation to compete and survive against its competitors. As discussed in the value chain concept, resource analysis needs to proceed along two parallel routes: value added and sustainable competitive advantage. Basically the resources of the organisation are those assets that contribute to the generation of value added. Lynch (2000) has divided the firm's resources into three main categories:

- Tangible resources: the physical resources of the organisation such as land, equipment, buildings, machinery and all the visible assets.
- Intangible resources: the non-physical presence that represents real benefit to the firm such as brand names, technology and patent.
- Organisational capability: the organisational capabilities that differ from firm to firm such as human resource skills, discipline and management style.

The basic role of the resources in an organisation is to add value. Value added is the difference between cost of input and market value of the output. From this point of view, value can be added in an organisation either by raising the value of its output (the price of the product or service in the market) or by lowering the cost of the inputs (the cost of raw materials and wages) into the firm. Usually organisations need to ensure that they do add value in the long term. Resource analysis determines the extent to which the resources of the firm add value and contributes to its profit profile.

Human resources and competitive advantage

Following the growth of interest in strategic analysis in the face of mounting competition in industry, human resources has been identified as a potential source of competitive advantage (Kakabadse *et al.* 1996). Some proponents of strategic human resource management (SHRM) argue that the management of human resources must fit within a suitable strategy (Mabey *et al.* 1998; Boxall and Steeneveld, 1999). An increasing number of studies have attempted to assess the linkage of HR and strategy process (Wright *et al.* 1998). A new paradigm of corporate strategy, which is referred to as the resource-based approach, has emerged to help companies compete more effectively in the ever-changing and globalising environment of the twenty-first century. This approach views competencies, capabilities, skills or strategic assets as the source of sustainable competitive advantage for the firm (Mabey *et al.* 1998). The link between human resources as a strategic asset of a firm and strategy can be assumed at different levels. There are four levels of linkage between HR and strategy: administrative linkage, one-way linkage, two-way linkage and integrative linkage (Golden and Ramanujam, 1985; Boxall, 1996). Anderson has argued that two fundamental and specific processes are available to HR people in order to help management to realise the full potential of the HR capabilities in support of their business objectives. These processes have been tested successfully at the Amoco Corporation. The first is linking people strategies to the company's strategic management process. The second is developing an HR strategy to support the corporation strategies (Anderson, 1997).

The attempts to link business planning and competitive strategy with HR planning have dominated the HRM literature (Salaman, 1992; Analoui, 2002). Human resources and the corporation management group should be engaged in a realistic strategic management process that can effectively link and ultimately bind the business strategy, organisational capabilities and people strategies. A well-developed business strategy identifies the need for specific organisational capabilities and reinforces the building of these capabilities as the primary focus of the people strategy (Kakabadse *et al.* 1996; Anderson, 1997).

Human resource involvement in the strategic management process has been thought to be effective in many cases. Its effectiveness, however, may vary with the firm's strategies. Strategic management is greater when senior managers view people as a strategic resource (Beer, 1997; Wright, *et al.* 1998). This relationship between regarding employees as strategic resources and the strategic involvement of the HR function may stem from differing levels of involvement required depending upon the overall strategy of the organisation. In this regard Wright, *et al.* (1998) contends that the relationship between HR involvement and both the perception of operation managers of HR effectiveness and the refinery performance varies considerably across different stages (Wright, *et al.* 1998).

Brockbank sums this up in some of his research findings:

> The challenge for the HR professional is threefold: first, examine and understand the context from which the business realities tend to derive; second, design critical, high value-added agendas; and third, ensure that broadly defined HR practices are exactly aligned and unified around these agendas. As these develop, HR will contribute a more strategic and high value-added presence as the firm competes in increasingly complex and changing contextual conditions.
>
> (Brockbank, 1997: 69)

Value chain analysis

Generally speaking the value chain analysis is a systematic approach to the costing of the business's process from the beginning to the end (Quayle *et al.* 1999) (Box 4.7). One of the determining strategic factors in the decision-making process is the cost of the products and services; producing the products at low cost can lead to high profit. The nature of organisations in terms of their size is different. An unprofitable product line in a big organisation may not lead to an

---

Box 4.7 Value chain analysis

- SMEs can gain high profit either by lowering production costs or increasing sales. Value chain management can help strategists to achieve these objectives.

- Value chain management is managing integrated information about product flow from input suppliers to end-users to reduce product costs, promote sales and improve customer satisfaction.

- Value chain is a systematic analysis of the businesses' processes and costs. It shows where value is added and costs are incurred.

immediate crisis but in a small business it is a different matter. In small businesses, if the business is not profitable it simply cannot continue.

More especially in the commodity-type businesses, competition tends to be based on price. If the firm cannot reduce the cost of the production, the price will be raised. Consequently, it will not be able to compete with the other firms which have efficient production systems and benefit from a more effective strategy. Understandably, the strategists must make sure that, in calculating overall cost – that is the cost of the raw materials, production, sale and distribution, and even after sales service cost – the firm is not placed in a weak position. Changes ought to be brought about so that observed weaknesses are strengthened and value chain management can help strategists to achieve these objectives. It can effectively manage the integration of disparate sources of information about product flow from suppliers to end-users to reduce product costs, sale promotion and improve customer satisfaction. The value chain concept has been developed by Porter (1985) and Figure 4.9 shows the main elements of value chain analysis.

Value chain is a rational and structured way of looking at a company's processes and costs (Lasher, 1999). It has also been suggested that the value chain is a representation of an industry chain. It assists firms to take strategic decisions when trying to acquire business segments where the highest values are allocated, or in increasing competitiveness through the reduction of those costs whose value is not completely perceived by customers (Morganti, 2002). Any firm has its own specific value chain activities. For example, in manufacturing firms, the main activities start with buying raw materials and preparing all the necessary equipment to start production operations. The second activity is production operation. Production includes the process in which the products are manufactured. Sales and marketing are considered as the next stage in value chain, which includes activities such as advertising, sale promotion, and pricing. The fourth stage in the value chain is distribution. According to Porter (1985), as is shown in Figure 4.9, the main idea behind the value chain is to identify overall costs based on stages along the product or service line, and compare the firm's performance at each stage with the performance of the competitors.

SWOT analysis

The next step in analysing the environment is determining the firm's strengths and weaknesses as well as opportunities and threats. This technique, known as SWOT analysis, shows what the firm can do very well and what it cannot do. The first two criteria, strengths and weaknesses, are calculated from analysis of the internal environment of the firm while the last two, opportunities and threats, come from analysis of the external environment of the firm (Box 4.8).

Figure 4.9	INPUTS	PRODUCTION	SALE	DISTRIBUTION	SERVICES
	Raw materials	Products	Marketing	Warehousing	Installation
Value chain analyses	Resources	Services	Pricing	Transportation	Parts

> **Box 4.8 SWOT analysis**
>
> SWOT is an analytical tool which can be used for both large and small organisations. It is often used to pinpoint the exact position of the firm prior to taking a major decision. When it is used for analysis of SMEs, it considers strengths and weaknesses alongside the opportunities and threats that the firm is likely to be faced with in the future. Strengths and weaknesses are gained from analysis of the internal environment of the firm, while opportunities and threats come from analysis of the external environment of the firm. SWOT analysis shows what the firm can do very well and what it cannot realistically accomplish. This technique is often used by strategists to make a list of internal strengths and weaknesses as well as a list of external opportunities and threats. Whilst the strength and opportunities provide the forward force the weakness and threats remind the strategist of the risks and inadequacies involved.

This technique helps strategists to make a list of internal strengths and weaknesses as well as a list of external opportunities and threats.

Strengths

As discussed earlier, a strength for an SME is a key success factor. Strengths could include the skills and abilities of the firm such as skilled and committed human resources, effective distribution channels, financial stability and technology know-how. Also patents, rights and reputation are considered as strengths of a small business. For example, consider the case of Gozal Travel. This is a small firm which operates within the tourism industry in Turkey. Because of its reputation and high quality services its customers are increasing on a steady basis. Gozal Travel's reputation, which generates a great deal of income annually, is clearly its strength. It should therefore be borne in mind that in the case of small businesses the distinctive competencies are usually considered as strengths. These competencies are the abilities which the firm possesses and its access to them. Evidently firms, especially SMEs, should explore and identify their strengths, exploit them fully and adapt to the environment. In other words, the firms need to fit their abilities (competencies) to the needs of the environment. As a rule, SWOT analysis reveals whether or not a firm possesses any distinctive competencies (strengths) or not. Accordingly, if the firm learns that it has strengths, these can be further developed. The business strategies are then based on the identified strengths. In contrast, where there is a lack of strengths related to the industry, the firm must either build up competences and develop its existing strengths or move to another industry (Box 4.9).

Weaknesses

Strategic analysis of the firm may well lead to finding its weaknesses. A weakness is something that a firm lacks or isn't as good at as its competitors. For instance, suppose that a small firm operates in the production and distribution

---

Box 4.9 Research note: strengths for SMEs in the electrical and electronic industries

In a recent study the industry strengths were examined using seven indicators: potential growth, market share, financial stability, resource utilisation, productivity, capacity utilisation, flexibility and finally adaptability. These indicators were measured using an ordinal scale from not important to essential. The result shows that financial stability (mean = 4.356, SD = 0.782) is the most important factor in determining industry strengths in the studied firms. In contrast market share (mean = 3.565, SD = 1.029) was reported as the weakest factor in determining industry strengths. It seems that turbulent environment of the industry and the changing expectations of the customers in the electronic industry push the firms to be more adaptable and flexible in developing business strategies. The importance of each factor in determining industry strengths was measured using the Likert scale.

Regarding the financial stability of the firms, 106 CEOs (87.9%) believed that, financial indicators are essential in determining industry strength. In contrast, only a few of the respondents (N = 3/2.3%) considered financial indicators as not important or of limited importance in determining industry strengths. The respondents considered adaptability (N = 103/78% as very important and essential) and flexibility (N = 87/65.9% as very important and essential) of the firm's strategies with customers' expectations as a determining factor. The flexibility of the firm in terms of coping with unexpected changes in the marketplace, managerial style and technology utilisation were considered as an essential factor in firm performance. Respondents prioritised the other factors in determining industry strengths including quality of products and services (N = 81/61% very important and essential) as the third priority, resources utilisation like HR and financial resources (N = 79/59% very important and essential) as the fourth priority, growth potential (N = 75/56% very important and essential) as the fifth priority, and market share (N = 71/53% very important and essential) as the sixth priority.

---

of fresh food. In comparison with its rivals, the firm produces high quality fresh food, but in the distribution of the product the firm faces some major problems. The fresh food needs to be delivered as soon as possible to the market; however, the firm lacks an efficient delivery system. In contrast, some of the existing rivals in the market could have already established the just-in-time system for delivering their products to the market. In the case of the former, the lack of an efficient delivery system ought to be considered as a major weakness for the firm.

SMEs should be involved in a continual process of analysis and assessment of their resources, skills, structure and leadership styles (Daft *et al.* 1988). This analysis can help the strategists in identifying the firm's weaknesses in comparison with the existing rivals in the industry. In identifying the weaknesses, the next step would be both recovering from those weaknesses quickly and strengthening the strategic weaknesses of the firm. The following points are some examples of the typical weaknesses in small businesses:

- Lack of financial resources
- Entrepreneurs' lack of managerial experience
- Entrepreneurs' lack of technical skills
- High labour costs
- Inefficient organisational structure
- Low production and services quality.

As discussed, the firm's weaknesses are identified by comparing the firm with its rivals. In other words, any weakness of the firm may be considered as a strength by competitors. Bearing in mind that by providing a strengths and weaknesses profile (SWP) we can analyse the small business's strategic strengths and weaknesses. Table 4.3 shows an example of such a profile.

By identifying the strengths of the business we will be able to formulate effective strategies based on the firm's strengths. Consequently, if we can recognise the strategic weaknesses of the firm, the next step will be adopting a course of action(s) to recover from and to strengthen the identified weaknesses.

Opportunities

At the beginning of the chapter we noted that the process of external environmental analysis leads to diagnosis of the opportunities or threats to the firm in its external environment. So, what are the opportunities of the firm? Opportunities are the situations in which the firm can improve its strategic

Table 4.3 The firm's strengths and weaknesses profile (SWP)	Internal environmental section	Effect of each factor	Assessment
	Resources	• Access to strong financial resources	↑ Strength
		• Strong family support	↑ Strength
		• High labour cost	↓ Weakness
		• Limited access to skilled human resources	↓ Weakness
		• High rate of profitability	↑ Strength
	Management	• Lack of managerial education	↓ Weakness
		• About eight years' experience in running small businesses	↑ Strength
		• High motivation in developing the business	↑ Strength
		• Tending to create a friendly environment in the firm	↑ Strength
	Marketing	• Access to effective advertising tools	↑ Strength
		• Poor marketing management	↓ Weakness
	Technology	• Poor adaptability with technological changes	↓ Weakness
	Structure	• Flexible organisational structure	↑ Strength

position (Lasher, 1999). For example, an increased market share for the firm in the international market (Wolff, 2000) or the firm's access to low price energy can both be considered as opportunities. The first step in the planning process is to be aware of opportunities. For small businesses, environmental scanning through which the firm can effectively determine its core competencies and opportunities acts as a major factor in the realisation of strategic management for the firm. Suppose our hypothetical firm is operating in a high tech industry. Any technological changes in the industry which can generate new sales opportunities or potential customers could be considered as an opportunity. If a firm is involved in either long or medium run planning, they have to have a clear vision of the future and the potential opportunities available. It is difficult to prepare an effective business plan without considering the opportunities. Therefore, small businesses usually succeed or fail based on how accurately they can identify the opportunities and benefit from these advantages. Since in the competitive environment the needs of the customers are changing, the firm's need to analyse the environment as often as possible.

Threats

Threats are the main obstacles and issues in the external environment of the organisation. Any changes in the external environment of the SMEs that have the potential to disrupt the firm's well-being could be considered as threats. For example, we recently witnessed rapid changes in technology and, as a result, in the business environment. Should the SME not be capable of adapting to these technological changes it will not be able to survive. In this case the changes in technology could be considered as a threat to the firm. For SMEs the environment is littered with threats to their survival. According to Lasher (1999) the following factors are some of the threats that SMEs typically experience:

- Unexpected entry of a large and more powerful competitor into the local arena.
- Technological innovation makes obsolete the way firms produce their products, making investments in equipment valueless.
- Union labour demands wages substantially higher than those paid by competitors in a non-union part of the country.
- Increasing cost of being in the business because of government environmental rules and regulations.
- Customer demand shifts away from the firm's products or services.

One of the techniques in recognising the opportunities and threats of the firm is providing an environmental threat and opportunity profile (ETOP). This consists of the environmental factors which could be considered as either opportunity or threat. Table 4.4 illustrates an example of an ETOP in a typical small business.

Bearing in mind that we can create the SME's ETOP for each environmental section separately, it would be possible to know exactly what the feasible economical opportunities and the potential threats to the firm in the market are. It is important to know that each firm will have its specific opportunities and threats profile. In other words, an opportunity for one firm could be a threat for another within the same industry.

How we can conduct a SWOT analysis in SMEs?

The wizardry of SWOT is the matching of specific internal and external factors which creates a strategic matrix that makes sense. It is essential to note that the internal factors are, by and large, within the sphere of the control of the organisation. These include operations, finance, marketing and areas related to the deployment of human resources. In contrast, the external factors are likely to be beyond the organisation's control, such as the political and economic factors, new technologies and its competitors (Weihrich, 1982).

As discussed earlier, prior to developing a strategy there is a need to analyse strengths, weaknesses, opportunities and threats of the firm. Conducting a SWOT analysis prepares the strategists for the formulation of business strategies. SWOT analysis can be carried out by both qualitative or quantitative methods or a combination of both. The quantitative method is more applicable and consists of the following procedures:

1. Choosing the factors indicating the opportunities and threats of the firm.
2. Choosing the factors indicating the strengths and weaknesses of the firm.

Table 4.4	External environmental section	Effect of each section	Assessment
An environmental opportunity and threat profile	Economical factors	• Increasing the firm's market share from local to national markets	↑ Opportunity
		• Possibility of energy substitute	↑ Opportunity
	Political–legal factors	• Increasing the minimum wage level	↓ Threat
		• New green issue regulations	↓ Threat
		• Small business links development	↑ Opportunity
	Technology	• Entering the new technology into the market	↑ Opportunity
	Rivals	• Entering a new large firm into the industry in a national market	↓ Threat
		• Developing a new production technology (patent) by the firm	↑ Opportunity
	Suppliers	• Increasing cost of raw materials	↓ Threat
		• Merging the main suppliers	↓ Threat
	Buyers	• Increasing the firm's reputation among buyers	↑ Opportunity
		• Increasing the customers' satisfaction from the firm's products	↑ Opportunity

3. Select the final strategic factors from stages one and two.

4. Score the firm and its selected competitors on each strategic factor.

5. Calculate a weighted average indicator for the firms listed in stage four.

6. Compare the findings and interpret the results.

It must be noted that in each stage the qualitative analysis can also be used to support the quantitative results. Here, we will go through the application of SWOT analysis for SMEs stage by stage, using a case study (see page 103).

Summary

- Environmental analysis is a process through which strategists study the environment of the firm and determine the strengths, weaknesses, opportunities, and threats (SWOT) of the firm. External analysis involves developing a better understanding of the industry while internal analysis is the study of the firm itself. Some of the reasons for the importance of the environment analysis in SMEs are CEOs' own awareness, uncertainty and changing environmental conditions, and determining the challenging environmental factors.

- The environmental factors of the firm could be classified into two main groups – external and internal. The external environmental factors are classified into two groups including general environmental factors and industry factors. The general environmental factors include four main societal environmental factors – political/legal, economical, sociocultural and technological. The industry environmental factors include those related to the industry itself such as suppliers, competitors, customers, government and shareholders. The internal environmental factors such as organisational structure, resources, management style and culture are those which are related to the firm itself. These factors are usually under the control of the management.

- PEST analysis looks at the impact of political, economical, sociocultural, and technological (PEST) factors on the strategy. The political environmental category includes factors such as taxation law, changes in employment law, green issues, political stability and war. Economical factors include the total GNP trends, inflation rate, exchange rate, employment level, interest rate, monetary and fiscal policies, banking policies and investment. Sociocultural variables include any factors related to the cultural aspects of the environment such as cultural changes, customers' values, demographic changes, birth and death rate, education level and health level and finally, the technological factors are those present in the environment in which the firm operates.

- The second step in analysis of the external environment of the firm is industry analysis. The aim of the industry analysis for SMEs is to determine the opportunities and threats facing the firm within the industry. It briefly includes industry profile analysis, competitive industry environment analysis, defining the strategic groups and determining the key success factors in the industry.

- Industry profile analysis, on the other hand, provides a clear general picture of the industry in which the firm operates. The task in profiling the relevant industry for a SME is to list its limits and boundaries with respect to customers, rivals, suppliers, production and services and any other relevant factors. It involves analysing the industry's profitability, market size and structure, industry life cycle and technological change.

- One of the most commonly used and famous techniques in industry analysis is the application of Porter's five-force model. It is suggested that in any industry, the role of competition is embodied in five competitive forces: the entry of new competitors, the threat of substitutes, the bargaining power of buyers, the bargaining power of suppliers and the rivalry among existing competitors. The five-force framework allows SMEs to see through the complexity and pinpoint those factors that are critical to competition in its industry.

- The last step in industry analysis for SMEs is developing strategic groups and key success factors (KSFs). A strategic group is a set of businesses that pursue similar strategies with similar resources. Categorising firms in any industry into a set of strategic groups is useful as a way of better identifying who the SMEs are competing with. Providing KSFs can help small business managers to focus on what they can do better than the competitors. Key success factors consist of the distinctive skills or abilities, normally related to the product or service or technology, which can be used to create a competitive advantage for the firm in the industry.

- Analysing the external environment of the organisation leads to the discovery of the opportunities and threats to the firm in the market. Analysing the external environment is not enough to provide a firm with a competitive advantage – firms need to assess their internal environment in order to identify their strengths and weaknesses as well. Analysing the internal environment of the firm is concerned with identifying and developing the firm's resources.

- The resource-based approach to organisational analysis has been regarded as the emergence of an important new conceptualisation in the field of strategic management. A resource is an asset, competency, process, skill or knowledge and is controlled by the organisation. A resource is a strength if it provides a SME with a competitive advantage. The resource-based approach to strategic management accentuates the link between the internal characteristics of the firm and that of the firm's performance. It has been proposed that a five-step, resource-based approach to strategy analysis should include identifying resources, identifying and appraising capabilities, evaluating sustainability of resources, formulating strategy identifying resource gaps and investment in upgrading weaknesses.

- One of the strategic factors in the decision-making process is the cost of the products and services. Producing the products at low cost can lead to high profit and value chain management can help strategists to achieve these objectives. Value chain management is managing integrated information about product flow from suppliers to end-users to reduce product costs and sales promotion and improve customer satisfaction. Value chain is a structured way of looking at a business's processes and costs.

- SWOT analysis shows what the firm can do very well and should engage in and what it cannot do and should avoid. The first criteria, strengths and weaknesses, are gained from analysis of the internal environment of the firm while the last two criteria, opportunities and threats, come from analysis of the external environment of the firm. This technique, as a managerial tool, helps strategists (managers and owner-managers) to list their firms' internal strengths and weaknesses as well as determining the external opportunities and threats. Strength for a SME is a key success factor. It can consist of the skills and abilities, competencies and committed human resources, effective distribution system or channels, financial stability and technological know-how. A weakness is something that a firm either lacks or isn't as good at as its competitors, such as a lack of spare financial resources, entrepreneurs' lack of managerial experience and technical skills, high labour costs, and inefficient organisational structure and processes. Opportunities are the situations in which the firm can improve its strategic position. Increased market share for the firm in the international market or the firm's access to low price energy could be considered as opportunities. In contrast, threats are the main obstacles and issues in the external environment of the organisation. Any change in the external environment of the SME with the potential to disrupt the firm's operation and well-being as a whole, could be considered as a threat. The entry of large and more powerful competitors into the local arena and technological innovation which makes the way firms' produce their products or provide their services obsolete are examples of threats for SMEs. It is important to remember that change in the environment does not necessarily have to be tangible or quantifiable. A change of customer preference or fashion could be a threat to the survival of a small business if it is unchecked and not acted upon.

Discussion questions

1. What is environmental analysis?
2. Why is environmental analysis so important for SMEs?
3. What are the environmental factors? Describe the two main categories of internal and external environments.
4. What is PEST analysis?
5. Which criteria should be considered in undertaking an industry profile analysis? List and explain at least three criteria.
6. Explain the industry life cycle theory in small businesses.
7. Explain Porter's five-force model and its implications for SMEs.
8. How are human resources considered as a competitive advantage?
9. Discuss the value chain analysis in SMEs.
10. What is SWOT analysis? Discuss the implications of SWOT analysis in SMEs.

Case study *SWOT analysis in SMEs*

Thomas Computer Limited (TC Ltd) is a small business concern operating in the Midlands. In terms of firm size, TC Ltd is considered to be relatively small with 55 employees and was originally established in 1995 with only 12 employees and £2 000 000 initial capital. Because of high market demand and lack of serious competitors TC Ltd has expanded its operations and activities and hence increased its market share. The last annual turnover of TC Ltd was £35 million. Recently two other companies including North Computers and High-tech were established in the Midlands. Thomas, the Managing Director of TC Ltd, who is a successful computer engineer with excellent knowledge in computer technology, is now facing the problem of two new firms entering the business arena. Last week, in an attempt to deal with new threats, he arranged a meeting with the management team as well as the management consultants to discuss the current problem. The board came up with the idea of immediate analysis followed by reformulating the business strategies. In order to analyse the current situation of the firm, the management consultant suggested a SWOT analysis exercise which consists of the following steps:

Step 1. Brainstorming the main questions about the current situation of the firm in the market. Thomas was asked to think about the current situation of the firm in comparison with the actual and potential competitors. He came up with some questions which were aimed at highlighting the positive and negative situations facing the firm. These are:

What are the internal positive and negative aspects of the firm *that are under the control* of TC Ltd?

- What do we do well compared with the two new entrants?
- What are our tangible and intangible assets?
- What experience do we possess?

- What is our production cost level?
- Do our resources need to be strengthened?
- Where do we lack resources?
- Where are we losing money?

What are the external positive and negative aspects of the firm *that are not under the control* of TC Ltd?

- What are the emergent needs of our customers that we can cover?
- What are the economical, political and technological trends that benefit us?
- What are the technological breakthroughs relevant to our processes and operations?
- What negative economic trends are likely to occur?
- What are the negative technological trends that we might face in the near future?
- Where are competitors about to bite us?
- How is our production quality compared with theirs (competitors)?

Step 2. Preparing the list of strengths, weaknesses, opportunities and threats and creating the SWOT matrix. Thomas and his management team listed these as:

Strengths:

- More than ten years' work experience in the industry
- Strong technical knowledge within computer industry
- Highly skilled computer engineers
- Managing director's educational level
- Established good network with customers.

Weaknesses:

- Lack of upgraded production tools
- Lack of long term goals and unclear mission
- Some financial problems
- Low employees' motivation
- Negative personal characteristics of the CEO such as a lack of discipline.

▶

Opportunities:

- Positive trends in computer technology
- TC Ltd's ability in adapting to technological changes
- Access to local network and marketing channels
- High reputation
- High quality of product.

Threats:

- The entry of two new firms to the industry in the Midland area
- High production costs
- Weak connection to national markets.

The management team worked on the strategic factors and summarised them in the following SWOT matrix:

Strengths	**Weaknesses**
• Work experience • Technical knowledge • Highly skilled employees • Educational level	• Lack of upgraded production tools • Lack of goals and mission • Financial problems • Low employees' motivation • Negative personal characteristics of the CEO
Opportunities	**Threats**
• Trends in computer technology • Adaptability with technological changes • Access to local network and marketing channels • High reputation • High production quality	• Entry of two new firms to the industry in Midland area • High production costs • Weak connection to national markets

Step 3. Developing a competitive ranking. After determining the strengths, weaknesses, opportunities and threats related to TC Ltd, Thomas developed a shortlist of important strategic issues from the SWOT matrix. Then he graded his own firm and its rivals on the important issues as follows:

Strategic issue	TC Ltd	North Computers	High-tech
Finance	6	10	9
Technological adaptability	10	8	9
Production quality	9	8	5
Production costs	6	9	10
Marketing	8	9	9
Local connections	10	2	3
Reputation	10	3	6

Step 4. Calculation of weighted average for competitors. Here, Thomas needed to calculate a weighted average grade for his own firm and the other two competitors. For this purpose, he wrote out the measures and the raw weights and then calculated weights for computation by dividing each raw weight by the sum of raw weights. The calculations are shown as follows:

Strategic issue	Raw weight	Weight
Finance	2	0.20
Technological adaptability	1	0.10
Production quality	1	0.10
Production costs	3	0.30
Marketing	1	0.10
Local connections	1	0.10
Reputation	1	0.10
	10	**1.00**

After calculating the weight for each strategic issue, the next activity was calculating the weighted average grade for each of the competitors. To achieve this, Thomas multiplied each competitor's grade on each strategic issue by the strategic issue's weighted and summed up each competitor to get the weighted average grade. The calculations are shown as follows:

Strategic issue	Weight	TC Ltd	North Computers	High-tech
Finance	0.20	$6 \times 0.2 = 1.2$	$10 \times 0.2 = 2$	$9 \times 0.2 = 1.8$
Technological adaptability	0.10	$10 \times 0.1 = 1$	$8 \times 0.1 = 0.8$	$9 \times 0.1 = 0.9$
Production quality	0.10	$9 \times 0.1 = 0.9$	$8 \times 0.1 = 0.8$	$5 \times 0.1 = 0.5$
Production costs	0.30	$6 \times 0.3 = 1.8$	$9 \times 0.3 = 2.7$	$10 \times 0.3 = 3$
Marketing	0.10	$8 \times 0.1 = 0.8$	$9 \times 0.1 = 0.9$	$9 \times 0.1 = 0.9$
Local connections	0.10	$10 \times 0.1 = 1$	$2 \times 0.1 = 0.2$	$3 \times 0.1 = 0.3$
Reputation	0.10	$10 \times 0.1 = 1$	$3 \times 0.1 = 0.3$	$6 \times 0.1 = 0.6$
	1.00	**7.7**	**7.7**	**8**

Step 5. Compare the weighted grades among the rivals and add the qualitative analysis. As can be seen from the calculations, the average weighted grade of the TC Ltd is less than High-tech but more than North Computers. Thomas realised that in order to develop effective business strategies TC Ltd needs to strengthen its financial resources. It also needs to decrease its production costs, at the same time upgrading the production system would help TC Ltd to decrease production costs. As we noted earlier high production cost is the main strategic issue that TC Ltd should face, solve and manage.

References

Amit, R. and Schoemaker, P. J. H. (1993) Strategic assets and organisational rent, *Strategic Management Journal*, 14, 33–46.

Analoui, F. (2002) *The Changing Patterns of Human Resource Management*, Ashgate, Aldershot, UK.

Anderson, W. R. (1997) The future of human resources: forging ahead or falling behind?, *Human Resource Management*, 36 (1), 17–22.

Andrews, K. (1971) *The Concept of Corporate Strategy*, Irwin, Homewood IL.

Bantel, K. A. and Osborn, R. N. (1995) The influence of performance, environment and size on the identifiability of firm strategy, *British Journal of Management*, 6, 235–48.

Barney, J. B. (1986) Organisational culture: can it be a source of sustained competitive advantage?, *Academy of Management Review*, 11, 656–665.

Barney, J. B. (1991) Firm resources and sustainable competitive advantage, *Journal of Management*, 17 (1), 99–120.

Beal, R. M. (2000) Competing effectively: environmental scanning, competitive strategy, and organisational performance in small manufacturing firms, *Journal of Small Business Management*, 38 (1), 27–47.

Beer, M. (1997) The transformation of human resource function: resolving the tension between a traditional administrative and a new strategic role, *Human Resource Management*, 36 (1), 49–56.

Berry, M. (1998) Strategic planning in small high tech companies, *Long Range Planning*, 31 (3), 455–466.

Black, J. A. and Boal, K. B. (1994) Strategic resources: traits, configurations and paths to sustainable competitive advantage, *Strategic Management Journal*, 15 (Special Issue), 131–148.

Boxall, P. (1996) The strategic HRM debate and the resource-based view of the firm, *Human Resource Management Journal*, 6 (3), 59–75.

Boxall, P. and Steeneveld, M. (1999) Human resource strategy and competitive advantage: a longitudinal study of engineering consultancies, *Journal of Management Studies*, 36 (4), 443–463.

Brockbank, W. (1997) Human resource's future on the way to a presence, *Human Resource Management*, 36 (1), 65–69.

Chandler, A. (1962) *Strategy and Structure*, MIT Press, Cambridge, MA.

Choo, C. W. (1999) The art of scanning the environment, *Bulletin of the American Society for Information Science*, Washington, 45 (3), 21–24.

Daft, R. L., Sormunen, L. and Parks, D. (1988) Chief executive scanning, environmental characteristics, and company performance: an empirical study, *Strategic Management Journal*, 9, 123–139.

Fahr, J. L., Hoffman, R. C. and Hegarty, W. (1984) Assessing environmental scanning at the subunit level: a multitrait-multimethod analysis, *Decision Sciences*, 15, 197–220.

Flynn, D. M. (1993) Sponsorship and survival of new organisations, *Journal of Small Business Management*, 31 (1), 51–62.

Gable, M. and Topol, M. (1987) Planning practices of small-scale retailers, *American Journal of Small Business* (Fall), 19–32.

Golden, K. and Ramanujam, V. (1985) Between a dream and a nightmare: on the integration of the human resource management and strategic business planning processes, *Human Resource Management*, 24, 429–452.

Goldsmith, A. (1995) Making managers more effective: Application of strategic management, Working Paper No. 9, USAID, March.

Grant, R. M. (1991) The resource-based theory of competitive advantage: implications for strategy formulation, *California Management Review*, 33 (3), 114–135.

Grant, R. M. (1998) The resource-based theory of competitive advantage: implications for strategy formulation, in H. Costin, (ed.) *Reading in Strategy and Strategic Planning*, The Dryden Press, London.

Green, P. G. (1997) A resource-based approach to ethnic business sponsorship: a consideration of Ismaili-Pakistani immigrants, *Journal of Small Business Management*, 35 (4), 58–71.

Hall, R. (1992) The strategic analysis of intangible resources, *Strategic Management Journal*, 13 (2), 135–144.

Hambrick, D. C. (1981) Environment, strategy, and power within top management teams, *Administrative Science Quarterly*, 26, 253–276.

Hitt, M. A. and Ireland, R. D. (2000) The intersection of entrepreneurship and strategic management research, in D. L. Sexton and H. A. Landstrom (eds) *Handbook of Entrepreneurship*, Blackwell, Oxford, 45–63.

Hoskisson, R. E., Hitt, M. A., Wan, W. P. and Yiu, D. (1999) Theory and research in strategic management: swings of a pendulum, *Journal of Management*, 25 (3), 417–456.

Jennings, D. E. and Lumpkin, J. R. (1992) Insights between environmental scanning activities and Porter's generic strategies: an empirical analysis, *Journal of Management*, 18, 791–803.

Kakabadse, A. K., Kakabadse, N. K. and Myers, A. (1996) Leadership and the public sector: an internationally comparative benchmarking analysis, *Public Administration and Development*, 16 (4), 377–396.

Kleindl, B. (2000) Competitive dynamics and new business models for SMEs in the virtual marketplace, *Journal of Development Entrepreneurship*, 5 (1), 73–86.

Lang, J. R., Calatone, R. and Gudmundson, D. (1997) Small firm information seeking as a response to environmental threats and opportunities, *Journal of Small Business Management*, 35, 11–23.

Lasher, W. (1999) *Strategic Thinking for Smaller Businesses and Divisions*, Blackwell, Malden, MA.

Leonard-Barton, D. (1992) Core capabilities and core rigidities: a paradox in managing new product development, *Strategic Management Journal*, 13 (Special Issue), 111–125.

Lynch, R. (2000) *Corporate Strategy*, 2nd edn, Prentice Hall, London.

Mabey, C., Salaman, G. and Storey, J. (1998) *Strategic Human Resource Management*, Sage Publications, London.

McGrath, R. G. and MacMillan, I. (2000) *The Entrepreneurial Mindset*, Harvard Business School Press, Boston, MA.

McKenna, S. D. (1996) The darker side of the entrepreneur, *Leadership and Organisational Development Journal*, November, 17 (5), 41.

Mehra, A. (1994) Strategic groups: a resource-based approach, *The Journal of Socio-economics*, 23 (4), 425–439.

Meyer, G. D. and Heppard, K. A. (2000) *Entrepreneurship as Strategy: Competing on the Entrepreneurial Edge*, Sage, Thousand Oaks, CA.

Miller, D. (1988) The relationship of Porter's business strategies to environment and structure, *Academy of Management Journal*, 37, 280–308.

Mintzberg, H. (1994) The fall and rise of strategic planning, *Harvard Business Review*, 72 (1), 107–114.

Morganti, F. (2002) The value chain in telecommunications, *Intermedia*, 30 (1), 18.

Niv, A., Jehiel, Z. and Isaac, M. (1998) Environmental scanning and information systems in relation to success in introducing new products, *Information and Management*, 33 (4), 201–211.

Pitts, R. A. and Lei, D. (1996) *Strategic Management Building and Sustaining Competitive Advantage*, West Publishing Company, New York.

Porter, M. (1979) How competitive forces shape strategy, *Harvard Business Review*, March—April, 134–145.

Porter, M. (1980) *Competitive Strategy*, Free Press, New York.

Porter, M. (1985) *Competitive Advantage: Creating and Sustaining Superior Performance*, Free Press, New York.

Quayle, M., Whithead, M. and Arkin, A. (1999) A small concern, *Supply Management*, 4 (22), 26–30.

Salaman, G. (1992) *Human Resource Strategies*, Sage Publications, London.

Sawyer, O. O. (1993) Environmental uncertainty and environmental scanning activities of Nigerian manufacturing executives: a comparative analysis, *Strategic Management Journal*, 14, 287–299.

Selznick, P. (1957) *Leadership in Administration: A Sociological Interpretation*, Harper & Row, New York.

Shay, J. P. and Rothaermel, F. T. (1999) Dynamic competitive strategy: toward a multi perspective conceptual framework, *Long Range Planning*, 32 (6), 559–572.

Spender, J. C. (1989) *Industry Recipes: An Enquiry into the Nature and Sources of Managerial Judgment*, Blackwell, Oxford.

Sven, H. (1998) Spontaneous environmental scanning, part two: empirical findings and implications for the organizing of competitive intelligence, *Competitive Intelligence Review*, Washington, 9 (4), 73–83.

Teece, D. J., Pisano, G. and Shuen, A. (1997) Dynamic capabilities and strategic management, *Strategic Management Journal*, 18, 509–533.

Thomas, J. B., Clark, S. M. and Gioia, D. A. (1993) Strategic sense making and organisational performance: linkage among scanning, interpretation, action outcomes, *Academy of Management Journal*, April, 239–270.

Tyler, B. B., Bettenhausen, K. L. and Daft, R. L. (1989) The use of low and high rich information sources and communication channels in developing and implementing competitive business strategy, paper presented at the annual meeting of the Academy of Management.

Weihrich, H. (1982) The TOWS matrix – a tool for situational analysis, *Journal of Long Range Planning*, 15 (2), 54–66.

Wheelen, T. L. and Hunger, J. D. (1998) *Strategic Management and Business Policy*, 6th edn, Addison-Wesley Publications, New York.

Wickham, P. A. (2001) *Strategic Entrepreneurship: A Decision-making Approach to New Venture Creation and Management*, 2nd edn, Prentice Hall, London.

Wit, B. D. and Meyer, R. (1998) *Strategy: Process, Content, Context*, 2nd edn, Thomson Learning, London.

Wolff, J. A. (2000) Internationalization of small firms: an examination of export competitive patterns, firm size, and export performance, *Journal of Small Business Management*, 38 (2), 34- 48.

Wright, P. M., McMahan, G. C., McCormick, B. and Sherman, S. C. W. (1998) Strategy, core competence, and human resource involvement as determinants of HR effectiveness and refinery performance, *Human Resource Management*, 36, 17–29.

Yasai-Ardekani, M. and Nystrom, P. C. (1993) Designs for environmental scanning systems: tests of contingency theory, Working Paper, University of Wisconsin-Milwaukee.

Zajac, E. (1995) SMJ 1994 best paper prize to Birger Wernerfelt, *Strategic Management Journal*, 16, 169–170.

Strategy formulation in small and medium-sized enterprises

The main objective of this chapter is to review and discuss the strategy formulation concept in SMEs. The chapter begins with a discussion on developing a vision and a mission statement as the first step in the process of strategy formulation (Bart, 2000). The second section reviews the current theories and provides practical examples in developing objectives and the third focuses on the process of planning strategically in SMEs. The chapter concludes with a discussion of generic strategies and business strategies at corporate level.

Strategy formulation in SMEs

Let's begin with the question, what is the nature of the strategy formulation task? In Chapter four we concluded that prior to formulating a strategy for a firm, SWOT analysis should be carried out in order to find out the internal strengths and weaknesses and the opportunities and threats that will be confronted externally. SWOT analysis pinpoints the position of the firm – where it is at present and how it can fit into the environment (Beal, 2000). It helps to generate basic and crucial information necessary for the formulation of the business strategies in SMEs. Indeed, formulating a strategy is one of the critical tasks of the managers (Hoskisson *et al.* 1999). Particularly in small businesses, the owner-managers or CEOs are those who are held responsible for the formulation of business strategies (Analoui and Karami, 2002a) – they are dealing with strategic decision-making within the SME. So it is essential to learn how SMEs' managers go about formulating and implementing business strategies.

Strategy formulation, as a phase in strategic management, is often referred to as strategic or long range planning and is concerned with developing an SME's mission, objectives and strategies (Bracker and Pearson, 1985; Rarick and Vitton, 1995). It has been proposed (Rarick and Vitton, 1995; Lasher, 1999; Lynch, 2000) that the strategy formulation task in organisations includes three main elements, developing vision and mission of the business, developing organisational strategic objectives and developing business strategies (Figure 5.1).

The first step in strategy formulation is defining the corporate mission (Germain and Cooper, 1990; Rarick and Vitton, 1995; Wheelen and Hunger, 1998). The mission statement promotes a sense of shared expectations among employees and conveys a public image to important stakeholder groups in the company's task environment. The second step in strategy formulation is specifying achievable objectives (Wheelen and Hunger, 1998). Objectives are the end results of any planned activity. Business objectives convert the mission statement into specific goals that shape the direction and activities of the business (Lowry *et al.* 1999). Finally, the third step in strategy formulation is developing strategies. Strategists tend to formulate strategies in light of the results of internal and external environmental analysis (SWOT analysis).

It is important to remember that approaches to business strategy formulation in SMEs have evolved over the past three decades. The result of research projects in this field collectively indicate that the SMEs that have been involved in formulating strategy for their firm, either formally or informally, are more likely to be successful than the firms which ignore the strategy-making task. For instance, Hambrick (1983) contends that the concept of strategy has been

Figure 5.1

The strategy
formulation task

Mission   Objectives

Strategy
formulation

Developing strategy

likened to a stream of decisions that involves internal and/or external alignments which affect SME's performances as the whole. The majority of the empirical studies within the field of strategic management in SMEs are expounding the various benefits of strategy formulation and point out the associated improved organisational performance as a result (Kudla, 1980; Bracker and Pearson, 1985; Aram and Cowan, 1990; Helms *et al.* 1997; Smith, 1998; Beal, 2000).

In contrast to propounders of the formal strategic camp, several studies emphasised the need for informal planning in SMEs. This chapter discusses the theoretical as well as practical aspects of the strategy formulation task in SMEs.

Developing a mission in SMEs

What is a mission statement?

Thompson (2001) has proposed that a vision statement describes what the company is to become in the future, while the mission statement reflects the noble purpose of the firm and provides an explanation for why it is in existence, the nature of the businesses it is involved in and the kind of customers it seeks to attract, serve and satisfy. Accordingly Scandura *et al.* (1996) suggest that a mission statement is but a summary of the essential aim or purpose of the firm; its fundamental reasons for being in business (Box 5.1).

A mission statement reveals the current reason for the existence of an organisation and, not surprisingly, is developed by the senior management of an organisation on the basis of the stated shared vision (Ackoff, 1987; Bart, 1998). A mission statement should be comprehensive and coherent so that it can be understood by both the internal and external stakeholders of the firm. Scandura *et al.* (1996) argue that externally the mission statement should provide a rallying point for all stakeholders. This includes shareholders, employees, suppliers and customers. Internally, mission statements are very important to an organisation because they provide employees with an understanding of the purpose and goals of the corporation. Finally, effective mission statements serve to align the strategy with the work culture of the organisation, a process which Campbell *et al.* describe as instilling 'a sense of mission' in the minds and hearts of employees – a feeling that what they do makes a difference in the world (Campbell *et al.* 1990).

Box 5.1 Mission statement definition

Mission statement

A statement that encapsulates the overriding purpose and objectives of an organisation. It is used to communicate this purpose to all stakeholder groups, both internal and external, and to guide employees in their contribution toward achieving it (*Oxford Dictionary of Business*).

Vision or mission?

It is prudent to distinguish between the terms vision and mission. Some prefer to consider vision and mission as two different concepts: a mission statement describes what the organisation is now; a vision statement describes what the organisation would like to become (Campbell, 1992). A clear vision defines the rules for acting incrementally and opportunistically. If a business is going to be successful today, creating a vision is a necessity, not a luxury – because no organisation can progress without an understanding of where it is going and what it should be trying to achieve (Kakabadse, 2001). A vision statement is developed by the senior management of an organisation to define the organisation's future state; it is a dream. A vision statement comes from the 'hearts' of top management and the best ones evoke emotion, that are easily remembered. It defines the future of the firm and creates a gathering point for all concerned with the organisation (Scandura *et al.* 1996). In this way, developing the vision statement is the very first step in developing a strategic plan for an organisation (see Figure 5.2). Professor Kakabadse (2001) in answer to the question, what is vision?, explains that, in management terms, the word visioning is used to describe an agreement among directors about the future of their organisation. It requires access to all relevant information, such as the present state of the company and its values. Everyone has some idea of where they are going and what they want to achieve, but their vision is often outdated, short-sighted or too long term. And when people have different visions there is dispute. A manager facing an unexpected situation can take a decision after asking himself the question 'will such an action further the company's vision?' Vision

Figure 5.2

Vision, mission and objectives

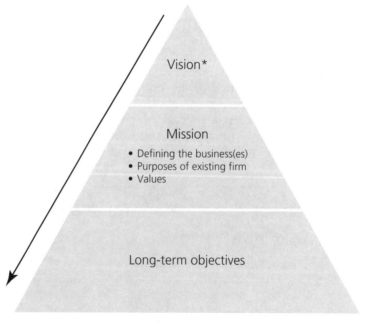

Vision*

Mission
- Defining the business(es)
- Purposes of existing firm
- Values

Long-term objectives

* A realisable dream

statements often embody the core values of the founding entrepreneur, and say something about the inspiration behind the company that would not be obvious from a reading of its business plans (Bowman and Faulkner, 1997). We define vision as a realisable dream, realisation of which is in part determined by the ability of the visionary to convey, convince and create commitment amongst all stakeholders – something they will believe in and be committed to in both known and unknown circumstances (Box 5.2).

Strategic vision, according to Sirower (1997), is where all acquisitions begin. Management vision of the acquisition is shared with suppliers, customers, lenders and employees as a framework for planning, discussion, decisions and reactions to change. Sirower argues that the vision must be clear to large constituent groups and adaptable to many unknown circumstances. In addition the vision must be a continuous guide to the actual operating plans of the company. If the vision does not translate into real actions, it can provoke damaging reactions from competitors (Wit and Meyer, 2001).

> A vision is an image of a better future, however defined; it is a state to which the company aspires, and therefore can at least logically be achieved ... Clearly a new vision needs to be adopted if the company is not to sink beneath the competitive waves, enthusiastically telling stories of past triumphs.
>
> (Bowman and Faulkner, 1997: 181)

Characteristics of an effective mission statement

The mission of any organisation reflects its essential purpose and its mission statement defines why a firm operates in a particular business environment. For instance, the mission of a firm in the restaurant industry will be different from that of a firm operating in a high tech industry.

Since the mission defines the ultimate objective of the firm and its philosophy of being in a particular industry, it is of the utmost importance that it is made

---

Box 5.2 Example of mission statement in small businesses

McMahon & McDonald, Inc. mission statement

We at McMahon & McDonald are dedicated to serving our principals and customers with the highest level of integrity in the retail, speciality foods classes of trade.

Encouraging open communication, an entrepreneurial spirit and a team approach, we are committed to achieving our common goals.

Maintaining the delicate balance between work, family and community, our people are our greatest asset. In the ever-changing food industry, they are the foundation of our success.

At McMahon & McDonald, *It's All About Attitude!*

http://www.teleweb.net/mcmahon/mmmiss.HTM

clear to all stakeholders both inside and outside the firm. It is important to emphasise here that a statement is only clear if it is understood by all concerned in the way it was meant to be. In that case, an effective and meaningful mission statement creates synergy and will provide a basis for increase in organisational performance. According to Ackoff (1986) a good mission statement should have five pertinent characteristics:

- Defining the business which the firm wants to be in.
- Differentiating the firm from its rivals.
- Enabling the firm in formulation of objectives.
- Exciting and motivating.
- It is relevant to all stakeholders inside and outside the firm.

Accordingly, Lynch (2000) believes that because organisations differ from each other so the mission statement ought to be regarded as personal to each organisation. Essentially a mission statement consists of five elements. These are:

- Consideration of the nature of the firm's business.
- Responses need to be considered from the customer perspective rather than that of the organisation itself.
- Reflecting the basic values and beliefs of the organisation.
- Reflecting the element of sustainable competitive advantage.
- The mission statement needs to summarise the main reasons for its choice of approach.

Therefore, an effective mission statement should clarify the purpose of the firm and define the business that the firm wants to be in. It should provide plausible answers to the question of why the firm exists (Analoui and Karami, 2002b). In some cases the firms categorise and locate themselves in wrong businesses. Suppose that a small firm produces cans of fruit juice – it can be categorised within either the drink industry or packing industry. So it is essential to define the kind of industry in which the firm wants to be located in future, and this is not necessarily the industry it is currently in.

Mission statements should differentiate the firm from its existing and potential rivals and competitors. For instance, the mission statement of KFC in the restaurant industry is different from that of McDonald's, although both firms are operating in the same industry. Mission statements should enable the firm to formulate its objectives and should cover the long term objectives of the firm (Pearce, 1982; Germain and Cooper, 1990). More importantly, the mission of the firm must be exciting and create motivation (buzz) in all employees of the firm. Increasing employees' motivation and their participation and contribution to the decision-making in the firm can help the firm increase its organisational effectiveness (Analoui and Karami, 2002a) (Box 5.3).

Finally the mission statement of the firm should be clearly understandable – make sense – to all stakeholders of the firm. Top management should avoid confusing the stakeholders regarding the purpose of the firm (Simpson, 1994; Kakabadse et al. 1996). As discussed earlier, if the firm's purpose and philosophy are clear to the stakeholders, it could be expected that the

Box 5.3 Priority of the components of the mission statements in the studied small and medium enterprises

Components	Priority
Long term profit, survival and growth	1
Customer satisfaction	2
Core technology	3
Market	4
Company philosophy and values	5
Product and services quality	6
Public image	7
Geographic domain	8
Self-concept	9
Concern for suppliers	10

Source: Adapted from Analoui and Karami (2002b) CEOs and development of a meaningful mission statement, Corporate Governance, *International Journal of Board Effectiveness*, 2 (3), p. 17.

stakeholders will support the firm (Want, 1986; Bart, 2000). In some cases, the firm's mission statement contains a long list of purposes. Top management try to put forward and explain some of the long term objectives of the organisation in a mission statement. This kind of mission statement will confuse the stakeholders and remove the focus from the real philosophy and purpose of the firm. In contrast, some mission statements are too short – clearly a happy medium is required!

Defining the business

Perhaps the most important step in developing an effective mission statement is defining the business in which the firm operates. Major problems will result from defining the business in the wrong way. Strategists should think in terms of benefits while writing their mission statement. Larson (1998) proposes that wise marketers know that customers buy benefits, not products. For instance, people don't buy shampoo, they buy the hope of shiny, tangle-free and presentable hair. They don't buy tyres, they buy safety, fast cornering and durability. Accordingly, Lasher (1999) suggests that in order to define the business strategists should have answers to three main questions:

1. What customer needs is the business aiming to satisfy?
2. What is the target market in terms of customer groups?
3. What technology is being used to satisfy the needs?

Investigating and answering the above questions determines the philosophy of an existing firm. In other words, answering those questions could be the first step towards developing a mission for the firm. The starting point of strategic planning is defining what sort of business the company is involved in – and this is not as simple as it sounds. The classical example is the railway industry (Larson, 1998). For a long time, railway companies believed they were in the railway business. They concentrated on tracks and trains, and all those things that go along with being in the railway business. For decades, the industry suffered poor financial performance. Eventually, some of the firms realised that they weren't really in the railway business; they were in the freight transportation business. The railway companies realised that when customers have materials to be shipped somewhere, they don't usually care how they get delivered. The customers do care that the shipment gets there on schedule, without damage, and at the lowest cost. The railway companies' emphasis on freight transportation made no difference in customers' minds. By defining their business as freight transportation, these firms made some rather dramatic changes. First, they stopped relying so completely on the railway. They started to view their business more through the eye of customer needs, as opposed to focusing on the technology that they used. Financial performance of this entire industry increased dramatically after this fundamental change occurred (Larson, 1998).

Roles of the corporate mission

It has been proposed that the corporate mission plays three important roles for businesses – direction, legitimisation, and motivation (Wit and Meyer, 1998). Let's discuss each of these briefly.

Direction

The mission statement defines the direction of the business. It determines where the business is most likely to go, thus it defines the ultimate objective of the firm. It has been commented that 'if you do not know where you are going, any road can take you there' (Collis and Montgomery, 1997). The mission statement can point the firm in a certain direction and lead it to achieve its goals and objectives strategically. By defining the corporate mission strategists will be able to craft suitable business strategies (a plan of action).

Legitimisation

The firm gains its legitimacy from the stakeholders who are involved in the firm's activities. The mission statement increases the firm's legitimacy with new stakeholders such as financial institutions and shareholders. Clarifying the firm's philosophy and its ultimate objective for the people both inside and outside the firm is a crucial factor in understanding and supporting the firm's strategy. It is also an important factor for the firm's stakeholders, in supporting the firm's strategies, to perceive that the firm is doing very well and it is following valuable goals and objectives. Therefore, as Wit and Meyer (1998) contend, when defining the mission of the firm, it is hoped that the stakeholders will accept and support the firm.

Motivation

The mission statement is important for promoting a sense of shared expectations among the firm and all employees (Shuman and Seeger, 1986; Analoui, 2000). The corporate mission can help by inspiring all the employees to work together in a particular way and increase their motivation in achieving the firm's goals and objectives.

Research in the mission statement

As discussed earlier, the first step in strategy formulation is defining the corporate mission (Germain and Cooper, 1990; Rarick and Vitton, 1995; Wheelen and Hunger, 1998). The literature available on mission statements in large firms and SMEs is both descriptive (Ackoff, 1987; Peters, 1988; Falsey, 1989; Campbell *et al.* 1990; Pearce and Robinson, 1994) and prescriptive (Pearce, 1982; Want, 1986; Pearce and David, 1987). Perhaps the research carried out in 500 SMEs by Pearce and David (1987) was the first attempt to study the relationship between mission statement and organisational performance empirically. They found that higher performance firms have a comparatively more comprehensive mission statement. Ackoff has observed that most mission statements 'consist largely of pious platitudes' (1987: 30).

There is an overwhelming consensus among writers that the development of business missions is fundamental for the survival and growth of any business (Peters and Waterman, 1982; Falsey, 1989; Germain and Cooper, 1990). For instance, Falsey (1989) argued that companies with mission statements which explicitly express a sense of responsibility for the community tend to perform well over a sustained period of time. Elsewhere, he concluded that companies that had prepared a written set of principles stating the philosophy of the company seem to have higher levels of performance.

It is argued in the literature that the benefits organisations derive from mission statements address many of the organisational and leadership problems that characterise growing SMEs. Calfree (1993) reminds us that messages of outward growth and profitability are usually better communicated to Wall Street than to those within the organisation upon whom the organisation's decision-making depends. Simpson (1994) too observed that mission statements are often vapid – 'we love our customers, we love our shareholders, we love our employees' and are often disconnected from the true capabilities and strengths of the firm. Finally, in their recent work O'Gorman and Doran (1999) concluded that as far as SMEs are concerned, high growth firms do not have any more comprehensive mission statements than low growth ones.

A mission statement allows the firm to articulate a strong vision for the organisation in order to communicate to its growing number of employees and professional managers. The mission statement promotes a sense of shared expectations in employees and conveys a public image to important stakeholders groups in the company's task environment. A fear of decreasing levels of customer service often prevents the entrepreneur from delegating day-to-day customer support activities. A mission statement focused on customer values can create a customer service culture and increase levels of customer satisfaction. Having said that, the benefits and usefulness of mission statements have been questioned in more recent empirical works (Piercy and Morgan, 1994; Simpson, 1994). Those who oppose mission statements do so on the grounds that they are empty public relations initiatives, that mission statement formulation and implementation are a lot more difficult than the literature makes out and that companies with a good business mission do not need to compress their aims into a statement.

The existence of a mission statement and its purpose in SMEs

In order to explore why SMEs have a mission statement, it would be useful to compare the result of the study in small businesses with the result of a similar study carried out in large firms. Baetz and Bart (1996) worked on the issue of developing mission statements in 135 large Canadian organisations. The results demonstrated that mission statements have by and large been used by more than three-quarters (86 per cent) of the firms involved in the study. They reported that the main reasons for having mission statements in their firm was to:

- Guide the strategic planning system.
- Define the organisation's scope of business operations/activities.
- Provide a common purpose/direction transcending individual and department needs.
- Promote a sense of shared expectations among all levels of employees, thereby building a strong corporate culture (i.e. shared value).
- Guide leadership style (Baetz and Bart, 1996: 528).

In the case of SMEs the role of entrepreneurs in developing mission statements cannot be ignored (Germain and Cooper, 1990; Ireland and Hitt, 1992; Karami and Analoui, 2001). In their study of mission statements in SMEs, Analoui and Karami (2002b) attempted to investigate whether or not SMEs have developed mission statements, and if they had what the main reason(s) for doing so may be. The results showed that the majority of the firms (78 per cent) have developed formal mission statements, as opposed to only 19 per cent that reported that they have not had any formal mission statements in their organisations. Only 2 per cent of respondents left the above question unanswered. These findings are very similar to that of previous studies. For instance, in Byars and Neil's (1987) survey of 208 firms, 68 per cent indicated that they had a mission statement. In his survey of the Business Week 1000, David (1989) reported that 41 per cent indicated that they had a mission statement.

Accordingly when Analoui and Karami (2002b) asked the CEOs involved in their study to outline the reasons for having a mission statement, the results strongly indicated that mission statements were being used in SMEs for different reasons. The main purposes of having mission statements, based on the respondent's priorities, are:

- Developing and planning business strategies.
- Increasing profit and growth rate.
- Promoting a sense of shared expectations among entrepreneurs and all employees.
- Providing clarity of direction for all categories of employees including entrepreneurs.

These results are also in accordance with the findings of O'Gorman and Doran's (1999) study of mission statements in SMEs. Analoui and Karami (2002b) discovered that in small businesses, like large firms, a formal mission statement is generally regarded and used as an important tool for strategic planning. In the case of SMEs mission statements were more related to strategy formulation than implementation of business strategies. Also, SMEs tend to use mission statements for increasing their profit and growth within the industry rather than for publicity. Based on the results of the Baetz and Bart (1996) research in large firms, the second reason for having a mission statement is to define the organisation's scope of business operations and activities. Promoting shared thinking and expectation among owner-managers, entrepreneurs and employees is further reason given by SMEs for having a mission statement. Finally, providing clarity of direction for the firm is the last of the four main reasons for having mission statements in SMEs.

The content of a mission statement in SMEs

It has been argued that a good mission statement tends to capture an organisation's unique and enduring reason for energising stakeholders to pursue common goals (Rarick and Vitton, 1995; Bart, 1998; Karami, 2001). It is also envisaged that it will enable a more focused allocation of organisational resources. Bart (1998), based on his findings, provided the content for what he thinks a good mission statement should include. Other empirical studies have similarly attempted to define and analysis the content of mission statements in either large firms or SMEs (for example, Campbell, 1992) using different approaches. Table 5.1 illustrates a sample of the main findings of major studies involved in identifying and analysing the components of mission statements. Pearce and David's (1987) research, for example, is probably the very first attempt empirically to identify the content of mission statements. They identified the specifications of target customers and the markets as the highest in terms of frequency, and the identification of the firm's desired public image as the lowest.

In their study of mission statements in 135 Canadian firms Baetz and Bart developed a number of categories for analysing the statements using the grounded theory approach. Concerning the content of the mission statements, they contended that a typical mission statement contains one or two of the following:

Table 5.1	Researcher(s)	Relevant country	Identified components
Components of mission statements identified by empirical researches	Pearce and David (1987)	USA	• The specification of target customers and markets • Principal products and/or services • The geographical domain • Core technologies used • Growth, survival and profitability • Company philosophy • Company self-concepts • Firm's desired public image
	Klemm *et al.* (1991)	UK	• Long term purpose of the organisation reflecting deeply held corporate views • Long term strategic objectives outlining desired direction and performance in broad term • Objectives in the form of quantified planning targets over a specific period • Scope and activities of the company in terms of industry and geographical spread
	Baetz and Bart (1996)	Canada	• Financial objectives • Non-financial objectives • Firm's value, belief and philosophy • Organisation's definition of success • Definition of organisation's strategy • Customers
	O'Gorman and Doran (1999)	Ireland	• Concern for survival • Product and/or services • Concern for customers • Geographical domain • Company philosophy • Concern for quality • Self-concept • Public image • Customer/market • Concern for suppliers • Core technology

Source: Adapted from Analoui and Karami (2002b).

- Financial objectives: for example, to enhance profitability and long term value.
- Non-financial objectives: for example, to provide a challenging work environment.
- A statement on values, beliefs and philosophy: for example, to be responsible.
- The firm's definition of success: for example, to meet or exceed customer's expectations. The organisation's number one priority – for example customer satisfaction.
- A definition of the organisation's strategy: for example, specific products or markets.
- Reference to one stakeholder: for example customers (Baetz and Bart 1996: 528).

Similarly, O'Gorman and Doran (1999) found that the mission statement in SMEs tends to place more emphasis on concern for survival, product or services than concern for the customers. Their findings are similar to that of Pearce and David (1987). O'Gorman and Doran (1999) also determined that the least important components of mission statements in SMEs are those that relate to the customer, market, concern for suppliers and core technology.

To take the debate one step further, Analoui and Karami (2002b) targeted the strategists and decided to identify the components of the firms' mission statement from the point of view of the CEOs and their perceived list of priorities. This method is very similar to that employed by previous researchers (Rarick and Vitton, 1995; O'Gorman and Doran, 1999; Bart, 2000; Karami and Analoui, 2001). Thus the respondents were asked to list the components of the mission statements of their firms in accordance to their perceived level of priority. An analysis of the data shows that the CEOs of the firms involved in the survey tended to emphasise 'long term profit, survival and growth' as the first priority in their mission statements (74 per cent). This result is similar to and in line with the findings of the other studies. For example, Baetz and Bart (1996) reported 'financial objectives' (46 per cent); and O'Gorman and Doran (1999) pointed to 'concern for survival' (72 per cent) as their first priority for content of mission statements. The results of our research show that CEOs placed little (9 per cent) emphasis on 'concern for suppliers' as a component of their mission statements.

Based on the analysis of the data collected, generally a mission statement in a SME typically contains: long term profit, survival and growth; customer satisfaction; core technology; market; company philosophy and values; product and services quality; public image; geographic domain; self-concept and concern for suppliers as main concerns for the CEOs involved. The 'customer satisfaction' component of the statement, which was the third most frequent (64 per cent) in O'Gorman and Doran's (1999) study, was the second most frequent component (67 per cent) in our study. More closely, the 'core technology' component, which was regarded as the fourth most frequent in Pearce and David's (1987) study in USA, and ranked as a non-financial element in O'Gorman and Doran's (1999) study in Ireland, was the third most frequent in our survey. Perhaps the technology-intensive nature of the electronics industry is the contributing factor influencing the results in our case. As for the least important components of the mission statement, the data analysis shows that geographic domain, self-concept and concern for suppliers score the lowest in order of perceived importance to CEOs (Box 5.4).

Developing the objectives

The second step in strategy formulation in SMEs is specifying achievable objectives. Hodgetts and Kuratko (2001) suggest that the owner-managers of the small businesses need to set objectives for their business on the basis of current and projected opportunities (Shuman and Seeger, 1986). These

---

Box 5.4 The importance of objectives in SMEs

A casual conversation between two owner-managers and long term friends leads to a more serious debate. 'I am in a very competitive business,' David explained to Andrew, defending the recent setbacks related to the poor performance of his firm. Andrew would not have any of this. He has spent nearly 20 years running a small business, quite successfully, in the printing industry. Andrew, unlike David, was a believer in planning, knowing exactly where to go and what to do to get there.

David went on to conclude, 'That's why I haven't been able to make much money over the last three years, though I think that things are going to get better this year. In fact, I am certain that profit will rise dramatically.' This argument did not sit well with Andrew. According to him, although several important reasons could be cited for David's poor performance, nevertheless, he was convinced that the major cause of it all is the failure to plan. Andrew thought it was high time to explain one or two things to David:

> You see David, you have no clear objectives, do you? That's why business is not working out well. And it's not just these days, it has always been touch and go with you. The reality is that you operate on a day-to-day basis. I have continually urged you to set a profit objective and then work backwards to determine how much you have to sell and with what type of mark-up. This is the logical way of doing things. But, as always, you prefer to just go along responding to daily events without any real strategy or plan. To be honest I do not understand how you have managed to hang on so long. Do you realise that it may be time to change before it is really too late. You have the resources, potential market and only a few competitors, ... you could be even more successful than I and that's the core of it.

This time David was convinced. For the first time, he understood the reality of setting clear objectives, not just for himself but for his staff and customers too. He realised that, with proper planning, the business could make a profit. He should no longer just wait for it to happen but plan for it. If Andrew could do it, so could he.

objectives should give firms direction for their future activities and investments. They go on to contend that strategies must be formulated, procedures designed and a budget must be drawn up: all however should be directed towards helping to attain the firm's stated objectives (Hodgetts and Kuratko, 2001). Without setting the objectives, the strategists in SMEs will be blind to the direction to be taken. In this sense, objectives could be regarded as the end result of a planned activity. It is business objectives which convert the mission statement into specific goals that shape the direction and activities of the business (Lowry *et al.* 1999).

In almost all cases, the objectives convert the generalities of the mission statement and turn them into specific commitment for the firm. Lynch (2000) believes that this will create a bridge between what needs to be done and when the objectives ought to be completed. On the whole, business objectives could be achieved in long-run, medium and short term periods. These could include profitability, employees' job satisfaction, production efficiency, organisational effectiveness, customers' satisfaction, social responsibility and technology development. Some place emphasis on a list of quantitative and measurable objectives, whereas others prefer a mix of both qualitative and quantitative objectives (Lasher, 1999). It is important to note that nowadays there are objectives such as employee job satisfaction and organisational effectiveness which cannot easily be quantified. Apart from the nature of the objectives, for small and medium-sized enterprises it is crucial to develop a mission statement and consequently outline a list of objectives (Smith, 1998). The emphasis here is on a rational step-by-step process rather the degree of the formality involved in decision-making.

Characteristics of the objectives

Generally, there is a danger that in small businesses objectives are developed based on the owner-manager's or CEO's personal objectives and preferences (Figure 5.3). Personal objectives and goals are highly subjective and may or may not be correct. However, the reality of business is an objective one. The stakeholders of a typical SME such as the customers, shareholders, banks and financial institutions, tax authorities and competitors will certainly view the business objectivity and subject it to detailed and careful analysis. To ensure a fair degree of objectivity, the objectives of the business, especially in the case of small businesses, should be developed on the basis of a carefully thought out mission statement which has emerged from a methodical SWOT analysis (Wheelen and Hunger, 1998).

In other words, the objectives of the firm should reflect the mission of the firm. Accordingly, the mission and vision statement of the firm should address the strengths, weaknesses, opportunities and actual or potential threats facing the firm. The strategic objectives of the firm should include answers to four main questions: What? Who? When? And how much? The objectives should include the outcomes and results (what), they should clearly indicate the target groups or markets (who), they should entail the conditions and time (when), and finally set out the standards and the criteria for performance assessment (how much).

Let's consider an example of an objective in SME. Suppose we are running a restaurant serving meals in West Yorkshire. Our objective could be concerned with: customers (who) have an enjoyable eating experience (what) every time (when) they eat at our restaurant (how).

Objectives and their characteristics have been considered from different perspectives. For instance Luffman *et al.* (1991) pointed out that many organisations state their objectives in terms such as 'a certain percentage of the market share', 'good quality product', 'a happy and well rewarded workforce' and so on. A prime purpose of objectives is to set targets or benchmarks against which performance can be measured. Thus, to be of worth to a SME, objectives should be measurable, achievable, realistic, explicit, internally consistent with each other, and communicable to others (Luffman *et al.* 1991).

In accordance with the above, Lowry *et al.* (1999) provide a definition of objectives from a marketing point of view. They propose that an objective should be:

- Acceptable to agency personnel – based upon the market realities and agency capabilities.

- Attainable in a specified time period within the reach of the agency and compatible with its strengths and weaknesses.

- Measurable – results can be measured against specific goals.

Figure 5.3

Developing
objectives

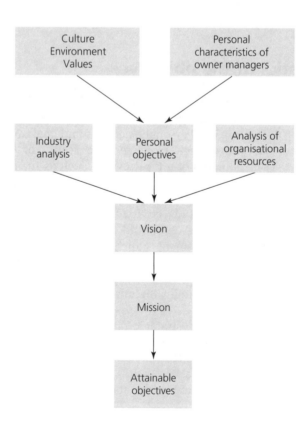

To enhance the probability of achieving the objectives, they should be feasible to obtain and completely accepted by agency personnel. A broad objective should be converted into several specific short-run goals. By completing all of these related goals within a certain time period, the objective can be attained. An indication of whether an objective was accomplished is determined by measuring the results of the efforts against the performance standard established for the objective. In this way, this measurement serves as a control device (Lowry *et al.* 1999).

Considering the results of the previous works, it could be concluded that in small and medium-sized enterprises, the owner-managers or CEOs should develop SMART objectives. Thus, an effective objective should contain the following characteristics, they ought to be

- **S**pecific
- **M**easurable
- **A**chievable
- **R**ealistic
- **T**ime bound.

In small businesses objectives should focus on the priorities of the business. They shouldn't just reflect a list of routine tasks (which you'll do anyway). Objectives should be goals that you can achieve; but you should have to reach for them. Small business managers should make the objectives SMART.

Benefits of the objectives

Clear objectives are needed wherever performance and results are central to an organisation's success. Often, it is observed that objectives are too vague or too weak to guide performance. There is no doubt that strong and precise objectives can lead to high performance and poor objectives lead to poor performance. It is for this reason that small businesses must get their objectives right. SMEs can benefit from developing proper objectives (see Figure 5.4). Some of the benefits of setting objectives are as follows:

Figure 5.4

Characteristics of effective objectives

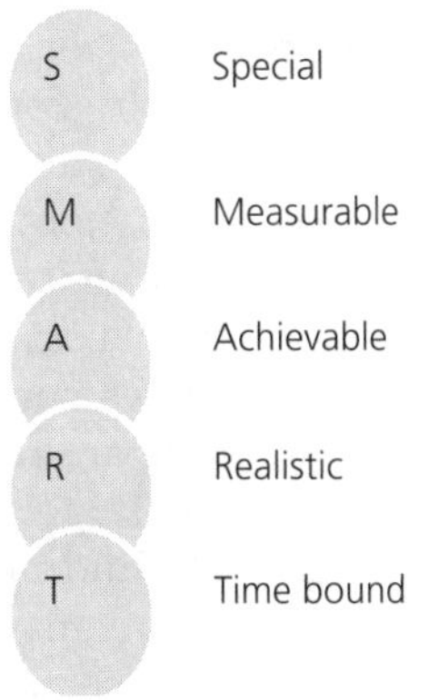

S	Special
M	Measurable
A	Achievable
R	Realistic
T	Time bound

- Setting effective objectives creates self-confidence in owner-managers.
- Motivation is central in SMEs management, and setting objectives increases motivation in managers and provides direction for the business.
- Setting objectives increases efficiency, which in turn leads to organisational effectiveness.
- Having formal business objectives provides criteria for the firm's performance evaluation.
- Setting objectives can help managers (or owner-managers) to control the process of organisational operations more effectively.

Types of objective

Objectives can be classified from different points of view. A typical organisation's objectives can be strategic or operational, quantitative or qualitative. In terms of a planning period, objectives can be long term, medium term or short term. Objectives can also be financial or non-financial.

Strategic versus operational objectives

From a managerial hierarchy point of view, objectives are classified as strategic, tactical and operational and in that order. Senior managers usually determine strategic objectives, while middle managers determine tactical objectives (Ledford *et al.* 1995). Consequently, supervisors and junior managers decided on the objectives appropriate to operational needs. Luffman *et al.* (1991) argue that objectives should ideally fit together, in that senior manager's decisions create the domain within which middle managers set their objectives. However, each level has specific concerns and the role of senior managers is vital in articulating the kind of objectives which create consensus amongst stakeholders. Whereas the role of middle managers is somewhat different, it is often concerned with implementing strategy and setting relevant functional objectives.

Quantitative versus qualitative objectives

Of course, objectives could be set either quantitatively or qualitatively. The nature of the indicators of the objectives usually determines their groupings. For example, the objectives set for financial indicators such as sale or production will be quantitative. In contrast, there are objectives indicators which are intangible and hard to subject to precise quantitative measurements such as effective performance, job satisfaction and increased commitment. These objectives have to defined qualitatively. As a rule, quantitative objectives are easy to define (mathematically) and easy to measure (Box 5.5).

Measurable objectives such as sales volumes are determined in quantitative scale. Suppose that we are running a small firm in the garment manufacturing industry and our sale target for the next two months is £2 million, or that our production target for children's clothing is 10 000 units per year. With this kind of target it would be relatively easy to measure the outcomes of sale and/or production and appraise the performance of the business as a whole. It is

---

Box 5.5 Measurable and less measurable objectives

Measurable objectives:

- To increase sales by 20 per cent within six months
- To reduce administrative overheads from 20 per cent to 13 per cent
- To achieve a net profit of 70 per cent of the total sales
- To produce 5000 units within next three months
- To increase total sale from £20 to £25 million within one year.

Less measurable objectives:

- To increase customer satisfaction
- To improve the firm's reputation for product quality
- To improve leadership quality
- To be more innovative.

---

important to note that the measurable objectives are not necessarily financial ones (Chell, 2001). For example, market share is a measurable but non-financial objective.

As much as quantitative objectives are easy to measure, the qualitative objectives are difficult to define and particularly hard to measure. Customer satisfaction and increased organisational performance are the obvious examples of less measurable objectives. Qualitative objectives either don't tell to what extent they are being achieved or they do not point to any particular action when they are not being achieved (Hodgetts and Kuratko, 2001). For instance, it would be difficult for the manager of a small business concern to determine the firm's increased effectiveness precisely. More importantly, even if it is arbitrarily decided that firm's target for effectiveness has not been increased, exactly what steps should be taken? The important point here is that the CEOs of the small businesses should, as far as possible, convert the less measurable objectives into measurable targets.

Long term versus short term objectives

Organisational objectives can be categorised as long term and short term. Long term objectives vary from firm to firm. The consensus is that usually long term objectives in SMEs are those that can be achieved within a period of three to five years. Essentially they are the strategic objectives of the firm and are created by senior management (Lasher, 1999). It has been observed that SMEs are seldom concerned with long term objectives. In contrast, short term objectives are naturally more financially oriented and they are more quantitative rather than qualitative in nature. Small businesses are frequently involved in setting short term objectives (Shuman and Seeger, 1986).

Strategic objectives can be divided into long term or short term (financial) objectives. The important point to bear in mind is that there should be a logical relationship between long term and short term objectives. Typically, the short term objectives should support the long term goals; otherwise the firm will not be strategically successful (Scandura *et al.* 1996). Also as we noted earlier the CEOs aim should be to balance long term goals and short term objectives. For instance, let's suppose a small business is in the early stages of its life cycle. Of course, it is expected that at this early stage there should not be too much concern with increasing profit, because the products and/or services are relatively unknown and have not been introduced properly to the market. However, gaining maximum profit is a financial objective and an appropriate combination of strategic and financial objectives should be established for each stage of the firm's product life cycle.

Setting objectives in practice for small business managers

In summary, the second step in the formulation of business strategies is developing a comprehensive set of goals and objectives for the firm. The goals and objectives should support the mission of the SME and should be SMART. In order to set objectives effectively, the small business managers should follow a logical process, therefore we have suggested a guideline for that purpose (Box 5.6).

The next step in the formulation of business strategies will be developing a strategy, which will be discussed in some detail.

Developing strategy

The third step in the process of strategy formulation is developing strategies (Porter, 1985). When strategists have managed to develop a mission statement

---

Box 5.6 Guidelines for setting objectives

- Determine the key people who should be involved in setting business objectives.
- Establish what must be done, when and who should be doing it.
- Develop a system for setting, reviewing, and managing business objectives throughout your company.
- Make the objectives SMART.
- Create business objectives that are clearly linked to the mission statement and strategic goals.
- Make sure that your businesses' objectives are taken together so that they result in an efficient use of funds and people in pursuit of broader business intentions.
- Train and involve all employees in your firm in the continuous process of setting, reviewing and meeting business objectives.

and to set the strategic objectives of the firm in light of environmental analysis, then they will be able to begin the task of developing business strategies. Strategy development usually involves determining how a firm can fit into its environment (Chell, 2001). The process deals with determining the firm's abilities as well as the needs of the industry so that the firm can meet those needs and fit into its surroundings. Approaches to business strategy formulation have evolved steadily since the 1970s and empirical research has proved that strategy development forms a prerequisite for the success of organisations – large or small. Developing an effective strategy is a difficult task. It requires awareness, especially on the part of the CEOs, of the environment and detailed analysis of the current situation of the firm – like all managerial skills it improves with practice. As we discussed earlier, business owner-managers or CEOs of SMEs are the ultimate strategic decision-makers in their firms.

In recent research Analoui and Karami (2002a) found that small business managers' strategic environmental awareness and experiences can play a significant role in developing a successful strategy. They observed that where the CEOs exhibited a distinct lack of strategic awareness, the firm performance was usually low.

In order to develop an effective strategy, strategists should answer some basic questions. Roth and Washburn (1999) contend that the strategy development process involves answering a series of ten basic questions that go beyond a SWOT analysis. These are:

1. What specifically does the firm sell?
2. Who are your customers? What is your market?
3. Why do buyers need your services?
4. Who are your major competitors? What is their share of the market?
5. What are your major competitors' strengths?
6. What are your major competitors' weaknesses?
7. What are the technical alternatives to your output?
8. What are your strengths?
9. What are your weaknesses?
10. In view of your answers to these questions, what strategies should be employed to use your strengths and take advantage of your competitors' weaknesses?

In order to develop a strategy, strategists in SMEs should be able to answer these questions considering the results of the industry analysis and the firm's resources, taking into account the strategic objectives. Roth and Washburn (1999) add that by answering the above questions, the strategy makers will have some statements to guide the way in which they conduct their practice.

Competitive advantage

What is competitive advantage? How do firms gain and develop their competitive advantages? Competitive advantage is a base for good strategy and in turn a good strategy should produce a competitive advantage. Competitive advantages are those factors that a firm needs to have in order to succeed in business. It has been defined as 'the ability of an organisation to add more value for its customers than its rivals, and thus attain a position for relative advantage' (Thompson, 2001: 1123). A competitive advantage can be the strengths or any type of ability a firm uses to beat its rivals. For example, some firms have skilled and motivated employees, while others have access to effective marketing channels and financial resources. Factors such as technology, marketing channels, skilled employees, unique competitive position and patent can be considered as competitive advantages for firms.

The recent access of SMEs to e-commerce can be considered as a competitive advantage (see Figure 5.5). Those small businesses that have access to the Internet and intranet will be able to develop better and more informed marketing strategies based on e-commerce advantages. In other words, access to the Internet as a strength for a small business will lead to the development of an effective marketing strategy which in turn will lead to developing e-commerce as a sustainable competitive advantage for the firm. Porter (1996) argues that, in general, sustainable competitive advantage is derived from the following:

- A unique competitive position
- Clear trade-offs and choices vis-à-vis competitors
- Activities tailored to the company's strategy
- A high degree of fit across activities
- A high degree of operational effectiveness.

He concludes that when activities complement one another, rivals will get little benefit unless they successfully match the whole system (Porter, 1996). Accordingly Lynch (2000) confirms that in seeking the advantages the strategists should examine the competitors as well as the firm itself and its resources. He has introduced nine sources of advantage in the organisations. These are:

- Differentiation
- Low costs
- Niche marketing
- High performance or technology
- Quality
- Service
- Vertical integration
- Synergy
- Culture, leadership and style of an organisation.

Figure 5.5

The firm's strategy and competitive advantages

Firm's strengths and distinguished advantages → Strategy → Firm's competitive advantages

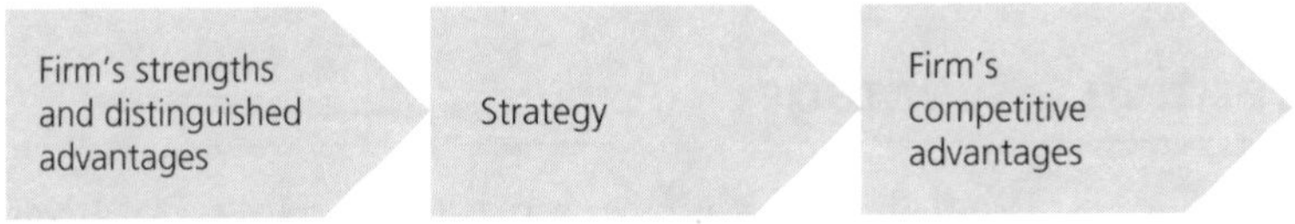

He concludes that there is no single route to achieve sustainable competitive advantage, however the achievement of a sustainable competitive advantage can be tested by three criteria. Consequently, a sustainable competitive advantage should be:

1. Sufficiently significant to make a difference.
2. Sustainable against environmental change and competitor attack.
3. Recognisable and linked to customer benefits.

Competitive strategies

Competition is at the heart of the success or failure of the business (Porter, 1985; Wickham, 2001). As Porter has aptly argued, competition determines the appropriateness of a firm's activities that can contribute to its performance, such as innovations, a cohesive culture or good implementation. Competitive strategy is the search for a favourable competitive position in an industry, the fundamental arena in which competition occurs (Porter, 1985). The business side of the corporate strategy framework refers to the industries in which a firm operates, as well as to the kind of competitive strategy which it adapts in each business environment. Industry choice is critical to the long term success of a corporate strategy. It has repeatedly been demonstrated that the best predictor of firm performance is the profitability of the industries in which it competes (Rumelt, 1991; Hoskisson, 2000).

A set of industries in which a firm operates also influences the extent to which it will be able to share resources across its business. The notion of relatedness may be used as a surrogate for a firm's ability to create synergy among its business. The particular competitive strategy a firm pursues in each industry also has an impact on corporate performance. While it may be unusual to find a corporation that pursues exactly the same source of competitive advantage in every one of its businesses, it is important to recognise that a corporation's resources are often only valuable when applied to similar generic strategies (Collis and Montgomery, 1997).

To understand how to achieve competitive advantage and how to generalise about the relative position of individual firms within an industry, Porter (1985) has developed the concept of generic strategies – categories of strategy that follow a particular pattern. Generic strategies became very popular in the early 1980s. There are two basic types of competitive advantage which the firm can process: low cost or differentiation (Porter, 1985). The two basic types of competitive advantage combined with the scope of activities for which a firm seeks to achieve lead to three generic forms of strategies for achieving an average performance in an industry: cost leadership, differentiation and the focus. The focus strategy itself is comprised of two variants – cost focus and differentiation focus.

Porter has suggested that each of the generic strategies involves a fundamentally different route to competitive advantage. He views a choice for type of competitive advantage sought and the scope of the strategic target in which competitive advantage is to be achieved as an important combination (Porter, 1985). The cost leadership and differentiation strategies pursue competitive advantage in a broad range of industry segments. Focus strategies, on the other hand, tend to vary widely from industry to industry. Competitive advantage is at the heart of any strategy, and achieving competitive advantage requires a firm to make a choice about the type of competitive advantage it seeks to attain and the scope within which it will attain it (Wit and Meyer, 1998). Collis and Montgomery (1997) thought that the idea of generic strategies ought to emphasise the consistency of a firm's activities and the need to tie each to the firm's overall mission and should also stress the importance of not getting stuck in the middle and ultimately failing to build a distinctive competence that creates a competitive advantage (Collis and Montgomery, 1997).

Cost leadership strategy

The low cost leader is a firm that can produce at the lowest cost and thus gain competitive advantage in any market from being able to provide the products and services at the lowest cost. Cost leadership may be the most appropriate strategy to pursue, if a firm can achieve this position (Lynch, 2000). The development of low cost production enables the firm to compete against other firms on the basis of lower prices. The profit advantage gained from the cost leadership strategy derives from the difference between average sale price in the marketplace and the cost of the production (Figure 5.6). Since the production cost of the low cost leader is less than the production cost of competitors, this company will be able to make more profit than its competitors.

Figure 5.6

Characteristics of the three generic strategies

1. *Cost leadership*. The cost leader is a company that is the lowest cost producer in a market, after judgement for quality differences. For cost leader low cost is a competitive advantage and its competitive scope is broad target.

2. *Differentiation*. Differentiation is a suitable strategy when the firm is able to differentiate its products and services based on attributes which customers value and the cost of doing so is lower than the extra revenue envisaged. For this strategy differentiation is a competitive advantage and its competitive scope is broad target.

3. *Focus*. In focus strategy, the firm concentrates on one or a limited number of market segments. Focus strategy exploits the differences in cost behaviour or the special needs of the customers in focused market segments. The competitive scope for both cost focus and differentiation focus is a narrow target. Lower cost is a competitive advantage for cost focus strategy and differentiation is a competitive advantage for differentiation focus strategy.

Because of the reliance of economies of scale cost leadership strategy is likely to be more sustainable in the long run (Channon, 2002). However, there are some risks associated with the cost leadership strategy. Porter (1980) believes that the cost leadership cannot be sustained if

1. Competitors imitate.
2. Technology changes.
3. Other bases for cost leadership erode.

Differentiation strategy

Differentiation is the second strategy of the Porter's generic types of strategies. When the firm cannot choose cost leadership strategy but is able to differentiate its products and services along some attributes which customers value, and the cost of doing so is lower than the extra revenue envisaged, then differentiation may be the appropriate strategy to pursue (Channon, 2002). Differentiated products and services satisfy the needs of the customers through a sustainable competitive advantage. This enables firms to focus on value that generates a comparatively higher price (Thompson, 2001). In other words, differentiation occurs when the products or services of a firm satisfy the needs of the customers better than the other firms' products and services. Therefore, the firm which differentiates its products will be able to charge a price that is higher than the average price in the marketplace. To pursue a differentiation strategy, the firm should define the target market properly and make sure that the customers are willing to pay for differentiation. Because of some of the necessary expenses, such as staffing and administrative costs, the price of the differentiator is usually higher than the average price in the marketplace. Although differentiation strategy has many advantages, there are still some problems associated with its pursuit (see Figure 5.7).

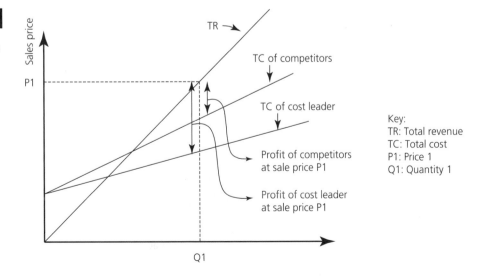

Figure 5.7

Low cost leadership average profit

Key:
TR: Total revenue
TC: Total cost
P1: Price 1
Q1: Quantity 1

As Lynch (2000) discussed, the first problem in pursuing differentiated strategy is the difficulty of estimating whether the extra costs can be recovered from the customers. The second problem, of course, is that successful differentiation may attract competitors to the industry to copy the products and/or services provided.

Focus (niche) strategy

According to Porter (1985) when neither a low cost leadership nor a differentiation strategy is possible for a firm a focus strategy, sometimes referred to as niche strategy, may be appropriate. By adopting a focus strategy the firm typically concentrates on finding a niche in the marketplace and will go about developing its competitive advantages for that niche. Here the firm focuses on a narrower segment of a market and develops its strategy to serve them in order to achieve a competitive advantage in its target segment. A niche strategy is often used by small and medium-sized enterprises (Lasher, 1999; Hoskisson, 2000).

There are two main problems associated with the focus or niche strategy. First, cost focus may be unachievable within an industry depending upon economies of scale, like the car industry. Second, in the long run the small, specialists niches could disappear as quickly as they appear (Wheelen and Hunger, 1998; Lynch, 2000).

The danger of being stuck in the middle

It has already been stressed that each of the generic strategies requires its own specific circumstances, for instance in terms of market size, skills and administrative structure of the enterprise. The strategists should make sure that they select one generic strategy. It is argued that if a firm pursues one or more generic strategies but fails to achieve any of them, then it will get stuck in the middle without a competitive advantage. This is of course an unenviable position to be in and resembles a boat without radar in stormy waters.

Porter's generic strategies in SMEs

Developing an effective competitive strategy is vital for SMEs. To help this view, Burns and Harrison (1996) considered some aspects of Porter's generic strategies in SMEs. Figure 5.8 shows the application of the three generic strategies in small businesses.

Cost leadership strategy is not attractive for SMEs. Cost leadership assumes that costs can be reduced, for example through economics of scale, and this is important to customers. Small businesses cannot achieve the economies of scale of large firms, so a cost leadership strategy is likely to pose an unattractive alternative as they seldom have the large capital to invest constantly in new technology.

Burns and Harrison (1996) emphasise that where the firm sets out to be unique by developing some dimensions that are specially and widely valued by customers, it has managed to develop a unique selling proposition (USP). In this way, the firm sets out to establish itself, in some ways, as a unique enterprise and to offer different products or services from that of its competitors. It can then charge a premium price. The risk associated with this is that the differentiation cannot be sustained for a long time as competitors begin to imitate or the USP becomes less important to customers. On the other hand if the premium charged is too high, customers may decide not to purchase the product or service at all. Having said that, USP is still an attractive strategy for smaller firms, particularly when it is combined with the third generic strategy where the firm focuses on a narrow target market segment combined with either of the other strategies. If the firm adapts a strategy of focused differentiation it is said to pursue a niche strategy. This is a very attractive strategy for SMEs. Focuses can also be used with cost leadership, where concentrating on certain market segments offers some cost advantages.

Burns and Harrison (1996) reported, in a survey of some 1500 smaller companies across Europe, that those companies that had seen their sales and/or profit grow in the 1990s were those which had better or different products or services, and this led to weak-to-normal levels of competition. Another survey into 3500 of Britain's 'super league companies' concluded that most of these high growth companies served niche markets. In other words, successful firms that follow a strategy of differentiation probably focused on target market segments.

Strategies at the corporate level

Corporate strategy defines what business the firm should be in. The corporate strategy of a firm determines its different product/market combinations and defines the scope of its activities. For instance, if it decides to enter new markets, the firm has to choose between several forms of market entry strategies such as export and joint venture. In smaller businesses, owner-managers or CEOs play a

Figure 5.8

The attractiveness of generic competitive strategies for SMEs

Cost leadership
Not attractive

Differentiation
Attractive

Cost focus
Possibly attractive

Differentiation focus
Very attractive

Priority of generic strategies for SMEs:
- First: Differentiation focus
- Second: Differentiation
- Third: Cost focus
- Fourth: Cost leadership

significant role in developing strategies at corporate level and determining the direction of the firm's activities. Corporate strategy in SMEs can be categorised into three main strands: specialisation and diversification, internationalisation and vertical integration/subcontracting (Bamberger, 1998). Each of these is discussed below.

Specialisation and diversification

Specialisation and diversification are fundamental strategies at corporate level and describe the diversity of the activities of the firm. Very often diversification and specialisation are defined by the variety of products and industries or strategic business units (SBUs) the firm is in. The importance of diversification is clearly related to its widespread adoption in many firms in the market economies (Hitt *et al.* 1997). There are two types of diversification:

- In related markets
- In unrelated markets.

When a firm diversifies, it moves out of its current markets and products into a new area. Diversification can be done in two ways. The first option is diversifying in related markets. There are risks associated with moving to a new market or attempting new production, but the risk in moving to a related market or producing related products is deemed to be low. There are three types of diversification in related markets:

- Forward integration: in which the firm extends its activities to the organisational output activities such as distribution.
- Backward integration: in which the firm extends its activities to the firms of its inputs such as suppliers of raw materials.
- Horizontal integration: in which the firm moves into activities related to its current activities.

Although synergy is the main reason for diversification in related markets, the firm may minimise this risk if it moves into related markets (Figure 5.9).

Figure 5.9

Product market matrix

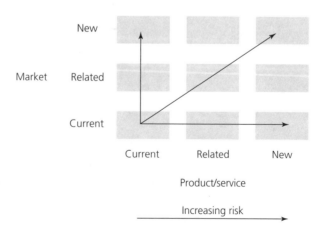

Increasing risk

The second option is diversifying in unrelated markets. Accordingly, when a firm moves to unrelated markets, it runs the risk of operating in areas where its detailed knowledge of the key factor for success is limited. Clearly, this will involve a step into the unknown and will carry a higher degree of business risks for the CEOs involved (Lynch, 2000). Specialisation and diversification have been central topics in strategy studies (Ramanujam and Varadarajan, 1989; Hoskisson and Hitt, 1994). Different studies of diversification of SMEs conclude that the strategic situation of SMEs is characterised by a number of related products or product groups.

Many scholars tried to study the linkage between diversification and other organisational factors. For instance, theoretical explanations of linking diversification and performance stem mainly from efficiency gains due to economies of scale and scope of the products or services (Chandler, 1990); learning and redefining (Mintzberg, 1988); risk reduction (Chandler, 1962); and top management strategic leadership abilities (Ohmae, 1982). The large body of literature in this field provides important insights into the motivation for diversification and its subsequent performance consequences (Ramanujam and Varadarajan, 1989; Datta *et al.* 1991; Hoskisson and Hitt, 1994). The results of other studies in the field of diversification in SMEs (Bamberger, 1998) show that diversification is a basic requirement for growth in SMEs. It has also been found that rising firm size is related to rising diversification of related product groups. Bagchi-Sen and Kuechler (2000) in their recent research examined the likely association between strategic planning and functional diversification (services and markets) in SMEs. They found that SMEs face considerable difficulty in overcoming both in-house and external barriers in accessing clients requiring non-traditional services (e.g. management consulting) and clients involved in international businesses. They reported that the proactive, functionally diversified and/or international-oriented firms outperform the reactive, functionally concentrated and local market-oriented firms. The competitive advantage for the former categories is based on flexible specialisation such as customisation of services for specific groups of clients, speed of delivery and specialised skills.

Another study of diversification in the banking industry in Europe (Bamberger, 1998), found a significant relationship between intended diversification and the bank's size, the CEO perception of competitive intensity and changing market preferences, and the bank's past variability in profitability. Finally, developing a market niche by differentiating a business from its competitors is a strategy that offers smaller firms a better chance of sustainable growth. Establishing a market niche is most effective when aimed at a narrowly defined market segment. Sometimes this can involve concentrating on gaps in the marketplace which are left by the larger companies.

Internationalisation

Internationalisation means that a firm is acting in one or several foreign markets and thus working in an international context. For SMEs internationalisation is a component of growing importance in their strategic behaviour (Bamberger, 1998; Meyer and Heppard, 2000). Internationalisation of SMEs must be considered with respect to the three levels of strategy proposed above and we will now review them. Several theories and concepts have been suggested to capture the process of internationalisation in SMEs. For instance Gankema *et al.* (2000) have introduced five stages of internationalisation of SMEs:

1. Domestic marketing
2. Pre-export
3. Experimental involvement
4. Active involvement
5. Committed involvement.

Internationalisation theories of SMEs are concerned with the choice of foreign target markets, products or services to be offered in selected foreign markets and the market entry strategies. Market entry strategies in the international field are concerned with export, licensing and management contracts as well as the establishment of sales or production subsidiaries. Forms and phases of internationalisation for SMEs are shown in Figure 5.10. With respect to SMEs export is mostly discussed. Market entry strategies are also concerned with internal development – development of resources, potentials within the firm – versus acquisition – buying of companies, merger – strategies and different owner strategies.

As far as ownership strategies are concerned, the use of joint ventures is of particular interest. Despite the importance of exporting for SMEs, it is only one

Figure 5.10

Forms and phases of internationalisation for SMES

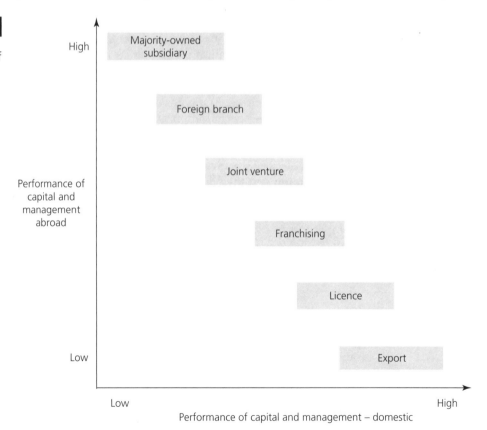

element and very often merely the first step in internationalisation process. In addition to indirect or direct exportation the process includes the creation of distribution agencies in foreign countries, the creation of own production facilities abroad, different production strategies as well as organisational strategies and internationalisation of management and capital. The strategies and the level of internationalisation should also be studied in relation to the entrepreneurial motivations, values, attitudes and objectives of the SME manager. For example, in a study of the internationalisation plans of Swiss SMEs (Bamberger, 1998) with the prospect of the western European economic integration, it has been found that most of the companies planned to push their exports to the EC and only a few planned to establish production facilities elsewhere abroad.

Exporting strategy

According to Masurel (2001) export and internationalisation are important to the survival of many SMEs because of their tremendous potential for enhancing sales growth, increasing efficiency and improving quality. In exporting, the goods are produced in the home country and exported to foreign markets. Exporting is becoming increasingly important for SMEs; for example fruits produced by small Spanish agricultural firms are exported to the UK market. Having access to the foreign markets' potential demands through intranets and business links enables small businesses to be more involved in internationalisation.

There are some advantages and disadvantages associated with the pursuit of exporting strategy. These are:

Advantages:

- Contracts with host country firm for distribution
- No need to establish operations.

Disadvantages:

- High transportation costs
- Tariffs changed
- Less control
- Local distribution fees
- Difficulty in customising products.

Although normally the exporting strategy is selected by manufacturing SMEs, recent research (Gankema *et al.* 2000; Masurel, 2001) indicates that increasingly small businesses in the service sector intend to pursue an export strategy for internationalisation. Masurel (2001) suggests that entrepreneurs of exporting SMEs in the service sector see international activities as high profit and low risk; a conclusion which confirms previous results of research carried out in the manufacturing sector.

Licensing strategy

Licensing is another form of internationalisation strategy for SMEs which enables SMEs to benefit from the technical expertise of the mother firms. The licensing firm grants rights to another firm in the host country to produce and/or sell a product and provides technical expertise to the licensee firm under this agreement. The licensee firm pays compensation to the licensing firm (Kotler and Armstrong, 1994). There are advantages and disadvantages for both the licensing and licensee firm (Box 5.7).

The advantage of the licensing agreement for the licensee firm is that there is a possibility for the firm to develop or adapt technology from the licensing firm. Therefore, the licensing firm should not license its distinctive competencies to the licensee firm.

Franchising

Franchising is one of the most popular forms of internationalisation of SMEs. A franchise is a system of distribution that enables the supplier to arrange for a distributor to distribute a specific product or service under agreed conditions. In a franchising strategy the contractor provides the licence with a preformatted package of activity. Normally the franchiser offers brand name and training services and the franchisee pays franchise fees as a percentage of turnover. McDonald's restaurants are the best example of a franchise. For small businesses, there are advantages and disadvantages in pursuing a franchising strategy:

Advantages:

- The franchise offers brand-name appeal
- The franchisee gets the benefit of training services provided by franchiser
- Receiving financial assistance from the franchiser
- Before entering to the franchise, the small business can see the track record of other franchisees showing proof of success.

Disadvantages:

- Franchise fees
- The control the franchiser exercises
- Unfulfilled promises of some franchisers.

Box 5.7 Advantages and disadvantages associated with a licensing strategy

Advantages:

- Licensee pays the costs
- Royalty payment for every unit produced/sold
- Least costly and risky.

Disadvantages:

- Less control
- Lower profit potential
- Licensee learns adapting technology.

Recently, franchising has proven to be one of the most important strategies for small and medium-sized enterprises. Box 5.8 shows the top ten franchises in 2002.

Basically franchise agreements can be categorised into two types – product or service franchise and business franchise. In a product franchise, the franchiser provides products and the franchisee sells them through a wholesale or retail outlet. Similarly, when a service is franchised, the franchisee receives a licence

---

Box 5.8 Top franchises for 2002

Top ten franchises for 2002

1 Subway
2 Jackson Hewitt Tax Service
3 Curves for Woman
4 7-Eleven Inc.
5 Yogen Fruz Worldwide
6 Quizno's Franchise Co.
7 McDonald's
8 Management Recruiters/Sales Consult/MRI Worldwide
9 Holiday Inn Worldwide
10 Jani-King

Top ten global franchises for 2002

1 Subway
2 Kumon Math & Reading Centres
3 McDonald's
4 Yogen Fruz Worldwide
5 Holiday Inn Worldwide
6 Curves for Women
7 Baskin-Robbins USA Co.
8 Mail Boxes Etc.
9 RE/MAX Int'l. Inc.
10 KFC Corp.

Top ten new franchises for 2002

1 Dippin' Dots Franchising Inc.
2 LA Weight Loss Centers Inc.
3 Priceless Rent-A-Car
4 Cruise Planners
5 Roly Roly Franchise Systems LLC
6 Sears Carpet & Upholstery Care Inc.
7 Home Helpers
8 Hangers
9 Schooley Mitchell Telecom Consultants
10 Wingstop Restaurant Inc.

Source: Entrepreneur.com (http://www.entrepreneur.com/Franchise_Zone)

---

for a trade name and the service to be sold. In either a product or service franchise, the franchiser does not control the franchisee business. The second type of franchising strategy is the business franchise. In a business franchise, the franchisee operates the business under a common trade name – Burger King is an example of business franchise. In a business franchise, the franchiser strongly controls the operations of the franchisee.

Joint venture and alliance strategy

A joint venture involves entering into the foreign market strategy by joining with foreign firms to produce or sell a product or services (Kotler and Armstrong, 1994). It is considered to be a successful strategy in the internationalisation of SMEs. In a joint venture contract, both foreign and domestic firms share assets and skills – however, it can take many forms. Joint ventures are also widely used by companies to gain entrance into foreign markets. The foreign companies generally bring new technologies and business practices into the joint venture, while the domestic companies already have the relationships and requisite governmental documents within the country along with being entrenched in the domestic industry. Kotler and Armstrong (1994) have categorised joint ventures into four types: licensing, contract manufacturing, management contracting and joint ownership.

Nowadays, joint ventures are a popular method of expanding business for small and medium-sized enterprises. A joint venture can turn under-utilised resources into profit. It can create a new profit centre for the business and enable the SMEs to enter the new least exploited markets, quicker and at less cost than trying it alone. Channon (2002) believes that joint ventures have several advantages, especially for smaller firms. Some of those advantages are:

- By pursuing a joint venture strategy smaller firms with poor finance and management skills can obtain the necessary resources to enter a new market.
- A joint venture reduces political friction against foreign-owned firms in a local market.
- A joint venture may provide knowledge of local markets, and marketing channels, and access to raw materials suppliers and local production facilities.
- Joint ventures reduce the risks of investment through sharing the project.

Although a joint venture has advantages for smaller businesses, there are still some disadvantages for firms when deciding to pursue a joint venture for the purpose of internationalisation. Channon (1999) observed that joint ventures are very difficult to integrate into a global strategy. A further problem arises when there is a mismatch between global management and local management. In other words, joint ventures can be difficult to manage because of the need to share, especially because parent companies may decide to interfere (Lynch, 2000). Many joint ventures also fail because of a conflict in tax interests between the partners. When considering the advantages and disadvantages of a joint venture, it soon becomes apparent that there is no single way to determine its long term success. However, despite the disadvantages, this strategy is growing rapidly within SMEs.

Vertical integration

Vertical integration and subcontracting strategies are the third dimension of corporate strategy in SMEs. Vertical integration refers principally to a strategy of acquiring control over additional links in the value chain of producing and selling products or services. Thompson (2001) argues that vertical integration is a situation in which the firms directly enter those parts of added value chain that is served by their suppliers or distributors. To achieve the potential benefits of vertical integration the firms need specialist and different skills (Channon, 2002). Vertical integration is one of the main corporate strategies in large firms. However, it is also an applicable corporate strategy for SMEs. In its simplest form, vertical integration means that a firm can integrate with either its supplier or distributor to create more value added. Suppose that a SME operates in baby food manufacturing industry. It buys the raw materials such as milk, fruits and additives from different suppliers and then produces, packages and markets the foods. Then it sells the finished products through different retailers nationally. In order to create more value added the SME could integrate with one of the suppliers or one of the retailers. This will lead to obtaining synergy by integrating two firms, each of which are specialised in their own field (Hitt *et al.* 1997). Vertical integration can be achieved in two ways.

Backward integration

In this strategy the manufacturing SME integrates with one of the raw material suppliers. Backward integration aims to secure supplies at a lower cost than its competitors. It is important to mention that after merger the firm should keep its competitive advantage on the supply side. Backward integration is shown in Figure 5.11.

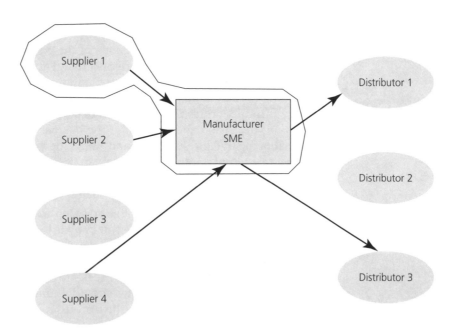

Figure 5.11

Vertical integration (backward integration)

Forward integration

If the firm has some problems with distribution of the product, it tries integrating with one of the distributors. This integration is called forward integration. Forward integration secures customers and guarantees product preference. The strategy of vertical integration is not limited to manufacturing SMEs. As Bamberger (1998) discuss, vertical integration relates to activities such as R & D, accounting, advertising, logistics, maintenance or services. In studying vertical integration strategies in SMEs, we have to bear in mind that vertical arrangements have to change over time depending on competitive conditions, corporate strategy objectives, technology and other environmental factors, to assess the type of vertical integration strategy that will be most appropriate at any particular time (Bamberger, 1998).

Subcontracting

Subcontracting is one of the most important strategies at corporate level of SMEs. In the case of a subcontracting strategy a SME begins to produce products and offer services for another firm, which retains responsibilities for its sale. In other words, a small firm produces goods and services for a larger firm as a customer based on the customer's needs and specifications. In a subcontract strategy, the contract work must meet negotiated standards and be done within a specific period of time. Generally speaking, the subcontractor should have a wealth of relevant experience, up-to-date skills (production and otherwise) and good communication and relating skills. Probably the main disadvantage of subcontracting is achieving lower margins because of the contractor's weak bargaining position.

Summary

- Making and formulating strategy is one of the critical tasks of the managers in small and medium-sized enterprises. Strategy formulation is often referred to as strategic planning or long-range planning and is concerned with developing an SME's mission, objectives and strategies. Therefore, the strategy formulation task in SMEs includes three main elements: first, developing the vision and mission of the business, second, developing organisational strategic objectives and, third, developing business strategies. The result of recent studies shows that small businesses which are involved in strategy formulation formally or informally tend to be more successful than the firms that ignore the strategy-making task.

- Developing vision and mission is the first step in strategy formulation. A vision statement describes what the company is to become in the future while the mission statement reflects the essential purpose for the existence of the organisation, concerning particularly why it is in existence, the nature of the business it is in, and the customers it seeks to serve and satisfy. A good mission statement has five characteristics: defining the business the firm wants to remain in, differentiating the firm from its rivals, enabling the firm in the formulation of objectives, exciting and motivating and its relevance to all of the stakeholders inside and outside of the firm. The corporate mission plays three important roles for businesses: direction, legitimisation and motivation.

- Perhaps the most important thing in developing a mission statement is defining the business in which the firm operates. In order to define the business strategists should determine first: what customer needs the business is satisfying? second: what is the target market in terms of customer groups? and third, what technology is being used to meet and satisfy the stated needs? The main purposes of developing mission statements in SMEs, based on the recent research findings, are:

  1. Developing and planning business strategies.
  2. Increasing profit and growth rate.
  3. Promoting a sense of shared expectations among entrepreneurs and all employees.
  4. To provide clarity of direction for the employees and managers/entrepreneurs.

- The second step in strategy formulation in small and medium-sized enterprises is specifying achievable objectives. Objectives are the end result of planned activity and they convert the mission statement into specific goals that shape the direction and activities of the business.

- The objectives of the business, especially in small businesses, should be developed on the basis of mission statement. Effective objectives should be SMART – **S**pecific, **M**easurable, **A**chievable, **R**ealistic and **T**ime bound. Some of the benefits of setting effective objectives for SMEs are:

  1. Creating self-confidence in owner-managers.
  2. Increasing motivation in managers and providing direction for the business.
  3. Increasing efficiency, which in turn leads to organisational effectiveness.
  4. Providing criteria for the firm's performance evaluation.
  5. Helping managers to control the process of organisational operations effectively.

- The objectives can be classified from different points of view. They can be strategic or operational, quantitative or qualitative. In terms of a planning period, objectives can be long term, medium term or short term, financial or non-financial.

- The third step in strategy formulation is developing strategies. Strategy development is concerned with determination of how a firm can fit properly into the environment. It deals with determining the firm's abilities as well as the industry need to fit the firm into its environment. In order to develop an effective strategy, strategists should answer some basic questions that go beyond a SWOT analysis as follows.

- Competitive strategy is the search for a favourable competitive position in an industry, the fundamental arena in which competition occurs. To understand how to achieve competitive advantage and how to generalise about the relative position of individual firms within an industry, the concept of generic strategies has been developed. This is concerned with categories of strategy that follow a particular pattern which consists of low cost leadership, differentiation and focus. The low cost leadership and differentiation strategies seek competitive advantage in a broad range of industry segments, while focus strategies vary widely from industry to industry, as do the feasible generic strategies in a particular industry. Small businesses cannot achieve the economies of scale of large firms, therefore cost leadership strategy is the most unattractive alternative for smaller firms. Differentiation is an attractive strategy for smaller firms, particularly when it is combined with the third generic strategy, where the firm focuses on a narrow target market segment combined with either of the other strategies. If the firm adapts a strategy of focused differentiation it is said to pursue a niche strategy. This is an attractive strategy for SMEs. Focuses can also be used with cost leadership, where concentrating on certain market segments offers some cost advantages.

- Corporate strategy in SMEs can be categorised into three main strategies: specialisation and diversification, internationalisation, and vertical integration/subcontracting.

- Specialisation and diversification are fundamental strategies at corporate level and describe the diversity of the activities of the firm. There are two types of diversification: in related markets and unrelated markets. When a firm diversifies, it moves out of its current markets and products into new areas. Developing a market niche by differentiating a business from its competitors is a strategy that offers smaller firms a better chance of sustainable growth.

- Internationalisation theories of SMEs are concerned with the choice of foreign target markets, the products or services they are to offer in the selected foreign markets and the market entry strategies. Market entry strategies in the international field are concerned with export, licensing and management contracts as well as the establishment of sales or production subsidiaries.

- Exporting is shipping commodities from the firm's home country to other countries for marketing or sale. The licensing enables SMEs to benefit from the technical expertise of the mother firm, which grants rights to another firm in the host country to produce and/or sell a product. Under this agreement the licensing firm provides technical expertise to the licensee firm and the licensee firm pays compensation to the licensing firm. Franchising is one of the popular forms of internationalisation for SMEs. In the franchising strategy the contractor provides the licence with a preformatted package of activity. A joint venture involves entering the foreign market strategy by joining with foreign firms to produce or sell a product or services. Joint ventures are generally considered to be a successful strategy in the internationalisation of SMEs. Vertical integration and subcontracting strategies are the third dimension of corporate strategy in SMEs. Vertical integration refers principally to a strategy of acquiring control over additional links in the value chain of producing and selling products or services. This will lead to obtaining synergy by integrating two firms, each of which has specialisation in its own field. Vertical integration can be done in two ways – backward or forward.

Discussion questions

1. What is the process of strategy formulation in organisations? Discuss the strategy formulation process in SMEs.

2. How do you define a mission statement? Discuss the differences between mission and vision statement in a firm.

3. How do you assess the characteristics of a good mission statement?

4. Explore the roles of developing an effective mission statement in small businesses.

5. What are the characteristics of effective objectives?

6. Explore the generic strategies in small businesses.

7. What are the corporate strategies in SMEs? Discuss the diversification strategy accordingly.

8. Discuss the internationalisation strategy in small businesses. List the internationalisation strategies in SMEs and explain one.

9. Explore advantages and disadvantages of exporting and franchising strategies.

10. Explain vertical integration strategy in SMEs. What are forward and backward integration strategies?

References

Ackoff, R. L. (1986) *Management in Small Doses*, John Wiley, Chichester.

Ackoff, R. L. (1987) Mission statements, *Planning Review*, 15, 30–31.

Analoui, F. (2000) What motivates senior managers? The case of Romania, *Journal of Management Psychology*, 15 (4), 324–6.

Analoui, F. and Karami, A. (2002a) How Chief Executives' perception of the environment impacts on company performance, *Journal of Management Development*, 21 (4), 290–305.

Analoui, F. and Karami, A. (2002b) CEOs and development of the meaningful mission statement, *Corporate Governance International Journal of Board Effectiveness*, 2 (3), 13–21.

Aram, D. J. and Cowan, S. S. (1990) Strategic planning for increased profit in the small businesses, *Long Range Planning*, 23 (6), 63–70.

Baetz, M. C. and Bart, C. K. (1996) Developing mission statements which work, *Long Range Planning*, 29 (4), 526–533.

Bagchi-Sen, S. and Kuechler, L. (2000) Strategic and functional orientation of small and medium sized enterprises in professional services: an analysis of public accountancy, *The Service Industries Journal*, 20 (3), 117–146.

Bamberger, I. (ed.) (1998) *Product Market Strategies of Small and Medium Sized Enterprises*, Ashgate Publishing Limited, Aldershot.

Bart, C. K. (1998) A comparison of mission statements and their rationales in innovative and non-innovative firms, *International Journal of Technology Management*, 16 (1–3), 64–77.

Bart, C. K. (2000) Mission statements in Canadian not-for-profit hospitals: Does process matter?, *Health Care Management Review*, 25 (2), 45–63.

Beal, R. M. (2000) Competing effectively: Environmental scanning, competitive strategy, and organisational performance in small manufacturing firms, *Journal of Small Business Management*, 38 (1), 27–47.

Bowman, C. and Faulkner, D. (1997) *Competitive Corporate Strategy*, Irwin, London.

Bracker, J. and Pearson, J. (1985) The impact of consultants on small firm strategic planning, *Journal of Small Business Management*, 23, 23–31.

Burns, P. and Harrison, J. (1996) Growth, in Paul Burns and Jim Dewhurst (eds) *Small Businesses and Entrepreneurship*, Macmillan Business, Basingstoke, 40–72.

Byars, L. L. and Neil, T. C. (1987) Organisational philosophy and mission statement, *Planning Review*, 15 (4), 32–35.

Calfree, D. (1993) Get your mission statement working!, *Management Review*, 82, 54–57.

Campbell, A. (1992) The power of mission: aligning strategy and culture, *Planning Review*, 20 (5), 10–14.

Campbell, A., Devine, M. and Young, D. (1990) *A Sense of Mission*, Hutchinson, London.

Chandler, A. D. (1962) *Strategy and Structure*, MIT Press, Cambridge, MA.

Chandler, A. D. (1990) *Scale and Scope: The Dynamics of Industrial Capitalism*, Belknap Press, Harvard University Press, Cambridge, MA.

Channon, D. F. (ed.) (2002) *Encyclopedic Dictionary of Strategic Management*, Blackwell, Oxford.

Chell, E. (2001) *Entrepreneurship: Globalization, Innovation and Development*, Thomson Learning, London.

Collis, D. J. and Montgomery, C. A. (1997) *Corporate Strategy: Resources and Scope of the Firm*, Chicago, McGraw Hill.

Datta, D. K., Rajagopalan, N. and Rasheed, A. M. A. (1991) Diversification and performance: critical review and future directions, *Journal of Management Studies*, 28 (5), 529–558.

David, F. (1989) How companies define their mission, *Long Range Planning*, 22 (2), 90–97.

Falsey, T. (1989) *Corporate Philosophies and Mission Statements*, Quorum Books, New York.

Gankema, H. G. J., Snuif, H. R. and Zwart, P. S. (2000) The internationalisation process of small and medium-sized enterprises: an evaluation of stage theory, *Journal of Small Business Management*, 38 (4), 15–27.

Germain, R. and Cooper, M. (1990) How a customer mission statement affects company performance, *Industrial Marketing Management*, 19, 47–50.

Hambrick, D. C. (1983) Some tests of the effectiveness and functional attributes of Miles and Snow's strategic types, *Academy of Management Journal*, 2 (6), 5–25.

Helms, M. M., Dibrell, C. and Wright, P. (1997) Competitive strategies and business performance: evidence from the adhesives and sealants industry, *Management Decision*, 35, 678–92.

Hitt, M. A., Hoskisson, R. E. and Kim, H. (1997) International diversification: effects on innovation and firm performance in product-diversified firms, *Academy of Management Journal*, 40 (4), 767–798.

Hodgetts, R. M. and Kuratko, D. F. (2001) *Effective Small Business Management*, 7th edn, Harcourt College Publishers, New York.

Hoskisson, R. E. (2000) Strategy in emerging economics, *Academy of Management Journal*, 43 (3), 249–268.

Hoskisson, R. E. and Hitt, M. A. (1994) *Down Scoping: How to Tame the Diversified Firm*, Oxford University Press, New York.

Hoskisson, R. E., Hitt, M. A., Wan, W. P. and Yiu, D. (1999) Theory and research in strategic management: swings of a pendulum, *Journal of Management*, 25 (3), 417–456.

Ireland, R. D. and Hitt, M. A. (1992) Mission statements: importance, challenge and recommendations for development, *Business Horizons*, 35 (3), 34–42.

Kakabadse, A. (2001) What is vision?, *Management Today*, 4–5.

Kakabadse, A. K., Kakabadse, N. K. and Myers, A. (1996) Leadership and the public sector: an internationally comparative benchmarking analysis, *Public Administration and Development*, 16 (4), 377–396.

Karami, A. (2001) Business strategy, environment analysis, and company performance: the evidence from the UK electronic industry, International Business and Economics Research Conference, October 8–12, 2001, Colorado, USA.

Karami, A. and Analoui, F. (2001) Strategy, mission statement and firm performance in small and medium sized enterprises (SME), Small Business and Enterprise Development Conference, March 29–30, University of Leicester, Leicester, UK.

Kotler, P. and Armstrong, G. (1994) *Principles of Marketing*, 6th edn, Prentice Hall Publications, New York.

Kudla, R. J. (1980) The effects of strategic planning on common stock returns, *Academy of Management Journal*, 23 (1), 5–20.

Larson, P. (1998) Strategic planning and mission statement, *Montana Business Quarterly*, 36 (3), 22–24.

Lasher, W. (1999) *Strategic Thinking for Small Businesses and Divisions*, Blackwell, Malden, MA.

Ledford, J., Wendenhof, J. and Strahley, J. (1995) Realizing a corporate philosophy, *Organisational Dynamics*, 23, 5–19.

Lowry, J. R., Avila, S. M. and Baird, T. R. (1999) Developing a niching strategy for insurance agents, *CPCU Journal*, 52 (2), 74–83.

Luffman, G., Sanderson, S., Lea, E. and Kenny, B. (1991) *Business Policy: An Analytical Introduction*, 2nd edn, Blackwell Business Publications, Oxford.

Lynch, R. (2000) *Corporate Strategy*, 2nd edn, Prentice Hall, London.

Masurel, E. (2001) Export behaviour of service sector SMEs, *International Small Business Journal*, 19 (2), 80–84.

Meyer, G. D. and Heppard, K. A. (eds) (2000) *Entrepreneurship as Strategy: Competing on the Entrepreneurial Edge*, Sage Publications, London.

Mintzberg, H. (1988) Generic strategies: toward a comprehensive framework, in R. Lamb and P. Shrivastava (eds) *Advances in Strategic Management Research Annual*, JIA Press, Greenwich, CT, 1–68.

O'Gorman, C. and Doran, R. (1999) Mission statements in small and medium sized businesses, *Journal of Small Business Management*, 37 (4), 59–66.

Ohmae, K. (1982) *The Mind of the Strategist: The Art of Japanese Business*, McGraw Hill, New York.

Pearce, J. (1982) The company mission as strategic tool, *Sloan Management Review* (Spring), 15–24.

Pearce, J. and F. David (1987) Corporate mission statements: the bottom line, *Executive*, 1, 109–116.

Pearce, J. and R. Robinson (1994) *Strategic Management: Strategy Formulation and Implementation*, 5th edn, Irwin, Boston, MA.

Peters, T. (1988) *Thriving on Chaos*, Pan, London.

Peters, T. and Waterman, R. (1982) *In Search of Excellence: Lessons from America's best-run companies*, Harper & Row, New York.

Piercy, F. and Morgan, N. (1994) Mission analysis: an operational approach, *Journal of General Management*, 19, 1–19.

Porter, M. (1980) *Competitive Strategy Techniques for Analyzing Industries and Competitors*, Free Press, New York.

Porter, M. (1985) *Competitive Advantage: Creating and Sustaining Superior Performance*, Free Press, New York.

Porter, M. (1996) What is strategy?, *Harvard Business Review*, November–December, 61–78.

Ramanujam, V. and Varadarajan, P. (1989) Research on corporate diversification: a synthesis, *Strategic Management Journal*, 10 (6), 523–551.

Rarick, C. and J. Vitton (1995) Mission statements make cents, *Journal of Business Strategy*, 16, 11–12.

Roth, B. N. and Washburn, S. A. (1999) Developing strategy, *Journal of Management Consulting*, 10 (3), 50–54.

Rumelt, R. P. (1991) How much does industry matter?, *Strategic Management Journal*, March, 167–185.

Scandura, T. A., Gitlow, H., Yau, S. C. and Greengraten-Jackson, J. (1996) Mission statements in service and industrial corporations, *International Journal of Quality Science*, 1 (1), 48–61.

Shuman, J. C. and Seeger, J. A. (1986) The theory and practice of strategic management in smaller rapid growth firms, *American Journal of Small Business*, 11 (1), 7–18.

Simpson, D. (1994) Rethinking vision and mission, *Planning Review*, 22, (5), 9–12.

Sirower, M. (1997) *The Strategy Trap: How Companies Lose the Acquisition Game?* Free Press, New York.

Smith, J. A. (1998) Strategies for start-ups, *Long Range Planning*, 31 (6), 857–872.

Thompson, J. (2001) *Strategic Management*, 4th edn, Thomson Learning, London.

Want, J. (1986) Corporate mission: the intangible contribution to performance, *Management Review*, August, 40–50.

Wheelen, T. L. and Hunger, J. D. (1998) *Strategic Management and Business Policy*, 6th edn, Addison-Wesley Publications, New York.

Wickham, P. A. (2001) *Strategic Entrepreneurship: A Decision-Making Approach to New Venture Creation and Management*, 2nd edn, Prentice Hall, London.

Wit, B. and Meyer, R. (eds) (1998) *Strategy, Process, Content, Context*, 2nd edn, Thomson Learning, London.

6 Strategic planning and developing a business plan

Learning objectives

By the end of this chapter you should be able to:

- Define the concept of planning and explain its significance for small businesses.

- Explain the process of business planning in SMEs.

- Explain different types of planning and their application in small businesses.

- Discuss the strategic planning in SMEs.

- Explore the content of an effective business plan.

- Develop a business plan for a new venture.

The main objective of this chapter is to review and discuss the strategic planning concept in SMEs. We start by defining the process of planning and go on to explore the importance of planning for small businesses. The second section of the chapter reviews the process of planning in small businesses in particular and discusses the types of the planning available to businesses. The third section reviews the theoretical background and practical application of strategic planning in SMEs. The chapter concludes with a discussion on how to provide an effective business plan for new ventures.

What is planning?

The terms plan, planning and strategic planning have become common concepts both in management literature and in our daily life (Zimmerer and Scarborough, 2002). So what is the meaning of planning and how we do define it in the context of small and medium-sized enterprises? Daft (2000) suggests that a plan is a blueprint for goal achievement and specifies actions like necessary resource allocations and tasks. In turn the word planning means determining the organisation's goals and defining the means for achieving them.

Planning is regarded as one of the most important management functions in large as well as small organisations (Bagchi-Sen and Kuechler, 2000). Every organisation and even individuals need to set a plan for their daily work. In organisation terms, however, planning has become a significant aspect of business life. Planning has been defined as the process of setting objectives and determining what should be done to accomplish them (Chell, 2001). Effective planning is good stewardship. Success in any endeavour requires careful preparation and planning. Without proper planning and adequate preparation, failure is almost guaranteed. In small businesses the owner-managers should have a clear plan and more importantly share it with the other employees. The involvement of the others will help to implement the plan more successfully.

The importance of the business plan for smaller firms

The literature strongly supports the argument that, in small business, planning is a key issue (see Figure 6.1). Planning is an emotional word for many people yet we all need to organise and plan our activities on a regular basis. This may include social, educational and business activities. It is not an exaggeration to claim that everyone uses planning, to a lesser or greater extent, to manage their daily life and the process may take formal or informal forms. The same is also true for the owners and managers of small businesses: undoubtedly they will all have plans for their businesses.

The importance of planning is partly due to the fact that it is essential to the success of a business venture. The first step to any successful venture is the preparation of the business plan. Without a doubt, careful planning will improve the business. There are many advantages associated with planning in SMEs. Chell (2001) listed five main advantages of planning in entrepreneurial firms. These are:

- Focus and flexibility: planning can help to know what business you are in, who are your customers and how you can serve them well.

- Improves performance: because planning is concerned with the best allocation and use of resources and it is result oriented.

Figure 6.1

The planning concept

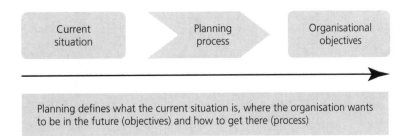

Planning defines what the current situation is, where the organisation wants to be in the future (objectives) and how to get there (process)

- Improved coordination: planning can improve the coordination between organisational divisions, by, for instance, translating strategic objectives into tactics at different levels of the organisational hierarchy.
- Improve control: planning is a powerful tool for organisational control, because it measures the achievements of the objectives.
- Time management: planning helps business owner-managers to decide what is important and how to allocate time to their commitments, so that longer term issues do not get overlooked.

It has been suggested that planning not only increases the success rate of the business but it also affects the level of performance of the firm (Rue and Ibrahim, 1996).

Although planning has many advantages for small businesses, there are also several barriers to its application for SMEs. For example, factors such as time pressure, continuing commitment or a fear of failure are but some of the reasons why managers of small businesses tend not to apply formal planning to their businesses activities (Box 6.1).

Why small and medium-sized organisations need a strategic plan

A plan for small business managers can be equated to a road map. Although much of the activities planned for will never need to actualise, preparing a plan can still help entrepreneurs to answer the three main questions: Where are we now? Where do we want to go? And how do we want to get there? Answering these three questions will help small business managers to develop their business objectives, carry out internal and external environmental appraisal, analyse the customers' needs, define the target market, develop a marketing strategy and finally determine the financial needs of the business. In this context, a strategic plan is a comprehensive plan that reflects the longer objectives and direction of the organisation (Chell, 2001). It forces SMEs' chief executive officers to develop their business plan and objectives in a systematic manner (Box 6.2).

Box 6.1 Why small business managers avoid planning

The following points highlight the reasons why some managers of small businesses tend to avoid formal planning in managing their firms:

- Fear of failure
- Time pressures
- Continuing commitment
- High costs consideration
- Lack of knowledge
- Lack of expertise.

> **Box 6.2 Significance of strategic planning in SMEs**
>
> Strategic planning is important to the long term growth and development of small high tech companies. Firms that employ strategic planning processes, whether formal or informal ones, exhibit enhanced corporate performance in relation to turnover, growth and attainment of corporate and profit objectives when compared with those companies in which no strategic planning is carried out.

In this way, after systematically developing a business plan, it can be refreshed and reviewed periodically. Strategic management is a vehicle to identify SMEs' weaknesses and strengths. As we noted in Chapter 5, without identifying the firm's weaknesses and strengths strategists cannot develop and formulate business strategies. Therefore, planning helps the strategists of SMEs to identify their strengths and competencies and create competitive advantages for their firms. Accordingly by identifying the firm's strengths and weaknesses the business owner-managers can go about formulating alternative strategies for competing with their rivals within the industry. Planning also prepares operational tools for small businesses to work with towards achieving their organisational and financial objectives. For instance, forecasting as a planning tool will enable small businesses to predict their future in terms of sales or production. Another example of a planning tool is scenario planning which involves identifying a range of possible futuristic development plans for dealing with predictable situations.

The business planning process

The process of business planning determines how business owners and managers transfer their personal objectives to business objectives and attempt to achieve them by following a logical process (Shuman and Seeger, 1986; Hatch and Zweig, 2001). Figure 6.2 illustrates a typical business planning process in SMEs.

The first step in the business planning process illustrates how owner-managers/CEOs' personal goals and objectives, along with corporate objectives, are determined through a judgement phase (Larson, 1998). Small business managers then analyse the internal and external environment of the firm to determine the business' strengths, weaknesses, opportunities and threats (SWOT) (Karami, 1999). The result of SWOT analysis will help managers to locate the business in the market and its competitors' strengths and weaknesses.

In light of the results strategists will be able to determine the firm's competencies and competitive advantages. The next step will be customer analysis which will determine the firm's target market and customer groups. The firm should then develop its marketing strategy and marketing mix accordingly (see Chapter 9 for more details).

Marketing mix shows what the business's product and/or services are. What are the pricing and promotion tactics? Where is the firm likely to operate and how does it distribute its products and services? The next step is developing an operational marketing plan and finally operational needs (Gable and Topol, 1987; Foster, 1993). As Lasher (1999) discussed the business plan is like a road map and as a tool, it shows the way from the starting point to the final destination. Thus Burns (2001) argues that the process of planning a business is just like map reading – decide on where you are, the destination you want to go

Figure 6.2

The business planning process

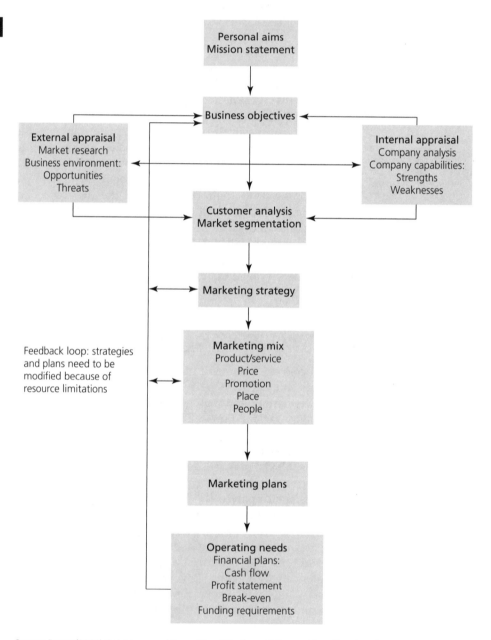

Source: Burns (2001) *Entrepreneurship and Small Business*, Palgrave Macmillan, London, p. 204. Reprinted by permission.

to; and then you can start to plan your route. The process of planning for a business attempts to provide answers to three main issues:

- Understanding where you are.
- Deciding where you want to go.
- Planning how to get there (Burns, 2001).

Types of business planning

According to Lasher (1999) there are four kinds of business planning. Small and medium sized-enterprises can adopt any of these planning tools to achieve their organisational objectives. They are:

- Strategic planning
- Operational planning
- Budgeting
- Forecasting.

As argued in Chapters 4 and 5, a strategic plan defines the action steps by which the firm intends to attain strategic goals (Daft, 2000). Lasher (1999) argued that strategic plans explain ideas and concepts and are frequently referred to as long-range plans. The application of strategic planning in small businesses will be discussed later in this chapter. Figure 6.3 compares the four types of planning.

The second form of business planning is operational planning. Operational plans are developed at the lower level of large organisations or the top level of small businesses to specify what action/steps are necessary for achieving operational goals. Normally, operational planning tends to prepare for the annual operation of the business and it tends to determine how to run the business on a

Figure 6.3

Four types of planning

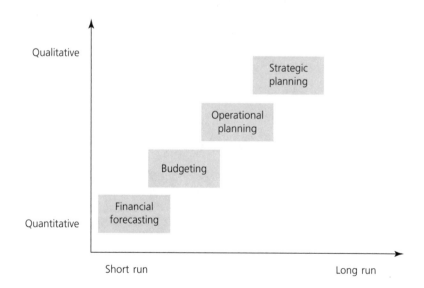

day-to-day basis. Functional objectives such as financial objectives, sales volume and annual production capacity are detailed in operational planning.

Budgeting is the third form of a business planning. A budget is a resource allocation plan that helps business performance at a functional level. A budget allocates resources for specific functions and presents standards against which action is measured (Fields, 1999). There are different budget types including revenue budgets capital budgets; and expenditure budgets (Bracker and Pearson, 1986). Budgeting is central to strategic management and planning in small businesses.

The fourth planning type is forecasting which estimates the financial results in the short run. Forecasting is more important with respect to cash flow in small businesses (Churchill and Lewis, 1983).

Now let's focus on the application of strategic planning in SMEs.

The application of strategic planning in SMEs

When we refer to long term planning in a business, we inevitably become involved in strategic planning. Strategic planning is a continuing process and one by which small business managers develop the firm's business strategies and maintain the firm's competitiveness in the market. According to Kuratko and Hodgetts (2001) strategic management in entrepreneurial firms is the formulation of long-range plans for the effective management of environmental opportunities and threats in light of a venture's strengths and weaknesses.

The application of strategic planning in small businesses is more or less limited. However the researches show (Berry, 1998; Analoui and Karami, 2002) that the SMEs' managers and executives should be involved in the process of strategic planning. One important reason for this is that usually the owner-manager of the business is seen as the ultimate strategist and decision-maker in the firm. Although many people at different levels in a business should be involved in the preparation of a business plan, only the business owner-manager/CEOs have the business perspective, the responsibility for setting the objectives, access to inputs from internal and external resources, and finally developing the business strategies of the firm (Box 6.3).

The application of strategic management in small businesses can be affected by organisational as well as environmental factors. Kuratko and Hodgetts (2001)

Box 6.3 Strategic planning in high tech firms

Recent research in the field of strategic planning in high tech firms suggests that:

Whether formal or informal strategic planning is carried out, managers should emphasise the substansive analytical elements of the process, namely: scanning the environment; analysing competitive activity; assessing strengths and weaknesses; identifying and evaluating alternative courses of action; reviewing and revising plans.

(Berry, 1998: 463)

argued that five main factors are likely to shape the strategic management activities of a growing company. These are:

- Demands on strategic managers' time
- Decision-making needs
- Issues of internal politics
- Environmental uncertainty
- Entrepreneur's vision.

Some scholars believe that in order effectively to use formal strategic management in small businesses the above issues ought to be considered carefully. While this approach has been criticised by others, by and large strategic planning models in small businesses can be grouped into two main streams of theories: rational models and intuitive learning models. Let's review the theoretical bases of both schools of thought in small businesses in some detail.

Strategic planning schools of thought in small businesses

During the last two decades many scholars have written about the importance of strategic planning in large as well as small firms. While some writers have concentrated on exploring strategic planning theory and developing a conceptual framework, others have chosen to study company planning practices and the way in which management could more effectively apply strategic planning theory. Although the interest in small business management has increased substantially and the literature available on strategic management in small businesses has also grown over the past 20 years, still much of it remains conceptual in approach. Considering the majority of works in strategic planning in small businesses, two distinct schools of thought are identifiable: rational and intuitive (Box 6.4).

The rational model of strategy considers strategy making as a formal activity. It focuses on the link between the external environment and the organisation and regards the task of achieving 'strategic fit' as an important goal for strategists (Hamel, 1996).

Box 6.4 Two models of strategy in SMEs

The rational model of strategy considers strategy making as a formal activity in the firm. It focuses on the link between the external environment and the organisation. Strategic fit is regarded an important goal for rational strategists.

The intuitive learning model of strategy focuses on the internal dimensions of the organisation such as culture, leadership and human resource policies. According to this model, formal strategic planning tends to lose its meaning over time especially in a dynamic environment, where innovation and flexibility are key conditions for survival.

Certain writers have presented the planning school of thought as being voluntary in nature, giving the impression of the presence of well-informed leaders choosing between clearly articulated alternatives. According to Hanlon and Scott (1995), the dominant perspective in relation to strategy in smaller organisations has been the rational planning model. Planning is often seen as the key to the company's success (Leidecker and Bruno, 1986; Monck *et al.* 1988). Researchers suggest that planning is contingent upon the nature of the business (Monck *et al.* 1988; Berry, 1998), skills of the owner-manager and his or her predisposition to planning, company size and stage of development/life cycle (Robinson and Pearce, 1984; Scott and Bruce, 1987). A survey by Berry (1998) of 257 companies found that small high tech firms do use strategic planning to direct their long term growth. However, it was found that the planning processes become more sophisticated as firms grow.

Other authors have questioned the value and applicability of strategic planning for small firms (Bhide, 1994). For instance, lack of financial resources and constraints on management time are seen as obstacles to strategic planning. It has been argued that strategic planning loses its meaning in a dynamic environment (Mintzberg, 1979) where innovation, flexibility and responsiveness to perishable opportunities are key conditions for survival. Carson *et al.* (1995) found that most entrepreneurs use neither formal planning nor strategy. The majority of researchers view formal planning as a necessity while acknowledging that planning in small firms tends to be different from that of large firms (Carson and Cromie, 1989). Within the rational planning school of thought, attempts have been made to identify the types of strategy associated with high growth SMEs (Covin, 1991; Smallbone *et al.* 1995). The empirical studies which do exist have been criticised on the grounds that they lack academic rigour and do not illuminate the perceived relationship between formal strategic management processes and organisational performance (Shrader *et al.* 1989).

The second model of strategic planning in small businesses is the intuitive learning model. McCarthy and Leavy's recent work (2000) is best placed in the discussion of the intuitive learning model of strategy. They have compared the rational planning and intuitive learning models of strategy (see Table 6.1).

Several writers have taken us well beyond the normative and rational planning models that have dominated the strategic management field for so

Table 6.1	*The rational planning model*	*The intuitive learning model*
A comparison between rational planning and intuitive learning models	Formal	Either formal or deliberate and/or emergent
	Focus on the external environment	Focus on the internal environment
	Linear model of strategy formulation	Non-linear model of strategy formulation
	Decision-making: hierarchical, top-down	Decision-making: top-down and bottom-up
	Rational	Rational and emotional
	Adaptive	Inventive
	Voluntarism	Neither overly voluntaristic nor overly determinist

Source: McCarthy and Leavy (2000).

long. Distinguished authors (Mintzberg and Waters, 1982; Mintzberg, 1987) have regarded strategy not so much as the outcome of point-in-time planning exercises but more as a pattern in a stream of decisions made over time. In the small firm literature, several researchers have started to focus on the internal dimensions of the firm (Hanlon and Scott, 1995; Meyer and Heppard, 2000). A study by Hanlon and Scott (1995) found that entrepreneurs were able to persuade others to 'buy into' their dream or vision which shaped the development of the firm.

Another study by Bouwen and Steyaert (1990), located in the resource-based school of thought, found that the values and core competencies of the firms tend to change in the growth phase. Not surprisingly, research in the small firm literature focuses on the personal characteristics of the founder; the entrepreneur is seen to have a crucial impact on company strategy, culture and performance of the firm (Kets de Vries, 1996). The authors further argue that entrepreneurs are rarely strategists acting according to rational principles. Instead they are more likely to act on the basis of instinct, a master plan or a vision and impulse. Thompson (1999), however, argues that entrepreneurs possess the qualities of successful strategic leaders; they go about systematically assessing opportunities and threats in the environment and adopt strategic positions. Several writers have highlighted the need for further research on how strategies are actually formed in small firms (Hanlon and Scott, 1995; Hendry *et al.* 1995; Boussouara and Deakins, 1999). For instance, Boussouara and Deakins (1999: 207) argue that in the high technology context, the formulation of marketing strategies and the learning process are not understood in the literature.

In recent years, the organisational learning concept has emerged as a strong theme in the small firm literature (Hendry *et al.* 1995; Boussouara and Deakins, 1999; Chaston *et al.* 1999). It is assumed that learning, which underpins diverse activities such as new product development, productivity, customer service, management styles and the like, is itself associated with firm performance. Not all studies can provide a set of clear statistically significant relationships between learning and performance (Chaston *et al.* 1999). Hendry *et al.* (1995) highlighted how organisational learning is often stimulated by crisis, although it has negative connotations for managers.

In summary, the treatment of strategy in the small business literature has lagged behind that of the mainstream strategic management literature. The majority of studies have been normative in orientation and firmly located in the rational planning school of thought. Recent studies suggest that an optimal strategy for all firms in a given context does not exist, due to variations in learning, culture, personalities, experiences and goals of actors within the firms.

The formality of strategic planning in SMEs

The majority of the empirical studies within strategic management in SMEs expound the benefits of strategic planning and stress the associated improved organisational performance (Aram and Cowan, 1990; Helms *et al.* 1997; Smith, 1998; Hoskisson *et al.* 1999; Beal, 2000). In contrast, a few studies tend to place emphasis on the use of informal planning in SMEs. Shuman *et al.* (1985) found from their empirical investigations examining 500 of the fastest growing privately owned SMEs in the United States that 95 per cent of firms without a formal and written business plan were operating at a profit in comparison to 84 per cent with a formal business plan. They reported the main findings of the research on strategic planning in SMEs management as follows:

- While the majority of firms did not have a formal business plan when they started, relying instead on personal experience and intuition, they adopted some form of planning once the company was in operation.
- As the companies have grown, the planning processes utilised have become more formal, structured and participatory, to ensure continued organisational effectiveness.
- The majority of the CEOs preferred an active and strong involvement in their companies' strategic planning, rather than delegating that responsibility to other members of management.
- Most CEOs felt that improved time efficiency, company growth and a better understanding of the market would be achieved through planning.
- The strategic planning activity tended to be primarily concerned with the short term, updated regularly, and operationally oriented.
- The absence of perceived benefits accruing to the company from planning endeavours negatively influenced the CEOs attitude toward planning in general, and the nature and extent of planning utilised in the future.
- Smaller company strategic planning is still in its formative period and its development will continue as more practical experience is acquired (Shuman *et al.* 1985: 49).

They also concluded that the higher the CEO in charge ranks planning as their prime responsibility, the higher their contribution to the enterprises. In contrast, during the 1990s we have witnessed a variety of empirical studies that have reported the benefits of engaging in strategic planning. Jenster and Overstreet (1990) focused on the formal planning of US credit unions. They observed from their study of 283 institutions that the propensity to plan is related to key organisational processes, structural configurations, administrative procedures, managerial perceptions of environmental predictability and multiple performance measures. One year later, Boyd (1991) published a long and detailed meta-analytic review, which involved the aggregation of 29 samples on a total of 2496 SMEs. Boyd concluded that the results of previous research were equivocal. He pointed out that existing research was subject to numerous measurement errors, which resulted in underestimation of the benefits of planning.

Second, although the average effect size was small, many firms do not report significant, quantifiable benefits from participating in the strategic planning process. During the rest of the 1990s, researchers have continued to investigate the benefits of planning (Lyles *et al.* 1993; Walters, 1993; Miller and Cardinal, 1994; Berry, 1998; Smith, 1998). In addition to formal planning having differing roles among various types of organisation, communication between management and board was seen as important for enhanced organisational performance. Lyles *et al.* (1993), in their study of 188 mixed firms, found that the planners' growth rate was twice that of the non-planners. In his study of 141 US exporting firms, Walters (1993) noted that a majority of firms were missing critical elements of formal planning. Despite not finding any statistical difference between planners and non-planners, he noted that those firms with the poorest sales growth planned the least. Miller and Cardinal (1994), using meta-analysis, found that strategic planning positively influences firm performance and that the method of study was primarily responsible for the inconsistencies reported in the literature.

Smith (1998), supporting this view in her study of 150 SMEs in the UK, concluded that to achieve and sustain a competitive advantage the SME should follow a number of formal measures which can be incorporated into its strategic planning processes. She suggested that strategic planning, as defined in business strategy literature, whilst relating primarily to large organisations can also be applied effectively to the new micro firm. She concluded that those small firms which use strategic planning in an effective manner will perform better, sometimes very much better, than those small firms which leave things to chance and deal with problems as they occur, on a reactive, rather than a proactive, basis (Smith, 1998: 869) (Box 6.5).

Simultaneously, Berry (1998) investigated the importance of strategic planning in small high tech companies in the UK. Her study focused upon the population of 487 small high tech firms identified from a database compiled by the UK Science Park Association. Berry (1998) reported that a significant correlation was found to exist between the perceived importance of business strategy formulation, accompanying planning formality and company size. Supporting the previous researches Analoui and Karami (2002) studied the strategy formulation in British SMEs. They examined formulation of strategies in SMEs by direct reference to the firm's mission statement, objectives and strategies. They found that mission, business objectives and functional strategies such as marketing strategy can be embodied in a business plan. Moreover, they argued that the majority of the SMEs studied (87 per cent) had a formal and written business plan (Figure 6.4).

In contrast only 13 per cent of the studied firms reported the lack of a formal business plan. Accordingly the research revealed a significant relationship

---

Box 6.5 Effective strategic planning in small businesses

Smith (1998) in her research on strategic planning in small businesses in Scotland found that using strategic management in an effective manner tended to increase the performance of the small business. She concluded that:

Of course, many businesses are run on a 'wing and a prayer'. Indeed, some business owners appear to prefer this course of action . . . those small firms which use strategic planning in an effective manner will perform better, sometimes very much better, than those small firms which leave things to chance and deal with problems as they occur, on a reactive, rather than a proactive, basis.

(Smith, 1998: 869)

between firm size and use of strategic planning. In other words, as the small businesses grow they become more involved in undertaking strategic planning activities. We will discuss the nature of strategic planning in small businesses in more detail in the next section.

The nature of strategic planning in SMEs

Strategy, its formulation or creation and implementation are recognised as key aspects of the management of large organisations (Ansoff, 1984). Small and medium-sized enterprises are urged to perform business and strategic planning for their survival (Ward, 1988; Bridge and Peel, 1999; Chan and Foster, 2001). However, most research on SMEs business planning tends to focus on succession planning rather than on business or strategic planning (Handler 1994; Upton and Heck 1997). The question which has been raised is that whether or not the CEOs in the studied firms have employed a strategic planning process. If so, what is the nature of such a strategic planning activity in SMEs?

Some authors are sceptical about the possibility of the existence of a clearly visible strategic planning process in many small business settings (Curran, 1996). In practice, some small businessmen may simply keep doing what they have done, assuming that market conditions will continue much as before and hope for the best. The sceptics may see this and interpret it as an absence of strategy (Shuman and Seeger, 1986; Shrader, Mulford and Blackburn, 1989; Rue and Ibrahim, 1996). Despite some research into the relative success of pursuing active policies of formal strategic planning or strategy formulation (Armstrong, 1982) there has been relatively little concern for the situations in which small businesses find themselves. Available research suggests that while SMEs should perform strategic and business planning, most tend to ignore this (Brown 1995; Rue and Ibrahim 1996). In a survey of 3033 small businesses (Anderson and Mutal, 1997) it has been discovered that 69 per cent of small businesses had no written strategic plan.

Analoui and Karami (2002) found in their recent research that the majority (83 per cent) of studied firms employed planning activities. As expected, the nature of employed planning activities varies from basic financial planning to formal strategic planning activities. This result supports the findings of Rue and Ibrahim (1996) who noted that SMEs are normally engaged in more planning than previously thought, with over half of their sample reporting written long-range plans, and 97 per cent reporting some specific plans related to their

Figure 6.4

Developing a business plan in SMEs

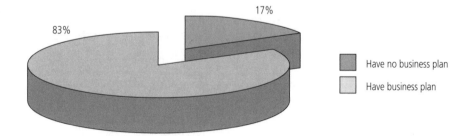

83%   17%

Have no business plan

Have business plan

growth. Ward (1998) also concludes that SMEs may not plan if the founder is preoccupied with a previously successful strategy. As well as the above studies, the findings of Analoui and Karami (2002) indicate the presence of a pattern very similar to the findings of Berry (1998) who reported that successful SMEs do employ strategic planning and run their business strategically.

Goodwin and Hodgett (1991) concluded that strategic planning brings major benefits to the companies that use it. However, many medium-sized companies confuse it with long term budgeting and miss out on its benefits. Their study examining the planning practices of 300 medium-sized companies in Australia revealed that over 86 per cent of all companies involved in the study prepare and use a strategic plan for their business. Analoui and Karami (2002) attempted to identify the type of planning activities and planning characteristics employed by SMEs. They categorised SMEs in terms of employing strategic planning into four categories (Table 6.2) as follows:

- No planning at all
- Financial planning alone
- Combined formal financial and informal strategic planning
- Formal strategic planning.

The first group of SMEs includes those firms which do not employ either formal or informal planning activities. In these firms, no planning activities were reported at all. Accordingly, no mission or objectives, either short or long term, are developed. In the second category, we see the SMEs which employ only financial planning. In this group, respondents rated formal financial planning as one of the essential activities which they undertake. CEOs stress the importance of tight financial controls and performance. It has also been found that these firms tend to develop short (up to one year) to medium-term (up to two years) financial objectives.

The firms in the second group were not engaged in strategic planning of any sort, however, they were involved in developing short-run forecasting plans as well as a quarterly budgeting exercise. The third group includes those involved in both formal financial and informal strategic planning. Respondents in this group firmly believed in the importance of informal strategic planning. However, they placed a great deal of emphasis on the monitoring and tight control on the financial planning and performance of the firm. It was revealed that these firms possess a mission statement and long term financial objectives specified over a two- to five-year planning horizon. In this group of the studied firms, mission statement, objectives and business strategies are not formalised in a business plan but clearly they are communicated and are known by all staff throughout the firm.

Finally, the fourth group of firms can be categorised as those concerned with formal strategic plans. In this group, management stressed the importance of a formal and explicit strategy formulation process, written mission statement and establishment of long term objectives over a two- to five-year planning horizon. Formal and written strategic plans were produced and reviewed on a six monthly or annual basis. In these firms, the developed formal strategic business plans are reflecting the management perception that significant benefit for the company will arise from this practice.

Table 6.2	Planning level	Characteristics
Planning levels and characteristics of the studied firms	Non-planning (17%)	Planning characteristics No mission statement No long term objectives Stress on short term objectives No formal or informal business plan Firm size Less than 10 employees Top management Not experienced but technically qualified
	Financial planning (21%)	Planning characteristics Emphasis on short to medium term 1 up to 2 years' financial objectives Stress on financial controls Strategic planning is not important Review the financial performance every one to three months Firm size Less than 100 employees Top management May have some experience but technically qualified, some managers have undergone management training
	Formal financial and informal strategic planning (38%)	Planning characteristics Emphasis on long term (2 to 5 years) financial objectives Stress on importance of strategic planning Informal mission statement Informal strategic objectives Firm size 100 to 200 employees Top management Have previous general management experience, technically qualified, have had management training
	Formal strategic planning (32%)	Planning characteristics Emphasis on long term objectives in relation to products or markets Written mission statement Stress on importance of formal strategic planning Reviewing strategic plans every six months or one year Firm size 200 to 499 employees Top management Have wide range of previous general management experience, multidisciplinary – marketing, technology, financial, strategic – management team

Developing a business plan

Entrepreneurs and small business managers setting up a new business need a business plan. A business plan allows entrepreneurs to crystallise their business ideas. It helps owner-managers to set business objectives and determine how to achieve them. In order to implement strategic plans in SMEs, it is necessary to operationalise them. In other words, there is a need and necessity to develop all of the necessary tactics such as marketing, pricing, technology development and budget, which will put the firm's overall strategic plan into action. All of these are put together in a document which is commonly referred to as the 'business plan'. There are many sources of help for developing a good business plan. Box 6.6 illustrates some of the Internet resources available for developing a business plan.

Let's first see what the characteristics of a successful business plan are and then study its content.

Characteristics of a successful business plan

As argued earlier, a business plan is a written summary statement of an entrepreneur's proposed business venture, its marketing strategy as well as operational and financial details. Zimmerer and Scarborough (2002) argued that a business plan serves two essential functions: first, it guides the firm's operations by charting its future courses and devising a strategy for following it; second, it attracts investors. A well-assembled business plan helps prove to outsiders that a business idea can be successful. An effective business plan helps entrepreneurs to avoid making business mistakes such as not developing a marketing plan, not knowing about the firm's customers, ignoring its cash position, ignoring employees, having no sales plan and finally giving up. Although there is not a single pattern for a business plan, successful business plans might have the following characteristics:

- Provides a good first impression of the business
- Demonstrates the enthusiasm of the entrepreneur about the venture

---

Box 6.6 Useful sources for developing a business plan

Some of the selected governmental and private web pages which provide information for developing a business plan include:
http://www.sbs.gov.uk/
http://www.business-plans.co.uk/
http://www.bbsrc.ac.uk/business/skills/plan/Welcome.html
http://www.smallbusiness.co.uk/
http://planmagic.com/
http://www.smallbusinessadvice.org.uk/sbas.asp
http://www.small-business-finder.co.uk/
http://www.uksmallbusinessdirectory.co.uk/

- Shows clearly who the firm's customers are
- Provides a clear, comprehensive evaluation of the risks and opportunities of the venture
- Presents information in an organised, concentrated format using visual aids
- Presents understandable technical information
- Uses a consistent style for ease in reading
- Outlines management experience and competence showing gaps that may need to be filled in.

Components of an effective business plan

What should a business plan cover? How we can create a perfect business plan and what should it look like? On the whole, there is no single format for a business plan – each would be particular to its business and will differ from other firms' plans. For instance, a business plan for a firm in the manufacturing industry will be different from that used in the insurance industry. Even a plan for the insurance industry in one part of the country may look different from a business plan developed for the same industry but in another part of the country.

However, there are essential points that ought to be observed when developing a typical business plan. Lasher (1999) argues that there is a great deal of difference in the substance of plans for different companies but a standard business plan may contain eight chapters: contents, executive summary, mission and strategy, market analysis, operations, management and personnel, financial projections and contingencies. Burns (2001), on the other hand, believes that a typical business plan should cover the following eleven areas:

- Business details
- Business goals and objectives
- Market information
- Strengths and weaknesses as well as competitive advantages
- Customers
- Marketing strategy
- Premises and equipment needs
- Key people and their functions and backgrounds
- Financial highlights – turnover, profit, break-even and so on
- Detailed profit forecasts
- Detailed monthly cash flow forecast.

This typical business plan could be suitable for small-scale start-up, however in the case of a larger undertaking there is a need to develop a business plan which contains a detailed forecast for at least three years. Recently, small businesses, by becoming involved in e-commerce and using Internet facilities for advertising and selling their products and services, have felt the need to use a dynamic format for their business plan. In this section we will outline a typical business plan for small businesses which may also be beneficial to the CEOs of firms involved in e-commerce. Let's discuss each section in some detail.

Coversheet

Preferably, the business plan should have a coversheet detailing the general information of the business. The key points included could be:

- Name of the firm
- Firm's address
- Name of contact person or owner-manager
- Contact phone and fax number
- Website and email address
- Logo
- Date of plan.

Table of contents

The table of contents is an outline of the entire document. This will guide the readers to their areas of interest as well as highlighted the organised nature of the plan.

Executive summary

The executive summary is an important section of the business plan and typically contains a summary of the main points of the business. It would normally provide the objectives and description of the business in an easy and coherent form. Bear in mind that the executive summary will be the deciding factor as to whether or not the investors continue to read the rest of the document. This section of the business plan should be prepared carefully and written in an interesting way with emphasis on the more important aspects of the plan. A typical effective executive summary should include the following key points:

- Brief description of the company
- Mission statement
- Business activities
- Management team and their capabilities
- Scope and potential market segment
- Competitive advantage and competitors
- Technical innovations
- Revenue and costs
- Resources needed, especially the financial needs of the business.

Introduction

The introduction explains the basic aspects of the business and provides an overview of the plan and vision of the firm. It also provides a brief history of the firm where applicable and will include specific information concerning the nature of the industry in which the firm wishes to operate. In the introduction, the nature and range of the product or services should be explained in some detail and the unique features, qualities and value to the consumers should be highlighted.

Market analysis

The market analysis or industry analysis provides a summary of any political, economical, social, or technological issues in general and the industry environment of the business in particular that will influence the firm. Some specific factors such as the target market, market size and potential customers should be also identified. It is, therefore, important to include the following points in this section:

- Growth trend of the industry
- Industry business life cycle and profitability
- PEST analysis
- Market value and structure
- Market size and location
- Key customers and their expectations
- Key success factors in the industry.

Competitive analysis and the marketing plan

The aim of the competitive analysis is to identify the competitors' strengths, weaknesses, opportunities and threats (SWOT analysis) and explain how your business will be better and more successful than your competitors. Marketing strategies such as pricing and advertising should be outlined in this part of the document. The main points which should be included are:

- Strengths
- Weaknesses
- Opportunities
- Threats
- Market segmentation for business-to-consumers (B to C)
  Business-to-business (B to B) or peer-to-peer (P to P)
- Description of the product
- Competitive advantages
- Pricing strategy
- Description of the distribution channel
- Advertising strategies.

Management and key people

In this chapter you should determine who will manage the business and what the capabilities and qualifications of the management team are. The management section is particularly important to the investors, because they are eager to know whether or not the management team is capable of running a high growth/high performance business. The significance of having consultants and high calibre employees ought not to be underestimated as these resources will undoubtedly be seen as significant factors for the increased success rate of any business. The main points in this part are:

- A comprehensive organisational chart
- Management team and their job descriptions
- Background of the management team
- Management team competencies and qualifications
- Key human resources such as consultants and specialists
- The legal form of ownership to be used and why
- List of licences and permits needed.

Technology, R & D and innovation

This part of the business plan is more important for the kind of businesses which operate in manufacturing as opposed to a service industry. The operation of a retail store is very different from a manufacturing firm. This part of the document, therefore, should include research and development leading to the product design, the type of production technology employed and innovative practices undertaken when developing the product(s). Attention ought to be paid to the major activities of the business operations such as machinery, raw materials suppliers, delivery time, quality control and production cost. Some of the main points which should be included are:

- Technology
- Product design
- Protection of intellectual property
- Business functions
- Location of the business and facility needs
- Production management
- Machinery
- Raw materials
- Costs of production and delivery
- Quality control.

Critical risks

The aim of this chapter is to identify margins of error from your assumptions. The critical risks should be identified and calculated. The business plan should consider the potential problems and obstacles of the business, identifying the potential risks and preparing proper scenarios to reduce the effects of those risks on the business and the allowing investors to judge how realistic your business plans are. This will provide a better assessment of the potential risks for the investment. The most crucial point here is to demonstrate that potential risks can be anticipated and controlled effectively.

Financial forecasting and management control

Financial forecasting and planning assists with the evaluation of whether or not the proposed business concept will be profitable and, more importantly, whether it can be financed adequately. Of course, one can seek assistance from outside consultants and accountants to prepare a comprehensive financial plan. The information can be summarised into pro forma financial statements, such as profit and loss account and cash flows. In this part of the document following points should be highlighted:

- Sales
- Cash flow (monthly and yearly totals)
- Break-even analysis for the first three years of operation
- Income statement
- Balance sheets
- Profit and loss statements
- Determination of financing needs
- Repayment of investors.

Implementation schedule

This section of the business plan determines the objectives and the expected timing of their accomplishment. Investors are very much concerned with the envisioning of the development of the business. The business planners' vision of the future for their firm and how they intend to get there will be a significant selling point. Therefore, it is of the utmost importance clearly to establish the milestones and deadlines. The implementation schedule will help the management to have access to a simple tool for tracking the progress based on established milestones and the expected time of accomplishment. Some business management tools such as programme evaluation review technique (PERT), critical path method (CPM) and Gantt charts can be effectively used to develop an implementation schedule for business plans. The implementation schedule therefore should include the following:

- Major milestones
- Timing for the business plan
- Deadlines for each stage of the business plan
- Critical activities.

Appendices

A lengthy business plan is not likely to be effective. However, there is some vital information that cannot be included in the main body of the document. This information, which is of a supplementary nature, such as drawings, detailed organisational charts, agreements, calculations, patents, CVs and other relevant company information, should be included in relevant appendices. This will provide the potential investors with a choice and opportunity to learn about the business should they wish to do so.

Summary

- Planning is one of the most important management duties in large as well as small organisations. The word planning means determining the organisation's goals and defining the means for achieving them. The importance of planning is essential to the success of small and medium-sized enterprises. The first step to any successful venture is the business plan. Planning not only increases the success rate of the business, it also affects the level of performance of the firm. Although planning has many advantages for small businesses, there are also several barriers in the application of planning for SMEs. For example, factors such as time pressures, continuing commitment and fear of failure are some of the reasons why small business managers hesitate to apply planning to their business.

- A strategic plan is comprehensive in nature. It reflects the longer objectives and direction of the organisation. It attempts to provide answers to three main questions: Where we are now? Where do we want to go? How do we wish to get there? Answering these three questions will assist the small business managers to develop business objectives, carry out internal and external environmental appraisal, analyse the customers' needs and define their target market, develop marketing strategy and finally determine the financial needs for the business. Therefore, it would be appropriate to claim that planning will normally help SMEs with the identification of their strengths and competencies, thus enabling them to create competitive advantages for the firm.

- The process of business planning determines how business owners and/or managers can transfer their personal objectives into business ones and go about achieving them systematically. The first step in the process of business planning is developing business objectives in light of the owner-managers/ CEOs' personal goals. The second step involves identification of the firm's strengths and weaknesses, opportunities and threats (SWOT analysis) to determine the firm's competencies and competitive advantages. The third step will be concerned with customer analysis which will lead to determining the firm's target market and customer groups. Then, accordingly, the firm should develop its marketing strategy and marketing mix. The fourth and last step is developing an operational marketing plan and finalising operational needs. There are four kinds of business planning in SMEs: strategic planning, operational planning, budgeting and forecasting.

- Strategic planning in entrepreneurial firms is concerned with the formulation of long-range plans for the effective management of environmental opportunities and threats in light of a venture's strengths and weaknesses. Application of strategic planning in small businesses is more or less limited. The application of strategic management in small businesses can be affected by organisational as well as environmental factors such as demands on strategists' time, decision-making needs, issues of internal politics, environmental uncertainty and the entrepreneur's vision.

- The majority of the empirical studies within strategic management in SMEs expound the benefits of strategic planning and the associated improved organisational performance which follows. The majority of SMEs have a formal (written) or unwritten business plan. Those small firms that use strategic planning in an effective manner perform better than those small firms who do not employ strategic planning tools. Strategic planning positively influences firm performance – as the small businesses grow they become more involved in strategic planning activities.

- Based on recent practical research SMEs, in terms of employing planning tools and planning characteristics, can be grouped into four categories. The first group of SMEs includes the firms which are not involved in either formal or informal planning activities. The second group is those firms only concerned with planning activities of a financial nature. The third group includes firms with planners concerned with formal financial and informal strategic plans. Finally, the fourth group of firms can be categorised as formal strategic planners. In this group management stress the need and importance of being engaged in the process of formal and explicit strategy formulation, written mission statement and having a long term objectives (over two to five years) planning horizon.

- Entrepreneurs and small business managers in setting up a new business need a comprehensive business plan which allows entrepreneurs to crystallise their business idea. An effective business plan describes clearly who the firm's customers are, the objectives and strategies of the venture and the management experience and credentials. An effective business plan should cover the main objectives and strategies of the venture. It should contain 12 sections including coversheet, table of contents, executive summary, introduction, market analysis, competitive analysis and marketing plan, management and key people, technology, R & D and innovation, critical risks, financial forecasting and management control, implementation schedule and finally appendices.

Discussion questions

1. What is a plan and how do you define the process of planning in SMEs?
2. Why do some small businesses avoid planning?
3. Explain the process of business planning in SMEs.
4. Discuss the four types of business planning in small businesses.
5. Why is strategic planning important for small businesses? Discuss the results of some empirical studies in the small business sector.
6. Compare the rational model with intuitive learning model of strategic planning in SMEs. Discuss the applications.
7. Discuss the characteristics of SMEs in terms of their involvement in planning.

8. What are the major advantages of a small business plan?
9. What is contained in the executive summary section of a small business plan?
10. What are the main parts of a typical business plan? How would a business plan for a small manufacturing firm differ from one for a small retailing firm?

Case study *Electronic Commerce Software (ECS) Ltd*

Electronic Commerce Software (ECS) Ltd
Business plan for start-up
October, 2003

Business Name and Address:
Registered Business Address:
Tel:
Fax:
Email:
Website:

1. Executive summary

This business plan outlines and highlights the objectives and strategies of Electronic Commerce Software (ECS) Ltd, for sales of office software to small and medium-sized companies. Electronic Commerce Software (ECS) will act as the main direct provider of office software in the northern region. We expect a high degree of profitability based on our marketing plan to key businesses in the area. Our management expertise in dealing with corporate decision-makers and our partner's reputation will be the cornerstone of our success.

Mission

Electronic Commerce Software (ECS) has been acting as the main office software distributor in the northern region within last three years, customising the client's individual needs. Although we recognise the intimate relationship between profitability and quality products, we are aware that our success is ultimately dependent on the well-being of our employees.

Objectives

- Market an office software package to small business managers and achieve £160 000 financial target in the first year.
- Earning profit of over £50 000 a year.
- Customise the software to the individual needs of each customer and provide training and after sales service to each customer.

Keys to success

The success of our company is dependent on our ability to:

- Anticipate clients needs.
- Adapt office software to these needs.
- Identify industries/corporations that need planning tools.

2. Introduction

Electronic Commerce Software (ECS) will be located in a home-based office in the Manchester region. This location is ideal, as it is close to the first potential customers' home

▶

offices. Electronic Commerce Software (ECS) will identify companies' software needs and work to address these needs. We guarantee the customer the right office software.

Products and services

Electronic Commerce Software (ECS) will provide small and medium-sized companies with office software solutions. We also will provide complete training for the use of solutions purchased from us.

2.1 Product and service description

Software

Electronic Commerce Software (ECS) software products consist of an office software package with proven quality in the consumer market. In fact, this product is described by *Daily Business* as the top-rated and best-selling small business office package to date. The enterprise version will be similar to the consumer version, however, it will be modified to fit the needs of different clients.

Consulting

Electronic Commerce Software (ECS) will perform as a consultant for all potential clients' degree of involvement in information technology. The goal of this consulting service is to ensure that all clients receive a solution that best fits their needs and capabilities. Whether they decide to purchase the product or not they will have an expert analysis of their information technology needs.

Training

Electronic Commerce Software (ECS) will provide further value to our customers, and ease the customer service burden on our partner, by ensuring that all product users are properly trained in the use of all software solutions.

Technology

The software package runs on Windows 95, 98, 2000, Windows NT and Macintosh platforms.

3. Market analysis

Competitive edge

Our greatest strength and competitive edge is the reputation and success of the desktop software product. This product is the market leader in sales and consumer ratings. Our success will rely upon building on those strengths. We will also rely on our experience of working with decision-makers at the corporate level.

Market trends

The most significant trend affecting our company is the growth of business-to-business e-commerce. More and more, firms recognise the need to take advantage of the exchange of information over the Internet and our products and services rely on this. The fastest growing segment of the e-commerce industry is the business-to-business sector.

Main competitors

There are currently several companies that provide office software for desktop applications. Additional competitors are companies which provide word processing, spreadsheet and collaborative planning software.

4. Competitive analysis and the marketing plan

We will operate in the business-to-business (B2B) as well as business-to-consumer (B2C) segment of e-commerce. In other words, our market is further segmented into small and medium-sized enterprises as well as home-based small business and individuals. Our product will allow the customers to make better and faster business decisions and receive quicker feedback from their end-customer.

Marketing strategy

We will first target the small businesses in retailing in the northern region and then expand our target market to small and medium-sized manufacturing enterprises in the next six months. We will attempt to establish a face-to-face meeting with SME managers (CFO, CIO, COO) where we will present a proposal tailored to their needs. If possible, we will also have this proposal reside on an extranet so that the client can modify the proposal and see first hand how the product and service work.

Pricing strategy

We will adapt a penetrating pricing strategy in the first year. However, in the second year we will slightly increase prices to cover the sale costs and achieve our profit objectives.

Advertising and promotion strategy

We will follow these tactics for advertising and promotion strategy:

- Personal contacts, with the individual and targeted small businesses as appropriate
- Advertising in local papers
- Develop our own website to advertise and introduce our products and services.
- Advertise on TV.

5. Management team and key people

David Yong has a BSc in computer science from the University of Leeds and an MBA in marketing and e-commerce from the University of Bradford. He has designed numerous successful business plans for companies in the manufacturing, e-commerce and entertainment sectors. David's work experiences are as follows:

- 5 years as senior consultant in the areas of business strategy, marketing and electronic commerce in both public and private sectors
- 2 years as business development manager
- 5 years as IT manager in manufacturing firms.

He consults with e-commerce and manufacturing companies in marketing strategies. He has travelled to different countries in Africa, Asia and South America and speaks French and Spanish fluently.

6. Financial forecasting

A balance sheet is a result of key assumptions and estimated sales/cash flows.

The key financial assumptions and statements including projected cash flow (Table 6.3), profit and loss accounts (Table 6.4) and balance sheet (Table 6.5) are as follows:

Table 6.3 Electronic Commerce Software (ECS) Ltd pro forma cash flow statement 2004/05

	May	June	July	Aug	Sept	Oct	Nov	Dec	Jan	Feb	Mar	Apr	Year end
Receipts													
Capital input	40 000						20 000						60 000
Sales			5000	8000	8000	15 000	20 000	20 000	15 000	16 000	7000	6000	120 000
Other													
Total	**40 000**		**5000**	**8000**	**8000**	**15 000**	**40 000**	**20 000**	**15 000**	**16 000**	**7000**	**6000**	**180 000**
Payments													
Direct costs of sale			1000	800	1100	1000	1300	2000	1200	950	300	350	10 000
Advertising	1400	1200	1200	1100	1350	1300	1600	1400	1300	1250	900	500	14 500
Salaries/wages	5800	5800	5800	5800	5800	5800	6200	5800	5800	5800	5800	5800	70 000
Travel	400		200	300	700	500	300	650	400	350	350	250	4000
Rent	400	400	400	400	400	400	400	400	400	400	400	600	5000
Insurance	200	110	110	110	110	110	110	110	110	110	105	105	1400
Heat/light/power	80	80	80	80	80	80	80	80	80	80	80	120	1000
Miscellaneous	200		50	100	100		350	75		100	50	75	1000
Total	***8080**	***7590**	***8840**	***8590**	***9640**	***9190**	***10 340**	***10 515**	***9290**	***9040**	***7885**	***7900**	***106 900**
Balance	31 920	(7590)	(3840)	(590)	(1640)	5810	29 660	9485	5710	6960	(885)	(1900)	73 100

*Balance denotes the difference between receipts and payments in each month.

Table 6.4	Sale	160 000		
	Direct costs of sale	(10 000)		
Electronic Commerce Software (ECS) Ltd pro forma profit and loss, April 2004	**Gross margin**		**150 000**	
	Gross margin (%)		93.75	
	Operational expenses			
	Advertising	14 500		
	Payroll expenses	70 000		
	Travel	4000		
	Rent	5000		
	Insurance	1400		
	Heat/light/power	1000		
	Miscellaneous	1000		
	Total operational expenses		**(96 900)**	
	Profit before interest and taxes		**53 100**	
	Taxes		(13 275)	
	Net profit			**39 825**
	Net profit/sale (%)			24.89

Table 6.5	**Assets**			
	Short term assets			
Electronic Commerce Software (ECS) Ltd pro forma balance sheet, April 2004	Cash	73 000		
	Accounts receivable	40 000		
			113 000	
	Total short term assets			
	Long term assets			
	Inventory	27 000		
	Office equipments	32 900		
	Total long term assets		59 900	
	Total assets			**173 000**
	Liabilities and capital			
	Accounts payable	5000		
	Current borrowing	8900		
	Long term liabilities	20 000		
	Total liabilities		33 000	
	Capital		139 000	
	Total liabilities and capital			**173 000**

References

Analoui, F. and Karami, A. (2002) CEOS and development of the meaningful mission statement, *Corporate Governance The International Journal of Effective Board Performance*, 2 (3), 13–21.

Anderson, A. and Mutal, A. (1997) *American Family Business Survey*, Family Business Centre, Houston, TX.

Ansoff, H. I. (1984) *Implanting Strategic Management*, Prentice Hall, Englewood Cliffs, NJ.

Aram, D. J. and Cowan, S. S. (1990) Strategic planning for increased profit in the small businesses, *Long Range Planning*, 23 (6), 63–70.

Armstong, J. S. (1982) The value of formal planning for strategic decisions, *Strategic Management Journal*, 1, (3), 100–111.

Bagchi-Sen, S. and Kuechler, L. (2000) Strategic and functional orientation of small and medium sized enterprises in professional services: an analysis of public accountancy, *The Service Industries Journal*, 20 (3), 117–146.

Beal, R. M. (2000) Competing effectively: environmental scanning, competitive strategy, and organisational performance in small manufacturing firms, *Journal of Small Business Management*, 38 (1), 27–47.

Berry, M. (1998) Strategic planning in small high tech companies, *Long Range Planning*, 31 (3), 455–466.

Bhide, A. (1994) How entrepreneurs craft strategies that work, *Harvard Business Review*, March/April, 150–161.

Boussouara, M. and Deakins, D. (1999) Market-based learning, entrepreneurship, and the high technology firm, *International Journal of Entrepreneurial Behaviour and Research*, 5 (4), 204–223.

Bouwen, R. and Steyaert, C. (1990) Constructing organisational texture in young entrepreneurial firms, *Journal of Management Studies*, 27 (6), 637–649.

Boyd, B. K. (1991) Strategic planning and financial performance: a meta-analytic review, *Journal of Management Studies*, 28, 353–374.

Bracker, J. and J. Pearson (1986) Planning and financial performance of small, mature firms, *Strategic Management Journal*, 7, 503–22.

Bridge, J. and Peel, M. J. (1999) Research note: a study of computer usage and strategic planning in the SME sector, *International Small Business Journal*, 17 (4), 82–87.

Brown, R. (1995) Family business: rethinking strategic planning, paper presented at the 40th Annual International Council on Small Business, June, Sydney.

Burns, P. (2001) *Entrepreneurship and Small Business*, Palgrave, London.

Carson, D. and Cromie, S. (1989) Marketing planning in small enterprises: a model and some empirical evidence, *Journal of Marketing Management*, 5 (1), 33–49.

Carson, D., Cromie, S., McGowan, P. and Hill, J. (1995) *Marketing and Entrepreneurship in SMEs: An Innovative Approach*, Prentice Hall, London.

Chan, S. Y. and Foster, J. M. (2001) Strategy formulation in small business: The Hong Kong experiences, *International Small Business Journal*, April–June, 56–71.

Chaston, I., Berger, B. and Sadler-Smith, E. (1999) Organisational learning: research issues and application in SME sector firms, *International Journal of Entrepreneurial Behaviour and Research*, 5 (4), 191- 203.

Chell, E. (2001) *Entrepreneurship: Globalisation, Innovation and Development*, Thomson Learning, London.

Churchill, N. C. and Lewis, V. L. (1983) The five stages of small business growth, *Harvard Business Review*, 61 (3), 30–50.

Covin, J. (1991) Entrepreneurial versus conservative firms: a comparison of strategies and performance, *Journal of Management Studies*, 28 (5), 439–462.

Curran, J. (1996) Small business strategy in M. Warner (ed.) *The Concise International Encyclopaedia of Business and Management*, International Thomson Business Press, London, 4510–4520.

Daft, R. L. (2000) *Management*, 5th edn, Harcourt College Publishers, Fort Worth, TX.

Fields, R. W. (1999) *The Entrepreneurial Engineer: Starting Your Own High-Tech Company*, Artech House, Boston.

Foster, M. J. (1993) Scenario planning for small businesses, *Long Range Planning*, 26 (1), 123–129.

Gable, M. and Topol, M. (1987) Planning practices of small-scale retailers, *American Journal of Small Business*, Fall, 19–32.

Goodwin, D. R. and Hodgett, R. A. (1991) Strategic planning in medium size companies, *Australian Accountant*, 61 (2), 71–83.

Hamel, G. (1996) Strategy as revolution, *Harvard Business Review*, July–August, 69–82.

Handler, W. C. (1994) Succession in family businesses: a review of the research, *Business Family Review*, 7 (2), 133–158.

Hanlon D. and Scott, M. (1995) Strategy formulation in the entrepreneurial small firms, in S. Birley and I. MacMillan (eds) *International Entrepreneurship*, Routledge, London, 17–38.

Hatch, J. and Zweig, J. (2001) Strategic flexibility: the key to growth, *Ivey Business Journal*, 65 (4), 44–47.

Helms, M. M., Dibrell, C. and Wright, P. (1997) Competitive strategies and business performance: evidence from the adhesives and sealants industry, *Management Decision*, 35, 678–92.

Hendry, C., Arthur, M. and Jones, A. (1995) *Strategy Through People: Adaptation and Learning in the Small-Medium Enterprises*, Routledge, London.

Hoskisson, R. E., Hitt, M. A., Wan, W. P. and Yiu, D. (1999) Theory and research in strategic management: swings of a pendulum, *Journal of Management*, 25 (3), 417–456.

Jenster, P. V. and Overstreet, G. A. (1990) Planning for a non-profit service: a study of US Credit Unions, *Long Range Planning*, 23 (2), 103–11.

Karami, A. (1999) Business strategy in context of managerial work: the case of British Airways Plc. Human Resource Development Practices & Practitioners Beyond the Year 2000: Two Day International Conference, University of Bradford, UK, May, 27–28.

Kets De Vries, M. F. R. (1996) The anatomy of the entrepreneur: clinical observation, *Human Relations*, 49 (7), 853–883.

Kuratko, D. F. and Hodgetts, R. M. (2001) *Entrepreneurship: A Contemporary Approach*, 5th edn, Harcourt College Publishers, Fort Worth, TX.

Larson, P. (1998) Strategic planning and mission statement, *Montana Business Quarterly*, 36 (3), 22–24.

Lasher, W. (1999) *Strategic Thinking Small Businesses*, Blackwell, Malden, MA.

Leidecker, L. and Bruno, A. (1986) Identifying and using critical success factors, *Long Range Planning*, 17 (1), 23–32.

Lyles, M. S., Baird, I. S., Orris, J. B. and Kuratko, D. F. (1993) Formalised planning in small business: increasing strategic choices, *Journal of Small Business Management*, 38–50.

McCarthy, B. and Leavy, B. (2000) Phases in the strategy formulation: an exploratory study of Irish SMEs, *IBAR*, 21 (2), 55–80.

Meyer, G. D. and Heppard, K. A. (eds) (2000) *Entrepreneurship as Strategy: Competing on the Entrepreneurial Edge*, Sage Publications, London.

Miller, C. C. and Cardinal, L. B. (1994) Strategic planning and firm performance: a synthesis of more than two decades, *Academy of Management Journal*, 37, 1649–1665.

Mintzberg, H. (1979) An emerging strategy of direct research, *Administrative Science Quarterly*, 24, 582–589.

Mintzberg, H. (1987) Crafting strategy, *Harvard Business Review*, July/August, 66–75.

Mintzberg, H. and Waters, J. (1982) Tracking strategy in an entrepreneurial firm, *Academy of Management Journal*, 25, 465–499.

Monck, C., Porter, B., Quintas, P., Storey, D. and Wynarczyk, P. (1988) *Science Parks and the Growth of High Technology Firms*, Croom Helm, Beckenham, Kent.

Robinson, R. and Pearce, J. (1984) The relationship between stage of development and small firm planning and performance, *Journal of Small Business Management*, April, 45–52.

Rue, L. W. and Ibrahim, N. A. (1996) The status of planning in smaller family owned businesses, *Business Family Review*, 9 (1), 29–43.

Scott, M. and Bruce, R. (1987) Five stages of growth in small business, *Long Range Planning*, 20 (3), 45–52.

Shrader, C. B., Mulford, L. and Blackburn, V. L. (1989) Strategic and operational planning, uncertainty and performance in small firms, *Journal of Small Business Management*, 27 (4), 45–60.

Shuman, J. C. and Seeger, J. A. (1986) The theory and practice of strategic management in smaller rapid growth firms, *American Journal of Small Business*, 11 (1), 7–18.

Shuman, J. C., Shaw, J. J. and Sussman, G. (1985) Strategic planning in smaller rapid growth companies, *Long Range Planning*, 18 (6), 48–53.

Smallbone, D., Leig, R. and North, D. (1995) The characteristics and strategies of high growth SMEs, *International Journal of Entrepreneurial Behaviour and Research*, 1 (3), 44–62.

Smith, J. A. (1998) Strategies for start-ups, *Long Range Planning*, 31 (6), 857–872.

Thompson, J. (1999) A strategic perspective of entrepreneurship, *International Journal of Entrepreneurial Behaviour and Research*, 5 (6), 279–296.

Upton, N. and Heck, R. K. Z. (1997) The family business dimensions of entrepreneurship, in D. L. Sexton and R. A. Smilor (eds) (2000) *Entrepreneurship*, Upstart Publishing, Chicago, 243–266.

Walters, P. G. P. (1993) Patterns of formal planning and performance in US exporting firms, *Management International Review*, 33 (1), 43–63.

Ward, J. L. (1998) The special role of strategic planning for family business, *Family Business Review*, 1(2), 105–117.

Zimmerer, T. W. and Scarborough, N. M. (2002) *Essentials of Entrepreneurship and Small Business Management*, 3rd edn, Prentice Hall, Upper Saddle River, NJ.

7 Strategy implementation in small and medium-sized enterprises

Learning objectives

By the end of this chapter you should be able to:

- Define strategy implementation.

- Explain the role of organisational structure in strategy implementation.

- Explore the strategic advantages and disadvantages of the different organisational structures for SMEs.

- Discuss the role of human resources in implementing a successful strategy.

- Explore the organisational culture and its importance in strategy implementation.

- Explain how budgeting can support strategy implementation in SMEs.

The main objective of this chapter is twofold: to discuss business strategies which are implemented in SMEs and to explore the constituent elements of successful strategy implementation. First the general definitions of strategy implementation will be discussed, referring to the theoretical models of strategy implementation. Then attention will be paid to the main elements of strategy implementation in SMEs, including organisational structure, leadership, human resources, culture and budgeting.

First, different organisational structures such as functional or matrix structure and their advantages and disadvantages for SMEs will be discussed. In the second section effective leadership and its role in strategy implementation will be explored in some detail; in the third section the importance of human resources in strategy implementation will be considered. Finally, the chapter contains a discussion concerning the need for effective management of the culture and budgeting as powerful tools for successful strategy implementation.

Implementation of strategy

The third aspect of strategic management in SMEs is the effective implementation of business strategies (Oladeji, 1998; Voss, 1998; Noble, 1999). It has been argued that well formulated strategies only produce superior performance for the firm when they are successfully implemented (Noble, 1999). Strategy implementation is not easy. It involves working with people and the structure of the organisation to make the visionary ideas developed earlier come true (Lasher, 1999). Many scholars believe that strategy implementation, particularly in SMEs, generates conflict and is time-consuming (Hale and Cragg, 1996; Lasher, 1999). This is true. It may lead to conflict situations because implementation is accompanied by organisational changes. There always are a few employees who are not in agreement with the introduction of change within the organisation. It is also time-consuming because it deals with organisational policies, procedures, timetables and budgeting and it has to be done throughout the entire organisation. Talking about the problems of implementation does not mean that it is not possible to implement strategies effectively. Solving the problems and preparing the possibilities of implementing business strategies are the managers' duty.

How can the strategy be implemented effectively? What organisational factors are involved in the process of strategy implementation? Generally speaking, there are many factors involved in strategy implementation; in this book we have selected five main elements that are believed to be essential for implementing a strategy, particularly in SMEs. These are:

- Organisational structure
- Leadership
- Human resources
- Managing culture
- Budgeting to support strategy.

In this chapter we will discuss all five elements in some detail. Now let us review some recent definitions and theoretical aspects of strategy implementation.

What is strategy implementation?

The implementation of business strategy has been the subject of an increasing number of studies and research works (Hauc and Kovac, 2000). In 1998, Kalai and Ledyard compared the traditional with the new paradigm of strategy implementation in organisations. They argued that in the traditionally static approach to implementation it is often impossible for strategists to enforce the optimal outcomes. And when restricting the choice to dominant strategy implementation, only the dictatorial choices of one of the participants are implementable. Recently, strategy implementation in SMEs as well as in large firms has been considered as a dynamic activity within the strategic management process (Box 7.1). Wheelen and Hunger (1998) consider strategy implementation

> **Box 7.1 Strategy implementation**
>
> - **Strategy implementation** simply means converting a selected strategy into action.
> - Effective strategy implementation consists of five essential **elements** including:
>   1 Organisational structure
>   2 Leadership style
>   3 Human resources
>   4 Managing culture
>   5 Budgeting.

as a process which might involve changes within the overall culture, structure and/or management system of the entire organisation. Grundy (1998) investigated strategy implementation in the context of project management. He concluded that a number of tools from strategic management, value management and organisational change can be imported into project management to enrich its traditional techniques considerably. These tools are particularly powerful when applied to complex, multifunctional projects when attempting to turn business strategy into implementation.

As discussed already, a review of the literature reveals the presence of few formal definitions of strategy implementation. Some of the differing views on strategy implementation are:

- The implementation stage involves converting strategic alternatives into an operating plan (Aaker, 1998).
- Implementation refers to the 'how-to-do-it' aspects of marketing. Implementation deals with organisational issues, with the development of specific marketing programmes and with the execution of programmes in the field (Cespedes, 1991).
- Implementation is the managerial interventions that align organisational action with strategic intention (Floyd and Woolridge, 1992).
- Implementation has been defined as 'the sum total of the activities and choices required for the execution of a strategic plan [...] the process by which strategies and policies are put into action' (Wheelen and Hunger, 1998: 183).

McKinsey's Seven-S framework

The review of the literature reveals that many scholars have highlighted various factors associated with strategy implementation such as the importance of the organisational structure, leadership style and resources (Goldsmith, 1995; Lorange, 1998; Noble, 1999; Hauc and Kovac, 2000). One of the early and most widely accepted frameworks for strategy implementation and organisation development is that of McKinsey (Seven-S framework). Based on discussions with consultants, academics and business leaders, the consultant firm of McKinsey & Co. has proposed the Seven-S framework (Figure 7.1) which identifies seven factors that are believed to be essential for successful implementation (Waterman *et al.* 1980). This framework provides a useful visualisation of the key components that managers must consider in making sure that a strategy permeates the day-to-day life of the firm (Robinson and Pearce, 1984).

McKinsey's consultants found that neglecting any one of the seven key factors could lead to an unsuccessful strategy implementation process – each is equally important and interacts with all the other factors. The framework is based on the assumption that a change of strategy will require a change in the organisation's skills and shared values (Waterman *et al.* 1980). This in turn will determine the requirements for the remaining factors. The Seven-S framework suggests that once the strategy has been designed the managers focus on six elements to ensure effective strategy implementation. The Seven-S model consists of strategy, structure, systems, shared values, skills, style and staff. Let's discuss these factors in some detail.

Strategy

Strategy is a general plan of action. It is the way a company aims to plan in response to anticipation of changes in its external environment, its customers and its competitors (Mintzberg *et al.* 1995). Strategy can be developed through

Figure 7.1

McKinsey's Seven-S framework

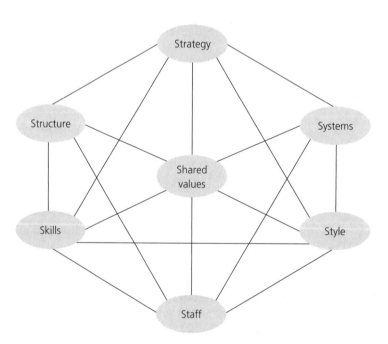

SWOT analysis and defining the firm's mission and objectives. The Seven-S model emphasises that, in practice, the development of strategies poses less of a problem than their implementation. Once the strategy is developed the strategists should consider the remaining six elements of the model to complement the process of implementing strategy successfully.

Structure

Developing an appropriate organisational structure and matching the structure to the strategy is a fundamental task of company strategists (Pearce and Robinson, 2000; Thompson, 2001). The structure of the organisation represents the vehicle for reaching the final destination, namely its objectives. The Seven-S model adds a contemporary perspective to the problem of organisational structure. The McKinsey consultants point out that in today's complex and ever-changing environment, a successful organisation may make temporary structural changes to cope with specific strategic tasks without abandoning basic structural divisions throughout the organisation (Waterman *et al.* 1980). This calls for flexibility and creative management to respond to and/or proactively take action to meet the new demands.

Systems

Systems consist of all the formal and informal procedures that allow the firm to work. Systems can overpower expressed strategies. This category includes organisational subsystems such as the Management Information System (MIS), training, budgeting, and accounting systems.

Style

Style refers to the pattern of actions (dominant managerial philosophy and shared values) undertaken by top managers in the organisations. Leadership style can either ease or create difficulties and problems in implementing a successful strategy.

Staff

Successful organisations view people as valuable resources that should be carefully developed, guarded, allocated and retained (Waterman *et al.* 1980; Analoui, 2002). Recent researches (Analoui and Karami, 2002) show that successful organisations consider human resources as a strategic asset. Thus, selecting key people for implementation of the developed strategies is a crucial task and the sole responsibility of top managers. Top managers should devote time and energy to planning the progress and participation of staff and more importantly the key people who are involved in strategy implementation.

Skills

The term skills refers to those activities that people do best and for which they are known. Nowadays this is referred to as a body of competencies that a firm (its human resources) possesses. Strategic changes may require organisations to add one or more new skills to their portfolio of competencies. Skills are categorised into three main groups including task-related skills, people-related skills and self-development skills (Analoui, 1999). In order to implement strategy successfully the organisations need to consider a combination of those three categories of skills (Box 7.2).

Shared values

This refers to culture, guiding concepts and the dominant set of values that unite an organisation in some common purpose. The mission statement is an example of a value which ought to be shared by all employees of the firm. In implementing the strategies there is a need and necessity to manage the organisation culture effectively – which in turn leads to creating synergy. This is an important task for the strategists.

By and large, considering the seven discussed factors can lead to successful strategy implementation – and naturally the costs of failed implementation efforts to the organisation will be enormous (Noble, 1999; Heracleous, 2000). Failure in implementing strategy successfully will result in waste of the organisation's scarce resources, money and time. Apart from that, Heracleous has argued that failed implementation efforts will result in lower employee morale and a diminished trust and faith in senior management, as well as creating a more inflexible organisation (2000). The question to address, therefore, is how the strategy ought to be implemented, particularly in SMEs. Organisational factors including structure, leadership, human resources and budgeting are believed to play a significant role in strategy implementation and will be discussed here in detail.

Box 7.2 McKinsey's Seven-S framework

- McKinsey's Seven-S framework is one of the early and most widely accepted frameworks for strategy implementation and organisation development. It suggests that once the strategy has been designed the strategists should focus on seven elements to ensure effective strategy implementation.
- The framework consists of seven elements as follows:
  1 Strategy
  2 Structure
  3 Systems
  4 Shared values
  5 Skills
  6 Style
  7 Staff.

Organisational structure and strategy implementation

Organisational structure has been considered as the basic element for the effective implementation of strategy. The purpose of an organisational structure is to enable managers to allocate the work, resources and administrative mechanisms that are necessary for the control and integration of the strategies of an organisation (Galbraith and Kazanjian, 1986). During the period of early development, a number of scholars (Selznick, 1957; Penrose, 1959; Chandler 1962; Cyert and March, 1963; Ansoff, 1965) have made significant contributions to the later development of the field of strategy implementation. In 1962 Chandler's work *Strategy and Structure* (Hoskisson *et al.* 1999), which focused on how enterprises develop new administrative structures to accommodate growth and how strategic change leads to structural change, was published. Chandler examines the growth and development of 70 of the largest businesses in the United States, including Du Pont, General Motors and Standard Oil. He observed a common pattern in their development. According to Chandler, strategy is:

> The determination of the basic long term goals and objectives of an enterprise and the adoption of courses of action and the allocation of resources necessary for carrying out the goals [and structure is] the design of the organisation through which the enterprise [can be effectively] administrated.
>
> (1962: 13–14)

Although organisations change their growth strategies to suit technological, economic and demographic changes, nevertheless new strategies may create administrative problems and economic inefficiencies. Structural changes are needed to solve these problems and to ensure the maximisation of economic performance (Stoner *et al.* 1995). Thus Chandler concluded that organisational structure followed and reflected the growth strategy of the firm. According to Chandler, organisations pass through three stages of development, moving from a unit structure to a functional structure and then to a multidivisional structure. He concludes that organisations do not really change their structure because their entrepreneurial founders excel at strategy but are generally neither interested in nor knowledgeable about organisational structure. It has been suggested that there are two approaches to strategy and structure: prescriptive and emergent (Lynch, 2000) (Figure 7.2).

Figure 7.2

Two perspectives on strategy and structure

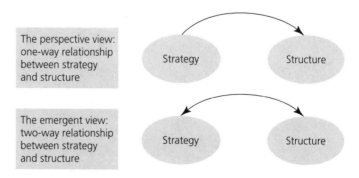

The perspective view: one-way relationship between strategy and structure

Strategy → Structure

The emergent view: two-way relationship between strategy and structure

Strategy ⇄ Structure

Galbraith and Kazanjian (1986) argue that, from a prescriptive view, the strategy is developed first and only then is the organisational structure defined. For the prescriptive strategist, organisational structure is a matter of how the strategy is implemented: it does not influence the strategy itself (Lynch, 1997). Lynch summarises the discussion by pointing out that it is first necessary to develop the strategy. When the strategy is developed, the organisation ought to be devised to deliver that strategy (Lynch, 2000). In contrast, from an emergent viewpoint, the relationship between strategy and structure is far more complex. From this perspective, the strategy and structure are more closely interrelated and hence the structure ought to be considered while strategy is being developed (Lynch, 1997).

Therefore, according to some modern strategists (Galbraith and Kazanjian, 1986; Mintzberg, 1991; Lynch, 2000) Chandler's concept of strategy first and then structure to deliver it may oversimplify the situation. Recently, Lynch (2000) summarised five major criticisms of the 'strategy then structure' process. These are:

- The structure may be too rigid to cope with the rapidly changing environment.
- The type of structure is just as important as the business area in developing the organisation's strategy.
- Value chain configuration that favours cost cutting or alternatively new market opportunities may also alter the organisation required.
- The complexity of strategic change needs to be managed, implying that more complex organisational considerations will be involved.
- Finally, the role of top and middle management in the formation of strategy may also need to be reassessed.

Organisational structures

Before embarking on the discussion of an appropriate structure for SMEs, it is helpful to review different types of organisational structures and explore their strategic advantages and disadvantages. There are different types of organisational structure including small organisations, functional organisation structure, multidivisional (M-form) or strategic business unit (SBU) structure and matrix and innovative organisation structure, each of which has advantages and disadvantages.

Small organisational structure

This organisational structure applies to the firms in micro level. Either small family businesses or firms employing less than ten employees are the best example of a small organisational structure. Suppose that as the owner-manager of a small food enterprise – a supermarket – Kevin and members of his family run the business together. Kevin plays the role of manager of the store and has the responsibility for the financial management of the business. Other members of the family each play different roles such as sales, purchase, cashier and delivery. From this example it is clear that the manager of the organisation acts as decision-maker and the other employees implement those decisions which have been made by the manager. Figure 7.3 illustrates an organisational structure for such a small firm.

Because of the small size of the organisation, the communication between manager and the employees is informal and very fast. They can see each other every day and talk about different issues related to the business. The employees can accept a variety of responsibilities and there are no restrictions in undertaking any task. Therefore, a main advantage is that the business can respond quickly to the changes in the market and customers' expectations. On the other hand, there are some difficulties associated with this kind of organisational structure. Since the owner-manager acts as the main decision-maker of the organisation, the degree of employees' contribution in strategic decision-making will depend largely on the management style of the manager. Since the employees have to undertake multiple tasks there may be confusion and even overlapping of the responsibilities. It also could be said that the organisational relationships are more informal.

Functional organisational structure

Functional organisation structure is applied to firms where the duties and responsibilities, because of their specialised and varied nature, have to be categorised into specific groups. These firms should carefully define the skills and areas of specialisations such as marketing, personnel, accounting and finance and operations. Categorising the organisational duties into functional specialities enables people to concentrate on one aspect of the work and develop their skills, expertise and competencies accordingly. The functional organisational structure is appropriate for firms which produce a main single product or service (Figure 7.4).

Generally, as a firm grows in terms of the number of employees or activities, the functional organisation structure can be adapted. Strategic advantages and disadvantages of the functional structure are illustrated in Box 7.3. In functional organisations the CEOs have strategic control over the firm's activities. Responsibilities and duties of the employees are defined clearly. Therefore, the firm can strive towards high efficiency through developing specialisation

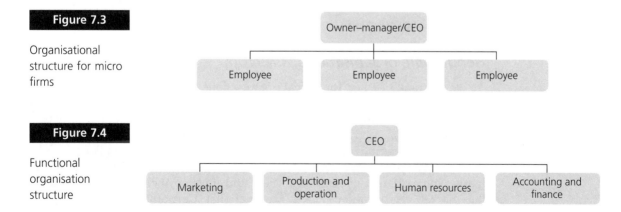

Figure 7.3

Organisational structure for micro firms

Figure 7.4

Functional organisation structure

> **Box 7.3. Advantages and disadvantages of the functional organisation**
>
> **Advantages:**
>
> - CEOs have strategic control over the firm's activities
> - Responsibilities and duties are defined clearly
> - Efficiency is achieved through developing functional expertise and skills
> - Task-related skills are increased in each functional section
> - Possibility of high quality training.
>
> **Disadvantages:**
>
> - Coordination problems
> - Limitations in development of general managers
> - Less flexibility in necessary changes
> - Potential conflict between functional areas
> - Develop a narrow specialisation.

and functional expertise. In functional organisations people are grouped according to the nature of their duties and report to the manager in charge of similar activities. For instance, all staff in the manufacturing section should report to the production executive and anyone whose work is related to marketing and sales ought to report to the marketing manager. Lasher (1999) argues that the functional organisation is the most common because strategically essential functions are defined along the functional lines. Low cost manufacturing and creative talent in marketing are some examples.

Along with advantages, there are some disadvantages with functional organisations. The functional organisation develops a very narrow specialisation in each department. Because there is some potential conflict between functional sections of the firm such as marketing and manufacturing, the task of coordination between functional areas will be made difficult for the chief executives. Moreover, functional organisations tend to show more concern for specialised units thus limiting the development and training of the general managers. Even with these disadvantages of functional organisations, it is one of the most appropriate structures for SMEs.

Geographic organisational structure

As we discussed earlier, functional organisations are the most popular form in single line firms. However, if the firm operates in different areas, it should use a geographic organisational structure. The geographic organisational structure focuses the firm's activities on local market conditions. In this structure, all functions in a specific region report to the same division manager. For example, firms which operate in national or international markets can divide the whole market into different geographical areas and develop their structure based on the market classification. Xerox Multinational Corporation operates in an international market and it has divided the international market into different areas (countries). For each area it has developed the subfunctional structure. Figure 7.5 illustrates the typical geographical organisational structure.

There are many advantages to geographical structure. By dividing the firm's resources into different areas, the firm will be flexible and responsive to changes in the local environments because each unit is small and tuned into the needs of its environment. Accordingly, the concern for customers' needs and expectations will be heightened. This structure enables the firm to develop general managers. It also enables chief executive officers to pinpoint responsibility for performance problems in different areas. Since each area is a self-contained unit, poor performance can be assigned directly to the manager of the area (Daft, 2000). Advantages and disadvantages of geographical structure are illustrated in Box 7.4.

There are some disadvantages associated with the geographical structure. Probably the main problem is duplication of resources and the high cost of running branches in different regions. The other main disadvantage is reduced technical skills and specialisation in each division. Because each division is small it is not economically viable to have technical training units in all

Figure 7.5

Geographic
structure

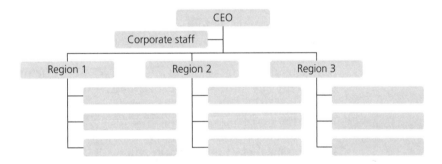

Box 7.4 Advantages and disadvantages of geographical structure

Advantages:

- High concern for customers' needs and expectations
- Development of general managers
- High flexibility in adapting with changes in the different local markets
- High coordination between functional departments in each division
- Possibility of comparing the efficiency of different divisions.

Disadvantages:

- High cost of running different divisions and duplication of resources across them
- Poor coordination across divisions
- Less CEO control over the divisions
- Less technical training and specialisation in divisions.

divisions. In terms of management control, since the local branch managers are authorised for decision-making to a certain level, the CEO may feel that they have less control over the local branches. The last disadvantage of having this kind of organisation structure arises because each division is located in a specific area in order to deal with local needs and customers and overall coordination between divisions may present a problem.

Multidivisional or strategic business unit structure

Functional structure is not appropriate for the firms which operate in different businesses or produce different main product lines. Pearce and Robinson (2000) claim that if the functional structure is retained in the firms which produce different main products, marketing managers may have to create sales programmes for vastly different products, production managers as a result may have to oversee the production of varied products or services, and top management may be confronted with excessive coordination demands. To avoid this, a new organisational structure is deemed necessary to meet the kind of decision-making requirements that result from increased diversity and size. The proper organisational structure for such diversified firms is a divisional or strategic business unit (SBU) structure. Thompson has defined the SBU as 'a discrete grouping within an organisation with delegated responsibility for strategically managing a product, a service or a particular group of products or services' (2001: 1128). Put simply, the firm which produces different main products and services ought to adapt a SBU structure. Figure 7.6 shows the typical divisional or SBU organisational structure.

In the 1970s, the US General Electric Company, in conjunction with McKinsey and Co., developed the organisational concept of the SBU and it was introduced widely throughout the world in the 1980s. A divisional or strategic business unit structure allows the CEO to delegate authority for the strategic management of strategic business units. There are many strategic advantages of having a divisional or SBU structure. Channon (1999) argues that the SBU structure can allow highly diversified corporations to optimise the strategic fit between related businesses and help to integrate the process of strategy formulation at both corporate and business level. The divisional or SBU

Figure 7.6   Divisional or strategic business unit structure

structure facilitates the coordination of the related activities within an SBU and allows strategic planning to be done at the most relevant level in the firm. Since the strategic decision-making at the business level is authorised to the SBU general managers, it frees the chief executive officer for broader strategic decision-making. It also provides excellent training for strategic managers. This will increase concentration on profitability in SBUs and allows for diversification of the products and services. Box 7.5 lists some of the advantages and disadvantages of the divisional or SBU structure.

Along with advantages, there are also some disadvantages associated with divisional/SBU structure. The business needs many general managers because each SBU is directed by a general manager. It creates difficulty in maintaining an overall corporate image and the strategic business units may begin to compete against each other. Finally, a divisional or SBU structure will have some difficulty in distributing central services to the functional areas.

Box 7.5 Advantages and disadvantages of divisional/SBU structure

Advantages:

- Focuses on the business area and products and markets
- Training for general and strategic managers
- Frees CEOs for strategic decision-making in corporate level
- Focuses on the accountability of the SBUs
- Focuses profitability on SBUs.

Disadvantages:

- Problem of distributing corporate overhead costs across SBUs
- Needs more general managers
- Potential competition across the functional divisions
- Less control of top management in SBUs
- Expensive duplication of functions across the SBUs.

Matrix organisational structure

It has been argued that in large firms increased diversity leads to a large number of products and services. Implementing strategies in such diversified large firms needs the adoption of a combined organisational structure called a matrix structure. Matrix organisational structures combine both the functional structure and the divisional/SBU structure simultaneously (Daft, 2000). Figure 7.7 shows the typical matrix organisational structure.

Probably the main difference between a matrix organisation and traditional organisations is that it has dual channels of authority, performance responsibility and control. A matrix organisation provides skills and resources when and where they are most needed (Robinson and Pearce, 1984). In the matrix organisation, there is decentralisation in strategic decision-making, moreover the middle managers are involved in the decision-making process. A matrix organisation prevents duplication of costs and allocates the resources effectively. Box 7.6 lists the advantages and disadvantages of the matrix organisations.

The matrix organisational structure also has some strategic disadvantages. As Robinson and Pearce (1984) commented, a matrix structure is easy to design but difficult to implement. They argue that the factors such as shared responsibilities and the use of resources can create misunderstanding among subordinates. Lasher (1999) has also noted that organisations with a matrix structure are expensive to run.

Factors affecting structure selection

Reviewing the organisational structures reveals that each structure has its advantages and disadvantages. In answer to the question, what is the best organisational structure?, it could be said that there is no single best organisational structure which could be generically applied to all firms. Obviously, each structure could only be applied in specific conditions. For instance, multidivisional or strategic business unit structure cannot be applied to small firms, however, the majority of SMEs can benefit from a functional organisational structure. There are many factors which influence the selection of organisational structure.

Figure 7.7

Matrix
organisational
structure

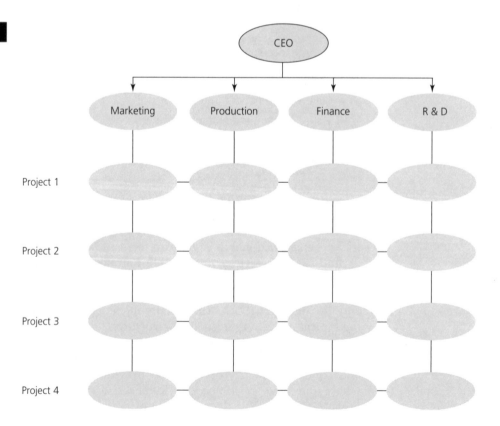

Box 7.6 Advantages and disadvantages of matrix structure

Advantages:

- Uses functional managers efficiently
- Decentralisation in decision-making
- Provides excellent training possibilities for strategic managers
- Involves middle managers in the strategic decision-making process
- Provides the possibility of involving the firm in variety of projects
- Uses the organisational resources where and when they are needed.

Disadvantages:

- May result in confusion and misunderstanding of responsibilities
- Too many meetings for decision-making which leads to a slow decision-making process
- Increased overall managerial costs
- May lead to competition between functional managers and project managers.

Size of the firm

The organisational size influences the choice of structure. For instance, large firms which operate in different markets or produce more than one main product cannot use the simple or functional organisational structure. In contrast the simple or functional structure seems to be more applicable in small and medium-sized firms.

Technology

Technology has been defined as the branch of knowledge that deals with applied science, applied engineering and electronics. However, in organisation and management theories, technology is defined as the knowledge, tools, techniques, and activities used to transform organisational inputs into outputs (Daft, 2000). Type and complexity of the technology also affects the organisational structure. For instance Woodward (1965), in her famous research in British manufacturing firms, found that manufacturing firms can be categorised according to three basic types of work flow strategy:

1. Small batch production technology which is designed for producing goods in batches of one or a few products designed to customer specification.

2. Mass production technology, which is distinguished by standardised production runs.

3. Continuous process technology which is a sophisticated and complex form of production technology with no human factor as a part of the actual production.

Woodward concludes that the structural characteristics associated with each type of technology are different. For instance, the organisational structure associated with small batch technology tends to be more flexible, it is characterised by less formalised procedures and a lower degree of centralisation in decision-making and low vertical and high horizontal communication. In contrast, the organisational structure associated with mass production technology is highly formalised and centralised, with vertical top-down communication and lesser horizontal communication. The mass production technology requires a rigid structure. Woodward discusses how continuous process technology is very similar to small batch technology in terms of discussed structural factors, so the structure must be designed to fit the technology.

The environment

Because of the interaction between the organisation and its environment, the two tend to mutually influence one another. As a rule, organisations must fit in and adapt to their environmental changes. For instance, a centralised structure is more suitable for a stable environment. In contrast if the organisation operates in a turbulent environment, a decentralised organisational structure would be more adaptable to emergent changes.

Many scholars have focused on studying the relationships between structure and environment. Daft's (2000) work in which the environment has been categorised into uncertain and certain conditions, and the structure have been categorised into vertical and horizontal, is worth examining (Figure 7.8).

Daft (2000) suggests that when the external environment of the organisation is more stable, the organisation should have a classic or traditional structure. Such an organisation can develop specialisation within the functional areas and centralised decision-making. Obviously the traditional structure emphasises on vertical control; when the organisation operates in an uncertain environment, a horizontal structure that emphasises low specialisation, decentralisation and less formal procedures is more appropriate. Daft (2000) concludes that when strategists adopt a wrong structure for the environment, this will result in reduced firm performance.

Strategy

As discussed earlier, strategy inevitably has impact on organisational structure, and in turn the organisational structure influences the strategy. Each strategy has

Figure 7.8

Two forms of correct fit between environment and organisational structure

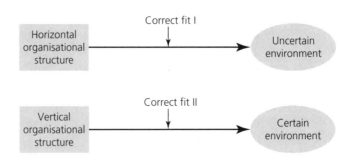

its goals and objectives. For instance, differentiation strategy aims at targeting the development of innovative products and services for the market, while a low cost leadership strategy attempts to increase internal efficiency. For each of these strategies, there is a need for developing an appropriate organisational structure.

As a result different factors affect the selection of an organisational structure. There is no single pattern of structure which could be used for all organisations and this is especially the case for SMEs. Apart from factors such as strategy, environment, size and technology, the philosophy and belief of CEOs is another considerable factor. Business owner-managers or CEOs of SMEs may combine different factors which affect the structure and develop the structure which is appropriate for their firms.

Strategy and structure in SMEs

The relationship between strategy and structure in SMEs has recently been investigated (Camille, 1994; Freel, 2000). The literature on large firms generally highlights the restrictions which they place on the entrepreneur and their initiatives. For example, Morse (1986) focuses more specifically on the consequences of cumbersome structures that generate bureaucratic systems which, in turn, freeze personal autonomy and individual creativity. Hill (1987) also refers to the control systems in large enterprises, which often become obstacles to innovation. The opposite is also true in SMEs, which are generally regarded as providing a friendlier environment where structures and processes are and must remain simple, flexible and adaptable (Camille, 1994).

In SMEs, decision-making is highly centralised. The fact that SMEs have very few levels of decision-making results in structural flexibility (Robinson and Pearce, 1984). A number of these same authors have also discussed the more limited resources of SMEs. In his (1994) research Camille concludes that large firms and SMEs are worlds apart in terms of structure and decision-making. If we take a closer look at these two very different worlds, one is more formalised and the other benefits from a more dynamic and adaptable structure, and it is less surprising to find that SMEs are often perceived as much more fertile than larger firms in terms of innovation. Moreover, it can be concluded that the importance of the role of SMEs in innovation is based on their ability to innovate more instinctively, more naturally and especially more efficiently (Adams and Brock, 1986). Given the distinctive features of SMEs mentioned above, it is no surprise to discover that entrepreneurial characteristics and organisational structure differ considerably between SMEs and large firms (Camille, 1994) (Box 7.7).

Another aspect of structure in SMEs is strategy implementation and re-engineering changes (Francis and McIntosh, 1997; McAdam, 2000). In comparison with large organisations SMEs have relatively informal, flatter and highly centralised structures (Hale and Cragg, 1996). Thus they should not experience the same degree of problems that large organisations have with regard to middle management resistance when attempting to implement strategy and re-engineering changes (Francis and McIntosh, 1997). Hale and Cragg (1996) concluded that SMEs have more chance of quickly forming a team based on process structure in line with re-engineering because of their informal style and natural cross-functional working style. McAdam (2000) argues that

> **Box 7.7 Strategy and structure in a small business**
>
> **Mini case study**
>
> Gary owns a small manufacturing firm. When he first started out, Gary used a functional departmentalisation arrangement. However, as the number of product lines increased and the business grew, Gary found the functional arrangement to be unwieldy. Recently he reorganised and moved into a product form of organisational structure. Under this new arrangement he is finding it easier to keep track of product line profitability. 'As you get larger,' he told a friend, 'it sometimes becomes necessary to reorganise. Under our new arrangement, I think we are a lot more efficient than we were before.'

cross-functional working in SMEs may be hindered by a lack of in-depth knowledge among the employees as mentioned earlier.

Most of the SMEs were seen as having a relatively simple structure. Thus, it was considered more straightforward to identify core processes for implementation and re-engineering and to drive re-engineering throughout the organisation than for large organisations.

Leadership and strategy implementation

The nature of leadership

Leadership is probably the most important factor to business success. Let's first see what leadership is and what is the difference between a leader and a manager. By reviewing definitions on leadership by different scholars, it is evident that many of the definitions used contain three terminologies: people, influence and goals. Leadership occurs among people (in a social context). A leader works with people at the different levels of the organisations and has to understand their needs, aspirations and expectations. Leadership is a people activity and a leader has influence on his or her people. A leader uses personal power rather than position power to manage the people with whom he works. Finally a leader attains the organisation's goals. Accordingly, Daft defined leadership as 'the ability to influence people toward the attainment of goals' (2000: 502). It could be said that modern leadership, rather than being autocratic, can be summed up as the ability to achieve the intended goals and objectives of the organisation through influencing and motivating people.

Many papers have been written about the differences between a manager and a leader. The main difference is probably the source of their power. The manager's source of power is the legitimate authority which comes with the position in the formal hierarchy of the organisation, whereas a leader, apart from position power, uses personal power to achieve the goals and objectives of the organisation. In this sense, an effective leader works *with* people and does not expect people to work *for* them (Analoui, 2002). Figure 7.9 illustrates the difference between a leader and a manager in attaining the organisations goals.

In terms of personal characteristics, leaders are more creative, flexible, innovative and likely to be visionary. In contrast, it could be said that a manager is persistent, a problem solver, analytical and rational. A leader initiates organisational changes while a manager stabilises the present situation (Daft, 2000). Leaders free people by involving them in organisational decision-making, and uses team or bottom-up decision-making patterns within the organisation, while managers use top-down and formal decision-making systems. Although there are differences between leaders and managers, it must be borne in mind that some people can exhibit a combination of leader/manager characteristics. Not surprisingly, leadership plays a significant role in implementing strategy within the organisations. By and large, it could be contended that should CEOs involve employees in strategy formulation, there will be more commitment on their part to implement the strategy successfully during the implementation stage. The reason for this is simple: if the employees are involved in the strategy formulation they will be more willing to commit themselves to the formulated strategies (Analoui, 2002) (Box 7.8).

Elements of entrepreneurial leadership

Entrepreneurs are managers, but with their own idiosyncratic characteristics. Probably one of the most important characteristics of the successful

Figure 7.9

Mechanisms used by leader and manager for achieving organisational goals

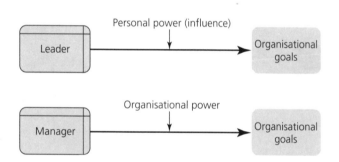

Box 7.8 Leadership and strategy implementation

- **Leadership** is the ability to influence people toward the attainment of goals.
- In terms of **personal characteristics**, leaders are creative, flexible, innovative and visionary. They use personal power in attainment of organisational goals and objectives.
- SMEs' leaders or CEOs play variety of **roles** as commander, architect, coordinator, coach, and premise setter in implementing strategy.
- There are six **barriers to strategy implementation**. These are a top-down leadership style, conflicting priorities, ineffective leadership team, poor vertical communication, poor coordination and inadequate down-the-line leadership skills and development.

entrepreneur is motivation – because they are often intrinsically motivated they know how to motivate other people. The leadership style is one of the most essential factors for successful strategy implementation in SMEs. Recently leadership in small businesses and entrepreneurial ventures has been investigated. Wickham (2001), in his recent work *Strategic Entrepreneurship* listed eight key elements of entrepreneurial leadership: personal vision, communication with stakeholders, organisational culture, knowledge and expertise, credibility, performance of the venture, leadership role and desire to lead (Figure 7.10).

He discusses how the entrepreneur's vision is the driving force behind leadership. So that person's vision must be rationalised and communicated with the people. The leader's vision should be clear to all of the stakeholders and should have the potential to create motivation among employees. Managing culture is another element of entrepreneurial leadership. Organisational culture is the set of key values, beliefs and norms that the employees of an organisation share. It is the entrepreneurial leader's role to shape the organisational culture by setting examples, the norms and standards and defining the values for the organisation. More importantly, in small businesses, the business owner-manager shapes the culture and determines what is and what is not allowed to take place. It is also expected that an entrepreneurial leader will have knowledge and expertise in the field. Since the leaders (strategists) in SMEs are the ultimate decision-makers, so they should be familiar with the technical aspects of the business. Accordingly, Wickham (2001) suggests that credibility is a critical factor in entrepreneurial leadership. A leader cannot create a

Figure 7.10

Factors in entrepreneurial leadership

Source: Adapted from Wickham (2001: 370).

motivated situation for implementing the formulated strategies, unless he or she has influence on the people and has credibility. Becoming a role model for others is one way of influencing their behaviour. Effective leaders practice what they preach (Analoui, 2002).

Finally, effective leaders desire to lead the organisation. No one can be an effective leader unless they really want to take on the role of a leader. Successful leaders are personally motivated to take up the role of leadership within the organisation. These entrepreneurial leaders prepare the tools and possibilities for implementing strategies successfully.

The role of leadership in strategy implementation

It has been suggested that top managers play a critical role in the implementation as well as the formulation of strategy (Hambrick, 1994; Noble, 1999). For instance, Hambrick has stated that:

> Top management teams are responsible for formulating adaptive responses to the environment, as well as implementing those responses. As such, the group sometimes is involved in discrete problems or choices ... however, the group also engages in ongoing, day-in/day-out administrative actions which collectively shape the organisation's form and greatly affect the types of problems and alternatives that are brought to its attention.
>
> (1994: 75)

Other works (Westley, 1990; Wooldridge and Floyd, 1990) have focused on middle management involvement in strategy implementation. They contend that implementation problems often arise due to a lack of understanding of and commitment to strategic decisions on the part of middle managers who are often excluded from the strategy formulation process.

Recent researchers (Hauc and Kovac 2000; Heracleous, 2000) concluded that it is the role of the top executives to ensure the smooth operation of the entire executive structure and to communicate effectively with that structure. In SMEs, the executives and business owner–managers play the main role in the formulation and implementation of business strategies.

There has been an evolution of approaches to strategy implementation, from purely autocratic to more participative ones (Bourgeois and Brodwin, 1998; Analoui, 2002). In studying the management practices of a variety of companies Bourgeois and Brodwin (1998) have found that CEOs approaches to strategy implementation can be categorised into one of the five basic descriptions. These categories are:

- The commander approach
- The organisational change approach
- The collaborative approach
- The cultural approach
- The crescive approach.

The first two descriptions represent the traditional approach to implementation. Here the CEO formulates strategy first and thinks about implementation later. The next two approaches involve more recent attempts to enhance implementation by broadening the base of participation into the planning process. The final approach takes advantage of managers' natural inclination to develop opportunities as they are encountered.

Similarly, the role of CEOs in implementing strategy has been studied (Heracleous, 2000). Heracleous argued that CEOs play a variety of roles – commander, architect, coordinator, coach and premise setter – in the implementing strategy (Box 7.9).

He argues that in each role the CEO uses distinctive methods for implementing strategy. In more turbulent and fast-moving environments, CEOs should act less as a commander or architect and more as a coordinator, coach and premise setter. The reason is that the first two roles separate thinking and acting, strategy formulation and implementation.

The wrong leadership style as a barrier to strategy implementation

A strategy or programme of change formed in the mind of one individual is much more problematic to implement than one which encompasses the input of others who have to live with its consequences. The question posed is, how does an effective entrepreneurial leader approach strategy implementation? In answer, Burns (2001) refers to the degree of changes in the environment and the degree of complexity of the task in hand. He introduces the different leadership styles used in entrepreneurial firms (Table 7.1).

Implementation of a strategy is usually sure to encounter the least difficulty if people feel that they have been involved in and have contributed to the emergence of strategy. If the employees in general feel that their concerns have

---

Box 7.9. Various roles of CEOs in strategy development and implementation

	CEO as
First role	Commander
Second role	Architect
Third role	Coordinator
Fourth role	Coach
Fifth role	Premise setter

Source: Heracleous, (2000).

been listened to and acted upon they are more likely to contribute to the development of the strategy and its implementation (Analoui, 2002). In this sense, implementation has already begun from the moment lower level managers and employees are involved in thinking about the future of the company. It has been suggested that CEOs are often baffled when they cannot seem to implement sound strategies. Beer and Eisenstat (2000) concluded that the root causes are six deep-seated barriers to strategy implementation – the six silent killers to strategy. These are top-down or laissez-faire senior management style, conflicting priorities, ineffective senior management team, poor vertical communication, the resulting poor coordination and inadequate down-the-line leadership skills and development. The top-down style included a discomfort with conflict, frequent absences to manage an acquisition and use of the top team for administrative matters rather than focused strategic discussions.

The second barrier, conflicting priorities, results in a divide between people and their performance. It literally tears the organisation apart.

An ineffective senior management team that operates within their own confined offices poses the third obstacle in implementing a strategy effectively. The so-called leadership team is in fact comprised of a group of insecure individuals who fear the loss of power should they face a situation where there is a need for cooperation and the sharing of ideas.

The fourth factor is the climate of poor communication and a lack of the skill of listening to the employees on the part of management. The fear of disapproval on the part of the employees and being judged rather than valued prevents the workers from communicating freely with their employers. Top management gives the impression that people at lower levels should keep their observations to themselves and in such an organisational climate cynicism tends to grow.

The next barrier to effective strategy implementation is poor coordination. A poor leadership style encourages individual rather than group and coordinated efforts in the organisation. This ensures the least participation and internal rivalry amongst the employees. In addition, the inability of management to see

Table 7.1 Leadership style in entrepreneurial businesses	Leadership style	Degree of environmental changes	Degree of task complexity	Organisational structure
	Paternalistic or autocratic	Low	Low	Hierarchical
	Paternalistic	High	Low	Flat but hierarchical
	Participative or consultative	Low	High	Team-based with protocols using matrix with hierarchy
	Team leadership	High	High	Innovative, flexible, decentralised, team-based using matrix with flat hierarchy

Source: Adapted from Burns (2001).

the organisation and its activities as a whole tends to trivialise the need for cooperation and coordination of efforts.

Finally, inadequate down-the-line leadership skills and development are the last barrier in strategy implementation. Lower level managers are not promoting the notion of skill development, neither do they promote the need for providing the employees with opportunities to learn and excel. When the status quo is preferred and the notion of change is frowned upon the need for coaching and training is deemed meaningless (Analoui, 2002; Burns, 2001). Should the entrepreneurial leaders be interested in successful development and implementation the firm's strategies, they must consider the following three points:

- Entrepreneurial leaders should not use an autocratic or dictatorial leadership style.
- Entrepreneurial leaders must be adept at using informal influence. They should meet and influence people.
- Entrepreneurial leaders must be adept at conflict resolution (Burns, 2001).

Human resources and strategy implementation in SMEs

We noted earlier that human resources play a significant role in implementing business strategies in SMEs. We discussed how the most important of the elements of corporate strategy in strategy implementation is the availability of corporate resources. The firm's resources are defined as the set of assets and capabilities, both tangible and intangible, which, when competitively superior, scarce and appropriate have the potential to create value from diversification (Collis, 1996). Commonly referred to as core competencies, the term resources actually covers a broader range of assets that can contribute to the competitive advantage of many different businesses. Resources are the critical building blocks of strategy. They determine not what a firm wants to do, but what it *can* do. Resources are inputs into a firm's production process such as capital, equipment, the skills of individual employees, patents, finance and talented managers. The main resources of the firm which corporate strategy rests on include the assets, skills and capabilities of the firm.

Probably the most important and strategic resource of SMEs is their employees. Alongside the proper organisational structure and effective leadership, motivated human resources significantly impact on the success of the strategy implementation. Having the right people in the key organisational positions is a crucial decision for strategy implementation (Analoui and Karami, 2002). Recently, employees have been considered as the competitive advantages of the firm. Pfeffer (1994) describes how changing market conditions have rendered many of the traditional sources of competitive advantage, such as patents, economies of scales, access to capital and market regulations less important in the current economic environment than they have been in the recent past. However, many scholars have considered motivated and skilled human resources as a unique source of competitive advantage for the firm (Lorange and Murphy, 1984; Lundy, 1994; Baird and Meshoulan, 1998; Storey, 1998; Boxall and Steeneveld, 1999; Analoui and Karami, 2002).

Human resources are a strategic asset of the firm – they turn a strategic plan into action. Unlike conventional assets, strategic human resources, as an intellectual or organisational capital, are largely invisible and therefore do not appear on the firm's balance sheet (Tomer, 1987). They are found in a skilled, motivated and adaptable workforce, and in a HRM system that develops and sustains it. Indeed, as intellectual capital has come to represent an increasing fraction of many firms' total assets, the strategic role of the human resources has also become more critical. Ulrich and Lake (1990) point to such an HRM system as the source of organisational capabilities that allow firms to learn and capitalise on new opportunities.

By and large, in order to implement the business strategies, the entrepreneurs and CEOs should absorb highly motivated people into SMEs and develop their competencies and capabilities. As Schell (1996) points out, 'the entrepreneur's single most important duty is to assemble a team of superstar employees by hiring and training, in game breaker positions'.

The strategic HRM concept

It would be useful to summarise the idea of strategic human resource management in this section, because managing human resources strategically is a part of the strategic management concept in SMEs. Much attention has been given to human resource management, yet often its varied roles within an organisation have been subject to neglect (Analoui, 1999). The mainstream concept of strategic human resource management (SHRM) is characterised by the importance which is placed first on the crucial role played by the senior management and second on the role of strategic HR policy and planning activities (Mabey, et al. 1998; Analoui, 1999). One of the key differences between traditional conceptions of HRM and SHRM is the extent to which human resource management is integrated into the strategic decision-making processes, which in turn tends to direct the organisational effort to cope with the environment (Guest, 1990; Analoui, 1997). From a business orientation point of view strategic HRM is defined as: 'those decisions and actions which concern the management of employees at all levels in the business and which are directed towards creating and sustaining competitive advantage' (Miller, 1989: 114). Strategic human resource management has been defined by Fombrun et al. (1984) as a set of techniques that enables interventions to be made within the business in order to improve performance. Therefore SHRM is an approach to making decisions on the intentions of the organisation concerning its people, an essential component of the organisations business strategy (Armstrong, 1996). In this context, SHRM is about the relationship between HRM and strategic management in the organisation and refers to the overall direction the organisation wishes to pursue in achieving its objectives through people (Box 7.10).

The SHRM perspective considers employees as strategic resources (Bennett et al. 1998). It has been proposed (Armstrong, 1996) that the concept of strategic HRM was first formulated by Fombrun et al. (1984), who wrote that there are three core elements that are necessary for firms to function effectively. These are mission and strategy, organisation structure and human resource management. According to Henry and Pettigrew (1986), one of the meanings of

> ### Box 7.10 Human resources as strategic assets for SMEs
>
> - **Human resources** are the strategic assets of the SMEs. They turn a strategic plan into action.
> - One of the **key differences** between traditional conceptions of human resource management and strategic human resource management is their approach to human resources.
> - **Strategic human resource management** considers human resources as a crucial element of strategy implementation.

SHRM is matching HRM activities and policies to some explicit business strategy. As a result, the new paradigm of strategic management considers human resources as a crucial element of strategy implementation.

The resource-based approach and strategy

In recent years there has been much concern for the resource-based view of the firm and strategy implication in SMEs (Lahteenmaki *et al.* 1998; Rangone, 1999; Analoui, 2000). This academic debate has been extended to the creation of a resource-based model of HRM (Boxall, 1996) which is seen as a foundation for organisational success (Kakabadse, 1999, 2001) and organisational effectiveness (Analoui, 1999). The new paradigm in the field of strategic management, earlier referred to as the 'resource-based approach', has emerged to help companies to compete more effectively in the ever-changing and globalised environment. This approach views competencies, capabilities, skills or strategic assets as the source of sustainable competitive advantage for the firm (Mabey *et al.* 1998). According to Prahalad and Hamel (1990) and Boxall (1992) a resource-based approach to strategy formulation and implementation focuses on costly to copy attributes of the firm as a source of economic rents, and therefore as the fundamental drivers of performance and competitive advantages. Generally there are various strengths associated with the adoption of a resource-based strategy. Boxall (1996) argues that the resource-based perspective implies the need to build strategic management processes. Indeed, most contemporary researchers concur that HR acts as a factor in determining the performance of the firm (Prahalad and Hamel, 1990; Hunt, 1995). For instance, Bennett *et al.* (1998) found that the integration of HR and strategy was greater when top managers viewed employees as strategic resources. Boxall concludes that:

> It seems safe to suggest, however, that what the resource-based perspective has stimulated is a re-balancing of the literature on strategy in a way that stresses the strategic significance of internal resources and capabilities and their historical development.

> (1996: 66)

The debate on strategic management and HRM reveals that the focus is centred on organisational success and effectiveness (Guest, 1990; Lahteenmaki *et al.* 1998; Analoui, 1999). As for strategic management, in recent years we have witnessed a major debate over the implication of the resource-based view of the firm for the theory of strategy. This debate also has implications for creating a strategic model of HRM (Boxall, 1996; Kakabadse *et al.* 1996). A typical way to approach SHRM is to define it as bridging the concept of business strategy and HRM (Lorange and Murphy, 1984; Boxall, 1991; Lundy, 1994; Lahteenmaki *et al.* 1998; Storey, 1998). There is some agreement at least on one point: there ought to be a link between a firm's strategy and the utilisation of its human resources (Lahteenmaki *et al.* 1998). What is HR strategy? Tyson (1995) defines HR strategy as the intentions of the corporation, both explicit and covert, towards the management of its employees, expressed through philosophies, policies and practices. Accordingly Schuler and Jackson (1987) have defined HR strategy very broadly to embrace three levels of activities – philosophies, policies and practices. Dyer (1984) defined HR strategy as the pattern that emerges from a stream of important decisions about the management of human resources, especially those decisions that indicate management's major goals and the means that are (or will be) used to pursue them.

According to Boxall (1992) there are two broad strands of meaning in the academic discourse on HRM. The first strand is based on the view that HRM constitutes a commitment-oriented model of labour management. In this context, HRM is seen as a distinctive approach to employment management (Guest, 1990; Pfeffer, 1994; Karami, 2001). As Boxall (1996) concludes, writers in this tradition are concerned with such questions as what practices constitute a high commitment model, is the model more likely to occur in unionised or non-union settings and are the outcomes of such a model actually superior?

The second strand of discourse in HRM is focused on the relationship between strategic management and employee relations in the firm (Hendry and Pettigrew, 1990; Boxall, 1996; Kakabadse *et al.* 1996; Wright *et al.* 1998). The concerns of writers in this school (Hendry and Pettigrew, 1990; Peck, 1994; Tyson, 1995; Boxall and Steeneveld, 1999) are spanning this intellectual boundary and thus the preferred definition of HRM is broad or generic, so as not to exclude any particular style of labour management (Boxall, 1996).

Human resources and competitive advantage

Following the growth of interest in strategic analysis in the face of mounting competition in industry, HR has been identified as a potential source of competitive advantage (Kakabadse *et al.* 1996). Some proponents of SHRM argue that the management of human resources must fit within a suitable strategy (Mabey *et al.* 1998). An increasing number of studies have attempted to assess the link between HR and strategy process (Wright *et al.* 1998). As we discussed earlier, a new paradigm of corporate strategy, which is referred to as the resource-based approach, has emerged to help companies compete more effectively in the ever-changing and globalising environment of the twenty-first century. This approach views competencies, capabilities, skills or strategic assets as the source of sustainable competitive advantage for the firm (Mabey *et al.*

1998). The link between human resources as a strategic asset of a firm and strategy can be assumed at different levels. There are four levels of linkage between HR and strategy: administrative linkage, one-way linkage, two-way linkage and integrative linkage (Golden and Ramanujam, 1985).

Anderson has argued that two fundamental and specific processes are available to HR people in order to help management to realise the full potential of the HR function in support of their business objectives. The first is linking people strategies to the company's strategic management process. The second is developing an HR strategy to support the corporation strategies (Anderson, 1997). The linking of business planning and competitive strategy with HR planning has dominated the HRM literature (Karami, 2002). HR and the corporation management group should engage in a strategic management process that links business strategy, organisational capabilities and people strategies. A complete business strategy in SMEs has three key components: an operating strategy, a financial strategy and people strategy. A well-developed business strategy identifies the need for specific organisational capabilities and reinforces the building of these capabilities as the primary focus of the people strategy (Kakabadse *et al.* 1996; Anderson, 1997).

HR involvement in strategy implementation

Human resource involvement in the strategic management process has been thought to be essential, to say the least. Its effectiveness, however, may vary with the firm's strategies. Strategic management is greater when top managers view people as a strategic resource (Wright *et al.* 1998; Analoui, 2002). This relationship between viewing employees as a strategic resource and the strategic involvement of the HR function may stem from differing required levels of involvement depending upon the strategy. As a result, it may be expected that the relationship between HR involvement in strategy formulation and implementation and SMEs managers' perceptions of HR effectiveness could be positive. In his recent research findings Brockbank (1997) summarised:

> The challenge for the HR professional is threefold: first examine and understand the context from which the business realities tend to derive; second, design critical, high value-added agendas and third, ensure that broadly defined HR practices are exactly aligned and unified around these agendas. As these develop, HR will contribute a more strategic and high value-added presence as the firm competes in increasingly complex and changing contextual conditions.
>
> (Brockbank, 1997: 69)

The desire to gain competitive advantage by integrating HR with business strategy and thus managing people more effectively is the main rationale behind strategic HRM thinking (Lahteenmaki *et al.* 1998). Human resource involvement in the strategy implementation process has been thought to be effective in many cases. The degree of its effectiveness may vary with the firm's strategies and it is has even been suggested that strategic management is greater when top managers view people as strategic resources (Wright *et al.* 1998).

As discussed earlier, HR involvement in the development and implementation of business strategies in small as well as large firms is one of the critical issues in studying HRM. To examine this thesis in UK manufacturing SMEs, the level of HR involvement in the process of formulation and implementation of strategy has been investigated (Analoui and Karami, 2002). The analysis of the data shows that human resources are more involved in strategy activities in high rather than low performance SMEs (Table 7.2). For instance in the high performance firms human resources were highly involved in strategy formulation (94 per cent), strategy implementation (96 per cent), long range planning (82 per cent), revising HR systems (78 per cent), and developing HR systems (91 per cent). Supporting the findings of Wright *et al.* (1998), the research result reveals a positive and significant correlation between HR involvement and firm performance in general in the studied SMEs.

The result of the data analysis reveals that the contribution of the human resources in the development and implementation of strategies is very much related to the CEOs' perception of HR as an important factor in a firm's performance. Overall, these results indicate that human resources are more involved in strategic activities such as developing HR systems, strategy formulation, long range planning and revising HR systems in those firms where their CEOs' perceive HR as a key source of competitive advantage. Therefore human resources as a factor for creating knowledge play an important role in increasing a firm's performance and its competitiveness in high performance SMEs (Analoui and Karami, 2002).

HR capabilities and implementation in SMEs

The importance of human resources in the distinctive sense of the term is based around the notion that people management can be a key source of sustained competitive advantage (Kakabadse *et al.* 1996; Mabey *et al.* 1998). This connection is, in turn, based on four main aspects – a human being's capability and commitment (Analoui, 1998), the strategic importance of human resources (Kakabadse *et al.* 1996), managing human resources by specialists and integration of human resource management and business strategy (Boxall, 1992). How do small business owner-managers perceive the importance of

Table 7.2			
	Factors	*Low performance SMEs* *	*High performance SMEs* **
HR involvement in strategy within high and low performance SMEs	Strategy formulation	42	94
	Strategy implementation	63	97
	Long range planning	39	82
	Revising HR systems	28	78
	Developing HR systems	44	91

*A percentage value indicates the percentage of the low performance firms (N = 39) in each category.
**A percentage value indicates the percentage of the high performance firms (N = 52) in each category.

human resources in the implementation of the business strategies? It is assumed that if the CEOs or business owner-managers perceive human resources as an important factor, then they will allow them to contribute to the decision-making process as well as strategy implementation. In our recent research we found that human resources have been perceived by CEOs as a crucial factor for strategy success in SMEs. For instance the findings of the research show that the majority of executives within the studied firms rated human resource capabilities as the key resource (71.2 per cent as very important and essential) (Figure 7.11). Accordingly, it has been assumed that if CEOs perceive human resources as a key resource they will put more emphasis on increasing the HR capabilities.

Consequently, it has been found that increasing human resource capabilities will lead to increased firm performance. Similarly, we found that high performance SMEs were involved in investment in the people, increasing training programmes for employees and management development programmes to develop human resource skills and capabilities. The chief executive officers were asked to rate the effects of the human resource capabilities on the firm's performance. The results confirm that the majority of CEOs believe that human resource capabilities, namely a skilled workforce (69 per cent), innovative human resources (59 per cent), effective human resources (78 per cent), human resource commitment (62 per cent), and training competent employees (81 per cent) have a high impact on increasing the firm's performance. It was found that utilisation of the firm's resources, particularly its human resources, could be related to the CEOs' perception of the importance of HR as a key resource of the firm. More specifically, a strong and positive relationship was discovered between a firm's performance and the HR capabilities in the studied firms. This thesis confirms the result of previous researches (Wright *et al.* 1998; Rangone, 1999) indicating that the firm's performance tends to positively relate to the core competencies of the organisation. Additionally, this result shows that one of the key competitive advantages of the firm is its human resources capabilities, which enable the generation of organisational effectiveness and high performance. Clearly any investment in increasing human resource capabilities must be considered as a crucial factor which in turn will increase the firm's performance.

Figure 7.11

Managerial perception of HR as a key resource of SMEs

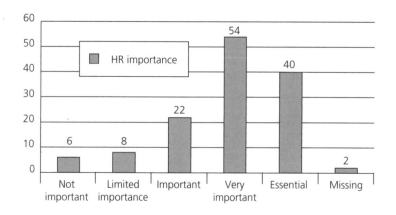

It can safely be concluded that increasing the HR competencies and capabilities of a firm will lead to a firm's success in achieving its goals and objectives in a competitive landscape. The prerequisite for this is of course the correct perception of the CEOs of the firms.

Toward the new strategic roles of HR in SMEs

Competition, globalisation and continuous change in market and technology are the principal reasons for the transformation of human resource management (Kakabadse *et al.* 1996; Beer, 1997). This competitive and global market has defined the new strategic roles for human resource management. Traditional HR ideas concentrate solely on physical skills, training covering only specific tasks, functional and subfunctional specialisation and concern for individual efficiency. The traditional perspective did not place emphasis on people and therefore paid more attention to task at the expense of people and their development (Analoui, 1998). The emerging human resource management ideas emphasise the total contribution to the firm, innovative and creative behaviour, overall effectiveness and cross-functional integration.

Finally, as a function of reduced transportation and information costs and of the removal of social and political barriers, the globalisation of business is proceeding at unprecedented and unexpected rates. Both the criteria and intensiveness of competition are changing as a result of globalisation (Brockbank, 1997). Globalisation is one of the essential reasons for the transformation of human resources management. In this case Beer has classified the main forces involved in changing human resources management in order to introduce its strategic role in a competitive advantage (1997). These forces are cost effectiveness, CEOs and development of new knowledge about the potential for organisations and their people to be a source of competitive advantage.

Managing the culture of the enterprise

Managing organisational culture is the third element of effective strategy implementation in small businesses. Organisational culture refers to the overall way the firm operates. It is the key component that gives any organisation that elusive, sustainable competitive advantage. What is culture? Culture is a company's value system. It is unwritten law, defining what is and what isn't done (Schell, 1996). Culture is like the personality of the firm. It includes the firm's history, its heroes and legends and everything that makes it what it is (Lasher, 1999). It is believed that the culture is a soft, intangible element that deals with people, trust, leadership and passion (Rinke, 1998). It is what people will do when no one tells them what to do. Organisational culture is composed of the shared values and beliefs of its members and is manifested in the ends sought by the organisation and the means used to achieve them (Hofstede, 1994). Bowman and Faulkner (1997) argue that culture is formed from three influences – organisational processes, cognitive processes and behaviour.

Organisational processes

Organisational structure and management style can influence culture. The power to make decisions is an important dimension for entrepreneurial organisations. The culture of sharing power by allowing greater participation of the employees will promote a contrasting culture to one which discourages and prevents greater involvement of the HR in decision-making and strategy formulation.

Cognitive processes

These are the values and beliefs and attitudes that employees hold in common. It could be assumed that in an entrepreneurial firm they can be developed by the personality of the entrepreneur or business owner-manager. The leadership style and dominant philosophy will be a determinant factor in forming the cognitive map of the employees and their subsequent preferences for behaviours and activities within the firm.

Behaviour

This is what actually happens in the organisations. Behaviour can be influenced by a variety of external factors but it reflects and reinforces culture. Analoui (2000), on the other hand, argued that often behaviour in the organisation is seen in its overt and most observable forms. Indeed, systematic observation has shown that the covert practices of the employees are both influencing and influenced by the culture of the enterprise and reflect the managerial style of the top management of the firm.

Schell argues that a small business's culture 'is a make-it-or-break-it element of success, because it is more than a collection of rules, regulations, company policies, guides and behaviour of the employees, including the entrepreneur' (1996: 161).

Culture elements for small businesses

Why is culture important for small businesses success? Rinke (1998) says that the firm's competitor can duplicate everything the firm does, but they can't duplicate the firm's culture. Competitors can duplicate the firm's pricing strategy, marketing and advertising tools, but they cannot behave as the firm does. Culture is everywhere in the organisations. All activities in the small businesses from production to marketing, administration and management are influenced by culture. Schell (1996) listed key elements of culture in small businesses which make up the entrepreneur's personality. These are:

- Values
- Perception
- Expense awareness
- Sense of urgency
- Time

- Accountability
- Follow-up
- Conflict resolution.

He argues that the entrepreneur can change the firm's culture as long as they understand that changes in culture '(1) require that the entrepreneur makes the change first, and (2) they take eons to occur' (1996: 167).

Now let's see how culture can help successful implementation of strategy.

Culture and strategy implementation in the entrepreneurial firms

Organisational culture supports and creates an environment in which to implement the developed strategy successfully; therefore the role of the entrepreneur is crucial in creating such a supportive culture in the firm. It has been suggested that an entrepreneurial culture needs to motivate people to do the right things, in the right way for the organisation as well as for themselves (Burns, 2001). Burns argues that in small businesses, the culture of a firm comes from the entrepreneurs, it reflects their personal values and belief. If the entrepreneur wants to plan and implement a strategy for success, they need to plan to achieve the culture they want. Rinke (1998) believes that managers can foster a positive culture and gives a few tips: give your credit away, listen more, talk less, create desire not fear, treat every employee like a volunteer, focus more on customer service, less on the bottom line, manage by appreciation, not by exception and finally – make work fun.

Accordingly, Lasher (1999) argues that the implementer's task is to implement the strategy with a minimum loss of human talent and expertise. He believes that 'the implementer should operate in two steps: first, identify areas in which the strategy and the culture are inconsistent. Second, develop a programme to change one or both so that they are reasonably consistent' (Lasher, 1999: 131). By and large, entrepreneurs should create a supportive environment and culture in which to implement the developed strategies successfully. In such an environment, the employees will be motivated to be involved in the formulation as well as the implementation of the strategy.

Budgeting for supporting strategy implementation

Allocation of resources is the task of strategists. They make decisions on which section of the firm should receive what resources. Resource allocation commits the organisation to implement the developed strategy. For instance, if the firm follows a product development strategy, the money and other resources have to be allocated to support the strategy activities such as research and development, product design and engineering. The main point in the allocation of resources is that the funds should be allocated to the departments in order to support the selected strategy. There are various approaches and methods to the allocation of resources. Budgeting is the main and most important tool for the allocation of the organisation's resources to support the strategy to be implemented.

Budgeting for entrepreneurial firms

In order to ensure implementation in SMEs, any business plan or strategy needs to be supported by adequate resources, in particular in financial terms. Budgets are plans as well as control tools and provide financial information about incomes and costs for CEOs. Budgeting shows how the CEOs are going to spend the money. Each department within the firm has its own operational plans which need money and financial support to be operationalised. As we discussed earlier, the first step in creating and operating a budget is the preparation of the sales forecast (Kuratko and Hodgetts, 2001). A sales forecast can be carried out by different forecasting techniques such as regression analysis. This will show what would be the amount of sales of the firm within a specific period of time. After a firm has forecast its sales for the budget period the expenses must be estimated. Manufacturing SMEs need to establish a production budget. Hence, the firms budget should contain the essential information on how money is to be allocated amongst its various departments and among different kinds of resources (Lasher, 1999). For instance, suppose that the sales department of a firm decides to increase the monthly sales by 10 per cent or the production department's target is to produce an exact number of items. In both cases, these plans need financial resources to secure their successful implementation. A firm's budget is normally viewed as a process that covers all departments of the firm. Budgeting often results in a formal, long range plan, normally expressed in terms of pounds over time, for example, the predicted revenues and expenses of a small business for 24 months. Long range budgeting, therefore, is a form of strategic planning. It may entail several years' financial projections, a coordinated management policy, and a control-and-correction mechanism that allows actual results to be compared to estimates.

Summary

- Strategy implementation is defined as putting the strategy into action. It includes five basic elements – organisational structure, leadership, human resources, managing culture and budgeting to support strategy.

- Organisational structure has been considered as the basic element of effective strategy implementation. The purpose of an organisational structure is to allocate the work and administrative mechanisms that are necessary to control and integrate the strategies of an organisation. There are different types of organisational structure including small organisations, functional organisations, multidivisional (M-form) or strategic business unit structure and matrix and innovative organisation structure, each having advantages and disadvantages.

- Small organisational structure applies to the firms at micro level. Because of the small size of the organisation, the communication between the manager and the employees is very fast and effective. The employees can accept a variety of responsibilities, there are no restrictions in undertaking any task and the business can respond quickly to the changes in the market and customers' expectations. In general, the degree of employees' contribution in strategic decision-making will depend on the management style of the owners or managers. Should employees be allowed to undertake a variety of tasks, there is a danger of role ambiguity and confusion of responsibilities.

- The functional organisation structure is usually applied in a SME. Here the total duties of the firm are categorised and clustered into specific groups. This type of structure is more appropriate for firms which produce one main (single) product or service. In functional organisations the CEOs enjoy a more extended strategic control over the firm's activities simply because the responsibilities and duties of the people are defined clearly. The firm achieves high efficiency through developing specialisation and functional expertise. The functional organisation develops a very narrow specialisation in each department. Coordination between functional departments is a difficult task for the chief executives. The functional organisation is the most appropriate structure for the SMEs.

- Geographic organisational structure focuses the firm's activities on local market conditions. In this structure, all functions in a specific region report to the same division manager. The firm will be flexible and responsive to changes in the local environments because each unit is small and tuned to its environment. The concern for customers' needs and expectations will be increased. This structure enables the firm to develop general managers and also it enables CEOs to pinpoint responsibility for performance problems in different areas. The main problem is duplication of resources and the high cost of running branches in different areas. The other disadvantages are fewer technical skills and less specialisation in each division and poor coordination between divisions.

- The proper organisational structure for diversified firms is the divisional or strategic business unit (SBU) structure. It allows the CEO to delegate authority for the strategic management of SBUs. The SBU structure can allow highly diversified corporations to optimise the strategic fit between related businesses and help to integrate the process of strategy formulation at both corporate and business level. It facilitates the coordination of the related activities within a SBU and allows strategic planning to be done at the most relevant level in the firm. It frees the chief executive officer for broader strategic decision-making. It provides excellent training for strategic managers. In contrast, it needs many general managers and creates difficulty in maintaining overall corporate image. Finally divisional or SBU structures have some problems with distributing central services to the functional areas.

- A matrix organisational structure combines both the functional structure and the divisional/SBU structure simultaneously. It provides dual channels of authority, performance responsibility and control. Matrix organisations provide skills and resources when and where they are most vital. In the matrix organisation there is decentralisation in strategic decision-making and more especially the middle managers are involved in the decision-making process. The matrix organisation prevents duplication of costs and allocates the resources effectively. In contrast, the matrix structure is easy to design but it is difficult to implement.

- There are many factors which influence the selection of organisational structure. Some of these factors are the size of the firm, technology, the environment and strategy. In SMEs, decision-making is highly centralised. The resulting structural flexibility is reinforced by the small number of hierarchical levels usually found in smaller organisations. SMEs have a relatively informal, flatter and highly centralised structure. They have more chance of quickly forming a team based on process structure, in line with re-engineering, because of their informal style and natural cross-functional working style. Most SMEs are seen as having a relatively simple structure.

- Leadership is the ability to influence people towards the attainment of goals. Probably the main difference between a manager and a leader is the source of their power. Leaders are creative, flexible, innovative and visionary. It could be claimed that a manager is persistent, a problem solver, analytical and rational. Leadership style is one of the most essential factors for successful strategy implementation in SMEs. Strategic entrepreneurship has eight key elements: personal vision, effective communication with stakeholders, organisational culture, knowledge and expertise, credibility, performance of the venture, leadership role and desire to lead. CEOs play a variety of roles as commander, architect, coordinator, coach and premise setter in implementing strategy in SMEs.

- There are six barriers to strategy implementation including top-down leadership style, conflicting priorities, ineffective senior management team, poor vertical communication, poor coordination and inadequate down-the-line leadership skills and development. Implementation is achieved with much less difficulty if the people feel that they have contributed to the strategy's emergence, and if the employees in general feel that their concerns have been heard in its development. Entrepreneurial leaders should not use an autocratic or dictatorial leadership style. Entrepreneurial leaders must be adept at using informal influence. They should meet and influence people. Entrepreneurial leaders must be adept at conflict handling and conflict resolution.

- Probably the most important and strategic resources of SMEs is their employees. Having the right people in the key organisational positions is a crucial element in strategy implementation. Human resources are the strategic assets of the firm and they are considered to be a competitive advantage of the firm. The entrepreneur's most important duty is to assemble a team of superstar employees by hiring and training, in game breaker positions.

- The new paradigm in the field of strategic management referred to as the 'resource-based approach' has emerged to help companies to compete more effectively in the ever-changing and globalising environment. This approach views competencies, capabilities, skills or strategic assets as the source of sustainable competitive advantage for the firm. It considers employees as strategic resources.

- The contribution of the human resources in the development and implementation of strategies is very much related to the CEOs' perception of HR as an important factor in a firm's performance. Human resources are more involved in strategic activities such as developing HR systems, strategy formulation, long range planning and revising HR systems, in those firms where their CEOs' perceive HR as a key source of competitive advantage. Emerging human resource management ideas emphasise the HR involvement in strategy, total contribution on the firm, innovative and creative behaviour, overall effectiveness and cross-functional integration.

- Managing organisational culture is the third element of effective strategy implementation in small businesses. Organisational culture refers to the overall way the firm operates. Culture is the key component that gives any organisation that elusive, sustainable competitive advantage. Culture is a company's value system. Culture is like the personality of the firm and is formed from three influences including organisational process, cognitive processes and behaviour.

- Culture is important for small businesses success because a firm's culture is unique and its competitors cannot duplicate it. The key elements of culture in small businesses which generally mirror the entrepreneur's personality are values, perception, expense awareness, sense of urgency, time, accountability, follow-up and conflict resolution.

- In small businesses, the culture of a firm comes from the entrepreneur – it reflects their personal values and belief. If the entrepreneur wants to plan and implement a strategy for success, they need to plan to create the kind of organisation culture which is conducive to success.

- The allocation of resources is the task of strategists. They make decisions on which section of the firm should receive what resources. Budgeting is the main and most important tool for the allocation of the organisation's resources to support the strategy implementation. Budgeting shows how the CEOs are going to spend the money. The firm's budget contains the information on how money is allocated among its various departments and among different kinds of resources.

Discussion questions

1. How do you define strategy implementation in SMEs?
2. What are the main elements in McKinsey's Seven-S framework? Discuss those elements in small businesses.
3. What are the main elements of strategy implementation?
4. Explore the organisational structure and its importance in strategy implementation.
5. What are the main differences between traditional organisational structures and a matrix structure?
6. What are the factors associated with selecting structures for SMEs?
7. Explain the basic elements of entrepreneurial leadership.
8. What are the main roles of leadership in strategy implementation?
9. What are the main barriers to effective leadership in small businesses?

10. Explore the nature of strategic human resource management.

11. How can human resources be considered as a competitive advantage of SMEs?

12. What are the new roles of the human resources in implementing an effective strategy?

13. Discuss the impacts of the culture in implementing strategy in SMEs.

14. Explain budgeting in entrepreneurial firms.

References

Aaker, D. A. (1998) *Developing Business Strategies*, 5th edn, John Wiley & Sons, Inc., New York.

Adams, W. and Brock, J. W. (1986) *The Business Complex: Industry, Labour and Government in the American Economy*, Pantheon Books, New York.

Analoui, F. (1997) How effective are senior managers in the Romanian public sector?, *The Journal of Management Development*, 16 (7), 502–516.

Analoui, F. (1998) Behavioural and causal influences on individual managerial effectiveness in the Ghanaian public sector, *The International Journal of Public Sector Management*, 11 (4), 300–313.

Analoui, F. (2000) Identification of clusters of managerial skills for increased effectiveness: The case of steel industry in Iran, *International Journal of Training and Development*, 4 (3), 217–234.

Analoui, F. (ed.) (1999) *Effective Human Resource Development: A Challenge for Developing Countries*, Ashgate, Aldershot.

Analoui, F. (ed.) (2002) *The Changing Patterns of Human Resource Management*, Ashgate, Aldershot.

Analoui, F. and Karami, A. (2002) How chief executives' perception of the environment impacts on company performance, *Journal of Management Development*, 21 (4), 290–305.

Anderson, W. R. (1997) The future of human resources: forging ahead or falling behind?, *Human Resource Management*, 36 (1), 17–22.

Ansoff, H. I. (1965) *Corporate Strategy*, McGraw Hill, New York.

Armstrong, M. (1996) *Personnel Management Practice*, 6th edn, Kogan Page Limited, London.

Baird, L. and Meshoulan, I. (1998) Managing two fits of strategic human resource management, *Academy of Management Review*, 13 (1), 116–128.

Beer, M. (1997) The transformation of human resource function: resolving the tension between a traditional administrative and a new strategic role, *Human Resource Management*, 36 (1), 49–56.

Beer, M. and Eisenstat, R. A. (2000) The silent killers of strategy implementation and learning, *Sloan Management Review*, 41 (4), 29–40.

Bennett, N., Ketchen Jr, D. J. and Schultz, E. B. (1998) An examination of factors associated with the integration of human resource management and strategic decision making, *Human Resource Management*, 37 (1), 3–16.

Bourgeois, L. J. and Brodwin, D. R. (1998) Linking planning and implementation, in B. D. Wit and R. Meyer (eds) *Strategy: Process Content and Context*, Thomson Learning, London, 682–691.

Bowman, C. and Faulkner, D. (1997) *Competitive Corporate Strategy*, Irwin, London.

Boxall, P. and Steeneveld, M. (1999) Human resource strategy and competitive advantage: a longitudinal study of engineering consultancies, *Journal of Management Studies*, 36 (4), 443–463.

Boxall, P. (1992) Strategic human resource management: beginnings of a new theoretical sophistication?, *Human Resource Management Journal*, 2 (3), 60–79.

Boxall, P. (1996) The strategic HRM debate and the resource-based view of the firm, *Human Resource Management Journal*, 6 (3), 59–75.

Brockbank, W. (1997) Human resource's future on the way to a presence, *Human Resource Management*, 36 (1), 65–69.

Burns, P. (2001) *Entrepreneurship and Small Business*, Palgrave, London.

Camille, C. (1994) Intrapreneurship in large firms and SMEs: a comparative study, *International Small Business Journal*, 12 (3), 54–67.

Cespedes, F. V. (1991) *Organising and Implementing the Marketing Effort*, Addison-Wesley Publishing, Reading.

Chandler, A. D. (1962) *Strategy and Structure*, MIT Press, Cambridge, MA.

Channon, D. F. (1999) *Encyclopedic Dictionary of Strategic Management*, Blackwell Business, Oxford.

Collis, D. J. (1996) Corporate strategy in multi-business firms, *Long Range Planning*, 29 (3), 416–18.

Cyert, R. M. and March, J. G. (1963) *A Behavioural Theory of The Firm*, Prentice Hall, Englewood Cliffs, NJ.

Daft, R. L. (2000) *Management,* 5th edn, The Dryden Press, New York.

Dyer, L. (1984) Studying human resource strategy, *Industrial Relations*, 23 (2), 227–247.

Floyd, S. W. and Woolridge, B. (1992) Managing strategic consensus: the foundation of effective implementation, *Academy of Management Executives*, 6, 27–39.

Fombrun, C. J., Tichy, N. M. and Devanna, M. A. (1984) *Strategic Human Rescue Management*, John Wiley, New York.

Francis, A. and McIntosh, R. (1997) The market, technological and industrial context of business process reengineering in the UK, *International Journal of Operations and Production Management*, 17 (4), 344–364.

Freel, M. S. (2000) Strategy and structure in innovative manufacturing SMEs: the case of an English region, *Small Business Economics*, 15 (1), 27–45.

Galbraith, J. R. and Kazanjian, R. K. (1986) *Strategy Implementation: Structure, System and Process*, 2nd edn, West Publishing, St Paul, MN.

Golden, K. and Ramanujam, V. (1985) Between a dream and a nightmare: on the integration of the human resource management and strategic business planning processes, *Human Resource Management*, 24, 429–452.

Goldsmith, A. (1995) Making managers more effective: Application of strategic management, Working Paper No. 9, March, USAID.

Grundy, T. (1998) Strategy implementation and project management. *International Journal of Project Management*, 16 (1), 43–50.

Guest, D. (1990) Human resource management and the American dream, *Journal of Management Studies*, 27 (4), 377–397.

Hale, A. and Cragg, P. (1996) Business process reengineering in the small firms: a case study, *Journal of Information*, 34 (1), 5–27.

Hambrick, D. C. (1994) Top management groups: a conceptual integration and reconsideration of the team label, in B. M. Staw and S. Cummings (eds) *Research in Organisational Behaviour*, JAI Press, Greenwich, CT, 16, 171–213.

Hauc, A. and Kovac, J. (2000) Project management in strategy implementation – experiences in Slovenia international, *Journal of Project Management*, 18 (1), 61–67.

Hendry, C. and Pettigrew, A. (1986) The practice of strategic human resource management, *Personnel Review,* 15, 2–8.

Hendry, C. and Pettigrew, A. (1990) Human resource management: an agenda for the 1990s, *International Journal of Human Resource Management*, 1 (1), 17–43.

Heracleous, L. (2000) The role of strategy implementation in organisation development, *Organisation Development Journal*, 18 (3), 75–86.

Hill, I. D. (1987) An intrapreneur-turned-entrepreneur compares both worlds, *Research Management*, 30 (3), 82–92.

Hofstede, G. (1994) *Cultures and Organisations: Software of the Mind*, McGraw-Hill, London.

Hoskisson, R. E., Hitt, M. A., Wan, W. P. and Yiu, D. (1999) Theory and research in strategic management: swings of a pendulum, *Journal of Management*, 25 (3), 417–456.

Hunt, S. (1995) The resource-advantage theory of competition, *Journal of Management Inquiry*, 4 (4), 317–322.

Kakabadse, A. (1999) Younger does not mean better, *The British Journal of Administrative Management*, Jan/Feb, 8–11.

Kakabadse, A. (2001) Dynamics of executive succession, *Corporate Governance*, 1 (3), 9–15.

Kakabadse, A. K., Kakabadse, N. K. and Myers, A. (1996) Leadership and the public sector: an internationally comparative benchmarking analysis, *Public Administration and Development*, 16 (4), 377–396.

Kalai, E. and Ledyard, J. (1998) Repeated implementation. *Journal of Economic Theory*, 38 (2), 308–317.

Karami, A. (2001) Strategy, HRM, and firm performance: the case of high tech SMEs in UK, 31st European Small Business Seminar, Dublin Institute of Technology, 13–14 September, Dublin, Ireland.

Karami, A. (2002) Corporate strategy: evidence from British Airways Plc, in A. Analoui (ed.) *The Changing Patterns of Human Resource Management*, Ashgate, London.

Kuratko, D. F. and Hodgetts, R. M. (2001) Entrepreneurship: a contemporary approach, 5th edn, Harcourt, Inc., Florida.

Lahteenmaki, S., Storey, J. and Vanhala, S. (1998) HRM and company performance: the use of measurement and the influence of economic cycles, *Human Resource Management Journal*, 8 (2), 51–65.

Lasher, W. R. (1999) *Strategic Thinking for Smaller Businesses and Divisions*, Blackwell Business, Oxford.

Lorange, P. (1998) Strategy implementation: the new realities, *Long Range Planning*, 31 (1), 18–29.

Lorange, P. and Murphy, D. (1984) Bringing human resource strategy into strategic planning: systems design considerations, in C. Fombrun *et al.* (eds) *Strategic Human Resource Management*, Wiley, New York.

Lundy, O. (1994) From personnel management to strategic human resource management, *The International Journal of Human Resource Management*, 5 (3), 687–717.

Lynch, R. (1997) *Corporate Strategy*, Pitman Publishing, London.

Lynch, R. (2000) *Corporate Strategy*, 2nd edn, Pearson Education Limited, Essex.

Mabey, C., Salaman, G. and Storey, J. (1998) *Strategic Human Resource Management*, Sage Publications, London.

McAdam, R. (2000) The implementation of reengineering in SMEs: a grounded study, *International Small Business Journal*, 18 (4), 29–45.

Miller, P. (1989), Strategic human resource management: what it is and what it isn't, *Personnel Management*, February, 46–51.

Mintzberg, H. (1991) The structuring of organisations, in H. Mintzberg and J. B. Quinn, *The Strategy Process*, Prentice Hall, New York.

Mintzberg, H., Quinn, J. B. and Ghoshal, S. (1995) *The Strategy Process*, (European edition), Prentice Hall International Ltd, London.

Morse, W. C. (1986) The delusion of intrapreneurship, *Long Range Planning*, 19 (6), 231–239.

Noble, C. H. (1999) Building the strategy implementation network, *Business Horizons*, 42 (6), 19–28.

Oladeji, S I. (1998) Technology policy and the development of small and medium scale enterprises in contemporary Nigeria, *Technovation*, 18 (2), 125–128.

Pearce, J. A. and Robinson Jr, R. B. (2000) *Strategic Management: Formulation, Implementation and Control*, McGraw-Hill International Editions, London.

Peck, S. (1994) Exploring the link between organisational strategy and the employment relationship: the role of human resource policies, *Journal of Management Studies*, 31 (5), 715–736.

Penrose, E. T. (1959) *The Theory of the Growth of the Firm*, Wiley, New York.

Pfeffer, J. (1994) *Competitive Advantage Through People*, Harvard Business School Press, Boston, MA.

Prahalad, C. and Hamel, G. (1990) The core competence of the corporation, *Harvard Business Review*, 68 (3), 79–91.

Rangone, A. (1999) A resource based approach to strategy analysis in small-medium sized enterprises, *Small Business Economics*, 12 (3), 233–246.

Rinke, W. J. (1998) How to build a positive organisational culture, *Food Management*, Cleveland, 33 (11), 17.

Robinson, R. and Pearce, J. (1984) The relationship between stage of development and small firm planning and performance, *Journal of Small Business Management*, April, 45–52.

Schell, J. (1996) *Small Business Answer Book*, John Wiley & Sons Inc., New York.

Schuler, R. and Jackson, S. E. (1987), Linking competitive strategies with human resource management practices, *Academy of Management Executives*, 1, 207–219.

Selznick, P. (1957) *Leadership in Administration: A Sociological Interpretation*. Harper & Row, New York.

Stoner, J. A. F., Freeman, R. E. and Gilbert, D. R. (1995) *Management*, Prentice Hall International Limited, London.

Storey, J. (1998) Do human resources really have a role in strategy?, *Financial Times Mastering Management*, 9, 14–18.

Thompson, J. L. (2001) *Strategic Management*, 4th edn, Thomson Learning, London.

Tomer, J. F. (1987) *Organisational Capital*, Praeger Publishers, New York.

Tyson, S. (1995) *Human Resource Strategy*, Pitman Publishing, London.

Ulrich, D. and Lake, D. (1990) *Organisational Capability: Competing from the Inside Out*, John Wiley and Sons, New York.

Voss, C. (1998) Made in Europe: small companies, *Business Strategy Review*, 9 (4), 1.

Waterman, R. H., Peter, H. T. and Philips, J. R. (1980) Structure is not organisation, *Business Horizons*, 23 (3), 14–28.

Westley, F. (1990) Middle managers and strategy: micro dynamics of inclusion, *Strategic Management Journal*, 11, 337–351.

Wheelen, T. L. and Hunger, J. D. (1998) *Strategic Management and Business Policy*, 6th edn, Addison-Wesley, New York.

Wickham, P. A. (2001) *Strategic Entrepreneurship: A Decision-making Approach to New Venture Creation and Management*, 2nd edn, Pearson Education Limited, Essex.

Woodward, J. (1965) *Industrial Organisations: Theory and Practice*, Oxford University Press, London.

Wooldridge, B. and Floyd, S. W. (1990) The strategy process, middle management involvement, and organisational performance, *Strategic Management Journal*, 11, 231–241.

Wright, P. M., McMahan, G. C., McCormick, B. and Sherman, S. C. W. (1998) Strategy, core competence, and human resource involvement as determinants of HR effectiveness and refinery performance, *Human Resource Management*, 36, 17–29.

8 Strategic control in small businesses

Learning objectives

By the end of this chapter you should be able to:

- Define strategic control.

- Describe the process of the control system.

- Explain the strategic surveillance and premise control.

- Explore implementation and special alert control.

- Discuss the methods of firm performance measurement.

- Explain the Z score model in organisational performance measurement.

- Discuss the three Es approach.

- Explore the balanced scorecard model.

- Discuss the implications of organisational performance measurement models in SMEs.

The main objective of this chapter is to review the concept of strategy evaluation and control in SMEs. It aims to answer the question, how can SMEs measure their performance and evaluate their strategy? Therefore, the chapter starts with a definition of strategic control and introduces the process of a control system within organisations. Then, in light of this, it describes the different types of strategic control employed in SMEs. In the third section the different approaches for measuring firm performance are explored.

Introduction

One of the main duties of management in small as well as large organisations is control and evaluation. As discussed earlier, evaluation and control constitute the last phase of the strategic management process. The formulation of strategic goals and the monitoring of their realisation is a complex exercise for any organisation. The use of systematic control procedures helps to ensure that organisations are making satisfactory progress toward their goals and that they are using their resources efficiently (Stoner *et al.* 1995). According to Hagen *et al.* (1998) strategic control refers to the corporate leaders' understanding of the strategies being implemented within the various business units. Therefore, strategic control focuses on the content of strategic actions in order to achieve appropriate outcomes.

In this chapter the process and the tools for employing strategic control will be discussed. In order to avoid any confusion, let's first define the concept of strategic control.

The definition of strategic control

How can SMEs ensure that the firms' actual activities conform to the planned ones? The question can be answered simply by defining management control. Control helps SMEs' managers to monitor the effectiveness of their firms. Before we define strategic control, let's first see how management control in general has been defined by other authors. Mockler (1984) suggests that management control is:

A systematic effort to set performance standards with planning objectives, to design information feedback systems, to compare actual performance with these determined standards, to determine whether there are any deviations and to measure their significance, and to take any action required to assure that all corporate resources are being used in the most effective and efficient way possible in achieving corporate objectives.

(1984: 2)

Strategic control, on the other hand, has been defined in different ways (Box 8.1). Essentially, strategic control encourages lower level managers to make decisions that incorporate moderate and acceptable levels of risk. According to Pearce and Robinson:

Strategic control is concerned with tracking a strategy as it is being implemented, detecting problems or changes in its underlying premises, and making necessary adjustment. In contrast to post action control, strategic control is concerned with guiding action as that action is taking place and when the end result is still several years off.

(2000: 443)

Hagen *et al.* (1998) argues that effective use of strategic controls by corporate leaders is frequently integrated with appropriate autonomy for the subunits so

Box 8.1 Types of control

Traditional process of control include four interrelated activities, which are defining performance standards, performance evaluation, diagnosing the deviations and system development.

Strategic control is concerned with tracking a strategy as it is being implemented, detecting problems or changes in its underlying premises, and making the necessary adjustments.

that leaders can gain competitive advantage in their respective markets. Strategic controls can be used to promote the sharing of both tangible and intangible resources among independent businesses within a corporate portfolio.

Strategy and operational plans

In SBU operational divisions of large firms, as well as the small and medium-sized enterprises, there must be a fit between strategy and the control systems. According to Shirley and Wolf (1994) effective strategy implementation requires integration with operational planning and control. As a rule, the operational plans should be consistent with the business strategies involved, bearing in mind that small businesses are more involved in operational plans. Consequently in small and medium-sized businesses the control activities should be related directly to the operational plan. In this way, the daily task of managing the business relates back to the strategic plan.

The process of control

The term control can be used as both a noun or a verb. Konsynski (1993) explains that the verb aspect of the control relates to checking, testing or verifying; exercising restraint. From this point of view the control is considered as a process. The noun form of the control relates to a state or measure of power and influence. The control process evaluates the organisational activities continuously and is closely related to the organisational structure and management style of the firm. Through the control process strategists determine whether or not the organisational goals and objectives are achieved. Traditionally, the process of control includes four interrelated activities. These are:

- Defining the performance standards
- Performance evaluation
- Diagnosis of the deviations
- System development.

Organisational control is the systematic evaluation of the organisational activities against organisational standards, determining deviations through gap analysis and developing the system. In the first step of the control process the strategist should define the standards set for performance. Performance standards can be qualitative, quantitative or a mix of both. Generally speaking, it is easier to define and evaluate quantitative performance indicators than qualitative ones. Volume of sales, number of production, return on investment (ROI) and amount of profit are all examples of quantitative standards.

The second step in the control process is evaluation and measurement of the actual organisational performance. Here, performance evaluation documents such as formal financial statements and performance appraisal are prepared. For instance, the profit and loss statement shows the sales volume, operational costs and net profit or loss for the performance period. Ordinarily, there are problems associated with the evaluation and measurement of the qualitative aspects of the organisational performance. However, management tools such as Total Quality Management (TQM) may provide alternatives for strategists for measuring the qualitative indicators.

The third step in the control process involves diagnosis and measurement of the deviations of the system by comparing actual performance to that of the defined standards. Application of this step reveals the probable gap between standards and actual performance. If there is no gap found between standards and actual performance, it would suggest that the planned organisational objectives have been achieved and the firm will not experience problems associated with strategic plan. For instance, suppose that a small business had a target to increase the sales volume by 15 per cent during the first six months of the year. At the end of the first six months, the financial statements show that the total sales volume has increased from £100 000 to £120 000. Therefore, this increase as an indicator suggests that the firm's sale objectives have been achieved.

The last step in the evaluation and control process is concerned with developing the system and taking any corrective action. This usually occurs when the managers find deviation between performance standards and actual standards. It must be borne in mind that system development may lead to changes either in employees' behaviour or performance standards. As illustrated in Figure 8.1, in cases where the firm fails to achieve the prescribed standard business managers may discover that either the performance standards have not been defined properly or that they have been set too low or too high.

It is important to note that undertaking the process of strategic evaluation and control is more than just reviewing the inventory of the processes and mechanisms of control. Control is the single most important part of the enterprise. Konsynski (1993) has suggested that, in judging strategic alignment, we need to consider the delivery mechanism for this critical management process or responsibility. Those systems that lead to a congruence of the strategic direction of the enterprise are thus key elements for strategic control.

As a final word, when implementing effective strategic control, strategists should consider either internal or external organisational factors which affect the organisational performance. They should determine the basic assumptions, strategic objectives and goals prior to defining the performance standards. If they discover any deviations, the strategic assumptions and objectives should be reviewed. It is of the utmost importance that a feedback mechanism has been correctly installed in the system so that strategists can ensure that all the deviations will be diagnosed and the whole system will be continuously improved.

Types of strategic control

According to Pearce and Robinson (2000) if we assume that a strategic management process includes strategy formulation and implementation, we can see four types of strategic control over the strategic management process. These are strategic surveillance, premise control, special alert control and implementation control. The first two strategic controls, strategic surveillance and premise control, cover both strategy formulation and implementation while the last two, special alert control and implementation control, cover the period of strategy implementation. Let's discuss each type of strategic control in some detail (Box 8.2).

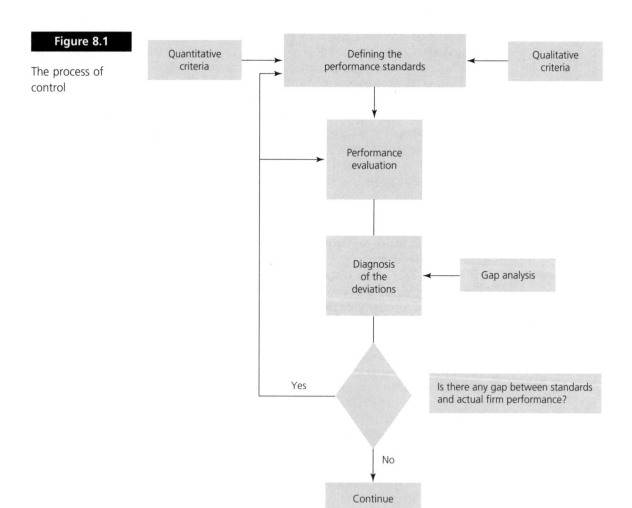

Figure 8.1

The process of control

Box 8.2 Types of strategic control

There are four types of the strategic control over the strategic management process:

- Strategic surveillance
- Premise control
- Special alert control
- Implementation control.

The first two strategic controls cover both strategy formulation and strategy implementation, the last two cover the period of strategy implementation.

Strategic surveillance

Strategic surveillance is an unfocused strategic control which helps the strategist to manage and control the strategy overall. In other words, strategic surveillance monitors the critical factors in either the firm's internal or external environment that are likely to have impact on the firm's strategy. As Schreyogg and Steinmann aptly defined it, 'strategic surveillance is designed to monitor a broad range of events inside and outside the firm that are likely to affect the course of its strategy' (1987: 101). By using strategic surveillance CEOs can have overall control on the firm's strategy. Establishing systematic environmental scanning can help strategists to be aware of critical environmental factors and consequently maintain a strategic surveillance over the SMEs' activities.

Premise control

The second type of strategic control is referred to as premise control. Strategists formulate strategies based on certain results of the environmental analysis, SWOT analysis and their assumptions or predictions of the future. It is clear that these assumptions and environmental circumstances may change from time to time, and strategists should review and change the firm's strategy if necessary. In other words, strategists may have to change the current strategy if a vital premise is no longer deemed valid. The strategic tool which helps managers to take such action is referred to as premise control. Premise identification techniques such as strategic assumption surfacing helps managers to uncover and understand the premises on which their strategies are based. As Pearce and Robinson observed, 'premise control is designed to check systematically and continuously whether the premises on which the strategy is based are still valid' (2000: 444). Basically premise control is concerned with monitoring two main factors – environmental and industry factors – involves continuous evaluation of the premises underlying strategy (Mark, 1994).

Environmental factors such as economical factors, technological changes and social and cultural factors play a significant role in the success of the firm's strategy. The firm's strategy is also influenced and affected by the industry factors. For instance, a competitor's strategy will impact upon the firm's strategy formulation and implementation. Premise control enables strategists to be aware of these shifts and hence to manage the strategy accordingly. When incorporated within an ongoing monitoring process which periodically checks and updates the premises, these techniques become particularly useful for indicating when major reconceptualisations of strategy are needed (Mark, 1994).

Implementation control

The third type of strategic control is implementation control. While strategic surveillance and premise control are concerned with exercising control over both strategy formulation and strategy implementation, implementation control is chiefly concerned with controlling the implementation of strategy in small as well as large organisations. Implementation of strategy is the process by which strategies are put into action through programmes, budget and procedures. This kind of control usually takes place as a series of activities that occur over an extended period of time and thus assesses the process of implementation phase by phase. 'Implementation control is designed to assess whether the overall strategy should be changed in light of the results associated with the incremental actions that implement the overall strategy' (Pearce and Robinson, 2000: 447).

The task of implementation control requires the reassessment of the firm's current strategic direction in light of its recent performance results (Mark, 1994). Implementation controls usually involve some form of milestone review process in which intermediate results of a strategic programme are compared with previously defined short term indicators of the programme's eventual long term success or failure. These controls can be used to make mid-course adjustments to strategy, to decide the appropriate level of resource support or to determine whether or not the strategic programme should be terminated.

Special alert control

Special alert control is used when unexpected events occur. If the firm suddenly faces a crucial factor that may significantly impact the firm performance, the current strategy should be reconsidered rapidly. Special alert control enables managers to reassess the firm's strategy and its current situation.

Strategy and the firm's performance

As discussed already, a typical strategic control system guides, monitors and evaluates progress towards meeting strategic goals and objectives. It steers the firm over the long term. Through a strategic control system, the performance of the firm is evaluated and measured. The traditional approach is to measure the effectiveness of an individual organisation in terms of its ability to meet and exceed its objectives in each of a number of specified areas (Smith, 1998). This model poses a number of issues in measuring especially qualitative variables in organisational effectiveness. For instance, problems in measuring qualitative or intangible success factors such as corporate image, technological competence, learning, corporate culture and employee morale are considerable.

The measurement of organisational effectiveness in administrative and service industries is particularly problematical because many of the outputs are intangible. The strategic planning literature recognises the inherent relationship between formulating strategic goals and the identification of the key success factors for any organisation. Any evaluation of organisational effectiveness could include an evaluation of relative performance compared to that of competitors. However, the critical factors for organisational success may be dependent on many variables, some of which are neither easily measured nor quantifiable. Where an overall integrated measure is difficult to achieve, the focus of attention is frequently shifted onto a few quantitative measures, simply because the alternative is just too complex to be considered seriously. Innovation, for example, may be ignored for these reasons.

In the area of financial performance, a simple earnings measure of effectiveness like return on investment (ROI) has been widely used. But this begs the question is it good enough? Problems associated with life cycles and accounting methods will make comparisons using such a measure difficult, even within the same industry. However, it could be argued that managers might reduce short term manipulation in pursuit of long term share price growth, especially if they are rewarded in terms of shares. There are specific techniques such as Z score model, the three Es approach and balanced scorecard that have been developed for measuring the performance of the firm. Let's discuss each of these techniques in some detail.

The Z score model

The Z score model measures the financial performance of the firm. In comparison to the other financial indicators such as share price and return on investment (ROI), which are too narrow for measuring firm performance, it offers an integrated measure of the financial performance of the firm. The Z score model therefore integrates financial features into a single score and can be used for the prediction of financial indicators in SMEs. For instance, the Taffler (1982) model combines four financial features into a single score:

$$Z = a + b \times x1 + c \times x2 + d \times x3 + e \times x4$$

While:

x1 = profitability measured as profit before tax/current liabilities
x2 = working capital, measured as current assets/total liabilities
x3 = leverage, measured as current liabilities/total assets
x4 = liquidity, measured by the no credit interval

The four diverse measures are combined using weightings (a, b, c and d) derived from a linear discriminate analysis with samples of failed and healthy companies. The overall Z score may be positive (for healthy companies) or negative (for companies subject to financial distress). The model is imperfect (Morris, 1998), like all similarly constructed models, in that it tends to over-predict failure; the distressed grouping includes many companies which do not fail, but that may be temporarily under performing. The Z score does give us a measure of overall financial performance, with which it is possible to rank all

UK companies and was constructed to measure solvency and indicate the likelihood of future survival, rather than the extent of overall well-being. Because it is confined to financial measures, even though it embraces aspects of profit and loss and balance sheet performance, its validity as a measure of overall organisational effectiveness is arguable.

The three Es framework

The Z score model only focuses on purely financial measures of the firm's performance, while the three Es framework includes non-financial variables in company performance measurement (Figure 8.2). The three Es framework consists of:

- Efficiency – concerned with the utilisation of equipment and the efficiency of the workforce.
- Economy – concerned with the optimum use of resources.
- Effectiveness – concerned with the achievement of outcomes.

This classification is particularly helpful in facilitating the generation of a host of suitable non-financial indicators.

The balanced scorecard

Rather than evaluating a corporation using just a few financial measures, Kaplan and Norton (1998) argue for a 'balanced scorecard', including non-financial as well as financial measures of organisational effectiveness (Figure 8.3). The balanced scorecard approach combines financial measures that tell the results of actions already taken with operational measures on customer satisfaction, internal processes, corporation innovation and important activities – the drivers of future financial performance (Wheelen and Hunger, 1998). The balanced scorecard provides an alternative which might offer improvements. Kaplan and

Figure 8.2

The three Es framework

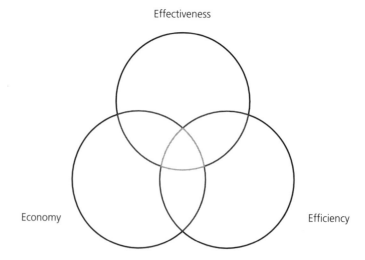

Figure 8.3 The balanced scorecard links performance measures

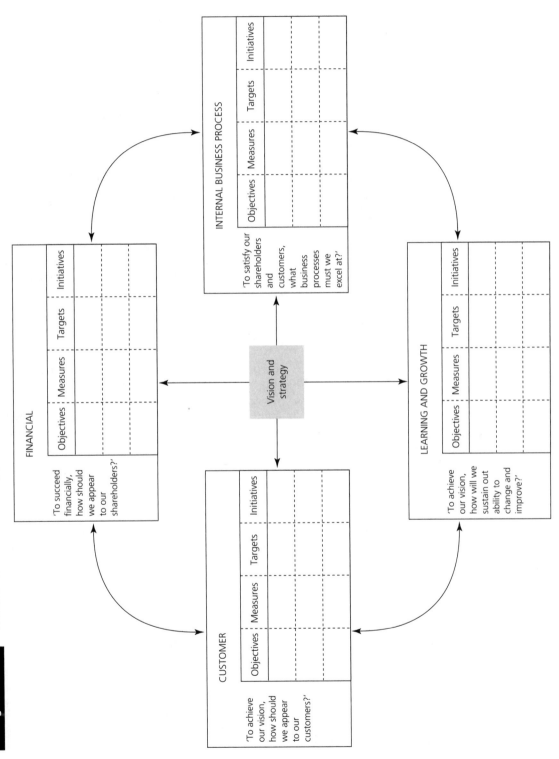

Source: Copyright © 1996, by the Regents of the University of California. Kaplan and Norton (1996). Reprinted from the *California Management Review*, Vol. 39, No. 1, by permission of the Regents.

Norton, in a series of articles, establish a multivariate approach which demands that the business be perceived both internally and externally. Management should develop goals or objectives in each of the four areas:

- Financial: How do we appear to shareholders?
- Customer: How do customers view us?
- Internal business perspective: What must we excel at?
- Innovation and learning: Can we continue to improve and create value?

Each goal in each area is assigned one or more measures, as well as target and initiatives. These measures can be thought of as key performance measures that are essential for achieving a desired strategic option. The balanced scorecard allows managers to look at the business from these four important perspectives.

Kaplan and Norton (1998), argue that giving senior managers information from four different perspectives, the balanced scorecard minimises information overload by limiting the number of measures used. Companies rarely suffer from having too few measures. The balanced scorecard forces managers to focus on the handful of measures that are most critical. Let us now discuss the different perspectives on the balanced scorecard approach.

Goals and measures

Today many companies have a corporate mission that focuses on the customer. 'To be number one in delivering value to customers' is a typical mission statement. How a company is performing from its customer's perspective becomes a priority of top management? The balanced scorecard demands that managers translate their general mission statement on customer service into special measures that reflect the factors that really matter to customers (Kaplan and Norton, 1998). Customers' concerns tend to fall into four categories: time, quality, performance and service cost. To put the balanced scorecard to work, companies should articulate goals for time, quality, performance and service cost, and then translate these goals into specific measures. Customer-based measures are important, but they must be translated into a measure of what the company must do internally to meet its customers expectations (Box 8.3).

Box 8.3 How the balanced scorecard helps SMEs' strategists

It combines the financial, customer, internal process and innovation and organisational learning perspectives and helps managers in:

- Understanding many interrelationships within the firm
- Transcending traditional notions about functional barriers
- Improved decision-making and problem solving.

The balanced scorecard keeps companies looking and moving forward instead of backward.

Managers need to focus on those critical internal operations that enable them to satisfy customer needs. The second part of a balanced scorecard gives managers that internal perspective. The internal measures for the balanced scorecard should stem from the business process that has the greatest impact on customer satisfaction factors that affect cycle time, quality, employee skills and productivity. Companies should decide what process and competencies they must excel at and specify measures for each.

The customer-based and internal business process measures on the balanced scorecard identify the parameters that the company considers most important for competitive success. Intense global competition requires that companies make continual improvements to their existing products and have the ability to introduce entirely new products with expanded capabilities. A company's ability to innovate, improve and learn ties directly to the company's value. That is, only through the ability to launch new products, create more value for customers and improve operating efficiencies continually can a company penetrate new markets and increase revenues and margins – in short, grow and thereby increase shareholders' value.

Ultimately, financial performance measures indicate whether there is a relation between the company's strategy and implementation and profitability, growth and shareholder value. Given today's business environment, should senior managers even look at the business from a financial perspective? Some critics go much further in their indictment of financial measures. They argue that the terms of competition have changed and that traditional financial measures do not improve customer satisfaction, quality, cycle time and employee motivation. In their view financial performance is the result of operational actions and financial success should be the logical consequence of doing the fundamentals well (Kaplan and Norton, 1998).

A number of performance measures are generated to reflect each of these four perspectives. Smith (1998) identifies 15: financial cash flow; sales growth; market share; customer sales from new products; on-time delivery; cooperative partnerships; internal technological ranking; cycle time; unit cost; yield; productivity; innovation – time to develop; time to market; process time and product focus. Much of this information will already have been collected; more will be available from internal sources. The remainder will emerge from customer surveys, benchmarking exercises and inter-company comparisons. Performance measurement of the kind advanced in the scorecard is a possible means of overcoming objectives in the short term, but still gives us no clear indication of a weighting system that would enable the four perspectives to be combined in a satisfactory manner to yield 'organisational effectiveness'. The question of comparability also remains unclear, because different market situations, product strategies and competitive environments will all require different scorecards.

Summary

- Traditionally, the process of control includes four interrelated activities – defining performance standards, performance evaluation, diagnosis of the deviations and system development. In the first step of the control process strategists should define the performance standard. Performance standards can be qualitative, quantitative or a mix of both. In the second step, performance evaluation documents, such as formal financial statements, and performance appraisal such as profit and loss statements are prepared. The third step in the control process involves diagnosis and deviations of the system by comparing actual performance to the defined performance standards. The last step in the evaluation and control process is developing the system and taking any corrective action.

- Strategic control is concerned with tracking a strategy as it is being implemented, detecting problems or changes in its underlying premises and making necessary adjustments. It is concerned with guiding action on behalf of the strategy as that action is taking place and when the end result is still several years off.

- There are four types of the strategic control over the strategic management process – strategic surveillance, premise control, special alert control and implementation control. The first two cover both strategy formulation and strategy implementation, the last two cover the period of strategy implementation.

- The Z score model measures the financial performance of the firm. It provides an integrated measure of financial performance; as a model it integrates financial features into a single score and can be used for the prediction of financial indicators in SMEs.

- The 'three Es' framework includes non-financial variables in the firm's performance measurement including efficiency, economy and effectiveness. This classification is particularly helpful in facilitating the generation of a host of suitable non-financial indicators.

- The balanced scorecard as a strategic control system combines financial as well as non-financial factors in organisational performance measurement. The scorecard puts strategy and vision, not control, at the centre. It establishes goals but assumes that people will adapt whatever behaviours and take whatever actions are necessary to arrive at those goals. The measures are designed to pull people towards the overall vision. By combining the financial, customer, internal process, innovation and organisational learning perspectives, the balanced scorecard helps managers understand, at least implicitly, about many interrelationships. This understanding can help managers transcend traditional notions about functional barriers and ultimately leads to improved decision-making and problem solving. The balanced scorecard keeps companies looking and moving forward instead of backward.

Discussion questions

1. How do you define strategic control?
2. Explain the traditional control process.
3. What are the four types of strategic control techniques? List and classify them into two groups in terms of their performance in the organisations.

4. Explain the nature and methods of strategic surveillance and premise control.

5. Explain implementation control in small businesses.

6. What is special alert control? Give an example.

7. Explain how the performance of SMEs can be measured. List the techniques and discuss the difference between financial and non-financial techniques.

8. Explain the application of the balanced scorecard in SMEs.

References

Hagen, A. F., Hassan, M. T. and Amin, S. G. (1998) Critical strategic leadership components: an empirical investigation, *Advanced Management Journal*, 63 (3), 39–44.

Kaplan, R. S. and Norton, D. P. (1996) Linking the balanced scorecard to strategy, *California Management Review*, 39 (1), 53–79.

Kaplan, R. S. and Norton, D. P. (1998) The balanced scorecard: measures that drive performance, in R. G. Dyson and F. A. O'Brien (1998) *Strategic Development*, John Wiley & Sons Ltd, Chichester.

Konsynski, B. R. (1993) Strategic control in the extended enterprise, *IBM Systems Journal*, 32 (1), 111.

Lysons, A. and Hatherly, D. (1996) Predicting a taxonomy of organisational effectiveness in UK higher educational institutions, *Higher Education*, 32 (1), 23–39.

Mark, K. F. (1994) Matching business-level strategic controls to strategy: impact on control system effectiveness, *Journal of Applied Business Research*, 10 (1), 25.

Mockler, R. J. (1984) *The Management Control Process*, Prentice Hall, Englewood Cliffs, NJ.

Morris, R. D. (1998) Forecasting bankruptcy: how useful are failure prediction models?, *Management Accounting*, May, 17–24.

Pearce, J. A. and Robinson Jr, R. B. (2000) *Strategic Management: Formulation, Implementation, and Control*, 7th edn, McGraw Hill, New York.

Schreyogg, G. and Steinmann, H. (1987) Strategic control: a new perspective, *Academy of Management Review*, 12 (1), 101.

Shirley, D. J. and Wolf, D. R. (1994) Strategic control systems for quality: an empirical comparison of the Japanese and US electronics industry, *Journal of International Business Studies*, 25 (2), 275.

Smith, M. (1998) Measuring organisational effectiveness, *Management Accounting*, 76 (9), 34–36.

Stoner, J. A. F., Freeman, R. E. and Gilbert, D. R. (1995) *Management*, Prentice Hall International Limited, London.

Taffler, R. J. (1982) Forecasting company failure in the UK using discriminant analysis and financial ratio data, *Journal of the Royal Statistical Society* (Series A), 145 (3), 28–34.

Wheelen, T. L. and Hunger, J. D. (1998) *Strategic Management and Business Policy*, 6th edn, Addison Wesley Longman Inc., New York.

Functional strategies in small and medium-sized enterprises

The main objective of this chapter is to review and discuss functional strategies in the realm of small and medium-sized enterprises. The chapter starts with the marketing strategy as the core strategy for small businesses. It continues with a discussion of the details of the pricing and advertising strategies, and the tactics in each strategy. The second section of the chapter reviews the contemporary theories and attempts to provide the details of financial strategies in SMEs. The chapter ends with a discussion concerning human resource strategies and their implication for small businesses.

Introduction

Strategies are formulated at three levels within the organisation. Corporate strategy, the first level, is formulated at the top. Business strategies are usually formulated and dealt with in strategic business units. Finally, functional strategies are formulated at the functional and operational levels of the organisation. It is imperative that a link is established between all three levels of strategy in the organisation (Figure 9.1).

In small businesses, the business owner-manager or CEO is the ultimate strategist who is inevitably involved in all three levels of strategy development. This chapter deals primarily with the functional level of strategies in SMEs. Functional strategy is defined as 'the approach taken by a functional area to achieve corporate and business unit objectives and strategies by maximizing resource productivity' (Wheelen and Hunger, 1998: 12). In SMEs, marketing strategies, financial strategies and human resource management strategies are all functional strategies and each will be discussed in this chapter in some detail.

Functional strategies in marketing for SMEs

Marketing is probably the strategic focus for SMEs (Shuman and Seeger, 1986). Small businesses will not be able to survive if they do not develop an effective marketing plan for their products and services. As discussed earlier, some of the strategic resources of the organisations – dedicated people, effective strategy and well developed marketing plans – are the main contributors to organisational success; but nowadays far more importance is attached to the marketing strategy. Observation shows that successful small businesses are committed to their marketing strategy and focus on the customers' needs. This

Figure 9.1

Strategy levels in organisations

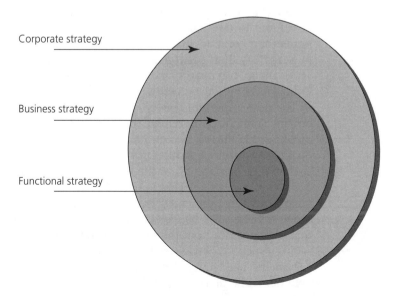

Corporate strategy

Business strategy

Functional strategy

raises the following questions: What is a marketing strategy? How can SMEs' managers develop a successful marketing strategy? What are the elements of a successful marketing strategy? Let's look at these questions and try to answer them in detail.

What is marketing?

People often confuse marketing with sales. It is imperative to establish that marketing is not solely concerned with selling or promoting a product or services. Selling and promotion are part and parcel of a larger marketing mix; a set of marketing tools that work together to affect the marketplace (Fields, 1999). Kotler and Armstrong have defined marketing as 'a social and managerial process by which individuals and groups obtain what they need and want through creating and exchanging products and values with others' (1994: 6). In contrast, selling is a developed art form which involves certain activities that directly effect the client's decision to purchase a product or service. Sales is a subset of marketing that carries out only those specific activities that are directly related to an actual sales event (Fields, 1999). From Kotler and Armstrong's definition of marketing, five basic elements can be observed. These are:

1. Customers' needs, demands and wants
2. Products
3. Value and satisfaction
4. Exchanges transactions and relationships
5. Market.

The basic concept underlying marketing is human needs. Human needs are referred to as human wants which are shaped by culture and individual personality and people satisfy certain aspects of their needs by purchasing products and services. Products in this sense of the word are anything that can be offered to the market to satisfy the customers' needs or wants. Kotler and Armstrong contend that customers are faced with a variety of products that might satisfy their need(s), each with specific different characteristics and value. They make buying choices based on their preferences which are largely influenced by their perception of the products' value.

The next important concept in marketing is exchange. Exchange is the act of buying something in return for something like money. The act of exchange occurs in the market, which has been defined as the set of actual and potential buyers of a product. Kotler and Armstrong equal the concept of marketing to a circle which is made up of the five elements of marketing (see above) linked to each other as a chain. That is why they define marketing as a process by which people buy what they need by creating and exchanging products with others. In order to distinguish between marketing and selling, Kotler and Armstrong argue that selling starts from the factory while marketing starts from the market. The selling function focuses on the existing products but marketing focuses on the customers' needs and demands. Selling usually ends with profit through sale volume, while marketing ends with profit through customer satisfaction.

The importance of marketing in SMEs has been investigated. In their recent research Murdoch *et al.* (2001) found that the SMEs managers' perception of marketing is very important and that they should be more concerned with marketing and concentrate more effort in that area. On the whole, companies seem to be aware of changes in their markets and how those changes are likely to impact on their business. Zimmerer and Scarborough also define marketing in small businesses as 'the process of creating and delivering desired goods and service to customers involves all of the activities associated with winning loyal customers' (2002: 180). They argue that the secret to successful marketing is to understand the customers' needs, demands and wants, offer them the product and service that satisfies their needs and provide them with convenience and value (Box 9.1).

In SMEs, the marketing function impacts on the whole firm's performance. All other functional areas of the firm such as finance and production should be coordinated by the marketing section (Bhide, 1994; Analoui and Karami, 2002). For instance, through analysis of market demand the marketing department determines what type of product should be produced; then the financial department allocates the necessary financial resources and budget to support and implement the intended marketing strategy. Similarly the HR department provides the skilled employees needed to produce the desired product. In this way, the marketing strategy could be considered as the core strategy which drives the firm towards its ultimate objectives. We have established that the type of marketing employed by a small firm largely depends on the life cycle stage of its product or services.

The first stage of the life cycle of SMEs is start-up. At the start-up stage business activity will focus on product orientation and gaining customer acceptance (Churchill and Lewis, 1983) and the marketing function should be appropriate to this. Carson (1985) aptly elaborates how the SMEs' marketing at the start-up stage is likely to be characterised and dominated by the reactive marketing practices of the firm. In other words, the quality and impact of the marketing can be determined by the way customer enquiries and market changes are responded to. As the business develops, much of the marketing will be characterised by experimenting or tinkering with a variety of marketing techniques. As the business becomes established over a number of years the entrepreneurs will develop their own marketing style and practice (Boussoara and Deakins, 1999).

In moving through the various life cycle phases, a SME will progress from a relatively uncontrollable marketing position to a relatively controlled marketing

---

Box 9.1 What does marketing mean for small businesses?

Marketing is different from selling. Selling is the process of delivering goods from factory to the customers, while marketing as a concept is getting the product from the market to the customers. Marketing in small businesses has been defined as 'the process of creating and delivering desired goods and services to customers and involves all of the activities associated with winning and retaining loyal customers' (Zimmerer and Scarborough, 2002: 180).

situation. By this stage, arguably, the enterprise's marketing will have become 'established' within certain boundaries. The entrepreneur/owner-manager will now know what kind of marketing works and what does not, and consequently will tend to adhere to the approaches to marketing that have paid off rather than experimenting with untried approaches (Carson and Gilmore, 2000).

Marketing strategy

The term marketing strategy has a different meaning within the overall marketing function. Most research in marketing in the field of SMEs suggests that some consider marketing strategy as an important factor to the firm's success (Carson and Gilmore, 2000). Murdoch *et al.* (2001) reported that there seems to be very little understanding of marketing as a strategic planning tool amongst Irish SMEs, and that the concept and practice of marketing has been employed by default rather than through planned effort within the studied firms. For most respondents in that study, marketing represented an action plan or series of activities, often as a support to selling. These activities were not only unplanned but were often an inconsistent series of reactions to situations.

Nowadays market conditions and the customers' needs and wants are subject to frequent and fast changes. Because of globalisation and internationalisation, the business environment for SMEs is becoming increasingly turbulent and small business managers and entrepreneurs should be more aware of the importance and impact of strategic marketing on the performance of their firms (Analoui and Karami, 2002). Although the marketing strategy is only one of the functional strategies of the firm, there is an overlap between the firm's overall strategy and its marketing approach. A marketing strategy enables SMEs to define their target market and choose a market mix approach. The marketing strategy looks at the customers' needs, wants and demands and determines how the firm can and should satisfy them.

In order to develop an effective marketing strategy for SMEs, entrepreneurs and small business managers should be innovative and creative (Box 9.2). The importance of creating an effective marketing strategy for SMEs is clear. But the question posed is what are the characteristics of the effective marketing strategy for SMEs? Zimmerer and Scarborough (2002) put forward five principles for developing a powerful and effective marketing strategy:

- Find a niche and fill it.
- Don't just sell, entertain.
- Strive to be unique.
- Create an identity for your business.
- Connect with customers on an emotional level.

Therefore, it is recommended that in developing a marketing strategy for small businesses a niche should first be found and focused on, avoiding head-on competition with larger firms. A niche strategy will allow the SME to maximise the advantages of being small. As we discussed in Chapter 5, the focus strategy is more attractive to small businesses than low cost leadership or

---

Box 9.2 Characteristics of an effective marketing strategy

An effective marketing strategy in small and medium-sized enterprises is concerned with:

1 Determining the needs, demands (wants) of the customers
2 Identifying target market of the business
3 Creating competitive advantages of the firm
4 Choosing a marketing mix.

---

differentiation. It is essential for CEOs to create a unique identity for the firm through developing an appropriate strategy for their marketing. Finally, in developing the marketing strategy managers of small businesses should realise that connecting deeply with customers and reacting to their views and comments are crucial factors for their success. An effective marketing strategy is concerned with the achievement of four main objectives – determining the needs, demands, and wants of the customers, identifying the target market, creating a competitive advantage for the firm and choosing a marketing mix.

We will now discuss each of the above objectives in some detail. Bearing in mind that for SMEs two main questions need to be answered before the marketing plan can be developed: for whom are you designing your product or service (market segmentation), and exactly what should that product or service mean to those in the marketplace (market positioning)?

Marketing research for small businesses

The first objective of the strategic marketing plan is determining the customers' needs, demands and wants. This can only be done by conducting market research. Marketing research can be defined as a tool for obtaining the information that serves as the foundation for creating a marketing plan. It involves the systematic collection, analysis and interpretation of the data pertaining to a small businesses' market, customers and competitors (Hart and Tzokas, 1999; Zimmerer and Scarborough, 2002). The marketing research gathers valuable information which the CEOs need in order to develop the firm's strategy. It shows what the customers' expectations, interests and needs are. Large firms regularly conduct market research to provide the necessary information for developing the firm's marketing strategies, but there are problems with marketing research in small businesses.

The extent of the importance of the market research for smaller firms is only revealed when managers realise that they must avoid mistakes because there is no margin for error if the firm's funds are scarce and budgets are tight. Kotler and Armstrong (1994) comment that managers of small businesses often think that marketing research can be done only by experts in large firms; but many of the research techniques such as observation, survey and experiment are also accessible to smaller firms. Small business managers can obtain information about their products and services simply by observing things around them. For example, a print shop manager can observe the advertisement methods and styles of his/her competitors in the local newspaper. Managers of small businesses can also gather the required data using an inexpensive but effective survey. For instance, the manager of a local restaurant can obtain customers' feedback about the quality of the service provided by developing a small questionnaire which accompanies the bill. Managers can also conduct their own simple experiments. For example, by varying the newspapers in which they advertise the manager of a sports centre can learn about the effects of the advertisement size, frequency and style.

Murdoch *et al.* (2001) found that none of the small business managers in the studied firms undertook formal information gathering, but many used a range of informal techniques. This included keeping up to date with general and specific media coverage, reading trade and consumer magazines, networking both formally and informally, and through membership of trade associations and business clubs. Managers understand the importance of marketing research in gathering data with which to develop an effective marketing strategy.

Marketing research and firm performance

Marketing information and marketing research are central to business success (Handler, 1994; Helms *et al.* 1997). Recently, we have witnessed efforts on the part of the scholars in the field of marketing in small businesses, to study the link between marketing research and company performance in the international domain. Several empirical studies have reached the conclusion that marketing research is indeed an important element in a firm's success. One of the notable studies in this field is that of Hart and Tzokas (1999) on the marketing research activities of small firms exporting from the UK. They reported that those SMEs that go about collecting greater amounts of background/infrastructure information about their export markets tend to exhibit higher export performance as measured by the ratios of export sales and profits to overall sales and profits. Hart and Tzokas (1999) concluded that:

- More formal marketing research activities are clearly related to higher ratios of both export sales and profits.
- Higher export profits are strongly related to information usage patterns. Initial evidence shows that decisions based on information collected may well contribute to export performance.
- Export marketing information, collected proactively and used seriously to aid decision-making in the export arena, is associated with higher levels of export performance.
- Particularly for exporting SMEs, the use of information relevant to the background/infrastructure of the import country could increase the firm's export profitability and the percentage of sales accounted for by its exports.

Similarly, Analoui and Karami (2002) in their recent work investigated the relationship between gathering environmental information and firm performance in the UK's SMEs. They found that successful SMEs do analyse environmental factors before formulating business strategies and developing marketing plans. High performance SMEs stress the importance of environmental analysis in the development of corporate strategy. In comparison, low performance firms have been shown to place less emphasis on formal and high frequency marketing research. They reported that there are different benefits from having a formal or informal marketing research and environmental analysis system. In this regard, a scanning system is seen as a necessity for the formulation and planning of business strategies, increasing profit and growth rate of the firm, and developing the firm's adaptability to unexpected environmental changes in a turbulent marketplace.

The strategic awareness of the CEOs plays an important role in the firm's performance. Where the CEO exhibits a distinct lack of strategic awareness and lack of information about the business environment the firm performance is low. As a result, the CEO's strategic awareness of the potential benefits of considering formal environmental scanning will be a significant determinant of the success and survival of the firm in the long term for SMEs.

The process of market research

The aim of marketing research is gathering data that are important for developing a strategic marketing plan. Marketing research can be carried out through a step-by-step process. This involves definition of the problem, collecting the data, analysing the collected data and finally drawing conclusions (Handler, 1994). Bear in mind that in small businesses all the mentioned research steps can be carried out either formally or informally (Box 9.3).

Step one: problem definition

The first step in the marketing research process is defining the problem – which is not always easy (Helms *et al.* 1997; Malhotra, 1999). Small business managers and entrepreneurs sometimes confuse a symptom with a problem. Typically, the entrepreneurs are not always aware of where the problem is until it is too late

---

Box 9.3 Marketing research in SMEs

Marketing research is the process by which small businesses can determine what their customers' demands, needs and wants are. It involves formally or informally collecting and analysing the data pertaining to small business environment and customers. Marketing research consist of the following steps:

- Problem definition
- Data collection
- Data analysis
- Conclusion and interpretation.

and the sales go down. For instance, when the firm loses its customers it signifies that there is a problem. In this case, taking up market research for the first time in order to find out the reason for the loss of customers and in an attempt to recover the lost businesses would probably be too late. In other words, it is much better to establish a practice of regular marketing research within the business to be forewarned of any potential problems. Therefore, the first task of the business is to define the problem.

Step two: data collection

In this stage, we have to determine how the data will be collected and how and by what methods they should be analysed to resolve the defined problem. Should we conduct a telephone survey, should we interview our customers, or arrange a focus group? There are different methods of data collection in marketing research (Malhotra, 1999). The data can be categorised into two main groups: primary and secondary. The primary data can be gathered through different methods such as observation, conducting interviews, questionnaire or an online survey. It has already been noted that in small business gathering data from individual customers (one-to-one) and then developing a marketing plan designed especially to appeal their needs, demands and preferences is more efficient. This approach requires the business owners to gather and analyse the detailed information about their target customers (Malhotra, 1999). Primary data can be gathered through the following techniques:

- Observation
- Questionnaire and customer survey
- Interview
- Telephone interview
- Focus groups
- Daily transactions.

Each of the data gathering methods has its advantages and disadvantages. Marketing researchers in SMEs can either select one specific method or combine different methods in order to gather the relevant primary data. For gathering secondary data, it has been suggested that small business researchers can use different resources including business directories, direct mail lists, demographic data, census data, forecasts, previous market research results, articles, local data and the World Wide Web (Zimmerer and Scarborough, 2002).

Step three: data analysis

The collected data in their raw form cannot be used for decision-making or developing business plans unless they are analysed and interpreted. The extent of the data analysis and interpretation of the results depend on the nature of the information sought or the problem being investigated. It is normally helpful to analyse the data descriptively first and illustrate the general picture of the data in tables, cross-tabulation, trends, bar charts and the like. Then the gathered data can be analysed for problem solving purposes.

Step four: conclusion and interpretation

Drawing conclusions and interpretations from the analysed data will complete the task of the market research. In a small business drawing conclusions is not as hard as in larger firms (Chaston *et al.* 1999). Suppose that the manager of a local firm manufacturing kitchen utensils realised that the sale of the products has been decreasing recently. The management team decide to investigate the problem. After contacting a sample of their customers, they realised the reason for the decrease in sales was due to a lack of after sales service. This realisation prompted the management team to revise their policy and ensure that the requested facilities were provided. The gradual increase in customer numbers points to the process of recovery.

Determine the target market of the business

The second step in developing an effective marketing strategy is determining the target market – the specific group of customers who are targeted by the firm for its products or services (Carson and Cromie, 1989; Burns, 2001). For instance, suppose that a small garment manufacturing firm produces only menswear. The target market for this firm is therefore men, and the marketing strategies of the firm should cover the needs and wants of men. As discussed in the last section, the important task is to determine what the needs, demands and wants of the customers are. Therefore, the firm should know *who* its customers are. In other words, the marketing research will help to identify the target market of the firm. A strategic marketing plan should determine a clear target market. If we do not know which group of people the firm should serve, we will not be able to formulate and implement a successful marketing strategy. Therefore, accurately defining the customer groups of the business is the prerequisite to developing a strategic marketing plan (Hanlon and Scott, 1995). Some small businesses fail to pinpoint their target market or tend to dismiss it as being too small; the irony of this is that small firms are more suited to reaching market segments that their larger rivals overlook or consider too small to be profitable (Zimmerer and Scarborough, 2002).

Because of financial constraints and budget limits, small businesses cannot afford to make big mistakes. They should have a clear picture of their customers, what they need and what they want. However, in certain cases, defining the target market is not easy. For instance, the PC games production firms used to target young people as their main customers, but new developments in computer technology have made games with realistic graphics and speed a reality and these kinds of game appeal to both adults and children.

The last point is that small businesses are at a significant disadvantage when competing with their larger counterparts. It is extremely difficult for a small growing company to compete with the larger more established names and brands in the market unless they learn how these larger competitors gain a sustainable advantage with identical products or services offered. Their market dominance, ideas and innovation stem from only one source – employee knowledge (Pangarkar and Kirkwood, 2002).

Developing a market-focused strategy can help SMEs that suffer from a lack of financial resources. In other words, SMEs can benefit from focusing on a specific segment of the market. Growing businesses tend to focus on their products or services rather than on the knowledge resources available to them. In this sense, the niche could be a good example. Basically, the target market concept is related to the differentiation concept. Small businesses can gain competitive advantages in the market by differentiation of their products and focusing on the niche. What small businesses need to learn from larger competitors is how to develop a dynamic learning environment which can propel innovation, strengthen market position and develop a true competitive advantage (Pangarkar and Kirkwood, 2002).

Determine the competitive advantages of the firm

Marketing strategy should consider the factors on which SMEs can build a competitive edge in the marketplace (Carson *et al.* 1995). Customer satisfaction is the ultimate objective of a strategic marketing plan. A competitive edge which leads to a high level of customer satisfaction is a crucial factor for the firm's success. Successful entrepreneurs use the advantages of the smallness of their firms to build a competitive edge over their larger competitors.

There are different bases on which SMEs can develop a competitive advantage. As we discussed earlier, focusing on customers' needs and wants can help small businesses in building a competitive edge. In this regard, Bagchi-Sen and Kuechler (2000) in their recent research compared two categories of resource in SMEs for creating competitive advantages. They concluded that competitive advantage is based on flexible specialisation such as customisation of services for specific groups of clients, speed of delivery, collaboration with other producer service firms, and specialised skills. Face-to-face interaction with clients continues to be the preferred mode of service delivery despite the increased adaptation of local area networks and other modes of information technology which are now used by the proactive, functionally diversified or internationally oriented firms. Other researchers suggest positioning as well as understanding customers' needs as a source of building a competitive edge for smaller firms. Hatch and Zweig (2001) argue that the essential components of a successful strategy include the following:

- A unique position
- A defensible position
- A clear customer need in a defined, significant target market.

Accordingly, Kuratko *et al.* (2001) studied quality practices for a competitive advantage in smaller firms. They argued that seven factors are important in gaining competitive advantages for smaller firms:

1. Leadership: as we saw in Chapter 7, the leadership style can be a source of competitive advantage for the small business. The leadership style involves how senior managers build and sustain a company-wide system dedicated to high expectations, high performance, individual development, initiative, organisational learning and innovation.

2. Strategic planning: addresses the planning undertaken by small businesses (Armstrong, 1982; Chan and Foster, 2001) – how a company develops and sets its strategic directions to gain its objectives and goals. Effective use of strategic planning includes passing higher level strategy and objectives to operations in order to develop operational systems for meeting business and customer performance requirements.

3. Customer and market focus: the customer is at the centre of quality strategies for small businesses. Understanding the customer and the marketplace involves listening to customers and studying customer satisfaction data (Zimmerer and Scarborough, 2002). Marketing research provides such customer satisfaction data.

4. Information and analysis: this category examines the central communication network of the high quality firm. Moreover, it is believed that effective use of information drives the firm's continuous improvement in performance and competitiveness (Malhotra, 1999).

5. Human resource focus: human resources are considered to be competitive advantages of the firm. Creating a high performance workplace and developing employees that embrace change are important aspects of the HRM function. Smaller entrepreneurial firms generally have key challenges with HRM because the small size of the firm often does not warrant hiring professionals exclusively dedicated to HRM activities (Analoui, 2002).

6. Process management: efficient and effective processes require integrated tasks from product/service design to post-sale customer service. For instance, just-in-time (JIT) operating systems may be appropriate for small and entrepreneurial firms by focusing on process improvement and increasing flexibility.

7. Business results: this category takes the form of data pertaining to customer satisfaction, company finances, supplier performance and company-specific operations. Smaller entrepreneurial firms usually do not require the information infrastructure that larger firms need (Kuratko *et al.* 2001).

According to Zimmerer and Scarborough (2002), for small businesses to achieve a high level of customer satisfaction they may have to rely on six important sources to develop a competitive edge: a focus on the customer, devotion to quality, attention to convenience, concentration on innovation, dedication to services and emphasis on speed.

Marketing mix

An effective marketing strategy should help in creating a marketing mix for SMEs. Once the firm has decided on its competitive marketing strategy, it is ready to develop the details of the marketing mix. The marketing mix has been defined as 'the set of controllable, tactical marketing tools that the firm blends to produce the response it wants in the target market' (Kotler and Armstrong, 1994). Marketing mix consists of four main elements known as the 'four Ps': product, price, promotion and place. Usually, the firm combines these elements to reach its target market. Figure 9.2 illustrates the four Ps in a marketing mix concept.

The four Ps of marketing are the main elements of the effective marketing strategy. Small and medium-sized enterprises should integrate these elements to maximise the impact of their products and services on the customers, and to increase customers' satisfaction. Let's review the marketing mix elements of the four Ps in detail here.

Product and service

A product means the goods and services which the firm offers to the market and whatever the firm sells. As mentioned earlier, the product must satisfy the needs and demands of the customers. The product is an essential element of the marketing strategy and travels through the various stages of the product life cycle (see Figure 9.3).

Figure 9.2

Marketing mix

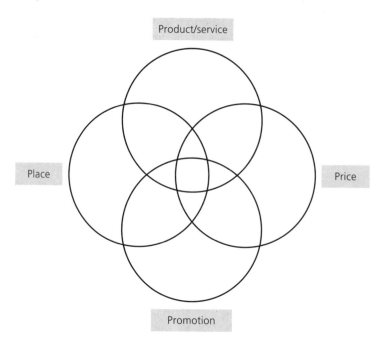

Figure 9.3

Product life cycle

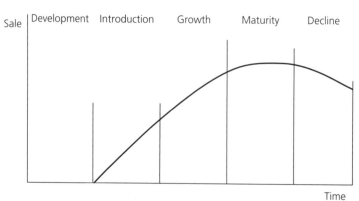

In each stage of the product life cycle the firm should follow a specific marketing strategy. A product life cycle consists of five stages. These are:

1. Product development
2. Introduction
3. Growth
4. Maturity
5. Decline.

The first stage of the product life cycle is the product development in which the firm finds and develops a new product idea (vision of a new product). During the product development stage the firm invests in developing the idea and creating the new products to satisfy the needs of the customers. Notice that there is still no sale in this stage. Once the firm has developed the new product, it introduces the new product to the market. Introduction takes time and in some cases it lingers for many years. In this stage, sales growth is very slow and the expenses of the distribution and promotion of the product are very high. Therefore, the profit in production stage is negative or very low. Here, SMEs can adopt one of several marketing strategies such as introducing the product to the market with a low or high price. The important point is that by choosing a proper strategy in the production stage the firm can introduce the product to the market effectively and increase the sales in the next stage. The advertising and promotion strategy which gives information about the new product and how to use it can help to introduce the new product to the market.

The third stage in the product life cycle is growth. Once the new product has been introduced to the market and has satisfied the potential customers' need, it will enter a growth stage. In this stage sales start to increase quickly. The profits increase during the growth stage as the promotion costs are spread over a large volume of sales. Bear in mind that at this stage potential competitors may try to enter the market.

During the maturity stage, sales volume continues to rise, but profit margins peak and then begin to fall as the other competitors enter the market. Competitors start to mark down prices and increase their advertising and sales promotion. These cause a reduction in the firm's profit. The firm can resort to different strategies at this stage to modify the market, product and marketing mix.

The last stage of the product life cycle is the product decline stage. Decline may be slow or rapid. Sales decline for many reasons such as technological changes, shifts in customer tastes and increased competition (Kotler and Armstrong, 1994). Of course, the time span of the stages of the product life cycle depends on the types of the products involved. For instance, the product life cycle for stable products such as cars lasts from ten to 14 years, while in the case of high fashion products it may last only four to six weeks (Zimmerer and Scarborough, 2002).

In conclusion, strategists in small businesses should consider the current stage of their products and services so that they can adopt an effective and appropriate marketing strategies (Karami, 2002).

Price

Price is the second element of the four marketing Ps. As we saw earlier, pricing strategy can impact on the decision of the customer to buy the firm's products or services or not. We all have experienced this, when we compare the prices of the same product offered by the different companies. In developing a marketing strategy small businesses should consider some basic points regarding the process of their products and services. For instance, Zimmerer and Scarborough (2002) believe that the right price for a product or service depends on three factors: first, the cost structure of the firm; second, an assessment of what the market will bear; and third, the desired image the company wants to create in its customers mind. Small businesses can use a number of pricing strategies to achieve their growth goal. Each has the potential of producing a profit, and most are tied to the critical relationship of price-to-sales volume. The pricing strategy for small businesses will be discussed in detail in the further sections of this chapter.

Promotion

The third element of the four Ps in marketing is promotion. Promotion involves both advertising and personal selling and covers all phases of communication between the seller and the potential customer. Promotions can be changed for specific market segment efforts. The major portion of a firm's promotion is advertising. Advertising has two basic functions: informational and persuasive (Lasher, 1999). The informational element provides any information about the firm and its products and services to the customers. Accordingly, the persuasive promotion aims at convincing people to buy the firm's products and services. Advertising with pricing creates an image of the firm and its product in the mind of the potential customers. This image can be positive or negative and this, to a large extent, depends on the selection and implementation of the proper advertising and pricing strategies by the SMEs. All advertising and other promotional activities should be in tune with the firm's stated position in the marketplace. This suggests that not only advertising themes but also media selection must be based on building and strengthening that position.

In summary, the importance of promotion in the overall marketing strategy suggests that managers should devote time to its written plan and constantly monitor the plan's performance. It is prudent to be creative but avoid being cute. As a rule, stick to the benefit approach and your customers will respond accordingly.

Place

Place is concerned with the distribution of the firm's products and services. SMEs should consider the proper distribution channels to deliver the products to the customers. The distribution channel is the route through which products are sent from manufacturer to the end-user. The simple procedure is for the manufacturers to sell the products or services directly to the consumers. For instance, some manufacturers sell their products through factory shops directly to the end-users. Or educational institutions sell their services directly to the customers known as the one-to-one approach.

In the second form of distribution channel, the manufacturers sell their products to the retailers and the retailers in turn distribute the products to the consumers. Finally, the distribution channel follows the pattern of manufacturer, wholesaler, retailer and consumer.

In the case of small businesses, selling products and services in the pattern of one-to-one has been considered an effective distribution method. These days with the aid of electronic selling through the World Wide Web small businesses can benefit from the Internet and intranet for selling their products and services globally. Generally speaking, product characteristics and customer characteristics determine the distribution plan for the firm's products and services. Additionally for most small businesses, especially those involved in retail, finding the best location at the lowest price becomes an important consideration.

Pricing strategy

One of the important functional marketing strategies in SMEs is the pricing strategy. Developing a proper pricing strategy along with an advertising strategy during the different stages of the product life cycle can help SMEs to satisfy their customers and increase their profit. The price is the monetary value of products and services in the market which can affect buyer choice. Holden and Nagle (1998) argue that price is the weapon of choice for many companies in the competition for sales and market share. The main reason for that is the short process of pricing. In other words, no other marketing tool can be deployed as quickly, or with such certain effect, as a price discount. Small business managers use different criteria for setting prices for products and services. The basis for pricing is the product or service cost. Small business managers should combine various criteria in setting prices rather than considering only product costs.

We will discuss the details of pricing strategy in SMEs in this section. Let's first examine the basic consideration on pricing in SMEs. Zimmerer and Scarborough (2002) argued that small business managers should consider the following factors in determining the final price for goods and services:

- Product/service cost
- Market factors – supply and demand
- Sale value
- Competitor's prices
- The company's competitive advantage
- Economic conditions
- Business location
- Seasonal fluctuations
- Psychological factors
- Credit terms and purchase discounts
- Customer's price sensitivity
- Desired image.

In small businesses the manager or entrepreneur should not be the only person who sets the price. More particularly, in high tech SMEs, the technical entrepreneur or any technical staff who play a main role in developing the new product idea should not solely recommend the price of the developed product or service. It is much better to set the price through a team discussion. This team could consist of members from the technical as well as marketing and financial departments. In this regard, Daly (1998) argues that for any product pricing decision, it's a good idea to get three perspectives:

1. The product owner or creator perspective
2. The financial/bottom-line perspective
3. The marketing or objective customer/member perspective.

Developing a pricing strategy: the basic considerations for SMEs

Once the firm has decided on offering a product or service to the market, it should decide on choosing a pricing strategy. What are the basic considerations for a pricing strategy? What should managers of the small business do before developing a pricing strategy for their firms? These are fundamental questions which should be answered prior to developing the pricing strategy for a product. The processes of developing a pricing strategy have been investigated (Daly, 1998; Kruglak, 1998). While pricing may seem a small detail, it can actually act as a basis for the success or failure of a new product in the marketplace. As Kruglak (1998) notes, the first step in pricing is to understand what you are providing. Daly (1998) suggests that a firm should be able to provide the answers to six critical questions before establishing its pricing strategy for any given service or product. These are:

1. What do you want your pricing strategy to accomplish?
2. What is the demand for your product?
3. Who are the competitors, what are they charging and for which features?
4. What are your costs?
5. What is the perceived value of the product?
6. Does your pricing strategy reflect the perceived value of the product while achieving your pricing goal?

Pricing strategy has also been considered from a customer value point of view. Kotler and Armstrong (1994) say that when buyers buy a product, they exchange something of value to get something of value. Effective customer-oriented pricing strategy considers how much value consumers place on the benefits they receive from the product. Small businesses may focus on the quality of their products and services in pricing. After all, product quality is important to customers. Holden and Nagle (1998) offer the 'five Cs' concept in pricing strategy development. They believe that marketers should adopt the five Cs of the value-based approach. These are:

- Comprehend what drives customer value.
- Create value in product, service and support.
- Communicate value in advertising.
- Convince customers of value in selling.
- Capture value in pricing strategy.

The five Cs concepts suggests that strategists should consider the customers values, their wants and needs; then they should begin developing the products and services which satisfy the customers' needs and values. Once the firm's product or service have been created, the firm should communicate these to the potential customers. From this point of view, advertising is giving the information to the customer about the product and service and how to use it.

The last point is selling and capturing the value in pricing strategy. Daly (1998) aptly suggests that the art of strategic pricing is identifying the perceived value of your product in the eyes and pocketbooks of the target audience.

Fundamental pricing strategy

Pricing strategies change as the product passes through its life cycle (Kotler, 2000). At the introduction stage, when the product is new to the market, developing a pricing strategy is more problematic. Apart from the product life cycle, the firm's objectives, perceived customer value, competition and price history may influence price strategies. Small and medium-sized enterprises may use a variety of pricing strategies and tactics in different situations (Box 9.4).

It must be remembered that when developing a pricing strategy in any circumstances it should be compatible with the firm's overall marketing strategy. Let's talk about the marketing strategies in some detail.

Box 9.4 Pricing strategies for SMEs

There is a variety of pricing strategies for small and medium-sized enterprises to be used in different situations. Each strategy has its advantages and disadvantages and could be applied in certain circumstances. Small businesses can combine different pricing tactics for developing an effective pricing strategy. Pricing tactics are:

- Skimming pricing
- Penetration pricing
- Discount pricing
- Price lining
- Leader pricing
- Geographical pricing
- Psychological pricing.

Skimming pricing strategy

Used when the firm introduces a new product into the market with virtually no competition in sight. In other words, small businesses can adopt a skimming pricing strategy for a product which is unique and for which people are willing to pay extra just to have it. This strategy also refers to the situation in which a firm has a strong patent position, or its product would be difficult to copy. Attracting competitors is the main disadvantage of a skimming strategy. In the skimming strategy profit is high because the sale price is much higher than the total costs. This particular advantage may attract competitors to copy the product or produce a cheaper version.

Penetration pricing strategy

Rather than setting a high price to skim off the market, a small business could set a low initial price in order to penetrate the market quickly. Penetration pricing strategy is the opposite of the skimming strategy; however, both are applied when a firm introduces a new product to the market. Penetration strategy is applied when a large number of competitors are selling the same product and entrance to the market is competitive. In such a situation the firm can introduce its product with a lower price than the market price (Thompson, 1999). The purpose is to discourage competition. In other words, the firm will break into the market to generate a high sales volume quickly. The result of low profit margins may discourage other competitors from entering into the market with the same products.

Discount pricing

In many cases small businesses reduce the prices of damaged or slow-moving goods. Small business managers use discount to encourage shoppers to purchase products before an upcoming season. There are different tactics for the discount strategy such as cash discounts, quantity discounts, seasonal discounts and allowances. Summer sale prices or Christmas discounts are examples of discount tactics.

Price lining

Price lining is a strategy whereby most retailers stock merchandise in several different price ranges. Each category of merchandise contains similar items in quality, cost and appearance or other features. For instance, some flower stores use price lines for their flowers to make it easier for buyers to select their needed items. Most lined products are categorised into good, better and best categories at different prices. The assumption in lining price is that people buy products with different uses in mind and with different expectations for quality. If small businesses do not carry a range of prices, they may lose those customers who cannot find the product at the right price.

Leader pricing

Leader pricing is a strategy in which a small business marks down the customary price of a popular item in order to attract more customers (Zimmerer and Scarborough, 2002). With leader pricing the small businesses temporarily price their products lower than the market price. The reductions have to be on recognised items purchased frequently that the customers know the prices of and can recognise the savings. For example, supermarkets price a few products as loss leaders to attract customers to the supermarket hoping that they will buy other items at normal prices.

Geographical pricing

If small businesses are required to deliver the sold merchandise to different geographical regions they adapt geographical pricing. In geographical pricing the seller should consider freight expenses (Docters, 1997). Zone pricing, in which the firm categorises its market into different zones and sets different prices for each zone, is the simplest method of geographic pricing. Suppose that a small retailer of electrical instruments, located in Leeds, operates in the Yorkshire area. It sells the same product at different prices to its customers in Leeds and Sheffield. Freight on board (FOB) is a well-known geographical pricing tactic in which the sale price includes all the shipping costs.

Psychological pricing

In psychological pricing SMEs consider the psychology of pricing as well as the economics. Small business managers prefer to set prices that end in odd numbers. Although the difference between actual price and psychological price is not very much, small differences in price psychologically attract customers to buy. Consider the case of a small retailer who sells a camera for £99.95 instead of £100. The actual price difference is only 5 pence but the psychological difference can be much greater.

Price is no object

In some industries the quality of the product or service is far more important than the price. In such cases the seller will set the price much higher than the normal level. For example, a well-known lawyer or doctor may charge their customers above the normal price. Another example is selling expensive automobiles or jewellery at very high prices.

Advertising strategy

The advertising strategy is one of the most important marketing strategies for small businesses. It is an effective method of promotion which provides the information about the firm's products and services for potential customers, who seek to know two kinds of information about the product they intend to buy. They first wish to know about the product or service itself and second how to use it. There have been many high quality products or services which have failed in the market simply because potential customers didn't know what they were or how to use them. The advertising strategy therefore helps SMEs to introduce their products and services effectively and promote the firm's sales.

These days with attention being paid to the development of electronic commerce and SMEs' access to the Internet, advertising plays an important role in the selling efforts of SMEs.

Advertising needs to be planned and implemented professionally. An effective advertising strategy should contain three main elements – advertising goals, selecting the media and advertising budget. Before we embark on discussing these elements, let's establish the meaning of the term advertising.

What is advertising?

Basically advertising has been defined as 'a communication that is paid for by an identified sponsor with the object of promoting ideas, goods or services. It is intended to persuade and sometimes to inform' (*Oxford Dictionary of Business*, 2002). Accordingly, Kotler and Armstrong have defined advertising as 'any paid form of non-personal presentation and promotion of ideas, goods or services by an identified sponsor' (Kotler and Armstrong, 1994: 487). As can be clearly seen, both definitions of advertising are part of a marketing strategy. Because it is a powerful communication tool, it enables the firm to communicate with its customers, simultaneously attract potential customers and establish a distinguished position for the firm with its competitors. As a part of an effective marketing strategy, advertising is considered an investment in the future of the business rather than extra expense.

Setting advertising goals

The first step in developing an effective advertising strategy is to define the advertising goals and objectives. These should be set based on the marketing strategy goals. Basically the marketing positioning and marketing mix (see previous section) define the task of the advertising plan. There are three main elements in setting advertising goals – the right message, the right people and the right time. In other words, the basic goal of an effective advertising strategy is to convey the right message to the right people at the right time (Figure 9.4).

First, we need to know what we want to say to our audience. What sort of information about our products and services should be given to the customers? Second, we have to define our customers. What are their characteristics? What are the expectations of our potential customers from the product or service they want to buy? Obviously any groups of customers, in terms of their characteristics such as gender and age groups, require different advertising plans. Third, we have to choose the right time for advertising – this is a very crucial element in the success of an advertising plan.

According to Kotler and Armstrong (1994), in terms of their objectives, advertising plans can be grouped into the following categories:

- Informative advertising
- Persuasive advertising
- Comparison advertising
- Reminder advertising.

The objective of informative advertising is to create a primary demand for the product or service which has just been introduced to the market. Here, the advertising goal might be to increase customer information about the product or service offered at a given price. Reminder advertising is used for mature products and services. The persuasive advertising strategy is aimed at increasing competition and attracting customers. It could be said that there is no one best advertising strategy for achieving all goals.

Who are the target customers?

Customers are central in developing an advertising strategy for small businesses (Carson and Cromie, 1989). As we discussed earlier, small business managers should determine the personal characteristics of the customers to whom the advertising is targeted (Chell, 2001; Analoui and Karami, 2002). Each part of the advertising plan should be matched with the characteristics of the targeted customers. Suppose that a small business operates in a region where the majority of people do not have access to the Internet. In such a market the World Wide Web as the major advertising tool will not be effective. By and large, the medium chosen should be directed to the characteristics of the target customer groups. It is important to know the customers' reasons for buying a specific product or service. In response, the managers of small businesses should analyse and come up with an answer to the question, why customers select one specific seller instead of another? Answering these questions helps to highlight the customers' expectations and benefits. Therefore, small businesses must develop advertising plans based on the targeted customers' wants and needs rather than the owners' opinions.

Figure 9.4

Three elements of advertising goal setting

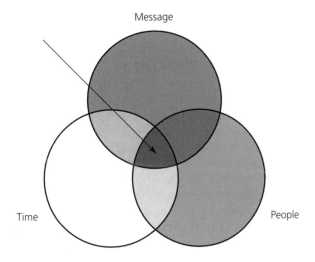

The advertising budget

The second step in developing an advertising plan for SMEs is determining and allocating the advertising budget. Once the goals and objectives of the advertising are clearly defined, an advertising budget ought to be prepared. An advertising budget determines how much a small business should spend in a specific period of time and preparing the advertising budget is not an easy task. Many factors such as the firm's stage in product life cycle and market share (Curran, 1996) influence the setting of the advertising budget. Small business managers employ different methods for preparing the advertising budget.

The percentage of sales is the most commonly used and easiest method for preparing the advertising budget – some percentage of the forecasted sales would be budgeted for advertising. Therefore, the amount of advertising budget will depend largely on the sales volume. The second and most successful method is linking the advertising budget to the business objectives. In this way, small business managers spend what it takes to get the job done, linking the advertising costs to specific objectives. As a result, business objectives should be established for the year ahead and the cost of accomplishing each objective ought to be reflected in a budget plan. An advertising budget should be planned for annually to cover a 12-month period. This helps the business to look ahead. Of course, splitting the annual advertising budget into the monthly and weekly expenditures basis will be an advantage for small businesses.

Selecting a medium

The third step in developing an effective advertising strategy is selecting the best medium to reach the targeted market. When selecting the advertising medium SMEs should consider crucial factors such as the characteristics of the targeted customer groups, market size and the advertisement costs. There is a variety of advertising media such as radio, local newspapers, the World Wide Web, television, cinema, parking meters, transport advertising, yellow pages and many other methods which are potentially available for SMEs. Each has its own advantages and disadvantages. It would be useful to develop a mix of types of media for advertising purposes. Let's discuss some of the selected advertising media for small businesses.

Newspaper advertising

Newspapers are one of the most popular advertising media for small business in local areas. Some businesses advertise on a regular basis in the local papers. The majority of homes in the UK receive a newspaper and in some cases the newspapers are delivered free of charge to the homes in residential areas. For most families and individuals reading the newspaper is a habit. Since the newspapers can cover a wide range of readers, it is a potentially effective advertising medium for small businesses. There are several advantages for SMEs to advertising in newspapers. Newspaper advertising can be flexible and convenient; hence advertisers can change the format of the ad, such as size, and often insert a new advertisement at short notice to suit their budget. Another advantage is the large variety of ad sizes newspaper advertising offers. Finally, newspapers cover a selected geographical region and in some cases selected groups of consumers. For instance, colleges and universities advertise in the *Times Higher Education Supplement* which is aimed at people involved or interested in higher education. There are of course some disadvantages to advertising in the newspapers. Newspapers usually are read once; consequently, the advertisement life is very short. Also there is no guarantee that those who buy the newspaper will read the ad and it could be argued that newspapers may not provide a proper medium for small ads because a small ad on a large page can be lost.

Magazine advertising

Magazines are another vehicle for advertising. Many of the same print-type principles which apply to newspaper advertising also apply to magazine advertising. However, there are some differences. For instance, newspapers are published daily while magazines are published on a weekly or monthly basis and are often reread and passed on. Advertising in magazines is more image oriented and the quality of pictures is better.

Radio advertising

Radio as a broadcasting medium offers a variety of information to different groups of the audience. For instance, it covers weather reports, sport, music and advertising. Advertising on radio is cheaper than on TV. Radio advertising is more active than printed ads and it can be used to support newspaper advertising. The disadvantage is that the audience cannot review a radio commercial. The important point in a radio ad is that you have to buy the right time for your commercial to reach the correct target consumers. For example, it is easier to catch people during their journey to and from work (from 6 am to 10 am in the morning and 4 pm to 7 pm in the evening).

Television advertising

Advertising in television can be considered as the main advertising medium. It uses sight, sound, pictures and colour, and combines them to create advertising. By advertising via the TV businesses can take their audience anywhere and show them anything. It covers different groups of consumers from children to elderly people. Many people spend a few hours a day watching TV, therefore it is possible to reach the targeted audiences by advertising on TV, for instance, children can be easily reached during cartoon programmes. The main disadvantage of TV ads is its high costs in comparison to the other advertising media.

World Wide Web

Recently advertising in the World Wide Web has become very popular for small as well as large firms. In Chapter 10 we will discuss the details of the application of the Internet and e-commerce for small business.

Yellow Pages

The Yellow Pages are a good advertising medium to reach the local market area for small businesses. It allows small businesses to place their business listing or ad in a selected classification within the book. The Yellow Pages are delivered free of charge to people's homes and it allows potential customers to contact you even if they didn't initially know your name.

Financial strategies for small businesses

One of the duties of the small business managers is financing the firm's activities. No business can survive without money. Any business needs money to support all of its short and long term activities. More importantly, small businesses need to be supported financially in the early stages of the business (Bracker and Pearson, 1986). Managers should make financial decisions as well as production or marketing strategic decisions in order to determine how the firm will have access to its financial resources. The term financing simply refers to raising money to make a purchase or run a business. We need money to buy a house, we raise money to change our car. In business we need financial resources or money to run the business. We also need some money to support our daily activities and to spend on long term assets like buildings. Lasher (1999) argues that the term strategic financing refers to the concept of raising money to start or expand a business.

Strategic financing is crucial to success. Money can power the engine of the business in the start-up stage and push the business forward successfully.

Initial considerations when financing the business

Getting money for small business involves a variety of financial and non-financial considerations. There are different resources for financing the small business. Having said that, small businesses cannot benefit from some of the financial resources which are available for large organisations. For example, the capital market for small businesses is imperfect and consists of a great variety of poorly organised financing sources. How can small businesses gain access to financial resources? In order to decide on selecting the financial resources, small businesses should consider some financial as well as non-financial factors in their financial decision-making. The main considerations for selecting the most suitable sources of funding for small business are the firm's financial profile, equity financing, debt financing and government resources:

- The small businesses' financial profile: this shows the firm's position in the business life cycle. It explains how your position in the business life cycle influences your financing options.
- Equity financing: explains how your form of business organisation can be used to bankroll your business, and the advantages and disadvantages of using venture capital.
- Debt financing: discusses where and how to get a business loan. What types of loan are available?
- Government resources: shows how the government can help to finance your small business, and describes other government financing assistance.

Equity financing

The first option in financing the business is equity financing. Equity financing requires that one sells an ownership interest in the business in exchange for capital. The most basic hurdle to equity financing is finding investors who are willing to buy into the business. In this context, an equity investor is someone who buys stock in the company. Investors are the part-owners of the firm who will have the right of control of the business. The amount of equity financing that can be undertaken may depend more upon a willingness to share management control than upon the investor appeal of the business. By selling equity interests in the business, small businesses sacrifice some of their autonomy and management rights. There are problems associated with financing small businesses with equity. Lasher (1999) argues that there is no market price on which to value the firm or a share of its stock. Second, the dividends are unlikely to be paid to shareholders for a long time.

Equity financing strategies for small businesses

There are different sources of equity financing for small businesses, each of which has their advantages and disadvantages. Let's look at each of these sources individually.

Personal sources

The first source of equity financing for a start-up venture is the entrepreneur's personal financial resources (Upton and Heck, 1997). Entrepreneurs can put their own savings into the business and this is may be the easiest and cheapest method of equity financing of the business start-up. There are, however, some risks associated with investing personal savings in the new business. The entrepreneurs will lose their own money if the business is not successful. However, equity financing from personal sources as seed capital will attract outside investors to invest in the business.

Angels

When personal financial resources are not sufficient to support the business, equity financing by individuals outside of the business who are interested in investing in the venture will be the second alternative. These wealthy individuals or private investors, who are called angels, are interested in investing in the business not solely for economic reasons but because they are seeking new business investments for a variety of economic and personal reasons. Angels can be a very good source of financing but this will not be available to every new business.

Business combinations

The third strategy of equity financing of the new business is to combine with another business. As discussed in Chapter 5, different forms of business combination such as joint ventures, strategic alliances or mergers and acquisitions can be employed to raise new funds and mobilise potential financial resources for the small businesses. The main advantage of business combinations is financing the business without cash debt. For example in a joint venture situation the small business can finance certain services or production functions by sharing expertise, assets, expenses and risk without necessarily incurring cash debt. In many cases equity financing is not the only reason for partnership. Most small businesses will benefit from partners that add value as well as bringing money to the new venture. For example, franchising with a well-recognised industry name can assist in advertising and marketing for the small business. On the other hand, in any partnership agreement, the entrepreneurs may lose some part of their control on the firm and should consider the advantages of partnership as well as the disadvantages of combining with the other firms.

Venture capital firms

Venture capital firms are the most popular financial resources for financing small and rapid growth businesses. Since there are no readily accessible sources of funding for small businesses, they look for any financial resources outside of the business for equity but will not be able to secure their financial resources for expanding and developing their businesses from the capital market. For instance, there is no established capital market for SMEs in the UK. In such a situation, venture capital firms can be a good alternative to support small businesses. Venture capital firms are large organisations that invest in small businesses for high profit. Zimmerer and Scarborough describe venture capital firms as 'private, for profit organisations that purchase equity positions in young businesses they believe have high-growth and high-profit potential, producing annual returns of 300 to 500 per cent over five to seven years' (2002: 371). Small business ventures in the high tech industry such as computers, biotechnology and e-commerce are the main targets for venture capital. They supply funding from private sources for investing in select companies that have a high, rapid growth potential and a need for large amounts of capital. The main disadvantage of financing small businesses by venture capital is the high price of financing. By and large, the cost of equity financing through venture capital is expensive, the advantage is that it offers a large amount of equity financing and provides qualified business advice in addition to capital.

Going public

Going to the public is another strategy for equity financing for SMEs. Going public means that a private SME sells its shares of stock to outside investors. Small businesses 'go public' through an Initial Public Offering (IPO) of their stock to the public for the first time. This financial strategy can generate funds for many uses such as working capital, repayment of debt or marketing. It is important to note that small businesses must meet some criteria before going public. According to Zimmerer and Scarborough (2002) small businesses should meet the following five characteristics in order to be considered by investment banks for going to public:

- High growth rate
- Strong record of earning

- Three to five years of audited financial statements
- A solid position in a rapidly growing market
- A sound management team.

A successful initial public offering increases the visibility of the firm and may lead to an increase in the demand for and value of the shares of the business.

Strategies of financing by debt for small businesses

Financing by debt refers to loans which entrepreneurs borrow from banks or financial organisation. The loans must be repaid with interest. A lender who lends to small business does not obtain any ownership claim in the small business as debtor. Compared with equity financing, the dept financing costs are normally fixed and small businesses do not have to sacrifice any ownership interests in their business (Box 9.5).

Thus debt financing is deemed to be more attractive than equity financing for the small business. SME managers can finance their business through two types of financing by debts – loans and bonds. Loans are the most important financing tool for small businesses (Bracker and Pearson, 1986), so let's discuss the financing of small businesses by loans first.

Nature of loans

Apart from the type of loan, any loan has two major characteristics: (1) the term of the loan and (2) the security to get the loan.

Term loans First, the 'term' of the loan refers to the length of time the small businesses have to repay the debt. Bank loans in terms of duration of loan can be either long or short term. Long term loans are normally used for buying fixed assets such as land or major machinery. Interest rates on long term loans are higher than those on short term loans.

Secured and unsecured loans Second, debt financing can also be secured or unsecured. A secured loan is a promise to pay a debt, where the promise is 'secured' by granting the creditor an interest in specific property (collateral) of the debtor. According to Lasher (1999) this type of loan is a dangerous feature

---

**Box 9.5 Some World Wide Web resources for accessing
debt financing information for small businesses in the UK**

www.business-barclays.co.uk
www.lloydstsb.co.uk
www.co-operativebank.co.uk
www.hsbc.co.uk
www.natwest.co.uk
www.dti.gov.uk

of financing with debt. If the debt service cannot be made regularly, the lender will be able to put the borrower into bankruptcy.

Types of loan

Banks and other financial organisations such as building societies, saving and loan associations, credit unions and insurance companies are the main sources of loans for small businesses. Apart from the nature of loans and debts, the most common types of loan given by any commercial and financial resources to start-up and emerging small businesses can be categorised as follows:

- Short term commercial loans: for start-ups and new small businesses, most bank loans will be short term. Short term loans are given for one to three years and used to purchase short term assets.
- Long term loans: long term loans are given for long term activities such as buying fixed assets, for example land, buildings and major equipments. Long term loans are usually secured by the asset being acquired.
- Lines of credit: with an approved line of credit small business managers can borrow up to an agreed ceiling at any time during the year. It sets a maximum amount of money available from the lender, to be used when needed by the small businesses.
- Equipment leasing: small businesses sometimes lease assets such as equipment, vehicles or office facilities. Leasing is a form of loan given by the banks to the small businesses to lease required equipment. The term of this loan is limited to the lease term.

Financial analysis: break-even point

Break-even point analysis is one of the most important financial tools which can help managers to understand the behaviour of costs in SMEs. Understanding the behaviour of costs in small businesses is crucial for strategists in charge of strategy development and strategic decision-making. It can be said that any of the functional and operational strategies in SMEs such as the pricing strategy, advertising strategy or HR strategies are linked to the costs (Boyd, 1991). Therefore, small business managers need to study the behaviour of the costs in order better to understand the fiscal workings of their business. Let's first explore the nature of the costs of the small businesses.

Fixed costs

Businesses' costs can be categorised into two groups of costs, fixed and variable. Fixed costs are those costs that will occur whatever the level of activity. In other words, fixed costs are not changed by the changing volume of business activity. Rent and equipments are examples of fixed costs. Suppose that a person decides to run a barber shop – she or he needs to rent a shop and buy some essential equipment. The cost of renting the shop will be the same whether she or he works and earns thousands of pounds or does not work at all; fixed costs are constant over a wide range of production or sales levels.

Figure 9.5 shows fixed costs and how they behave as the volume of business activity changes.

Variable costs

Variable costs include those expenditures which change in line with sales. In other words, variable cost rises or falls in direct proportion to any growth or decline in output volumes (Barrow, 2001). In small manufacturing firms, raw material costs and labour costs are examples of variable costs. The manufacturing firms will pay more for materials if they increase the production volume. Delivery costs and sales commission are examples of the variable costs in small businesses. Figure 9.6 shows how variables costs will increase if the volume of sales increases.

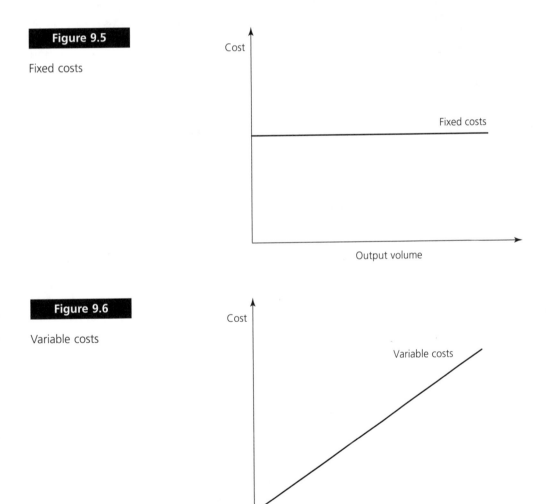

Figure 9.5

Fixed costs

Figure 9.6

Variable costs

Semi-variable costs

Understandably, not all costs can be fitted into either fixed or variable costs. There are some costs which are referred to as semi-variable which have both fixed and variable costs elements. Heat, light and telephone costs can be considered as semi-variable costs in workshops.

Break-even point

We can calculate the total costs of the business by adding the fixed costs to the variable costs. The difference between total revenue and the total costs of the firm determines the profit or loss. Obviously if the total revenue is greater than total cost the difference will be profit, otherwise it will be loss. The break-even point is the state in which the total revenue of the firm is exactly equal to the total costs. Figure 9.7 shows the break-even point graphically.

The point where the total revenue line crosses the total cost line is named the break-even point – the area after break-even point is profit. In other words, it is only when the break-even point has been reached that a business can start to make a profit. Consequently, it is important for small business managers to find out the business's break-even point when taking a decision on sales strategy. Box 9.6 clarifies the calculations for break-even points analysis by an example.

Functional strategies in human resource management

Human resources strategies are of a functional nature, like finance and marketing (Walker, 1992; Bowman and Kakabadse, 1997). The strategic importance of functional strategies in HRM has become more widely accepted in recent years (Morden, 1993; Karami and Analoui, 1999). The human resources that are available in an organisation actually determine the manner in which the enterprise can implement its strategies. Morden has argued that human resource strategies derive from the result of human resource audit and analysis,

Figure 9.7

Break-even point

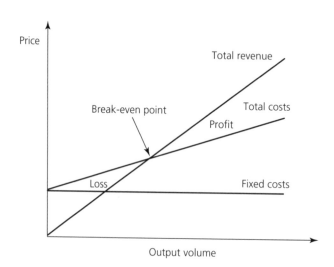

Box 9.6 Break-even point calculations

Suppose that a small business operates in selling TVs and other electronic appliances. The total costs of the business during a year are £60 000. The unit selling price of a TV is £800 and the variable costs per unit TV are equal to £500. Now the small business manager wants to know at what level of sale the business can reach the break-even point. The break-even point is calculated by following equation:

$$BEP = \frac{\text{Fixed costs}}{\text{Unit selling price} - \text{Variable costs per unit}}$$

$$BEP = \frac{£60\ 000}{£800 - £500} = 200$$

As we can see 200 units of sales is the break-even point. By selling 200 units of the TV the firm's total sale revenue will be equal to £160 000. Accordingly the total costs of the firm by selling 200 units of TV will be equal to £100 000. Therefore the firm's profit in the same sale level is equal to zero. The following calculations show the details.

Total sale revenue = Total number of sale × Unit selling price
Total sale revenue = 200 × £800 = £160 000

Total costs = Fixed costs + (Total number of sale × Variable costs per unit)
Total costs = £60 000 + (200 × £500) = £160 000

Profit = Total sale revenue − Total costs
Profit = £160 000 − £160 000 = 0

the result of staff appraisal, HR forecasts and plans and the degree to which staff competence is perceived to yield competitive advantage in the market (Morden, 1993; Hendry *et al.* 1995).

Functional HR strategies should guide the effective utilisation of human resources to achieve both the firm's annual objectives and employee satisfaction and development. Human resource strategies in SMEs can be categorised into four basic functional strategies. These include recruitment and selection, training and development, retention and finally evaluation and control strategies (see Box 9.7).

In this section we will explore each of the HR strategies in some detail.

Recruitment and selection strategy

The aim of a recruitment and selection strategy is to decide how quality people can be attracted to the business (Analoui, 2000). According to Pearce and Robinson (2000) the recruitment and selection strategy should answer some basic questions. These are:

> ## Box 9.7 Key functional strategies in HRM
>
> Human resource management strategies in SMEs can be categorised into four basic strategies as follows:
>
> - **Recruitment and selection:** what key people are needed and how can the firm recruit them?
> - **Training and development:** how can the business help its employees to develop their capabilities and competencies?
> - **Retention strategy:** how can the business motivate the employees through an effective payment system?
> - **Evaluation and control:** how can the firm improve its performance through an effective evaluation and control system?

- What key people are needed to support the business strategy?
- How can the firm recruit the needed key people?
- How sophisticated should the selection process be?

Armstrong and Spellman (1993) have summarised the factors which the recruitment strategy should take into account. First, the firm should consider those factors which are likely to attract or deter people from joining the organisation such as career opportunities, access to higher level education and training, reputation of the organisation for innovation and high level of involvement. Second, the business should determine the basis upon which it competes with its competitors for high quality staff or competitive resources. Third, the firm should consider the alternative methods of meeting the human resource requirements such as flexibility, training, career management and productivity planning. Finally, the recruitment strategy should normally cover the selection techniques.

Human resources development strategies

Human resource development strategies should be designed to support the need for new or enhanced skills and the increase in competence required to achieve business strategies (Analoui, 2002). Development of skills and competencies and staff training are based on the identification of training needs. Analoui (2000) developed a comprehensive model of human resources skills in large as well as small organisations. This model includes self-development skills, people-related skills and task-related skills. Thus it is argued that small business managers should consider a comprehensive combination of the three categories of required skills when developing their human resource development strategy. Human resource development consists of training and management development strategies (Analoui, 1993).

Training strategy

Small business managers should consider following five factors in developing training strategy (Analoui, 1990, 1993):

- Why do small businesses need to develop a training strategy?
- What strategic issues in SMEs should be covered?
- The training needs of small businesses for either the short or long term.
- The availability of resources for developing an effective training strategy.
- Finally, how the training strategy should be implemented successfully.

Management development strategy

Analoui (1994) argues that management development strategy depends on some variables that affect the managerial style. Some of the variables which should be considered in a management development strategy consist of the firm's ownership structure, the quality of the employee, environment, culture and staff involvement in operational decision-making (Morden, 1993).

Retention and compensation strategy

What is the appropriate payment system for the small businesses? And how can small and medium-sized firms motivate and retain good and highly skilled people? These important questions are answered in the retention and compensation strategy (Analoui, 1998). Retaining highly skilled employees within the firm is the most important challenge faced by the SME managers. Most importantly, in cases of labour shortage it is the effectiveness of this policy that ensures the continued operations of the firm (Analoui, 1999). According to Armstrong and Spellman (1993) strategies for improving retention are in the areas of pay, reward, performance, commitment and team building:

- Pay: small business managers should ensure that all employees, particularly key people, are paid according to their market worth.
- Rewards: a reward strategy can help companies to identify rewards that may be applicable to certain target groups in the organisation. Morden (1993) has indicated that policy decisions on pay and reward are key determinants of employee productivity, commitment and willingness to accept change.
- Performance: as argued in Chapter 7, in small businesses employees take on a variety of responsibilities. If the business fails to establish a performance management system, in order clearly to define the employees' responsibilities and appraise their performance, it may lead to demotivation of the employees.
- Commitment: is defined as identification with the organisation and a desire to remain with it. Commitment can be enhanced by explaining the organisation's missions and encouraging comment on them (Armstrong and Spellman, 1993).
- Team building: team building is a strategy for success in small businesses (Analoui, 1998). It is often thought that a small number of employees will automatically provide the basis for team work. This is a misconception. Managers of SMEs should attempt to select, train, develop and manage their employees in self-directed teams.

Performance appraisal and evaluation strategy

Performance appraisal compares an individual job performance to standards or objectives developed for the individual position (Analoui, 1991). As discussed in Chapter 8, for the purpose of the evaluation and appraisal process the standard of behaviour is systematically defined, the actual performance of the employees (including managers and CEOs) are measured and accordingly the actual performance is compared with the set standards. If the performance is lower than expected it may prompt corrective action, such as additional training, while high performance may merit a reward (Analoui, 2002). It would be more effective if the businesses were to establish a formal appraisal system within the firm. Stoner *et al.* have classified the purposes of the formal appraisal into four major categories:

1. To let employees know formally how their current performance is being rated
2. To identify employees who deserve merit raises
3. To locate employees who need additional training
4. To identify candidates for promotion (Stoner *et al.* 1995: 396).

To evaluate the effectiveness of the HRM process within an organisation, the Harvard researchers have proposed a 'four Cs' model:

- Competence
- Commitment
- Congruence
- Cost effectiveness.

By shaping HRM strategies to enhance commitment, competence, congruence and cost effectiveness, an organisation increases its capacity to adapt to changes in its environment (Milliken *et al.* 1990; Kakabadse *et al.* 1996). Increased commitment means better communication between employees and managers and a high level of competence implies that employees are versatile in their skills and can take new roles as needed. Cost effectiveness means that the human resource costs are kept equal to or less than those of competitors. Finally, higher congruence means that all stockholders share a common purpose and collaborate in solving problems (Stoner *et al.* 1995).

Summary

- Strategies are formulated at three levels within organisations – corporate strategy, business strategy and functional strategy – there should be a link between the three levels within the organisation. In small businesses, the business owner-manager or CEO is the ultimate strategist who is involved in developing these three levels of strategy. Marketing strategies, financial strategies and human resource management strategies are examples of functional strategies in SMEs.

- In SMEs the marketing strategy impacts on the whole firm's performance. The secret to successful marketing is to understand the customers' needs, demands and wants, offer the product and service that will satisfy the customers' need and provide customer services, convenience and value. All of the other functional areas of the firm, such as the financial department or production, should be coordinated by the marketing section. The marketing strategy is one in which SMEs define their target market and choose a market mix. It is recommended that in developing a marketing strategy small businesses choose their niche and focus on that to avoid competing with larger firms. A niche strategy will allow SMEs to maximise the advantages of their smallness.

- Market researchers gather valuable information which CEOs need for developing the firm's strategy. Market research shows what the customers' expectations, interests and needs are and marketing information and market research are central to the success of the business. Successful SMEs do market research when formulating marketing strategies and developing marketing plans. High performance SMEs stress the importance of market research in the development of corporate strategy. Market research can be carried out through a step-by-step process. These are a definition of the problem, collecting the data, analysing the collected data and finally drawing the appropriate conclusions.

- The target market is the specific group of customers that the firm targets with its products or services. The market research identifies the target market of the firm and a strategic marketing plan should determine a clear target market to be served. Developing a market-focused strategy can help SMEs which suffer from a lack of financial resources to benefit from focusing on a specific segment of the market. Growing businesses tend to focus on their products or services rather than on the knowledge resources available to them.

- An effective marketing strategy should help in creating a marketing mix for SMEs. The marketing mix consists of four main elements known as the 'four Ps' – product, price, promotion and place – which the firm combines to reach its target market. The four Ps of marketing are the main elements of an effective marketing strategy. SMEs should integrate these elements to maximise the impact of their products and services on the customers and increased their satisfaction.

- Developing a proper pricing strategy along with an advertising strategy during the different stages of the product life cycle can help SMEs to satisfy their customers and increase their profit. In small businesses the business manager or entrepreneur should not be the only person who sets the price. SMEs may use a variety of pricing strategies and tactics in different situations. Skimming pricing strategy is used when the firm introduces a new product into the market with no competition; penetration strategy is applied when a large number of competitors are selling the same product and the condition for entering into the market is competitive. Discount pricing encourages shoppers to purchase products before an upcoming season and price lining is a form of strategy where most retailers will be stocking merchandise in several different price ranges. Leader pricing is a strategy in which a small business marks down the customary price of a popular item to attract more customers. In geographical pricing the seller should also consider freight expenses. In psychological pricing, small and medium-sized enterprises consider the psychology of pricing as well as its economics.

- Advertising is an effective method of promotion which provides the information about the firm's products and services to potential customers. Nowadays, with attention being paid to the development of electronic commerce and SMEs' access to the Internet, advertising has become an important part of small businesses' selling efforts. Advertising needs to be planned and implemented professionally. An effective advertising strategy should contain three main elements – advertising goals, selecting the medium and advertising budget.

- The term financing simply refers to raising money to run a business. There are different resources for financing the small business, mainly equity financing and debt. Equity financing requires that you sell an ownership interest in the business in exchange for capital. The entrepreneur's personal financial resources, angels, combining with the other businesses such as joint ventures, strategic alliances, mergers and acquisitions, venture capital firms and going public are the main resources for equity financing for small businesses. Financing by debt refers to loans which entrepreneurs borrow from any bank or financial organisation. The loans must be repaid with interest. Small and medium-sized enterprise managers can finance their business through two types of financing by debt: loans and bonds. Any loan has two major characteristics: the term of the loan and the security to get the loan. There are five types of loan: short term, commercial loans, long term loans, lines of credit and equipment leasing. Break-even point analysis is one of the most important financial analyses which can help the entrepreneur to understand the behaviour of costs in SMEs. Understanding the behaviour of costs in small businesses is crucial to strategists for developing strategies and strategic decision-making.

- Human resource management strategies in SMEs can be categorised into four basic strategies. Recruitment and selection: what key people are needed and how the firm can recruit them? Training and development: how can the business help its employees to develop their capabilities and competencies? Retention strategy: how can the business motivate the employees through an effective payment system? Evaluation and control: how can the firm improve its performance through an effective evaluation and control system?

Discussion questions

1. How do you define marketing strategy for small businesses?
2. What characteristics should an effective marketing strategy have? List four and discuss at least two factors.
3. Discuss the importance of marketing research and explain its process in SMEs.

4. Discuss determining the target market and competitive advantage as main aspects of the marketing strategy in SMEs.

5. What is the marketing mix concept? Discuss components of marketing mix in small businesses.

6. What should small business managers consider in developing a pricing strategy?

7. List the pricing strategies and discuss penetration and lining strategies in small businesses.

8. Discuss developing the advertising strategy in small businesses. What are the main elements of an effective advertising strategy?

9. Discuss two main financial strategies including equity financing and debt financing in SMEs.

10. What are the functional human resource strategies? Discuss HR development strategy in SMEs.

References

Analoui, F. (1990) Managerial skills for senior managers, *International Journal of Public Sector Management*, 3 (2), 26–38.

Analoui, F. (1991) Toward achieving the optimum fit between managers and project organisations, *Project Appraisal*, 6 (2), 217–222.

Analoui, F. (1993) *Training and Transfer of Learning*, Avebury, Aldershot.

Analoui, F. (1994) *The Realities of Management Development Projects*, Avebury, Aldershot.

Analoui F. (1999) Eight parameters of managerial effectiveness: a study of senior managers in Ghana, *Journal of Management Development*, 18 (4), 36–39.

Analoui, F. (2000) Identification of clusters of managerial skills for increased effectiveness: the case of steel industry in Iran, *International Journal of Training and Development*, 4 (3), 217–234.

Analoui, F. (ed.) (1998) *Human Resource Management Issues in Developing Countries*, Ashgate, Aldershot.

Analoui, F. (ed.) (2002) *The Changing Patterns of Human Resource Management*, Ashgate, Aldershot.

Analoui, F. and Karami, A. (2002) How chief executives' perception of the environment impacts on company performance, *Journal of Management Development*, 21(4), 290–305.

Armstong, J. S. (1982) The value of formal planning for strategic decisions, *Strategic Management Journal*, 3, 100–111.

Armstrong, M. and Spellman, R. (1993) *Gaining a Competitive Advantage in the Labour Market*, Coopers and Lybrand, London.

Bagchi-Sen, S. and Kuechler, L. (2000) Strategic and functional orientation of small and medium sized enterprises in professional services: an analysis of public accountancy, *The Service Industries Journal*, 20 (3), 117–146.

Barrow, C. (2001) *Financial Management for Small Businesses*, 5th edn, Kogan Page Limited, London.

Bhide, A. (1994) How entrepreneurs craft strategies that work, *Harvard Business Review*, March/April, 150–161.

Boussouara, M. and Deakins, D. (1999) Market-based learning, entrepreneurship, and the high technology firm, *International Journal of Entrepreneurial Behaviour and Research*, 5 (4), 204–223.

Bowman, C. and Kakabadse, A. (1997) Top management ownership of the strategy problem, *Long Range Planning*, 30 (2), 197–208.

Boyd, B. K. (1991) Strategic planning and financial performance: a meta-analytic review, *Journal of Management Studies*, 28, 353–374.

Bracker, J. and Pearson, J. (1986) Planning and financial performance of small, mature firms, *Strategic Management Journal*, 7, 503–522.

Burns, P. (2001) *Entrepreneurship and Small Businesses*, Palgrave, London.

Carson, D. (1985) The evolution of marketing in small firms, *European Journal of Marketing*, 19 (5), 7–17.

Carson, D. and Cromie, S. (1989) Marketing planning in small enterprises: a model and some empirical evidence, *Journal of Marketing Management*, 5 (1), 33–49.

Carson, D. and Gilmore, A. (2000) Marketing at the interface: not 'what' but 'how', *Journal of Marketing Theory and Practice*, 8 (2), 1–8.

Carson, D., Cromie, S., McGowan, P. and Hill, J. (1995) *Marketing and Entrepreneurship in SMEs: An Innovative Approach*, Prentice Hall, London.

Chan, S. Y. and Foster, J. M. (2001) Strategy formulation in small business: the Hong Kong experiences, *International Small Business Journal*, April-June, 56–71.

Chaston, I., Berger, B. and Sadler-Smith, E. (1999) Organisational learning: research issues and application in SME sector firms, *International Journal of Entrepreneurial Behaviour and Research*, 5 (4), 191–203.

Chell, E. (2001) *Entrepreneurship: Globalisation, Innovation and Development*, Thomson Learning, London.

Churchill, N. C. and Lewis, V. L. (1983) The five stages of small business growth, *Harvard Business Review*, 61 (3), 30–50.

Curran, J. (1996) Small business strategy, in M. Warner (ed.) *The Concise International Encyclopaedia of Business and Management*, International Thomson Business Press, London, 4510–4520.

Daly, N. R. (1998) Strategic pricing practices, *Association Management*, 50 (7), 38–43.

Docters, R. G. (1997) Price strategy: Time to choose your weapons, *The Journal of Business Strategy*, 18 (5), 11–15.

Fields, R. W. (1999) *The Entrepreneurial Engineer: Starting Your Own High-Tech Company*, Artech House, Boston, MA.

Handler, W. C. (1994) Succession in family businesses: a review of the research, *Business Family Review*, 7 (2), 133–158.

Hanlon, D. and Scott, M. (1995) Strategy formulation in the entrepreneurial small firms, in S. Birley and I. MacMillan (eds) *International Entrepreneurship*, Routledge, London, 17–38.

Hart, S. and Tzokas, N. (1999) The impact of marketing research on SME export performance: evidence from the UK, *Journal of Small Business Management*, 37 (2), 63–75.

Hatch, J. and Zweig, J. (2001) Strategic flexibility: the key to growth, *Ivey Business Journal*, 65 (4), 44–47.

Helms, M. M., Dibrell, C. and Wright, P. (1997) Competitive strategies and business performance: evidence from the adhesives and sealants industry, *Management Decision*, 35, 678–92.

Hendry, C., Arthur, M. and Jones, A. (1995) *Strategy Through People: Adaptation and Learning in the Small-Medium Enterprises*, Routledge, London.

Holden, R. K. and Nagle, T. T. (1998) Kamikaze pricing, *Marketing Management*, 7 (2), 30–39.

Kakabadse, A., Kakabadse, N. and Myers, A. (1996) Leadership and the public sector: an internationally comparative benchmarking analysis, *Public Administration and Development*, 16 (4), 337–396.

Karami, A. (2002) Corporate strategy: evidence from British Airways Plc, in Analoui, F. (ed.) (2002) *The Changing Patterns of Human Resource Management*, Ashgate, Aldershot, 46–64.

Karami, A. and Analoui, F. (1999) New human resource management initiatives in the enterprise sector: a strategic approach, Human Resource for Development: People and Performance Conference, University of Manchester, UK, June, 27–30.

Kotler, P. (2000) *Marketing Management, The Millennium Edition*, Prentice Hall, London.

Kotler, P. and Armstrong, G. (1994) *Principles of Marketing*, 6th edn, Prentice Hall International, London.

Kruglak, A. (1998) Six steps to pricing service agreements, *Security Distributing and Marketing*, 28 (4), 71–76.

Kuratko, D. F., Goodale, J. C. and Hornsby, J. S. (2001) Quality practices for a competitive advantage in smaller firms, *Journal of Small Business Management*, 39 (4), 293–311.

Lasher, W. (1999) *Strategic Thinking Small Businesses*, Blackwell, Oxford.

Malhotra, N. K. (1999) *Marketing Research: An Applied Orientation*, 3rd edn, Prentice Hall, New York.

Milliken, F. J., Dutton, J. E. and Beyer, J. M. (1990) Understanding organisational adoption to change: the case of work family issues, *Human Resource Planning*, 13 (2), 91–108.

Morden, T. (1993) *Business Strategy and Planning: Text and Cases*, McGraw Hill, London.

Murdoch. H., Blackey, H. and Blythe, J. (2001) Beliefs and attitudes of Welsh SMEs to marketing, *Journal of Targeting, Measurement, and Analysis for Marketing*, 10 (2), 143–155.

Oxford Dictionary of Business (2002) 3rd edn, Oxford University Press, Oxford.

Pangarkar, A. M. and Kirkwood, T. (2002) Building a corporate learning culture with limited resources, *CMA Management*, 76 (2), 30–33.

Pearce, J. A. and Robinson, Jr, R. B. (2000) *Strategic Management: Formulation, Implementation and Control*, 7th edn, McGraw Hill, New York.

Shuman, J. C. and Seeger, J. A. (1986) The theory and practice of strategic management in smaller rapid growth firms, *American Journal of Small Business*, 11 (1), 7–18.

Stoner, J. A. F., Freeman, R. E. and Gilbert, D. R. (1995) *Management*, Prentice Hall International Limited, London.

Thompson, J. (1999) A strategic perspective of entrepreneurship, *International Journal of Entrepreneurial Behaviour and Research*, 5 (6), 279–296.

Upton, N. and Heck, R. K. Z. (1997) The family business dimensions of entrepreneurship, in D. L. Sexton and R. A. Smilor (eds) (2000) *Entrepreneurship*, Upstart Publishing, Chicago, 243–266.

Walker, J. W. (1992) *Human Resource Strategy*, McGraw Hill, New York.

Wheelen, T. L. and Hunger, J. D. (1998) *Strategic Management and Business Policy*, 6th edn, Addison Wesley Longman Inc., New York.

Zimmerer, T. W. and Scarborough, N. M. (2002) *Essentials of Entrepreneurship and Small Business Management*, 3rd edn, Prentice Hall, Upper Saddle River, NJ.

10 Strategic issues for small businesses

Learning objectives

By the end of this chapter you should be able to:

- Review the strategy concepts of SMEs.

- Classify the strategic characteristics of SMEs.

- Discuss the main strategic issues in small businesses.

- Explain the need and importance of managing strategic changes in small businesses.

- Analyse approaches to strategic change.

- Explain the nature and importance of innovation in small businesses.

- Discuss globalisation and SMEs.

- Explore the stages of internationalisation in SMEs.

- Discuss the importance of electronic commerce in small businesses.

- Explore electronic commerce and SMEs strategies.

The main objective of this chapter is addressing the emergent strategic issues in SMEs. The first section of the chapter reviews the concept of the strategic changes that have recently occurred in small and medium-sized enterprises. The next section focuses on globalisation and small businesses. Then, the concept and the applications of electronic commerce in the small business will be considered. Finally the strategies for growth and success in small business will be explored. Accordingly, the characteristics of successful SMEs will also be discussed.

Introduction

This chapter reviews some of the emergent issues in SMEs. It highlights the strategic needs of small businesses to survive and succeed in the marketplace. Managing strategic changes poses fundamental issues for small businesses. How can the firm adapt to the environmental changes? Developing and applying the strategic management concept enables the strategists to meet the change requirement with confidence.

Globalisation and internationalisation are another set of strategic issues to be considered by the CEOs of small businesses. To what extent is globalisation important for small businesses? And why do SMEs go to international markets? It should be noted that there is still no very clear answer to such questions. However, we are witnessing many efforts by researchers and serious scholars to investigate globalisation and its impacts on the success of the small businesses.

Finally, rapid developments in information technology (IT) as well as electronic commerce (e-commerce) are further strategic issues with which SMEs are nowadays confronted. In this chapter, we review these and related strategic issues which impact on SMEs. The chapter will end with some practical thoughts about strategic management for managers and practitioners.

Strategy and SMEs

Strategic management is an emergent concept in management practice. As a growing field of enquiry, strategic management typically deals with large organisations, but SMEs can no longer be ignored. Small businesses play a significant role in the well-being of the country's economy. Despite the importance and growing recognition of SMEs and their contribution to job creation, innovation and business development, the importance of strategic management to the SME sector has not been recognised and acknowledged until recently.

Accordingly, scholars have now begun to focus on the investigation of strategy formulation and implementation in SMEs. Despite government support, every year a significant number of SMEs fail or cease trading. The underlying problem appears to be an overall lack of strategic management skills and related competencies, which leads to the inability to develop an adequate control system.

Why business owner-managers in SMEs refuse to use strategic management

There are many reasons why managers of small businesses are avoiding the use of strategic management:

- Lack of knowledge about strategic management and its advantages for SMEs.
- Lack of skills and competencies to use strategic management.

- The involvement of SME managers in daily operating issues.
- Lack of trust.

There are numerous advantages for the SMEs in approaching their business strategically. Establishing a strategic management approach can assist SMEs in developing realisable business vision and mission statements which can be operationalised to achieve the set objectives. Normally, in small firms, managers make decisions based on their own experience and perception of the business performance and market. This may or may not work, is very risky and often ends in tears. An established strategic management approach provides a guide for top management and strategists to make decisions based on facts rather than pure feelings.

Finally, strategic management, in its holistic sense, matches the firm's abilities and output to the demands of environment, thus enabling managers to cope with change strategically. Research has shown that successful businesses and small firms tend to practise strategic management either formally or informally.

Managing strategic change

Managing strategic change is an emergent issue for small and medium-sized enterprises. Let's discuss this issue in more detail. Nowadays, organisations are facing substantial changes in their environment. Years ago, firms were operating in a more stable environment characterised by the lack of email, personal computers, Internet and intranet, cellular phones and electronic office equipment. Today, we live and work in an ever-changing world. No business, small or big, can exist let alone remain successful without adapting to the changes in the environment. Not surprisingly, successful firms are constantly striving to come up with new products and services (Daft, 2000).

Managing strategic change helps strategists to adopt the new ideas and behaviours quickly and systematically. By observing and monitoring external trends, for instance in technology, market situations, customer expectations and competitors' strategy, strategists can formulate strategies to use planned change to help their firms to adapt to external changes. It is important to note that forces for change exist both in the external environment and within the internal environment of the firm (Box 10.1).

In the following section the concept of strategic change is explored and the way to manage change strategically is briefly considered.

What is strategic change?

As discussed in Chapter 3, in today's turbulent environment organisations in general, and small and medium-sized enterprises in particular, need to adapt continuously to the emerging new situations. In increasingly competitive markets, organisations need to be able to change quickly and purposefully. Successful organisational change can lead to customer satisfaction, profitability, growth of small businesses and an overall improvement in organisational performance. Strategic change helps managers to achieve the organisational

> **Box 10.1 Managing strategic change**
>
> Managing strategic change is a strategic management tool that helps small and medium-sized enterprises to adopt the new ideas and behaviour. Strategic change may be undertaken using either prescriptive or emergent strategic approaches. The underlying theory of strategic change is based on consideration of five interrelated factors. These are:
>
> - Environmental assessment
> - Leading change
> - Linking strategic and operational change
> - Strategic human resource management
> - Coherence in the management of change.

strategic goals and objectives. According to Lynch 'strategic change is the proactive management of change in organisations to achieve clearly identified strategic objectives. [This] may be undertaken using either prescriptive or emergent strategic approaches' (2000: 291). Therefore, strategic change management enables people to contribute to the organisational change that in turn will lead to improved and compatible firm performance.

The central factor in any strategic change is people and the tasks that they perform in the organisation. In other words, strategic change is fundamentally about people. For change to take hold in an organisation, especially in SMEs, the strategic plan for change must be led by the key people (stakeholders) and those who best understand the firm – the people who work in it (Analoui, 1999).

The importance of strategic change in SMEs

As discussed in Chapter 4, the role and direct involvement of the entrepreneurs and business owner-managers in the process of strategic planning in SMEs is a critical one. Often these key people tend to manage the entire business single-handedly and be responsible for the formulation and implementation of the business strategies in their firms. Since strategic change involves almost all people and their tasks, especially in SMEs, it would be realistic to expect some resistance on their part to slow down and possibly halt the process – a case of the fear of the unknown.

Of course, there are many reasons why people resist organisational change. For instance, people's unfamiliarity with the new conditions, fear of losing their job and lack of technical skills can be perceived as consequences of a change. In such circumstances, people tend to stick to the current situation and attempt to prevent any organisational change. According to Daft (2000) there are four main reasons for resistance to change:

- Self-interest
- Lack of understanding and trust

- Uncertainty
- Different assessments and goals.

Strategic change management helps people to become involved in the process of change and facilitates its implementation by adapting to new environmental conditions. For instance, getting involved in information technology (IT) and using the Internet is a new challenge for small businesses. Many small business managers' lack the necessary technical skills and expertise which discourages them from becoming involved in IT and the Internet. In such a situation, business managers should attend short and intensive IT courses which may open up a new avenue for the sales of their product and services worldwide.

Causes of strategic change

Understanding and knowing the roots and causes of strategic changes will help strategists to manage it successfully. As we discussed earlier, the forces for change come from the external as well as internal environments. Any essential change in the external environmental factors, such as technology or competitors' strategy, may lead to changes in the firm's strategies and policies. In the case of small and medium-sized enterprises, for instance, globalisation is a new challenge. It presents the managers with choices and decisions about becoming involved or not and what benefits they would derive from a much bigger market. On the other hand, there are some internal factors such as goals, organisational structure and the firms' needs, which force SMEs to change from within. One of the earlier works in managing strategic change (Tichy, 1983) suggests four main causes for strategic changes. These are:

- Environment
- People
- Technology
- Business relationships.

Any substantial changes in the sociocultural environment, such as changes in economical and political factors, can lead to demand for strategic changes. Industry environmental factors such as competitive pressures, suppliers and labour unions may lead to strategic changes within the firms.

Another cause for strategic change is people. When new people join the organisation they may bring with them new ideas, innovative and strategic thinking which can lead to the emergence of strategic change. More importantly, in SMEs, key people often play a significant role in managing the business and consequently forcing change.

Suppose for a moment that the management of a small business which has firmly believed in an autocratic leadership style and personal decision-making system has received a new recruit: a CEO, graduate from a well-known business school, who believes in a participative leadership style and the development of team work. He likes to encourage people to take risks and be more innovative when carrying out their tasks. Under this management, inevitably there will be strategic changes introduced throughout the firm resulting from the new style.

The change in this case may require strategic planning implementation, maybe through training and development and maintenance.

The third force for strategic change is technology. Any change in the technology can have a substantial impact on the content of the work and even the survival of the small firm. If the firm cannot adopt the new changes in the technology, it will not be able to compete with competitors that have already done so and are enjoying the competitive advantage.

Finally, the last cause of strategic change is business relationships. New business relationships such as mergers, alliances, franchises and any other significant developments may require substantial changes in the organisation in order to take advantage of the newly established business relationships. For instance, when a small business decides to join a franchise, it will probably require some adjustment to new regulations and procedures on the part of the firm and its human resources. Had the change been anticipated, planned for and effectively implemented the chances are that the firm would benefit from its new partners.

If the change is introduced and managed carefully, it will result in sustainable behaviour and/or performance change.

Approaches to the management of strategic change

In the process of strategic management the managers should know how they would deal with strategic changes – how they will introduce and implement the change strategically. Basically, there are two main approaches to managing strategic change. The first is employing a prescriptive approach to strategy, which can be considered as top-down process. This approach considers managing change as a step-by-step process. The second is the emergent approach to managing strategic changes. Within the realm of emergent theory there is no one single best practice or answer to a problem. In this way, the strategic change is seen as a learning opportunity: a challenge rather than a crisis.

Learning theory and the five factors theory of strategic changes are the most basic but essential theories related to the emergent approach to strategic change. In this section, we will briefly review these approaches.

Unfreezing and refreezing attitudes: the prescriptive approach

The unfreezing and refreezing attitudes approach considers organisational change as a three-step process. This approach to change was originally developed by Lewin (1952). He introduced three steps for implementing organisational change. These are:

- Unfreezing current attitude
- Moving to a new level
- Refreezing attitudes at the new level.

In the first step the assumption is that for change to take place, the old attitudes or behaviour must be seen as unsatisfactory and should be abandoned.

The important point, however, is that the prescribed feeling of unsatisfactory behaviour cannot be imposed on the individuals or groups. Experience shows that people should feel and decide for themselves that their behaviour is not satisfactory.

In the second level, the assumption is that once people realise that their behaviour is unsatisfactory, they will search for a new behaviour by examining different alternatives. Finally, once the satisfactory behaviour has been found refreezing will take place at the new level. Positive reinforcement and supporting the change is a crucial factor for refreezing behaviour successfully.

The five-factor theory of strategic change: the emergent approach

The second group of theories for managing strategic change are classified as emergent approaches to change. In general, according to Lynch (2000), within emergent theories there is no one single approach. Some theorists place emphasis on the ability of the firm to respond satisfactorily to the changing environment. In the other words, managing strategic changes will have to focus on the effective and quick response of the firm to changes in the immediate or extended market. Other theories concentrate on the long term need to change organisational factors such as the skills and competencies of the human resources over a long period of time. Pettigrew and Whipp (1991) have developed one of the most well-known theories of strategic change in which they suggest that the management of strategic change consists of five interrelated factors. These are:

- Environmental assessment
- Leading change
- Linking strategic and operational change
- Strategic human resource management
- Coherence in the management of change.

They argue that each of the factors should be considered in relation to the others. In other words, not only should each factor not be regarded as a separate factor but there should also be an interlink between the five factors in order to manage the strategic change successfully. Generally speaking, the emergent theories to strategic change take a long term approach, while the prescriptive theories stipulate a short term approach. It could be also argued that in comparison with the prescriptive approach, the emergent approaches to strategic change are less disruptive and are likely to be least costly (Lynch, 2000).

Therefore, the application of each of these approaches to SMEs depends on the strategy chosen by the firm. For instance, if the firm faces short term strategic crises the emergent model of strategic change may not provide an effective solution. As Chell (2001) concluded, there is no one route to change and development for SMEs or a division of a multinational company. Essentially the key is having the right culture, which means the things are done as and when they are required. A prescriptive approach is more tempting but likely to yield unsatisfactory results in the future.

Globalisation and SMEs

Globalisation is an emergent strategic issue for SMEs. Let's see first what we mean by the term globalisation. The term globalisation has been considered from different perspectives. Nowadays, SMEs are increasingly active in international markets (Haahti, Hall and Donckels 1998). According to Graham (1999) the process of the internationalisation of the production and distribution of goods and services, and the associated trade and capital flows, have been loosely described as 'globalisation'. He argues that:

> The term 'globalisation' is an imprecise one, despite its current popularity, but is broadly accepted as that set of activities associated with the multinational/direct foreign investing firm which integrates its activities across national borders in the sense of making decisions to maximise the profits or interests of the group.
>
> (1999: 89)

From this point of view the term globalisation applies to the SMEs' involvement in operating in foreign markets such as exporting and foreign investment (Box 10.2).

As Graham (1999) and Gankema *et al.* (2000) suggest, if globalisation is defined as being the broader opening up of national economies to the international marketplace, then it will have several implications for small firms as well as large. Therefore, the increased participation of small firms in the international marketplace can be seen as an important part of globalisation. Since SMEs differ from the large firms in terms of their managerial style, independence, ownership and scale of operation, the study and understanding of globalisation and internationalisation and their involvement in the global market is of the utmost importance.

Box 10.2 Globalisation and SMEs

Globalisation and involvement in foreign markets is an emergent strategic issue for small and medium-sized enterprises. The process of the internationalisation of the production and distribution of goods and services, and the associated trade and capital flows, has been loosely described as globalisation. Internationalisation for SMEs consists of five stages:

- Operating only in the domestic market
- Searching for feasibility of exporting
- Involvement in exporting to the foreign market on a low scale
- Active involvement in exporting
- Committed involvement in multinational foreign markets.

Stages of globalisation for SMEs

Globalisation for SMEs has been considered as a process of internationalisation. Gankema *et al.* (2000) consider the internationalisation of a firm to be a process analogous to the stages of product adoption. They argue that the innovation-related models (I-model) of internationalisation consider each subsequent stage as an innovation for the firm. They extended their discussion of globalisation for SMEs based on the stages of the internationalisation process originally proposed by Cavusgil (1980) (Figure 10.1).

According to Cavusgil there are five stages of internationalisation for SMEs. These are:

- Domestic marketing. In this stage the firm operates only in the local market and is not involved in exporting at all. Operating in the domestic market may apply either to organisations in the early stages of the firm's life cycle or firms in the micro level. These firms lack the facilities and experience for going abroad.

- Pre-export. In this stage the SMEs search for information about internationalisation and study the feasibility of exporting and should ideally make a decision on the level of their involvement in internationalisation. Details of the internationalisation levels of SMEs have been discussed in Chapter 5. At this level the ratio of the export is at or near to zero.

- Experimental involvement. In this stage the firm starts to be involved in exporting on a small scale to the low risk markets. Morally, the firm targets the markets that are known to the firm. As the firm is experiencing a new market, it should be familiar with the market's characteristics.

- Active involvement in exporting. In this stage the SMEs are actively involved in internationalisation through export to markets in different countries.

Figure 10.1

The degree of SMEs' involvement in globalisation

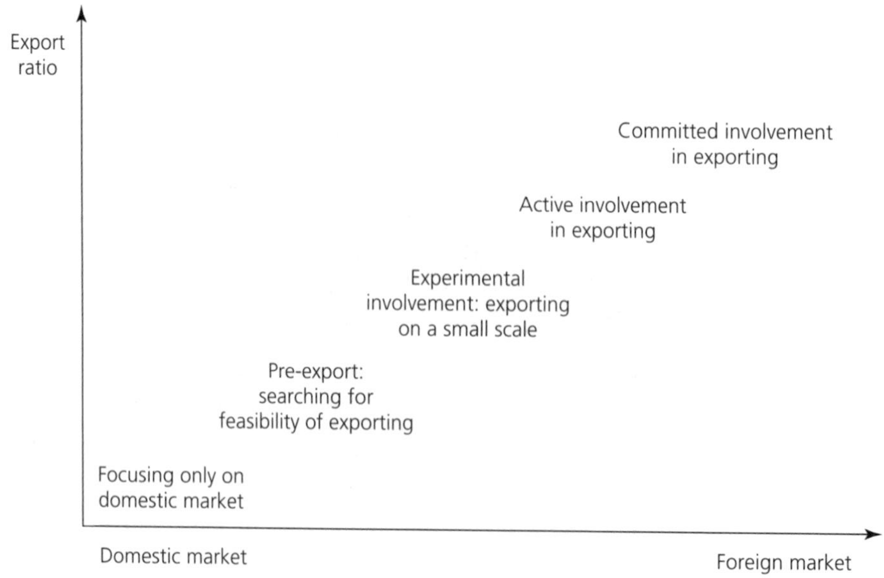

According to Cavusgil (1980) the export ratio of the firms at this stage is 10 to 39 per cent.

- Committed involvement. In this stage the firm operates in foreign markets rather than local markets. In other words, the firm depends heavily on international business activities. Direct investment in the foreign markets is an example of SMEs committed to involvement in internationalisation.

Information technology

Technological innovation, information technology (IT) and related issues have immense impact on SMEs in turbulent and rapidly changing business environments. Small and medium-sized firms face special problems in the formulation of their strategies due to deficiencies arising from their limited resources and range of technological competencies. These days the Internet and the World Wide Web (WWW) are having a major impact on how businesses operate. The size of the company and the perceived importance of e-commerce to business functions have been noted consistently as possible factors in determining whether or not businesses get involved in e-commerce (Beveren and Thomson, 2002). Today a businesses cannot avoid using IT tools and e-commerce. For instance, the World Wide Web allows customers to search and find competitive information and new sources of supply easily. Buyers can easily compare the prices of different suppliers and have access to detailed information about the suppliers. There are no business hours and the buyers can purchase products any time and anywhere ignoring time zone differences (Da Costa, 2001). E-commerce has many advantages for buyers as well as suppliers, but the reality is that for SMEs, moving into e-commerce may require a major change in the commerce models that the businesses use. Moreover for SMEs, not surprisingly, the transaction costs involved in developing online businesses are high.

Electronic commerce

Electronic commerce has been defined from different perspectives. From a communications perspective it is the delivery of information, products/services or payment over telephone lines, computer networks or any other electronic means. From a business process perspective it is the application of technology toward the automation of business transactions and workflow. From an online perspective e-commerce provides the capability of buying and selling products and information on the Internet and other online services (Turban *et al.* 2000). As discussed, e-commerce has many advantages for consumers. E-commerce enables customers to shop or do other transactions 24 hours a day from almost everywhere. It provides the customer with more choices from any vendor, more products and less expensive products and services, and allows them to shop in many places and conduct quick price comparisons. E-commerce allows quick delivery and customers can receive relevant and detailed information in seconds, rather than days or weeks. It also makes it possible to participate in virtual auctions and allows customers to interact with other customers in electronic communities, exchanging ideas and comparing experiences.

Finally e-commerce facilitates competition, which results in substantial discounts (Adam and Yesha, 1996). Regarding the benefits of e-commerce to the organisation, it expands the marketplace to national and international markets and decreases the cost of creating, processing, distributing, storing and retrieving paper-based information. Electronic commerce allows reduced inventories and reduces telecommunication costs and the time between the outlay of capital and the receipt of product and services (Komenar, 1997; Turban *et al.* 2000).

The different types of electronic commerce

The nature of the relationship between the business and consumers forms the type of e-commerce. There are four major types of e-commerce:

- Business-to-business (B2B): most e-commerce today is of this type. It includes information flow among two or more businesses.

- Business-to-consumer (B2C): these are retailing transactions with individual buyers. For instance providing banking services to the customers through the Internet is a B2C type of e-commerce.

- Consumer-to-consumer (C2C): in this category the consumer sells directly to other consumers. Examples are individuals using classified ads to sell residential property, cars, knowledge, expertise and advertising personal services.

- Consumer-to-business (C2B): this category includes individuals who sell products or services to the firms as well as individuals who seek sellers, interact with them and conclude a transaction.

Figure 10.2 illustrates the e-commerce matrix that explains the electronic relationship between business and consumers.

There are two other types of e-commerce – non-businesses e-commerce and intrabusinesses. Non-business e-commerce is concerned with using e-commerce in non-business organisations. Many non-business organisations such as academic institutions, not-for-profit organisations, religious organisations, social

Figure 10.2			
Four types of e-commerce	Consumer	Consumer-to-business (C2B)	Consumer-to-consumer (C2C)
	Business	Business-to-business (B2B)	Business-to-consumer (B2C)
		Business	Consumer

organisations and government agencies are using various types of e-commerce. Intrabusiness (organisational) e-commerce includes all internal organisational activities, usually performed on the intranet, that involves the exchange of goods, services or information (Turban *et al.* 2000).

Electronic commerce and SME strategies

As Turban *et al.* (2000) argue, the environment changes such that market requirements, technological changes and pressures force organisations to respond to these changes. Traditional responses may not be sufficient due to the magnitude of the pressures and the frequent changes involved and organisations must frequently use innovations and re-engineer their operations. In many cases, e-commerce is the major facilitator of organisational responses. While SMEs typically do not have the capital and human resources of larger competitors, many appear to be making significant investments in information technology. Companies with 500 or fewer employees purchased over $200 billion worth of technology products and services in 1998, over five times as much as was spent by larger companies (Caldwell and Wilde 1998; Wilde 1998).

Small and medium sized enterprises are developing Websites, intranets and using email at close to the same percentages as larger businesses. However, they have been slower to adopt e-commerce applications (Wilder 1999). This could be due to the high cost of setting up and maintaining e-commerce applications. A viable option for SME e-commerce is to outsource to a third party (De Soto 1998). Recent research by Kleindl (2000) highlighted the importance and roles of online systems in developing SMEs' strategies as follows:

1. Improved customer services: online systems enable the firm to provide more facilities for its customers. It improves customer services and allows consumers to gain access to product and inventory information.

2. Electronic commerce: online services enable the firm to adopt e-commerce. E-commerce in turn allows SMEs access to larger markets without the cost of setting up new distribution systems. It also allows SMEs to target narrow markets faster than larger competitors.

3. Customer relationship management application: online connections between the SME and its customers increase the speed of response and allow for close to instant communication.

4. Increased business-to-business connections (extranets): SMEs can act as an intermediary linking larger businesses with very small suppliers (Kleindl, 2000).

Major technology strategies are recommended for SMEs attempting to compete in the contemporary global environment. Relative to larger firms, smaller businesses that make effective use of Internet opportunities may also find that they can be more innovative, faster in responding to environmental demands and better able quickly to change or adapt business models to gain competitive advantage. Using IT in order to improve customer services through online systems can be considered as a new strategy for SMEs. Increased business-to-business (B2B) connection has been considered as another strategy for SMEs (Engler, 1999).

In summary, SMEs are facing change in their competitive environment that will force them to modify or completely abandon many current business practices. SMEs must consider new business models that take advantage of existing and emerging Internet-based technologies in order to stay competitive. Their willingness to adopt new technologies is also likely to influence their ability to hire and retain new talent. While internal development may not be feasible for many resource-poor SMEs, the use of IT can provide SMEs with the ability to compete.

Final thoughts: strategic characteristics of SMEs

One of the objectives of this book was to identify the characteristics of the successful SMEs, which employ a strategic management process. We have discussed how strategic management can be considered as the process of formulation and implementation of business strategies in SMEs. Such a process involves environmental scanning (SWOT analysis) in order to determine the strengths, weaknesses, opportunities and threats of the firm, developing mission and objectives, formulation business strategies and finally implementation and evaluation of the strategies.

As discussed in previous chapters, SMEs are different in terms of their strategic characteristics. In order to identify these characteristics, SMEs can be categorised into two groups – high performance and low performance firms. From the analysis of the case studies, the key strategic characteristics or attributes of high performance versus low performance firms are illustrated in Table 10.1.

Table 10.1 compares the environmental analysis (SWOT), goals, strategic planning and implementation and some general characteristics of high performance firms with those of low performers and therefore enables a clear set of prescriptions to be enunciated. This set of prescriptions may be useful not only to practitioners but also to academic analysts of strategy in SMEs. For instance high performance SMEs have written, formal and clearly defined objectives. In contrast, the objectives of the low performance SMEs are more informal and usually exist in the head of the business owner-manager. Moreover, in high performance SMEs, commitment, motivation, quality and organisational effectiveness is high while the research reveals that the same variables in low performance firms is at a moderate level.

Recalling our earlier discussion of strategic management theories as well as case studies and the findings of the other researches through the book, it should be possible to prescribe strategies and suggest patterns of behaviour, which should when implemented, help the firms to achieve their objectives. First regarding environmental awareness, the firm should scan the environment and collect the information of rivals on a regular basis and be aware of the industry and their competitors. The firm also must be aware of its strengths and weaknesses and be ready to exploit its strengths and improve its weaknesses.

Reacting to the customers is an important point that SMEs should never forget. Box 10.3 provides some guidelines regarding environmental awareness for SMEs.

Regarding the mission and objectives, SMEs should develop a clear mission statement and make sure that it is clear to all of the employees. It would be helpful if small businesses aim for long term profit and growth and set business rather than personal goals.

Table 10.1		Characteristics	
	Variable	*High performance firms*	*Low performance firms*
Strategic characteristics of low versus high performance SMEs	Environmental analysis (SWOT)		
	Awareness	Very good	Poor
	Frequency of industry analysis	High	Low
	Reaction to customers' comments	Fast and precise	Slow
	Goals		
	Mission	Written and formal	Informal
	Objectives	Clearly defined	Personal
	Period of objectives	Medium or long term	Short term
	Strategic planning		
	Employing strategic management techniques	High	Not at all
	Business plan	Formal	Informal
	Planning level	Strategic planning	Financial planning
	Managerial involvement in strategic decision-making	Multidisciplinary management team	Top management
	Emphasis on long term strategic plans	High	Low
	Emphasis on ongoing evaluation in strategic planning	High	Low
	HR involvement in developing business plans	High participate	Low participate
	General considerations		
	Commitment	High	Moderate
	Communications	Quick	Formal
	Motivation	High	Moderate
	Quality	High	Variable
	Information technology	Exploited	Not used extensively
	Organisational effectiveness	High	Moderate

> ### Box 10.3 Some practical guidelines for SME managers for developing their environmental awareness and organisational objectives
>
> #### Environmental awareness
>
> - Develop an awareness of the industry and competitors.
> - Scan the environment and collect information about rivals on a regular basis.
> - Be aware of your firm's strengths and weaknesses and be ready to exploit your strengths and improve your weaknesses.
> - Be aware of your firm's opportunities and threats in formulating your strategies.
> - Be aware of new products and keep up to date with changes in the market.
> - Frequently analyse the industry in which you operate and your competitors' business strategies.
> - React to your customers' comments quickly and precisely.
>
> #### Organisational objectives
>
> - Develop a clear mission statement and make sure that it is clear to all your employees.
> - Develop quantifiable financial goals.
> - Set long term and clear objectives and targets and work toward them.
> - Aim for long term profit and growth.
> - Set business rather than personal goals.

Regarding strategy formulation and implementation, the development of formal business plans and the employment of a multidisciplinary management team in strategic decision-making process is recommended. Taking into account employees' suggestions to increase their motivation and involving the employees in developing business plans is very important in the implementation of strategies. Commitment to the strategic plans and following them through is a further crucial factor in strategy in SMEs.

Finally, it is strategically important to implement and update technology and learn how to use it correctly. Using IT for the planning and implementation of business plans and up-to-date IT systems for the budgeting and financial management of the business plays a significant role in SMEs' performance. The last point is developing team work in order to increase organisational effectiveness.

> **Box 10.4 Some practical guidelines for SME managers for strategy formulation and implementation**
>
> **Strategy formulation and implementation**
>
> - Develop formal business plans.
> - Employ a multidisciplinary management team in the strategic decision-making process.
> - Be flexible and adaptable in developing your business plans.
> - Learn from your and others' experiences in strategic decision-making.
> - Be self-critical and carry out an ongoing evaluation in your strategic planning.
> - Take into account employees' suggestions to increase their motivation.
> - Involve employees in developing business plans.
> - Implement and update technology and learn how to use it correctly.
> - Use IT for the planning and implementation of your business plans.
> - Use and update IT systems for the budgeting and financial management of the business.
> - Provide high quality products or services for long term customer satisfaction.
> - Commit to your strategic plans and follow them through.
> - Keep communication efficient and speedy rather than formal and slow.
> - In order to increase effectiveness, develop teamwork in the organisation.

Summary

- Managing strategic change is an emergent issue for SMEs. Managing strategic change helps strategist to adopt new ideas and behaviours within their firms. Successful organisational change can lead to customer satisfaction, profitability and growth of small businesses and overall improvement in organisational performance. Strategic change helps managers to manage achieving the organisational strategic goals and objectives within the changing environment. According to Lynch, strategic change is the proactive management of change in organisations to achieve clearly identified strategic objectives. The forces for change come from the external as well as internal environments (sources). Four main causes for strategic changes are environment, people, technology and business relationships.

- Strategic change may be undertaken using either prescriptive or emergent strategic approaches. The unfreezing and refreezing attitudes theory is a prescriptive approach that considers organisational change as a three-step process: unfreezing current attitudes, moving to a new level and refreezing attitudes at the new level. In contrast, the second group of theories for managing strategic change are classified as emergent approaches. The five-factor theory of strategic change is one of the emergent approaches that considers the management of strategic change a combination of five interrelated factors – environmental assessment, leading change, linking strategic and operational change, strategic human resource management and coherence in the management of change.

- Globalisation is an emergent strategic issue for SMEs. One of the important aspects of globalisation for SMEs is their involvement in foreign markets. The process of internationalisation of the production and distribution of goods and services and the associated trade and capital flows has been loosely described as 'globalisation'. From this point of view the term globalisation applies to SMEs' involvement in operating in the foreign markets such as exporting and foreign investment. Therefore the increased participation of small firms in the international marketplace can be seen as an important part of globalisation.

  Internationalisation for SMEs consists of five stages – domestic marketing, pre-export, experimental involvement, active involvement in exporting and committed involvement.

- Technological innovation, information technology (IT) and related issues have immense impact on SMEs in turbulent and rapidly changing business environments. IT and e-commerce can help SMEs make a rapid response to the environmental changes. Today businesses cannot avoid using IT tools and electronic commerce although moving into e-commerce may require a major change in the commerce models that businesses use.

- E-commerce provides the capability of buying and selling products and information on the Internet and other online services. Enabling customers to shop at any time, providing the customer with more choices, allowing quick delivery, the possibility of participating in virtual auctions, providing the facilities for customers to interact with other customers in electronic communities and finally facilitating competition are major advantages for customers. On the other hand, e-commerce also has many advantages for the organisations. It expands the marketplace to national and international markets and decreases sale costs. There are four major types of e-commerce, business-to-business (B2B), business-to-consumer (B2C), consumer-to-consumer (C2C) and consumer-to-business (C2B).

- Small and medium-sized enterprises have to use innovations and attempt to re-engineer their operations in order to respond to the environmental changes and market requirements. In many cases, online services are the major facilitator of organisational responses. Online services may help SMEs to develop their strategy successfully in order to improved customer services, e-commerce, customer relationships, management application and increased business-to-business connections (extranets). Small businesses that make effective use of Internet opportunities may also find that they can be more innovative, faster in responding to environmental demands and better able to quickly change or adapt business models to gain the competitive advantage.

- In practice, in order to formulate and implement the business strategies successfully, the firm should establish an effective environmental scanning system. The firm must also be aware of its strengths and weaknesses and be ready to exploit its strengths and improve its weaknesses. Regarding the mission and objectives, SMEs should develop a clear mission statement and make sure that it is clear to all of the employees. It would be helpful if small businesses aimed for long term profit and growth and set business rather than personal goals. Developing formal business plans and employing a multidisciplinary management team in the strategic decision-making process are recommended. Taking into account employees' suggestions to increase their motivation and involving the employees in developing business plans is very important in the implementation of strategies. Finally the SMEs should use, update and learn how to use IT correctly. The last point is developing team work and managing people effectively in order to increase organisational performance.

Discussion questions

1. Discuss the importance of strategic management for small businesses.
2. What is strategic change? List causes of strategic change.
3. Explain the approaches to management of strategic change.
4. Explore the importance of strategic change in SMEs.
5. Discuss the impacts of globalisation on SMEs' performance.
6. Explain the importance of the IT and e-commerce in SMEs.
7. Discuss e-commerce and developing strategy in SMEs.
8. What are the strategic characteristics of the successful SME?

References

Adam, N. and Yesha, Y. (1996) *Electronic Commerce: Current Research Issues and Implications*, Springer, New York.

Analoui, F. (1999) *Effective Human Resource Development: A Challenge for Developing Countries*, Ashgate, Aldershot.

Beveren, J. V. and Thomson, H. (2002) The use of electronic commerce by SMEs in Victoria, Australia, *Journal of Small Business Management*, 40 (3), 250–253.

Caldwell, B. and Wilde, C. (1998) Emerging enterprises, *Information Week*, June 29, 53–60.

Cavusgil, S. T. (1980) On the internationalisation process of firms, *European Research*, 8 (G), 273–281.

Chell, E. (2001) *Entrepreneurship: Globalization, Innovation and Development*, Thomson Learning, London.

Da Costa, E. (2001) *Global E-Commerce Strategies for Small Businesses*, MIT Press, Cambridge, MA.

Daft, R. L. (2000) *Management*, 5th edn, The Dryden Press, Fort Worth, TX.

De Soto, R. (1998) Creating an active internet presence: a new alternative, *Telecommunication Magazine*, December, 73–75.

Engler, N. (1999) Small but nimble, *Information Week*, January 18, 57–62.

Gankema, H. G. J., Snuif, H. R. and Zwart, P. S. (2000) The internationalisation process of small and medium sized enterprises: an evaluation of stage theory, *Journal of Small Business Management*, 38 (4), 15–27.

Graham, P. G. (1999) Small business participation in the global economy, *European Journal of Marketing*, 33 (1/2), 88–102.

Haahti, A., Hall, G. and Donckels, R. (eds) (1998), *The Internationalisation of SMEs: The Interstratos Project*, Routledge, London.

Kleindl, B. (2000) Competitive dynamics and new business models for SMEs in the virtual marketplace, *Journal of Developmental Entrepreneurship*, 5 (1), 73–86.

Komenar, M. (1997) *Electronic Marketing*, John Wiley & Sons, New York.

Lewin, K. (1952) *Field Theory in Social Science*, Tavistock, London.

Lynch, R. (2000) *Corporate Strategy*, 2nd edn, Pearson Education, London.

Pettigrew, A. and Whipp, R. (1991) *Managing Change for Competitive Success*, Blackwell, Oxford.

Tichy, N. (1983) *Managing Strategic Change*, Wiley, New York.

Turban, E., Lee, J., King, D. and Chung, H. M. (2000) *Electronic commerce: A Managerial Perspective*, Prentice Hall International Limited, London.

Wilde, C. (1998) Internet levels the field, *Information Week*, June 29, 64–66.

Wilde, C. (1999) E-business work status, *Information Week*, January 4, 53–54.

Author Index

Subject Index